BOMBER BARONS

5TH BOMBARDMENT GROUP HEAVY

Turner Publishing Company
Publishers of Military History

Co-published by
Mark A. Thompson, Associate Publisher

Pre-Press work by M.T. Publishing Company, Inc.
Graphic Designer: Diana F. Butcher

Author: The 5th Bombardment Group Association

Library of Congress Catalog
Card No. 98-61818

ISBN: 978-1-68162-270-5

Limited Edition

Page 1 photo: 30 September 1944. First mission to Balikpapan. Pandansari refinery. Mission was supposed to be 13th Air Force and 5th Air Force; however, the 5th Air Force had back luck and did not get to the target. The 31st Squadron of the 5th Bomb Group with Col. Tomas Musgrave in the lead did hit the target.

TABLE OF CONTENTS

HISTORY

5TH BOMBARDMENT GROUP (H)

THE 5TH BOMBARDMENT GROUP (H)

This document is intended to cover the history of the Fifth Bombardment Group from the era immediately preceding WWII, through the war years until V-J Day 1945. It is presented against a summary background of the entire life of the organization.

The group was originated and activated in Hawaii on the island of Oahu on 19 May 1918 as the Second Observation Group. On 12 April 1921 it was redesignated as the Fifth Group (Observation) and later on 21 June 1922 as the Fifth Group (Pursuit and Bombardment). Effective 1 May 1923 it was reorganized as the Fifth Group (Composite) at Luke Field, Oahu. The units assigned were Headquarters, Fifth Group; 65th Service squadron; 41st Air Intelligence Section; 11th Photo Section; 6th Pursuit Squadron; 23rd Bombardment Squadron and the 72nd Bombardment Squadron. On 25 March 1938 it was redesignated as the Fifth Bombardment Group, again as the Fifth Bombardment Group (M) on 26 December 1939 and finally as the Fifth Bombardment Group (H) on 20 November 1940.

Following the end of WWII, the Fifth was redesignated the Fifth Reconnaissance Group, Very Long Range, Photographic on 11 March 1947. On 1 July 1949 the Fifth Reconnaissance Wing was established. On 14 November 1950, the group was redesignated the Fifth Reconnaissance Wing (H). The wing was redesignated the Fifth Bombardment Wing (H) on 1 October 1955. In the year 1999 it resided at Minot AFB, North Dakota and operated B-52H aircraft.

During its life the group has had two official and one unofficial group insignia. At the time WWII began it was a winged death's-head on a blue background. The death's-head was white with black eyes, nose and teeth outline. The wings were gold and were joined at the bottom by a gold banner bearing the inscription: *Kiai O KaLewa*, which is an expression in the Hawaiian language meaning *Guardians Of The Upper Regions*. During 1944-45 the group adopted the name of *Bomber Barons* with an insignia which included a death's-heads figure, clothed in maroon and gold, smoking a cigarette in a long holder and wearing a black top hat. The figure was shown against a blue shield having a broad gold stripe running from the upper left hand to the lower right hand corner, with the letter B located on the stripe at the two corners. This insignia was never officially adopted.

The emblem adopted by the Fifth Bombardment Wing features a winged death's-head against a shield which is divided vertically by a nubbly line. The area to the left of the line is green and the area to the right is black. The deaths head is blue with gold wings. The lower part of the shield is enclosed with a banner carrying the *Kiai O KaLewa* motto.

5TH BOMBARDMENT GROUP HEAVY

In its long history, going back to the earliest days of what eventually became the Air Force, the Group/Wing maintained and flew a variety of aircraft as illustrated by the following list.

Aircraft	Years	Aircraft	Years
DH-4	1919-1924	A-3	1936-1939
HS-21	1919-1926	B-18	1937-1942
N-9	1919-1920	B-17	1941-1943
R-6	1919-1920	B-24	1943-1945
FD-VIII	1920-1926	LB-30	1942
JN-6	1920-1929	B-29	1946-1952
MB-3	1920-1926	C-46	1947-1948
NBS-1	1922-1929		
LB-5	1923-1929		
SE-5	1924-1926		
PW-9	1927		
B-4	1929-1937		
LB-6	1929-1937		
OA-1	1929-1937		
0-19	1929-1937		
P-12	1930-1937		
B-12	1934-1939		
BB-10	1934-1940		
C-47	1945		
B-25	1945		
A-24	1945		

The following distinguished officers have commanded the Group/Wing over the years.

Lt. Col. Millard F. Harmon	Oct 1936 - Sep 1938
Colonel Shepler W. Fitzgerald	Sep 1938 - Aug 1941
Lt. Co. Edwin B. Bobzein	Aug 1941 - 1942
Colonel Arthur W. Meehan	1942 - 1 Nov 1942
Colonel Brooke E. Allen	1 Nov 1942 - 10 Aug 1943
Colonel Marion D. Unruh	10 Aug 1943 - 31 Dec 1943
Lt. Col. Joseph E Reddoch, Jr.	31 Dec 1943 - 4 Apr 1944
Colonel Thomas C. Musgrave, Jr.	4 Apr 1944 - 21 Apr 1944
Colonel Joseph E. Reddoch, Jr.	21 Apr 1944 - 15 Aug 1944
Colonel Thomas C. Musgrave, Jr.	15 Aug 1944 - 6 Jan 1945
Major Albert W. James	7 Jan 1945 - 15 Mar 1945
Colonel Isaac J. Haviland	15 Mar 1945 - 5 Jul 1945
Lt. Col. Albert W. James	5 Jul 1945 - 9 Sep 1945

In September 1939 World War II began in Europe. Shortly thereafter the United States Army Air Corps (later the Army Air Force) began to build and train toward a stronger organization. The Fifth Group moved from Luke Field on Ford Island in the middle of Pearl Harbor to their new home at Hickam Field. Hickam provided a beautiful, new, three-story, concrete barracks for the enlisted men and new homes and apartments for officers and senior non-commissioned officers. At Hickam the Fifth was joined by the recently activated Eleventh Bombardment Group (H). As new enlisted men arrived from the mainland, they were sent to specialty schools and following completion of classes were assigned to combat crews. The group comprised the 23rd Bombardment Squadron, the 31st Bombardment Squadron, the 72nd Bombardment Squadron and the 4th Reconnaissance Squadron.

The group was equipped with the Douglas B-18 medium bomber, a twin engined plane with a very rugged structure. Those sent to Hawaii were equipped with flotation compartments in the wing as well as having a bilge pump. They were lightly defended for an aircraft expected to go into combat: three .30 caliber machine guns and no power turrets. The B-18s however served a useful purpose in 1940. Combat crews normally flew five days a week, Monday through Friday from 0800 hours until 1200 hours. Many of the flights

Hickam 1909-1939 30th Anniversay, US Air Corps B-18s.

were navigation exercises to various other islands in the Hawaiian Group. The many hours aloft built up valuable experience for every member of the crew. Many flights were for the benefit of the bombardiers. At that time all bombardiers were enlisted men, primarily senior non-commissioned officers. The Norden bombsights were classified secret and were kept in a special vault in the hanger which was guarded 24 hours a day. One never saw the bombsight. When the crew came to the aircraft, the bombardier was carrying it in a canvas bag. The squadrons annually spent two weeks at the South Cape of the big island, Hawaii for record bombing using the 100 pound practice bomb. There was a short runway there which could handle the B-18 and wooden barracks, which was kind of roughing it after the comfort of the new barracks at Hickam. There was also the opportunity to gain experience in handling live bombs at the bombing range on the island of Kahoolawe. This is a small and at that time uninhabited island near Kauai. Rumor had it that one person, a goatherd, lived on the island but that seems unlikely. This activity went on regularly through the spring of 1941. Each squadron also retained a Martin B-10, and there was an occasional flight in it. The B-10 was a pretty, low wing, twin-engined monoplane. As a note of the advancement of technology from the B-10 to the B-18, the B-10's engine instruments were in a small panel on the inboard side of the engine nacelles. The pilot needed sharp eyesight.

In November of 1940 the group was redesignated from a medium bombardment group to a heavy, and in May of 1941 received its first B-17s. The squadrons each retained a couple of B-18s but the regular crews found themselves with three added members and flying in a B-17. These were the C models, lacking tail guns and effective belly guns. Nevertheless they were a valuable step up for all personnel. Flying went on in the regular schedule of 0800 to 1200 five days a week. Now however the emphasis was on bombing, usually from an altitude of 20,000 feet. Combat crews gained experience in operating at altitude, on oxygen and even in Hawaiian skies, dressed in the Air Corps heavy flying suit. (An especially difficult task was using the relief tube, which was in the bomb bay, just ahead of the radio cabin door, with the bomb bay doors open. Remember the aircraft was neither heated nor pressurized. Sounds trivial, but on a real mission it could become a problem if not solved.)

Experience went beyond that obtained in flying. The combat crews were required to do regular routine maintenance on the aircraft, and so crew members became competent in keeping the aircraft air ready. This was a crucial skill in later times at distant bases in the South Pacific. There were times when a crew on an island and far from an Air Depot or hanger personnel, accomplished such major tasks as an engine change or the change of a main landing gear. This depended upon skills which had been honed by the many hours spent with the aircraft in the air and on the ground. In addition to his own particular skill, every crew member became familiar with the field stripping and maintenance of the .30 caliber and .50 caliber machine guns.

In September of 1941 the Fifth Bombardment Group assisted in equipping the Ninteenth Bombardment Group (H). Each squadron in the Fifth and the Eleventh Groups gave up an aircraft, a combat crew and ground support personnel. These aircraft and personnel then proceeded to Clark Field in the Phillipines. Many of those who survived the Japanese capture of the Phillipines later met old friends when the Fifth and Nineteenth met briefly in New Guinea in 1942.

AT WAR AGAIN

By Madonna Yancey

World War I had been called *The War to End All Wars*. After all the terrible loss of life and destruction, there was a belief that the world would never again see war waged on such a massive scale. Yet a mere 20 years later, battles were once again raging throughout Europe, North Africa, China, and Southeast Asia.

For its part, the United States had adopted an isolationist policy, preferring to distance itself from the affairs of the world and concentrate on rebuilding from the Great Depression. Yet there were some in our government and military who had a premonition of what would soon come, including President Roosevelt, who sounded a cautionary note when he suggested that, *America must become the arsenal of democracy.*

The war in Europe had begun in 1939, when Germany launched an attack on Poland. In quick succession, the Germans took control of Holland and Belgium, then France and finally North Africa.

The Germans had also set their sights on England, but Britain's Royal Air Force proved a formidable foe. For nearly three months, the skies over England were dark with Luftwaffe planes seeking to bomb the British into submission. But England refused to be conquered. Hitler then took a new tack, again sending German bombers to the skies over England to attack civilian targets. Germany's next goal was to conquer Russia, the only thing standing between Hitler's army and Japan, their ally in the East.

For some time prior to the beginning of World War II, the Japanese had been undertaking their master plan to gain control of the other half of the world. That was only part of the plan for the Japanese believed that if they could first conquer the Far East, eventually they would come to dominate the world. By 1930, the plan was in motion. The Japanese occupied strategic positions throughout the Asian mainland. As well, they controlled islands off the coast of China and many Pacific Islands that were small but that would be of tremendous strategic value in the war that was to come.

The Japanese set about to bring the rest of Southeast Asia, more of the Pacific islands and, finally, China under their control. The battle for China had begun in 1931, when Japan wrested control of the province of Manchuria from the Chinese. When the League of Nations voted to place sanctions against the Japanese, Japan simply resigned from the organization. By 1937 most of the Chinese mainland was under their control.

Eventually, French Indo-China would fall under Japanese control, once France had been defeated by the Nazis. The Japanese also had a treaty with Thailand, which virtually assured their control of that part of the world along with its vast supply of natural resources. Piece by piece, the Japanese were acquiring the strategic locations and the raw materials they would need to complete their master plan. Nor were American interests safe from the Japanese master plan, even at this early date. A United States gunboat, the *Panay*, was bombed and sunk by the Japanese, who claimed that the incident was unintentional. During this time period the Japanese also captured the islands of Hainan and Spratley. Located near both the Philippines and Borneo, these islands were of immense strategic importance to the Japanese. On 27 September 1940, Japan officially joined the Axis Powers. The only thing that stood between the Germany and Japan and their joint goal of world domination was the United States. If America entered the war, the balance would shift. Still, in spite of the aggression on the part of the Axis Powers, the United States remained in an isolationist mood.

All the while, the United States was in negotiations with Japan in an attempt to bring about peace. As Japanese diplomats sat across the bargaining table from their American counterparts, the Japanese military was making other plans. The Japanese devised a strategy that would catch the Americans off guard and inflict heavy casualties and damage on their forces in Hawaii, thereby preventing, or at least delaying, America's entry into the war.

In late November 1941 the Japanese Navy's attack fleet, under the command of Admiral Yamamoto, set sail on a course that would take them to a launching site in the Pacific Ocean, about 230 miles north of Oahu. From there, they would attack the American installations at Pearl Harbor and other sites on the island of Oahu. If this strategy worked, the Japanese would catch the Americans by surprise and inflict heavy casualties and damage.

On the morning of 7 December 1941, the ships of the Pacific Fleet were lying at rest in Pearl Harbor. Just before 8 a.m. the early morning calm was shattered as the first wave of Japanese fighters and bombers approached their target. Their commander radioed these words back to the waiting fleet: *Tora, Tora, Tora*. The coded message was a signal that the attack had begun.

The attack was swift and deadly. Fifteen minutes after the attack began, the *USS Arizona* exploded when she was hit by an armor-piercing bomb. Nine minutes later she was at the bottom of the harbor. The *Arizona*'s entire crew, 1,177 men in all, were killed in the attack.

Four other battleships — the *USS Oklahoma, USS California, USS West Virginia*, and *USS Utah* — joined the *Arizona* in her watery grave. The *USS Maryland, USS Pennsylvania* and *USS Tennessee* were also severely damaged.

The radar station at Opana Point had picked up signals of incoming planes early that morning, about an hour before the attack began. A flight of B-17s from the mainland had been expected that morning, so the men at the radar station assumed the signals were from friendly aircraft.

The Japanese also attacked other American military installations on the Island, including the Naval Air Station at Kaneohe Bay, a Marine Corps Air Station, and the airfields at Bellows, Wheeler and Hickam.

Less than an hour after the first attack, a second wave of Japanese planes struck, inflicting even more damage on the American installations. The *USS Nevada* attempted to reach open water, but was hit and beached. While severely damaged, she did avoid the fate of the other battleships moored at Pearl Harbor.

The Americans, though unprepared for the attack, struck back at the invaders. Some pilots from the Army Air Corps were able to take off and shot down several enemy planes.

The previous night five midget Japanese subs had attempted to slip into Pearl Harbor. Four of them were sunk, and the 5th was captured when it ran aground.

The attack was over in just two hours. But the toll was heavy. Eighteen ships had been sunk at Pearl Harbor, and more than 2,400 men had lost their lives there. More than 1,100 other had been wounded. Hundreds of planes had been destroyed on the ground at the Oahu airfields, with many more deaths and injuries. Now, the United States had no choice but to enter the war against the Axis Powers.

Admiral Yamamoto was reported to have said in the aftermath of the attack on Pearl Harbor, "I fear we have only awakened a sleeping giant."

Admiral Yamamoto's fears were quickly realized. While the Japanese had inflicted considerable damage, it could have been much worse. The Navy's aircraft carriers were not in port at the time of the attack. While the facilities at Pearl Harbor had sustained heavy damage, they had not been destroyed. And the oil storage facilities on the island had not been destroyed, which was, perhaps, the biggest failure of the Japanese attack. Had the attack on the oil storage facilities met with success, the Navy's ships would have had to be moved, and America's ability to wage war in the Pacific would have been made much more difficult.

Later that day, at 2100 hours, Eastern Standard Time, Japan formally declared war on the United States. The following day the United States declared war on the Axis Powers. All of the training and preparation the men of the 5th Bombardment Group had undertaken would now be put to test in battle. All of their skill and bravery would be needed to overcome a formidable and determined enemy.

PEARL HARBOR DAY

As remembered by some of the men of the 23rd Squadron, 7 December 1941 began peacefully. Most of the 23rd were on base, a result of there having been a beer party in the hanger the night before. The commander of the 23rd was Major Laverne G. (Blondy) Saunders. Saunders was a former West Point All American tackle who believed the troops should have a beer party about every three months. Usually these had been at some Oahu beach location, but he may have had good reason for keeping most of the men on base that night.

The 23rd occupied the third floor of a wing of the barracks which was oriented somewhat east and west. The windows on the north side of this wing faced directly toward Pearl Harbor. Several of the men had been to morning chow at the big, consolidated mess hall and were idling about their bunks. There was the sound of aircraft from outside, however this was no cause for alarm. It seemed that the Navy had something airborne every Sunday which was a puzzle because the Army Air Corps at Hickam never flew on Sunday. Being young and entranced with just about anything airborne several of them strolled over to the windows to see what in the world the Navy was up to. What they saw was a formation of three aircraft at about 10,000 feet. As they watched, the formation pushed over into a long dive. When they pulled out a moderate quantity of smoke was seen in the direction of Ford Island. From their vantage point a direct view of the ships on battleship row was obscured by the three-story Marine barracks which was just inside the Pearl Harbor fenced area adjacent to the Hickam area. Someone commented that the Navy must be using very large spotting charges in their practice bombs. (A spotting charge was normally a pound of black powder with an igniter placed in the base of a practice bomb. At the time of impact of the bomb in the target area the black powder is ignited, releasing a cloud of smoke which is photographed by the scoring camera in the dropping aircraft.) The next aircraft to come into view was a lone float plane which came in toward Pearl Harbor from the direction of Barber's point to the west. After it disappeared from view behind the Marine barracks, a geyser of water was seen to rise high in the air. Now that just did not look right. Sure enough it was a torpedo plane, not a float plane; although they did not figure that out for about a minute. At the end of that minute, the first three aircraft came over the Hickam barracks at rooftop level, displaying their big red, round insignia and instantly everyone knew they were at war.

There was a big rush to get out of the barracks, most people guessing that it would shortly become a target. Several ran out into the street to the north of the barracks. By that time it seemed that there were strafing aircraft everywhere. They dropped their bombs or torpedoes and then came over and strafed targets at Hickam. There were no sure slit trenches at Hickam that day so some took cover behind the street curbs, but when they made themselves as flat as possible and one eye could see over the curb, it appeared that somewhere else would be better.

"Someplace else" was the hanger. There were guns there, offering the possibility to shoot back. The available gun mounts were quickly manned and a lot of guys left over. Two of these decided to take a run across the main runway to where two of the squadron's B-18s were dispersed. The idea was to arm it with a .30 caliber machine gun. They went to the armament shack where one of them took a machine gun while the other carried a 100-round ammunition can. (The aerial .30 caliber was designed to have the 100-round am-munition can mounted on the gun and made for quick change when that can was empty.) They set out running as hard as they could to cover the half-mile distance to the B-18. The scene outside was chaos. The Japanese planes seemed to be everywhere, and the Navy was doing a busy job of trying to shoot them down. Their anti-aircraft shells were exploding all over the place at an altitude of about 200 feet, or so it seemed. The fuses from the nose of the anti-aircraft shells came down as a unit about six inches in diameter and weighing several pounds. One quickly became more concerned about being wounded by one of these than by the Japanese. In the midst of this lively environment there appeared several new B-17s, mixing in with the Navy's anti-aircraft fire and the Japanese, who were probably as confused at this unexpected turn of events as the B-17 crews since the Japanese did not shoot any of them down. They had no ammunition and their guns were still in cosmoline. Word later was that they all found a safe landing place somewhere on the island.

Finally, with tongues hanging out, our two warriors reached their objective. To their surprise it was found that the aircraft had guns and ammunition. The ammunition was in fabric belts rather than the normal aerial ammunition belt. (The latter is made of steel and is so constructed that when a round is fired the part of the belt which brought it to the gun is discarded. The fabric belt can be made to work in the aerial machine gun with a little effort). One man took the rear crank-up turret while the other took the nose turret. The aircraft was pointed in an easterly direction. Our intrepid runners had barely reached their destination when, from the direction of Honolulu, off the right wing of the B-18 an aircraft appeared, flying at tree-top level. This was a single engine aircraft, therefore it must be Japanese. As he came in range, approaching them head on, they began firing. At that angle about the only target is the engine; many rounds went into his engine but the aircraft kept going. After he had passed they did not turn to follow him because almost immediately his buddy appeared from the same direction. He was given the same treatment; however, he returned the fire with his 20mm cannon. He scored several hits along the trailing edge of the B-18 but failed to scratch either of our gunners. The situation was such that one wondered if there would soon be more Japanese planes or if this thing would go on all day, or what. Finally at about 1000 hours, a formation of 20 to 30 planes came over at an altitude of about 10,000 feet. They dropped from that altitude and their target was Hickam. The barracks and many of the hangers were hit. Many of the B-17s were damaged beyond repair by the strafing which had occurred in the first attack. Several were lost when a bullet struck the panel of Very pistol flares on the fuselage wall in the radio cabin. The aircraft simply burned in half and it was a sad and sorry sight to see these great planes sitting with broken backs. Naturally a standard task for combat crews was added. The Very flares were carried in a .50 caliber ammunition box and the first man off the aircraft after landing was tasked with taking the box of flares out of the plane and to a safe distance away.

Much of the barracks, perhaps all, could not be occupied. A fire had started in the roof structure under the copper cladding and this burned for two or three days. In the combat crews many of the senior non-commissioned officers had apartments away from the barracks and in those cases whole crews bunked with them. The mess hall had suffered a direct hit and was unusable. A temporary mess hall was set up along side Pearl Harbor Channel and served cheese, bread and coffee on Sunday night.

Headquarters Seventh Air Force
13 June 1942
Subject: Air Force Employment at Midway

1. By order of Cincpac, The VII Bomber Command came under the operational control of PatWingTwo. Until 1 April 1942, all planes of the VII Bomber Command were, because of the tactical situation, assigned either to search or striking force, which permitted little training of bombardiers and aerial gunners. On that date, approximately 25 percent of the planes of the VII Bomber Command were made available for limited training daily.

2. On 18 May 1942, the 7th Air Force was placed on a special alert in preparation for meeting a threatened enemy attack. At that time 34 B-17s were on hand, of which seven were Cs and Ds which were not sufficiently armed to utilize on combat missions. That left a total of 27 B-17s suitable for combat service. From the 18th to about the 28th of May no B-17s were used on search missions but were held loaded with five hundred and six hundred pound demolition bombs as a striking force.

3. From 18 May to 10 June, 60 B-17s arrived in this department and were assigned or attached to the VII Bomber Command. This, of necessity, required a radical reassignment of equipment to the tactical squadrons, some of which received new equipment only one or two days prior to 3 June. Bombers arriving from the Mainland in the early part of the morning were turned over immediately to the Depot, where extra ferry tanks were removed, auxiliary tanks installed in the radio compartment, and equipment and armament checked. The planes were then made available to the tactical units within 24 hours. To accommodate this large increase in planes, it became necessary to convert the 72nd Squadron from a B-18 to a B-17 squadron. This reequipping of the 72nd Squadron with B-17s began on 4 May when two airplanes of this type were assigned to them. They were not fully equipped until about two days before they were committed to combat. Obviously no opportunity existed for the proper training of this unit

4. Upon arrival of the additional equipment, all squadrons were brought up to Tables of Organization strength. Little opportunity existed for combat crews and maintenance personnel to familiarize themselves with the new equipment, particularly the ball-type turret. During the action several cases of malfunctioning of the bomb release mechanisms were reported, and it is believed these can be directly attributed to the short time available to personnel to become familiar with their material. During combat it was found that some ball turrets when operated to maximum traverse, pulled away their electrical fittings, necessitating manual operation of the turrets.

5. Because of the time and space elements, it was necessary for combat crews to accomplish to a large extent their own servicing and maintenance at Midway. Crews returned from long and trying combat missions to find that they must reservice their own planes and accomplish essential maintenance. As a result they went into the air on some missions in a very exhausted condition.

6. After a two weeks period of alert, the first actual combat mission began when one squadron of six airplanes was ordered by PatWingTwo to proceed to Midway. This squadron arrived at Midway on the 30 May and flew two search missions on the following two days to a distance of 800 miles and return. On 31 May another squadron of six airplanes was ordered to Midway and, after making a tank change to comply with local instructions, was sent on a search mission on 31 May and 1 June. These airplanes were flown on distant search missions to 800 miles and return with an installation of one bomb-bay tank and one-half bomb load. Combat crews flew approximately thirty hours in two days before the beginning of actual hostilities, in addition to accomplishing their own maintenance.

7. On 3 June actual combat began and six additional airplanes were flown to Midway to assist in attack on a reported force of Japanese vessels. The first combat began on 3 June at 1623 hours, when nine B-17s were ordered to attack a force bearing 265 degrees and 570 miles from Midway. This force was reported by pilots conducting the bombing operations to consist of five BBs, or CAs and other warships and transport vessels estimated to be about 45 in number. The attack was conducted by elements from an altitude of 8000 feet, and dropping thirty-six 600 pound demolition bombs having 1/10 second delay fuses, in train at 120 foot interval. A total of five hits, one probable hit and four near misses, was observed on two BBs or CAs and two large transports. One BB and one transport were observed aflame. One waterline hit was made on the other transport.

8. On 4 June the Japanese fleet was located bearing 225 degrees and 180 miles from Midway, and four B-26s armed with 2000 pound torpedoes were dispatched. This force attacked two carriers in the face of extremely heavy fighter opposition and anti-aircraft fire from all caliber guns of the fleet. Two of the B-26s were shot down, but one of the lost airplanes was observed to have launched its torpedo before being shot down. The other two B-26s successfully delivered their attack and reported torpedoes launched true for the target and combat crews reported two hits. They returned to Midway and made crash landings on the airdome. Both planes were riddled with bullet holes throughout. It is interesting to note that one leakproof tank had approximately fifty bullet holes in it and apparently operated successfully for at least 180 miles on the return flight.

9. Fourteen B-17s were dispatched at 0415 NT 4 June and proceeded on course to attack the same body bombed the previous afternoon. Enroute to the target, at a distance of approximately 200 miles, a message was received in the clear, stating that another enemy task force complete with many carriers was approaching Midway from 325 degrees at a distance of 145 miles. The bomber formation was directed to intercept, and climbed to 20,000 feet. Interception was effected at 0732 MT. At 0810 two carriers were seen to emerge from beneath broken clouds. The order to attack by flights was given at 0814. The first two flights attacked with a total of forty-four 500 pound bombs. They obtained one hit on the stern of a carrier. The hit was obtained by the second element and the photographs previously furnished headquarters were taken at this time. The third flight of three B-17s obtained one hit on the port bow, one waterline hit amidship, one possible hit and five near misses. The fifth element of two planes attacked this second carrier and obtained one hit, one possible hit and two near misses. The three B-17s of the fourth

element attacked the third carrier and obtained one hit and two near misses. Three carriers were reported on fire after this attack. Anti-aircraft fire was heavy and at the proper altitude but generally behind. Enemy fighters were not anxious to close, but of those that did, two Zeros were shot down.

10. Six B-17s, each with half a bomb load and one bomb bay tank, were dispatched by PatWingTwo from Oahu to Barking Sands early on 4 June. There airplanes were then ordered from Barking Sands to Midway, and attacked the carrier force at 1830 hours before landing at Midway. This attack was conducted on one CV and one DD from an altitude of 3600 feet. Eight bombs were dropped, resulting in one hit and two near misses on the carrier, which was already aflame. One hit was made on a destroyer and the destroyer sank. Heavy anti-aircraft fire was experienced during this attack, and eight Zero fighters made interception with the bombing force. Four of these fighters were shot down and one was damaged. The bombardier's window in one ship and a hole approximately 19 inches in diameter from an anti-aircraft shell in the wing of another airplane was the only damage to the bombing force. Considerable difficulty was experienced with bomb racks on this flight and about nine bombs hung on the racks. The two damaged B-17s were unable to drop any of their bombs.

11. Six B-17s took off from Midway and made contact with the previously mentioned CV force at about 1830 hours on 4 June. Four of these airplanes attacked a cruiser, dropping twenty-eight 500 pound demolition bombs and observed one hit, one probable hit and two near misses. This attack was made from 25,000 feet and reported no anti-aircraft fire. The cruiser was left smoking heavily and aflame. No interception by fighters was made. The remaining two planes attacked a BB and a burning CV from 10,000 feet, dropping sixteen 500 pound demolition bombs. One hit and two near misses were observed on the BB and two hits and three near misses on the CV. The carrier slowed down sharply, and anti-aircraft fire stopped from both the BB and the CV. Several Zero fighters intercepted these planes and three Zeros were shot down and one damaged. No damage was reported to the B-17s.

12. On 5 June, three squadrons of six airplanes each were dispatched by PatWingTwo from Oahu to Midway. Four B-17s took off from Midway and made contact at 0830 hours with two BBs or Cas, bearing 270 degrees and 130 miles from Midway. These airplanes dropped nineteen 500 pound observing two probable hits and three near misses. The attack was made from 20,000 feet and results were not observed. Heavy anti-aircraft fire was reported but no fighter opposition. No damage was done to the B-17s. Four additional B-17s attacked a second BB or CA of this force immediately after the first attack from the same attitude and dropped twenty 500 pound demolition bombs, reporting one hit on the stem and four near misses. No fighter interception was made, and no damage was reported to the B-17s.

13. Seven B-17s made contact at 1825 hours on 5 June with one large cruiser bearing 300 degrees and 300 miles from Midway. Four of these airplanes attacked from 16,000 feet and dropped thirty-two 500 pound demolition bombs. Two hits and three near misses were reported. Anti-aircraft fire did not damage the B-17s, and there was no fighter opposition to this force. Three of these airplanes dropped twenty-four 500 pound demolition bombs from 14,500 feet on this same cruiser, reporting one hit and one near miss. Damage as

a result of this bombing was not observed, and the same report relative to anti-aircraft fire and fighter opposition was made.

14. Five B-17s attacked a heavy cruiser at 1825 hours on 6 June, bearing 320 degrees and 435 miles from Midway. This squadron dropped fifteen 600 pound and eight 300 pound bombs from altitudes ranging from 9000 to 12,500 feet. The damage was not observed, but extremely heavy anti-aircraft fire was reported. One B-17 in this flight was seen to drop its bomb-bay tank, probably as a result of anti-aircraft fire. This airplane failed to return from the mission, and to date its crew has not been recovered. A fact of interest is that this airplane was named the City of San Francisco and was an airplane donated to the government by the citizens of that city. One other B-17 landed in the ocean as a result of fuel shortage. This crew was located and picked up, but one member of the crew was killed.

15. On 6 June, 12 additional B-17s were ordered to Midway from Oahu. About 1140 on 6 June, six B-17s made contact with a large submarine that was mistaken for a cruiser. Twenty 500 pound demolition bombs were dropped from an altitude of 9500 feet and photographs of the pattern showed several near misses. The submarine was friendly and was not damaged. No other contacts were made with enemy surface forces after this date.

16. During the entire operation, a total of 55 B-17 plane missions were flown, and three hundred and fourteen 500 hundred or 600 pound bombs and eight 300 pounds bombs were dropped from altitudes varying from 3600 to 25,000 feet. These bombs were dropped on an accumulated total seven BBs or CAs, seven CVs, one DD and two transports. Twenty-two direct hits, six probable hits, and 46 near misses were reported. Contact with 18 Zero type fighters was reported, and of this number, ten were shot down and two damaged. Two B-17s were lost at sea and two were damaged. Four B-26 plane missions were flown with four topedoes, scoring three hits on two carriers. Two B-26s were lost at sea and two made crash landings at Midway, badly damaged. Very heavy antiaircraft fire was reported throughout and up to altitudes of 20,000 feet.

The following comments and recommendations are deemed pertinent and have been derived from personal observation, official reports and interviews with combat personnel.

Incidents and conclusions reached which should be of value to training establishments.

A. Servicing and maintenance conditions, as well as the general living conditions on small Eastern island at Midway were poor, due to lack of provision for greatly augmented airplane strength. Combat crews consistently flew long, grueling missions daily and were forced to do their own servicing and necessary maintenance to a large extent. As a result of this condition and because of continuous search missions from the beginning of the attack, many of the combat crews fought missions in an exhausted physical condition. Only damaged aircraft were returned to Oahu during the battle, and many crews were used continuously throughout the operations.

B. During the attack by Japanese aircraft on Midway, the powerhouse on Eastern Island was destroyed, resulting in complete disruption of one of the systems for refueling. The servicing of aircraft immediately became a serious and tedious proposition, and overworked crews spent long hours servicing by hand from cans and drums. More than one method of servicing should be planned at all bases that might be under attack. The enemy could have sent a second wave of attackers to destroy our aircraft on the ground during the slow servicing and refueling due to disrupted installations.

C. Power equipment is a vital necessity for clearing debris from runways and operating areas of any airdrome under attack. Many airplanes were disabled from tire punctures caused by shell fragments and coral thrown up on the runway.

D. Attack with torpedo bearing aircraft must be well coordinated with dive bombing or high level bombardment attack unless heavy loss of torpedo bombers is to be suffered. Fighter support if the range permits should always be used.

E. Adequate ground crews and equipment for servicing, maintaining and care of aircraft must be provided in order not to over-fatigue combat crews. Every consideration should be given to adequate underground facilities for messing and sleeping combat crews. It is believed that rest and comfort of combat crews is one of the most important factors in their accomplishment of assigned missions.

F. Adequate air transport service facilitates supply and maintenance to bases distant from supply points. During this operation, an already over-burdened transport service was forced into almost continuous operation.

G. Japanese carrier forces proved to be highly maneuverable in their efforts to avoid bomb patterns. In some instance, complete circles, combined with turning maneuvers, were employed to avoid high level bombers. Photographs of one large carrier showed a turning radius of about 1700 feet. They made continuous efforts to secure cloud cover.

H. Anti-aircraft fire from carriers and from the immediate escorting vessels proved to be more accurate than from other surface ships.

I. For operations against fighter aircraft and in strafing operations it is believed that the current belly loading of ammunition does not contain a sufficiently high percentage of tracer ammunition. Combat personnel believe that tracer ammunition should be as one in three.

J. LB-30 aircraft is considered suitable for search operations, but is believed that the use of PBYs for search in the face of the enemy is not desirable, due to their particularly slow speed and vulnerablility to fighter aircraft.

K. The new ball turrets on the B-17Es proved to be a very successful installation and caused only minor electrical difficulty in their operation. In planning the use of electrically operated turrets it should be considered that such installations are a continuous drain on the electrical system of the airplane. Some provision should be made to augment the present source of electrical power since these turrets are in almost continuous operation during combat missions. All fields where bombardment airplanes are stationed should have extra turrets for instruction in maintenance and operation.

L. Coordination with carrier based aviation is an extremely difficult problem for ground based aircraft because carriers normally operate under conditions of radio silence. Every effort should be made to plan attacks well in advance.

M. No great difficulty was experienced in hitting surface ships at altitudes of 4000 to 25,000 feet. The Japanese apparently have the reverse of a bombsight mounted on their surface craft and can estimate the time at which the bombardier making his run will have to release his bombs. At this point the ship begins to maneuver, adding to the difficulty of hitting it by precision bombing. In order to aid in this computation, enemy fighter planes appeared to be stationed above the fleet for the purpose of giving the exact altitude of our bombers to the ships in the fleet. This aided them in calculating the time of bomb release and also was a great aid in anti-aircraft fire. The anti-aircraft fire of the Japanese fleet was heavy but ineffective. The only serious hit obtained by the guns was on the wing of a B-17. On the other hand, the fire of automatic weapons was quite accurate and caused some losses.

N. Pilots consider the B-17 to be an excellent combat airplane. With the addition of two .50 caliber machine guns in the nose of this airplane would be capable of taking care of itself against almost any opposition encountered. The airplane is particularly tough. The major deficiency is its range and every effort should be made to produce and deliver the B-29 and B-36 types to this area. The B-26 is considered satisfactory as a torpedo bomber but training for crews and ordnance personnel in use of torpedoes must be accomplished and ample supply of reinforced torpedoes kept on hand.

O. The Japanese avoided damaging the runways at Midway. If they had been bombed it would have added greatly to the difficulty of our operation.

P. Liaison communication was uniformly excellent and no jamming was apparent. Interplane communications on command frequencies unsatisfactory due to three types of transmitters which could not overlap to provide a common frequency.

Q. At our bases scattered throughout the Pacific we must not only have an ample supply of fuel, bombs, and ammunition, but a supply of spare parts, special equipment and enough maintenance personnel to take care of the equipment likely to be based there until reinforcements can be brought in.

R. Vital installations where dispersion and concealment are impractical must be protected against air attacks.

The time immediately following Midway was one of relative quiet for the 5th Group and the last such until the end of the war. That quiet was broken in late summer of 1942. The United States made the strategic decision that it was necessary to stop the expansion of the Japanese Empire before it captured Australia. The place where they were to be stopped was the medium-sized island of Guadalcanal in the Solomon Group.

The Navy landed a Marine combat force on the island on 7 August 1942. Shortly thereafter the 11th Group was ordered to the South Pacific. Meanwhile the Fifth Group remained on Oahu as an organization but its planes and combat crews were sent to the South Pacific and attached to the 11th Group. The 11th was commanded by the former commander of the 23rd Squadron, Lt. Col. LaVerne G. Saunders. He had been promoted to Lt. Col. at the end of December 1941 and given command of the Eleventh group. With the move to the South Pacific, he was promoted to Colonel. He was a very aggressive commander and frequently flew with his squadrons as Command Pilot. While flying with the 31st Squadron on a mission up the "slot" the pilot of his plane was killed and the co-pilot severely wounded. Saunders took control of the plane and successfully ditched it on a reef. He and the surviving crewmembers were rescued the following day. The crew of the 5th as well as the 11th got a great deal of combat experience under his leadership. In December 1942 he was promoted to Brigadier General, and was at that time the youngest BG in the Army.

With Colonel Brooke Allen commanding, the 5th Group moved to the South Pacific in November 1942. Most made the long trip in the Liberty ship Peter H. Burnett, taking along everything that one imagined would be needed to survive in a jungle environment. The planes and combat crews were retrieved from the 11th Group. Two squadrons, the 23rd and 72nd, set up home bases on the island of Espiritu Santo on the New Hebrides group while the 31st and the 394th set up home bases at Henderson Field on Guadalcanal. The exercise was to spend a month at the home base and to then change locations with the other two squadrons. When you were at Guadalcanal (usually shortened to *Canal*), you flew one day and you rested and did what maintenance your plane required the next. When at Santo some reconnaissance missions were flown and heavy maintenance work done on the planes as required.

In 1942 and early 1943 operations were out of Henderson Field which was shared with Navy SBDs among others. Living conditions were primitive. Some sleeping accommodations were available at a transient camp maintained by the Marine Corps. This became unpopular after a night in which a Marine patrol chased a Japanese patrol through one of the tents at about midnight. Many of the crews carried quartermaster cots with them from Santo and slept at the plane. In early 1943 the shortage of food was such that the daily ration consisted of corn flakes for breakfast and tomato soup for lunch and dinner. During this period of time American ground forces controlled Henderson, the fighter strip and a perimeter area, and enemy troops were close enough so that small arms fire could be heard. By the end of February Japanese troops had been cleared from the island and in the spring of 1943 conditions at the *Canal* were greatly improved with the opening of Carney Field for heavy bombers. Throughout this time the enemy played the *Charley* game which consisted of sending a lone medium bomber to the *Canal* at about 2200 hours at 20,000 feet. He seldom hit anything of military value and naturally the searchlights got on him and the 90mm AA began banging away and making so much noise that it was impossible to sleep even if one did not take refuge in a slit trench. That was the purpose of the *Charley* game ... keep everyone awake.

Frequent targets for bombing missions were Kahili airfield on the southern tip of Bouganville (also known as "Buggerville" because the buggers might get you up there) and nearby Shortland Harbor and Treasury Island; Munda Point on New Georgia and a fighter strip at Buka Passage at the northern end of Bouganville. First timers at the *Canal* were usually scheduled for a milk run to a lightly defended seaplane base at Rekata Bay on Choisel. Information from Coast Watchers frequently noted that the day after the 5th had successfully bombed an airstrip the enemy had repaired it and operated from it. (Coast Watchers were mostly Australian plantation owners or civil servants who lived in the Solomons prior to the outbreak of war. When the Japanese came, they took to the hills (most of the area on most of the islands was hilly) with a squad of Fiji Scouts and a portable radio set and supplied valuable information on enemy positions, results of our

strikes and assisted in the rescue of downed crews.) This required many repeat missions to the enemy airfields in the area. The runways were not the only targets at these bases and many stores were destroyed and many planes destroyed on the ground.

Throughout the early part of 1943, all missions flown were during daylight, sometimes with fighter escort but more often without. This did not prove to be a serious problem. The B-17 was heavily armed with .50 caliber machine guns, both hand held and in power turrets, and it had a useful trajectory to 1000 yards. The hundreds of hours of flight experience in the B-17 which the 5th brought to this conflict resulted in such tight formations in combat situations that it was difficult for enemy fighters to penetrate the defense, and damage to planes and personnel casualties were light during this period.

There were many changes during the spring of 1943. The 11th Group was relieved and replaced with the 307th Group. The 13th Air Force was activated and all Army Air Force groups became part of it. The 5th, which had belonged first to the Hawaiian Air Force, then the 7th Air Force, was now part of the 13th. At the working and flying level these command changes meant little. During the whole time the 5th Group had been the family and the squadron the home.

The 307th Group was equipped with new B-24s, an aircraft which surpassed the B-17 in speed, range and bomb load. The remaining B-17s were old and nearing the end of their useful life and were gradually, with their combat crews, gathered into the 23rd Squadron. They were committed to night missions as the other 5th Group squadrons gradually acquired B-24s and new combat crews. Night missions were a great change from daytime. Gunners were pretty much unable to see if anything threatening the plane was out there. The guns were all manned just the same. The night flyers then took up the *Charley* game but improved over the one played by the Japanese. The planes carried a full load of 300 pound bombs and take-off was made at half-hour intervals. These missions were almost all carried out against Kahili, usually at an altitude of 12,000 to 14,000 feet. When the objective was reached, several bombing runs were made and on each, one or two 300 pounders dropped. Meanwhile their AA pounded away and never seemed to hit anything. By the time all planes had kept their schedule, the enemy below were kept awake for most of the night and many fires started. There was concern for the possibility of encountering night fighters, and the concern was that it seemed that it would be impossible to defend against them. Finally after several nights of these missions a B-17 was seen by a following plane to explode. It was never certain whether it was a victim of a night fighter or of a direct hit by an AA shell.

The Guadalcanal era was coming to an end. At the end of July every plane which could carry a bomb and every surface vessel which had a cannon rendezvoused near New Georgia Island and delivered their explosives on Munda Point in preparation by an amphibious landing by the Army ground forces.

MISSIONS

NEW GEORGIA AND TARAWA ISLANDS

New Georgia Island was another important stronghold for the enemy. Their grip was being loosened, however, as American ground forces had landed on the island and were preparing

for a drive on Munda Airfield. For the first time, the 23rd and 72nd Squadrons would be called on to attack enemy troops on the ground in support of an American ground offensive. It was a highly successful mission.

Meanwhile, the 31st was preparing for a strike against Tarawa in the Gilbert Islands. Taking off from a base on Ellice Island, the 31st Squadron's planes flew 700 miles to reach their target. Once again, it was a successful mission, though the re-

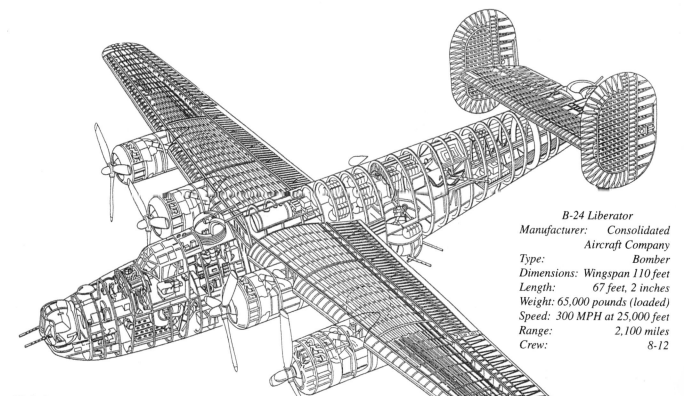

B-24 Liberator
Manufacturer: Consolidated
Aircraft Company
Type: Bomber
Dimensions: Wingspan 110 feet
Length: 67 feet, 2 inches
Weight: 65,000 pounds (loaded)
Speed: 300 MPH at 25,000 feet
Range: 2,100 miles
Crew: 8-12

turn flight home was an eventful one. One plane had to land in the ocean, 100 miles from the base at Funafuti, while two others did not have enough fuel to taxi to the revetment area after landing.

The 5th Group was beginning to receive more and more of the new B-24s. These planes would be used in an entirely new type of mission, a mission that the 394th was selected to carry out. These B-24s, nicknamed *Snoopers*, would use radar to bomb their target — the *Tokyo Express*. This was the nickname given to the Japanese shipping operations between Rabaul and the Solomon Islands.

The *Snoopers* augmented an already powerful arsenal of men and planes. On 12 September, they hit an enemy sub and destroyer. Two weeks later, they sank one ship and damaged three others in the *Tokyo Express* route. The *Snoopers* continued their precise and deadly hits throughout the summer and fall, attacking shipping in Bougainville, north New Britain and south New Ireland, sinking five ships and damaging nine others in September, and in another show of their power and prowess, sinking six enemy ships and damaging another ten during early October.

As the year drew to a close, strikes from the 5th's squadrons encountered less and less resistance. Kahili and Kara had become easier targets. And the *Tokyo Express* was taking a thorough beating. On 3 November, B-24s from the 23rd and 72nd Squadrons once again took aim on those shipping routes, attacking a Japanese naval task force en route to New Ireland. When the bombing had stopped, one of the huge Japanese transports was stopped dead in the water and six Zekes had been shot down. As 1943 drew to a close, the 23rd and 31st Squadrons continued their bombardment of targets on Bougainville and throughout the Solomon Islands. In conjunction with aircraft from the 307th, they destroyed two runways on Nauru Island.

RABAUL, NEW IRELAND

In late November, squadrons from the 5th and the 307th Groups joined in a Joint Army-Navy Attack on Japanese shipping in Simpson Harbor, Rabaul. This was the 5th's first strike on that island. Carrier-based aircraft hit first, followed by aircraft from the 5th and 307th bombing from altitudes as high as 20,000 feet. Swarms of Japanese planes crowded the sky, trying to intercept the American planes, and fierce anti-aircraft fire came from the ground. Still the men of the 5th would not be denied. Col. Unruh, of the 23rd, brought his squadron's planes down to 8,500 feet to bomb a cruiser lying in the harbor. Planes from the 23rd also shot down four enemy fighters; two more were listed as probably destroyed.

The *Snoopers* also had a large role in the strikes against Rabaul. On 24 and 25 November, a Snooper caught sight of the Tokyo Express, shadowing the enemy vessels until Allied naval units could intercept them; in all, four enemy ships were sunk. In late December, a Snooper inflicted heavy damage on a Japanese sub.

The 5th continued delivering heavy blows against Rabaul all through Decemb r, although they sometimes encountered poor weather conditions. The Lakauna Airdrome at Rabaul suffered extensive damage and Rabaul Town was also hit several times. The deadly accurate bombs rained down on Rabaul by the forces of the 5th Bombardment Group set three Japanese ships on fire; one sank, another was severely damaged and probably sank, while nothing was left of the third but a smoking hull. The Bomber Barons even delivered a special Christmas package to the enemy at Rabaul in the form of some accurately placed bombs.

The Japanese continued to send their fighters up and after the planes of the 5th, but more often than not, they found themselves on the losing end of the fight. And despite the fierce defenses the Japanese mounted, the 5th Bombardment Group did not suffer a single fatality over that three-month period until Col. Unruh and his crew were shot down over New Ireland.

On 28 December of that year, the *Snoopers* left the 5th Group and moved to Munda, where they were redesignated as the 868th Bombardment Squadron.

As 1943 drew to a close, the Allies had retaken many of the strategic islands that once were in Japanese hands. They controlled New Georgia and had successfully invaded the Solomon Islands. New Britain, Tarawa and Bougainville had been wrested away from the enemy. The Japanese had been driven from Salamana. The Marshall and Gilbert Islands were being battered by the 7th Air Force. The 23rd and 31st Squadrons continued to pound away at enemy targets. New Ireland, Buka and Bougainville all felt the 5th's bombs. Rabaul was besieged by relentless day and night bombing raids. With each attack, the enemy was growing weaker, its offensive and defensive capabilities diminishing day by day.

In January 1944, the 23rd and 72nd Squadrons began operating from Munda, which allowed their B-24s to carry larger bomb loads, delivering even more severe blows to the Japanese. They hit and destroyed grounded aircraft and turned enemy runways into strips of giant craters. Ground installations and airfields were left in smoldering ruins. The American forces and their allies had the skills, the equipment and the will needed to win the war, as well as having a righteous cause on their side. And bad weather be damned! The Fighting Fifth would make it through and complete their missions.

Rabaul was one of Japan's most important holdings. To strike at the heart of the enemy's installations and forces in Rabaul would deal a serious blow to their ability to continue the fight. Losing Rabaul would also deliver a serious blow to the morale of the already beleaguered Japanese forces. And so the fusillade continued.

The Group's ground crews worked non-stop to repair damaged planes quickly and send them back into the air. In a briefing to the 394th, published in a history of the 5th Bombardment Group, Col. Reddoch praised the work of the 5th, saying, "Without resorting to our records, I believe I can safely say the 5th Group in the past two months has dropped more bombs more accurately on major targets than at any time in its history. The idea is to be long-faced over a mediocre mission and to aim at nothing short of perfection."

There was much more to come. Rabaul had just been a warm-up for the next great battle:

Damaged B-24 on 7 June 1944 in Truk, pilot Lt. Denver D. Campbell.

Damaged B-24 on 7 June 1944 in Truk, pilot Lt. Denver D. Campbell.

The strike against Truk was carried out to support a Naval Task Force operation in the Palau Islands. The Japanese would defend the island with all their strength, but it would not be enough to overcome the skill and determination of the 5th Group.

TRUK

On 27 March, a formation set out for Truk. Huge weather fronts prevented them from reaching their intended target, but they bombed an alternative target.

The following week, a formation of B-24s from the 5th Group struck Dublon Town, on another of the islands in the Truk Atoll. Again, the weather interfered with the scheduled plans. One squadron was unable to reach its intended target. Still, the Bomber Bar-

(l to r) Front row: Sgt. Satterfield (tail gunner), Sgt. Barrow, S/Sgt. Daywalt (third engineer), T. Sgt Bigley (radio), and S/Sgt. Trutter (engineer). Back row: T.Sgt Jones (engineer), 1st Lt. Riley (bombardier), 1st Lt. Mossberg, 1st Lt. unknown (copilot), and 1st Lt. Bolton (pilot).

ons blasted away at Dublon Town in the face of fierce enemy defenses. Another important target was Moen Airfield.

In June, Truk once again felt the wrath of the Bomber Barons. There was an important fighter base and repair facility on Eton Island, as well as a major installation on Dublon Island, both in the Truk Atoll. Destroying or severely damaging those facilities would add another weak link to an already weakening chain. Furthermore, the Truk Atoll was one of the keys to Japan's hold on the Philippines; a successful strike would loosen the enemy's grip on the Philippines.

On 15 June, American Marines staged an invasion of Saipan, with support from the U.S. Navy fleet. Carrier-based enemy aircraft attacked the fleet, but were met with fierce defenses from American planes. Again, the Japanese suffered heavy losses: 428 planes lost, five ships sunk, two others probably sank and 11 damaged.

The 5th Group attacked Yap Island in support of the Saipan invasion. Any enemy naval vessel which attempted to refuel or take refuge in those waters became an instant target.

THE CAROLINE ISLANDS

The first strikes at Truk had been costly ones for the 5th Group. Many of the group's planes were badly damaged. In the raid on 2 April, three crews were lost. And when the battle was over, it was time for the 5th Group to make its next move. The 5th's Group Headquarters and squadrons made the move from Munda and Guadalcanal to Los Negros, an island in the Admiralty Group. From there, they would hit Woleai Island in the Caroline Island Group.

Los Negros had been invaded by the 1st Cavalry Division not long before the 5th Group moved to the island. It was the first time since the war began that the entire 5th Group was stationed in the same place. The battle for Los Negros had been hard-won. The bodies of enemy soldiers lying about the airfield bore testament to the fierce fighting that had just taken place. From Los Negros, the 5th Group would strike the Woleai Atoll. Woleai Island itself was of tremendous strategic importance to the Japanese. Search planes and naval vessels were based there, and the island was located along a major supply route for aircraft and supplies. A successful strike against Woleai would play an important role in plans for an invasion of New Guinea and Saipan.

In all, the 5th Bombardment Group made 13 strikes against the Woleai Atoll, nine of them against the island. These were long missions, ten hours in all, and completely over water. The bombers were all alone, with no fighter cover to help protect them. For their heroic efforts, they received a Distinguished Unit Citation.

BIAK

The pace of the war continued to quicken, as American forces time and again pushed the enemy back farther and farther toward their homeland. General MacArthur made a successful invasion of Dutch New Guinea in the early spring of 1944, and Truk, Satawan, Wake Island and Ponape were hard hit by Carrier Forces. In May, the 5th made more strikes against Truk and Woleai, but their primary objective was to pound Biak in preparation for the D-Day invasion.

(l to r) Front row: Paul Thompson, Loren Hobart Pocoacom, Vernon Jackson, Frank Martmurano, and Karl Freese. Back row: Howard Kurtz, Raymond Bowen Decensen, John Moffett, Billy Lacy, unknown, and Dave Porter.

Photo taken in 1944 on Wakde Island, Bill Lonas pilot.

Biak was an important supply base for the Japanese, and its beach was heavily defended. The 5th pounded the beach defenses, runways and the supply and personnel installations at Bosnek Town in a relentless barrage, which turned the whole target area into a massive inferno. They set fire to the enemy's gasoline supply on the island and reduced the headquarters building of their Army Air Flotilla to a pile of rubble.

Later in the month, the 5th staged another bombing raid on Bosnek Town; and this time, the infantry followed right behind. One by one, they overtook islands and installations that had once been in Japanese hands.

During the battle for Biak, the 5th did sustain some losses, as several B-24s were shot down and several crew members were injured.

YAP ISLAND

Yap Island, in the Carolines, had been the scene of previous 5th Group strikes. By late June, it was time for the B-24s to revisit the island to bomb supplies and personnel based there. On 22 June, Liberators set out for Yap Island. It was the first daylight strike on the target made by land-based aircraft. The primary targets were Japanese Navy vessels. When the Bomber Barons failed to find any ships, they turned their sights and their bombs on the Yap Airdrome and Yap Town itself. In addition to inflicting heavy damage on their targets, they also destroyed 16 enemy aircraft on the ground.

Throughout July and on into early August, the 5th continued the attack on Yap, as well as on Woleai Island. These long and dangerous missions were flown without the benefit of fighter escorts. The Japanese would not give up Yap without a long, hard fight. The air base and maintenance facilities were far too important to their war machine. Time and again, the enemy sent their fighters up to challenge the Bomber Barons. Several aircraft and several crews from the 5th were lost during these missions.

Between their missions to Yap, the 5th was also called upon for a pre-invasion bombing raid on Noemfoor Island, New Guinea. Their successful mission helped General MacArthur's ground forces to take the island with little opposition from the Japanese.

PALAU ISLANDS

The next target for the 5th Bombardment Group was the Palau Islands, part of the Caroline Islands Group.

So far, Saipan was in American hands and Guam had been successfully invaded. American forces had also taken Tinian in the Mariannas. Tinian was particularly important to our strategy for winning the war, for it was from that island that American bombers would strike at the heart of the Japanese homeland. And it was from Tinian that the Enola Gay would take flight to deliver the war-ending blow at Hiroshima.

The Palau Islands were the westernmost islands in the Carolines Group, the last major obstacle preventing the Allies from retaking the Philippines. They were also an important supply and command center, crucial to the Japanese war machine and, therefore, one of the war's most important targets.

In August, the 5th Group moved to Wakde Island, off the coast of western New Guinea to prepare for the strikes on the Palau Islands. Many new combat crews were arriving at this time, replacing the crews that had fought so hard and won so many battles.

These new crews had a difficult task ahead of them. Their job was to destroy Koror Town, an administrative headquarters for the enemy, and to wipe out the airdromes on Peleliu, Negsbus and Babelthaup. Because of strategic operations, the time for successfully completing these missions was limited. Time limits, weather and enemy defenses were once again no match for the Bomber Barons. By the time they had finished, the Palau targets were nothing but piles of useless rubble.

HALMAHERA ISLANDS

The Palau missions accomplished, it was on to the Halmahera Islands for the men of the 5th. Located south of the Philippines, the Halmaheras were vitally important to the enemy because of their numerous airfields and harbors. The islands also provided protection for Borneo, home to Japan's extensive oil and gas industries.

Again, heavy weather made the Bomber Barons' task more difficult. But no matter. They hit the airfields at Galela and

On 10 January 1945 the Group flew to Grace Peak north of Manila. Due to severe screw ups, our crew was low on gas and landed at this grass strip on the way back to Morotai, Halamahera Island. The "24" in the photo is Masr-a-Raider, the very same plane we had landed at Didorog.

Luhur A/S, Cebu City, P.I. Six planes, 31st Bomb Squadron, 5th Bomb Group. Excellent bombing.

Miti, at Lolobata and Hatataboka. And while the Bomber Barons were finishing their task, Marines were landing at Peleliu Island while General MacArthur and his troops were landing at Moratai. Now enemy targets in the Philippines could be hit by bombers stationed in the Palau Islands. Japan's grip on the South Pacific had been loosened even further. Soon, they would have to let go.

Following the bombing raids on the Palau and Halmahera Islands, the 5th struck personnel and supply targets in the Ceram Islands. In one strike, Amahai Town was almost annihilated.

BORNEO

In September, combat crews, planes and maintenance crews made another move, this time to Noemfoor Island, where they awaited word of their next mission. Soon they learned the intended target: Balikpapan, Borneo, home to Japan's most important source of aviation fuel and lubricating oil. To successfully strike this target would deal a near-death blow to the enemy's

ability to continue fighting. And even more than the strikes at Yap, Balikpapan would be a test of men and machinery. The flight to Borneo and back covered 2,610 miles, and the gross load carried by the B-24s would be in excess of 68,000 pounds. In addition, each plane's ammunition load would be cut in half, reducing their ability to ward off enemy fighter defenses. But the B-24 was a marvel of engineering and design. Several test take-offs and flights showed that the overloaded B-24s should be able to perform. As for the Bomber Barons, no mission had proved too difficult for them throughout the course of the war.

The 5th's first target was the massive Pandansari Refinery, with an 18,500 barrel-per-day capacity. On the night of 30 September 1944, planes from the 5th and 307th Groups of the Jungle Air Force, along with the 5th Air Force's 90th Bombardment Group, took off from Noemfoor bound for Balikpapan, once again flying without fighter cover.

The Japanese had a welcoming committee awaiting their arrival. In the face of these heavy defenses, the forces of right prevailed. The B-24s delivered a message loud and clear, written in blazing hot fire and thick black smoke. The Pandansari Refinery was all but obliterated.

The enemy's planes and anti-aircraft fire inflicted considerable damage. The 5th lost three of their B-24s, and many others limped home full of holes and with engines feathered. For their efforts, the 5th Group received a Presidential Unit Citation.

In October, the Bomber Barons paid another visit to Balikpapan, again hitting their targets with deadly accuracy. On a third strike, the group had the welcome support of the 18th and 347th Fighter Groups in their P-38s and P47s. After two more strikes, the oil-producing capacity at Balikpapan had been severely damaged. With replacement parts difficult to come by, the Japanese war machine had been dealt a devastating blow.

Meanwhile, carrier-based planes were pounding enemy targets at Luzon, Manila and Subic Bays, Panay, Cebu, Leyte and the Negros Islands. The stage was being set for an invasion of the Philippines.

On 18 October, planes from the 5th turned an oil separation and tank farm at Tarakan, Borneo, into another blazing inferno, destroying the main pumping station, the power plant and nine other buildings.

On 16 November 1944, all four squadrons returned to Borneo, this time to Brunei Bay where a task force of four enemy battleships, two heavy and four light cruisers, five destroy-

such an important prize. The Japanese fleet was gathering in hopes of repelling the coming invasion.

On 22 October 1944, bombers from the 5th Group staged a successful strike on the Lahug airdrome on Cebu Island.

Meanwhile, reconnaissance aircraft from Noemfoor swept over the Pacific in a near-constant search for enemy vessels. And when they were found, it was the Bomber Barons' turn. In the meantime, ground forces had landed on the east coast of Leyte Island.

Eight crews and planes from the 72nd Squadron, along with ground personnel, were sent to Morotai. For five straight days, they flew ten to 12-hour missions, protecting the troops on Leyte from an onslaught by enemy ships.

On 30 October, the 5th Group began an assault on enemy airfields in the Negros Islands. Again, the Bomber Barons were successful. Six airdromes on Negros Island were destroyed. They hit the Lahug Airdrome on Cebu, the Lumbia and Licanon Airfields on Mindanao and Puerta Princesa Airfield on Palawan. Japanese aerial defenses for the Visayan Islands and for the shipping lanes in the China Seas had been knocked out. In addition, the enemy was unable to launch air attacks against American ground forces. And the constant hammering of Japanese shipping kept supplies and reinforcements from reaching the Philippines.

On 2 November, the Bomber Barons were flying in the vicinity of Ormoc Bay when they found a group of Japanese ships carrying reinforcements. They struck at the enemy ships, sinking a 10,000 ton transport and sending 10,000 enemy soldiers to a watery grave.

The enemy fought back, sending their own bombers to Morotai. They were able to cause some damage and injuries, but they couldn't stop the Bomber Barons.

Throughout the remainder of 1944, the 5th hit enemy airfields, oil installations and ships throughout the Philippines, Celebes, Halmaheras and Borneo.

All during this time, Allied Forces were continuing their relentless march through the South Pacific. They struck at Iwo Jima, Manila and Luzon. They landed strike forces at Palawan, Ormoc Town and Mindoro Island, with bombing support from the 5th. General MacArthur controlled Leyte and Samar. Most of the Visayan Islands were under Allied control or in the hands of Filipino guerillas. Time was growing short for the Japanese.

It was now 1945, and the war was entering its final stages. The 5th continued their bombing attacks on enemy targets in the Philippines and the Halmahera Islands. By the time they received orders for a strike on Nichols Field at Luzon, Admiral Halsey's fleet had so thoroughly devastated the enemy defenses on the island that the Bomber Barons encountered no resistance. Their bombs rained down until Nichols Field was no longer recognizable; it was a series of enormous craters. Other airfields in the vicinity were also bombed during this mission.

The next target of the Bomber Barons was Cavite Naval Base, also on Luzon. From 24 January until 4 February, they pounded at the enemy installation until nearly every building on the base was no more than a pile of rubble. When bad weather prevented some of the 5th's aircraft from reaching Cavite, they turned their attention to Corregidor, giving the Japanese a taste of what was soon to come.

1st Lt. Hanna (standing on the right) and his B-24 crew in the Philippines.

ers and five merchant ships was waiting. Despite fierce opposition, the Bomber Barons sank one heavy cruiser and damaged a battleship and one light cruiser. Once again, the battle took a toll on the 5th, with three B-24s shot down and almost all planes in the group suffering damage.

THE PHILIPPINES

If the Allies could recapture the Philippines, the Japanese empire would be cut in half. It would almost certainly be a death knell to their war efforts. They would lose important naval bases. It would also be a heavy blow to the enemy's morale to lose

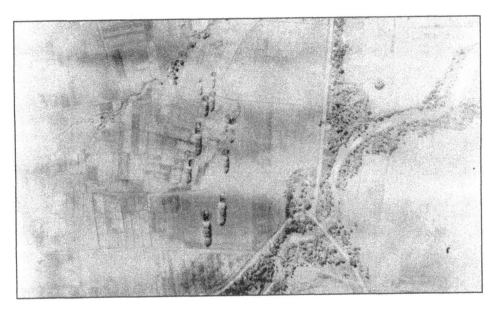

November 1944, the above three photos show bombs falling toward and exploding on Talisay Airdome on Negros Island, Philippine Islands. This island was ringed with many airdromes. Our job was to keep them neutralized by cratering the runways. This helped to minimize enemy air action against MacArthur's landings on Leyte and other nearby islands.

January 1945, Nichols Airdome at southern outskirts of Manila, Luzon, P.I. Note bombs walking down runway. Manila Bay to right.

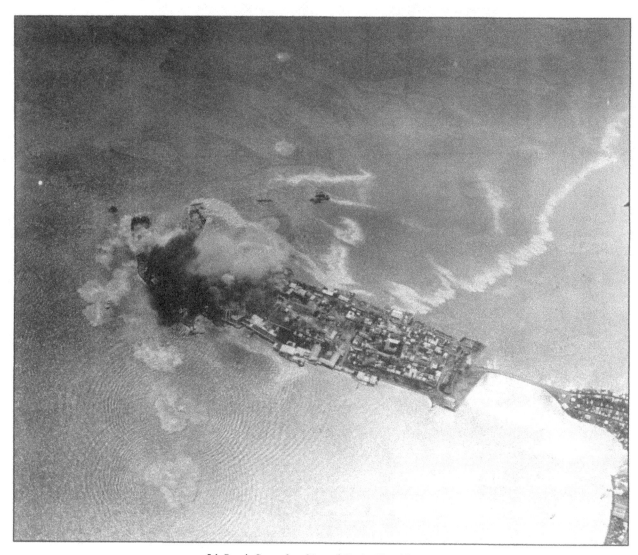

5th Bomb Group bombing of Cavite Naval Base.

February 1945, Bombs falling on fortifications on Corregidor, Luzon, P.I. This was just prior to U.S. paratrooper landing to retake the island.

A series of strikes against Corregidor began on 9 February, with the 5th taking out the enemy's gun emplacements on the island. By this time, the enemy was putting up very little resistance. American ground troops were taking the Philippines piece by piece. By the end of January, Clark Field was in American hands, the 8th Army had invaded Bataan and the 6th Army was inching closer to Manila. By the time the strikes on Corregidor began, General MacArthur's troops occupied Manilla.

Borneo, too, continued to stagger under the weight of so many packages delivered by the Bomber Barons. These packages were quickly depleting the enemy's ability to put up a fight against the relentless American assault from the sky, from the sea and from the ground.

In early March, the 5th Group moved to Guiuan, Samar, in the Philippines, where they remained until V-J Day. From their new base, the Bomber Barons supported landing operations at Mindanao and Panay and Cebu.

B-24s from the 5th Group also conducted photo reconnaissance missions over Saigon, prior to bombing the Thu Dau Mot Airdrome near the Japanese-controlled city. And they continued their strikes and search missions on targets throughout the Philippines. These missions required surgical accuracy on the part of the bomber crews, as American troops were always in the vicinity of the bombing targets.

The Bomber Barons not only supported the invasions by American troops, they also supported Australian operations in Borneo and Tarakan, as well as an invasion of Borneo by Australian and Dutch troops.

BORNEO INVASIONS

The next missions for the 5th Group were to take out the Japanese airfields in southwestern Borneo. Pontianak, Kotawaringen, Kuching and Sinkawang were devastated in a series of strikes. Then they blasted away at beach defenses and supply stations on Labuan Island and Bioaketon, which soon fell into the hands of Australian troops, troops who were very grateful for the deadly accuracy of the Bomber Barons.

The next target was a familiar one: Balikpapan. After first wiping out the Japanese anti-aircraft batteries, they struck at the enemy's beach defenses. Again, these missions were in support of Australian troops, who made a successful landing on Balikpapan on 1 July.

Japanese airfields in Borneo and the Celebes Islands were next on the Bomber Barons' hit list. Following a series of successful strikes against these airfields, the 5th once again flew support missions for Australian and American ground forces. They also flew strikes against small groups of enemy troops who were concentrated in the mountains of Negros Islands.

FORMOSA

The tide of the war had completely turned in the Allies' favor. Still, there were a few enemy strongholds that needed to be taken out. New crews, unused to the heat of battle, had been arriving from the mainland. They would soon get a taste of the fighting that the Bomber Barons had developed their reputation on since the early days of the war.

On 1 August, the huge Takao railroad marshaling yards on Formosa suffered a heavy blow at the hands of the Bomber Barons. Other targets on Formosa were also hit during the period from 7 August through 12 August.

Thoroughly weakened and demoralized, the Japanese were ready to begin peace negotiations. Their very homeland was aflame from daily strikes by America's mighty B-29 bombers.

The Bomber Barons continued to conduct patrol missions, but their bombing missions that had played such a significant role in turning the war to the Allies' favor, had come to an end. From the first day of the war, they had put President Roosevelt's words into action. They had hit the enemy wherever and whenever they found him.

CITATIONS AND COMMENDATIONS

In all, the 5th Bombardment Group flew approximately 1,000 combat missions. They fought from across the vast reaches of the South Pacific, driving their bombs into the heart of the enemy's defenses. Members of the 5th Bombardment Group received more than 13,300 decorations. Theirs is a most glorious history, filled with words of praise and commendation for their courage and determination.

In the early days of the war, the Bomber Barons received a commendation for their strike from Munda against the Lakunai Airdrome at Rabaul:

> My compliments to all hands concerned on damaging air blows of 26th and 27th. Keep 'em burning, wrote Admiral Halsey.

The American Navy's forces expressed their gratitude for the 5th Group's strikes on Rabaul in the following message, which reads, in part:

> Heartiest congratulations to you and all concerned on the Rabaul air strikes. The relentlessness of the attacks and their effectiveness have aroused great admiration and enthusiasm everywhere.

So effective were the Bomber Barons' missions against New Ireland, New Britain, Bougainville, Truk and Rabaul, that on 5 April 1943, Admiral Halsey once again sent a commendation:

> With the announcement of the virtual completion of the South Pacific campaign, except for mopping up and starving out operations, I can tell you that no greater fighting team has ever been put together. From the desperate days of Guadalcanal to the smooth steam-rolling days of Bougainville and the easy seizure of Green and Emirau, all U.S. and Allied services put aside every consideration but the one goal of wiping out the Japanese. As you progressed, your techniques and teamwork improved until at last Amphibious, Sea and Air Forces were working as one beautiful piece of precision machinery that crushed and baffled our hated enemy in every encounter. Your resourcefulness, tireless ingenuity, co-operation and indomitable fighting spirit form a battle pattern that will everywhere be an inspiration. And a great measure of sky blazing, sea sweeping, jungle smashing of the combat forces goes to the construction gangs and service organizations that bulldozed bases out of the jungle, brought up the beans and bullets and supplies. You never stopped moving forward, and the Jap[anese] never could get to launch a sustained counterattack. You beat them wherever you found them, and you never stopped looking for them and tearing into them. Well done.

In April and May 1944, the 5th Group carried out a series of 13 strikes on Woleai Island and other targets in the Caroline Islands Group. These strikes were so devastating to the enemy, so masterfully carried out, that they earned the 5th Group a Distinguished Unit Citation, which states:

> For outstanding performance of duty in action during the period 18 April to 15 May 1944. Almost immediately after arriving at Los Negros, Admiralty Islands, the 5th Bombardment Group (H) was assigned the task of neutralizing the Woleai Island group, a key base in the Japanese inner defense circle. Located there were an airfield, bivouac areas, supply and storage depots, a radio direction finder station, and a number of antiaircraft positions. The airfield was an important base for the staging of enemy tactical aircraft between Japan and the vital naval base at Truk.

After describing in detail the destruction to enemy installations and aircraft caused by the Bomber Barons, the citation continues as follows:

> Often braving intense antiaircraft fire, navigating and bombing with superior accuracy, the 5th Bombardment Group (H), in less than a month, was largely responsible for reducing to shambles a base upon which the Japanese had depended for an uninterrupted flow of supplies and aircraft for the strategic defense of Truk, Palau, and the western Caroline and Marianas Islands. All during this period the ground echelon worked steadily and efficiently to keep the aircraft in peak operational condition. The exemplary courage and devotion to duty displayed by the personnel of the 5th Bombardment Group (H) reflect great honor upon the Armed Forces and the United States.

The importance to the war effort of the Jungle Air Force, including the 5th Bombardment Group, was not lost on America's ground and sea forces. After the attacks on Yap and Woleai, Lt. General R.K. Sutherland, General Headquarters, Southwest Pacific Area, wrote the following message to Major General St. Claire Street, Commanding General of the 13th Air Force:

> I have just had a letter from Admiral Carney, Chief of Staff, Third Fleet, in which he said that the 'damned 13th Air Force has just about spoiled the war for our carriers, particularly at Yap; Davidson's command, Task Force 38, left Yap in disgust after the first day because our old Ex-So. Pac. 13th Air Force had left no decent targets.' We all feel good with you to see such a comment.

In June 1944, the 5th Bombardment Group was transferred from the command of Admiral Halsey, who was greatly admired and respected, to FEAF under the command of General Kenney. Admiral Halsey, in turn, held the Bomber Barons in the highest regard, as he conveyed in his farewell message to the 5th Bombardment Group:

> Proudly I send this parting 'well done' to my victorious all-services South Pacific Fighting Team. You have met, measured, and mowed down the best the enemy had on land and sea and in the air. You

have sent hundreds of Tojo's ships, thousands of his planes, tens of thousands of his slippery minions whence they can never again attack our flag, nor the flags of our Allies. You beat the Jap[anese] in the grim victory at Guadalcanal; you drove back and hunted him out; you broke his offensive spirit in those smashing Bougainville-Rabaul blows at his ships and planes in November 1943; and you have smashed him and rolled over him to easily occupy Emirau. And now, carry on the smashing South Pacific tradition under your new commander, and may we join up again farther along the Road to Tokyo.

The Bomber Barons' successful missions against Balikpapan won admiration and praise from General MacArthur and a Presidential Unit Citation for the 5th Bombardment Group. General MacArthur wrote:

Please express to all officers and men involved my admiration for their resolute determination in pressing home the attacks on Balikpapan in the face of extraordinary difficulty and hazard. It shows up the finest tradition of the Air Force.

The Presidential Unit Citation describes in detail the onerous task facing the Bomber Barons in their missions against Balikpapan and recognizes the significant contributions made by maintenance crews and ground personnel to the success of the mission, stating in part:

Credit for the success of this history-making mission must go not only to the gallantry and skill of the air crews but also to the outstanding devotion

to duty of the maintenance crews and other ground personnel, without whose determined efforts the strike could not have been made. The achievements of the 5th Bombardment Group have brought great honor to the Armed Forces of the United States.

The squadrons who flew fighter cover for the 5th Group's bombing missions also recognized the significance of the Bomber Barons' contributions to winning the war. Lt. Col. Edwin A. Doss expressed his admiration in the following excerpt from his commendation:

To provide fighter cover for missions handled in this manner, it was merely a matter of our own squadrons being on time at the rendezvous. The work of your planes over target was an inspiration to our pilots, and never did they return from one of these missions without pointing out the precision and effectiveness of your formations.

And following missions in support of the Australian invasion of Borneo, W. Dostock of RAA Command, Allied Air Forces, sent this message:

I desire to express my appreciation of the magnificent work performed by your command in support of our operations. The Australian Forces landed without sustaining casualties in the beachhead area and this outstanding achievement is almost entirely attributable to the pre-assault bombing operations in which the 5th Group played a predominating role. Without your support success of the land operations would have been in grave doubt.

18 November 1944, strike on Main pumping station, Taraken.

A TRIBUTE TO GROUND MEN

This history would not be complete without paying just tribute to the ground men of the 5th Bombardment Group (H).

There is nothing glamorous about the ground man's job. The work is almost monotonously the same, day after day. The hours are long and many times irregular. Yet the very lives of combat men and the fighting efficiency of the airplanes depend on how well these men do their job. The ground men of the 5th Bomb Group have done a superior job despite all kinds of disappointments and hardships.

The role played by the 5th Bomb Group ground crews is a glorious one. They have put our Flying Fortresses and Liberators into the air despite lack of equipment and parts. The ground man has improvised newer and quicker methods by which our bullet-and-shrapnel-riddled airplanes were more quickly made serviceable. Lacking parts, he scoured junk piles, so that he could patch up these bombers. He has improvised newer and safer devices for protection of combat crews. He helped improve bombing accuracy by constant improvement and maintenance of the bombsight. He has made many improvements which increased operational efficiency. Finally, he has fed, clothed and cared for the welfare of the combat man. He has done all this and more despite many hardships.

The glory of the ground man lies in the fact that he has been able to accomplish all this in the face of bombings, disappointments, jungle heat, bugs, mosquitoes, malaria, dengue, poor food and long overseas service.

The end of the war found many ground men of this group overseas for periods ranging from 24 to 36 months, living on hot jungle islands. The so-called 18-month rotation policy for overseas service never seemed to apply to them. Home had become an obsession with many of them. They were disheartened and disillusioned. The length of their overseas time under a hot tropical sun changed many of them from bright young boys to weary old men. Some of them became physical wrecks. Others had their home life in the States completely disrupted. Yet these men continued to exert maximum efforts to keep the Fortresses and Liberators flying.

Constant nightly bombings on Guadalcanal and Morotai kept them up all night; then they worked all day. Some men were killed and others wounded by these bombings. Constant diets of "C" rations and Spam for long periods of time made these foods hateful. Eating became an unpleasant necessity.

Constant movement of the group from jungle island to jungle island uprooted any small comforts they might have acquired. At one period of time this group achieved four moves in five months, scarcely giving the ground man a breathing spell. He had to tear up the old camp and hack a new camp area out of the jungle.

All this time either the hot tropical sun beat down on him or the tropical rains drenched him. Many times the ground man lived in mud with rivers of rain running through his sun-baked, humid tent. Perhaps the following parody (to right) can give the reader a visual picture of the so-called South Pacific Paradise.

During this whole time very few men received rest leaves. Some of the men hadn't had a rest leave in two years.

Perhaps the only thing that kept these men going was the fact they were Americans, Americans who had a sense of humor which overcame all obstacles. Somehow they always managed to laugh at something.

South Pacific Post

Somewhere on a South Sea Island
Where the sun is like a curse
And each long day is followed
By another slightly worse.
Where the coral dust blows thicker
Than the shifting desert sands,
And the white man dreams of
Finer colder land:

Somewhere in the South Pacific
Where a woman is never seen,
Where the sky is never cloudy and
The grass is never green.
Where the Nips bomb nightly
Robbing man of blessed sleep,
Where there isn't any whiskey
But two cans of beer per week.

Somewhere in the Blue Pacific
Where the mails are always late,
Where Christmas cards in April
Are considered up to date.
Where we always have the payroll
But never have a cent,
Though we never miss the money
'Cause there's no place to get it spent.

Somewhere in the Southern Ocean
Where the gooneys moan and.cry
And the lumbering deep sea turtles
Come up on the beach to die
Oh, take me back to New York, the
Place I love so well,
For this God-forsaken Island is
Awful close to hell.

-Anonymous

The folks back home can never really visualize the hardships and disappointments of the ground man—crew chief, assistant, ordnance man, armament man, clerk, cook, supply man transportation man or any other. But higher headquarters recognized the many difficulties of the ground man of the 5th Bomb Group. They realized that on many occasions he had to exer almost superhuman efforts to get the bombers into the air. I almost every commendation and in every Unit Citation, the Ground Man was cited for his excellent achievement.

No, the ground man does not appear glamorous but he ha achieved a glorious record. In the background he has been the backbone of the fightingest Heavy Bombardment Group in the Pacific. His excellent maintenance records reflect the importar part he played in Bomber Baron's relentless attack and drive o the Nips.

THE 5TH BOMBARDMENT GROUP SQUADRONS

HISTORY OF THE 394TH BOMBARDMENT SQUADRON (H)

A complete overall history of our squadron with all of the pertinent highlights over a period of years could hardly be consolidated into the brief account that follows.

Aviation has come a long way since the days that aircraft were designed and put through the original experimental stages and our squadron has had the experience of nursing a goodly share of this equipment from its infancy to its present all powerful war winning weapon.

A review of the records reveals that the activation of the 394th starts out with an argument. One historian has contended that the birth of the squadron was in 1917 and another argued that the birth was in June 1919. The records, however, seem to bear out the fact that May 1917, at Aviation Camp (now in Kelly Field), San Antonio, Texas, the 4th Aero Squadron (that's us in those days), Signal Corps was born. It served within the continental limits of the United States during World War I. During the year of its activation, it was redesignated Squadron "B," and moved to Post Field, Fort Sill Oklahoma. In January 1919 the squadron was merged with several other alphabetically designated squadrons to form the Flying School Detachment at the same field. Later during this same year the Flying School Detachment was demobilized.

On 23 June 1919, at Hazenurst Field, Long Island, New York, 1st Lt. Harry H. Young, Air Service (Aeronautics), was attached to the 4th Aero Squadron and directed to organize that squadron, without delay, for service in the Philippine Islands. (Some 26 years later we finally got there.) Naturally enough of the first contingent of men was recruited from New York and the New England states.

Very shortly after activation, the squadron was ordered to Ford Island, Pearl Harbor, Hawaii. Arriving in Honolulu on 24 January 1920 it started a continuous tour of overseas service which proved (without official confirmation) to be the longest continuous overseas stretch of any Corps outfit.

The 394th Bombardment Squadron (H), came into being at a time when ideas of the true work of military aviation were undergoing great and fundamental changes; and in its history the Squadron epitomizes this transition and its outcome. Just as the first American military flying was done for observation purposes as an adjunct of the Signal Corps, so also the 394th was activated as an observation squadron; and while bombardment was emerging as the center of air power strategy, the 394th moved through changes in designation, equiptment, training and function, to become a thorough going bombardment squadron whose weight has since been felt generally all over the Pacific.

The original designation was the 4th Aero Squadron but in 1924 this unit was changed to the 4th Observation Squadron and still later in the same year the name was slightly changed again to the 4th squadron (Observation). This name was retained until 1938 when another change in designation converted us to the 4th Reconnaissance Squadron, which name we retained until 1942 when the squadron was officially designated the 394th Bombardment Squadron (H). From the 4th Reconnaissance Squadron came the squadron insignia which we still retain. The four (4) points of the star signify readiness for action in the four corners of the earth and the yellow and blue colors represent observation by daylight and in darkness. The changes in relation to higher commands were even more numerous than the changes in its designation. The principle organizations to which the 394th belonged in its earlier years were the 2nd Observation Group; the Air Service, Hawaiian Division; the 17th Composite Group, and the 5th Composite Group. Its present position was determined in 1940, when the 394th was assigned to the 5th Bombardment Group (H), and in 1942 when the Group became a part of the 13th Air Force.

S-4 Section, 5th Bomb Group, Headquarters at Carney Field in Guadalcanal, Solomon Islands in late 1943. (l to r) Front row: (5) Cpl. Capetta, (6) Cpl. Loosbrock, and (7) Cpl. Bornstine. Second row: Capt. Yehtter, Maj. Brown, Capt. W.S. Bralley, and Capt. Cameron. Back row: (5) Sgt. Phipps, (7) Sgt. Leak, and (8) Sgt. Brown.

Japanese ship off Guadalcanal. Photo taken on 10 December 1943.

For the first several years the squadron duties could be classed as more or less routine but in the early days that routine was well loaded with hazards. Most of the planes, known officially as DH-4's, were referred to as *Flying Coffins*. The airstrips of those days were a far cry from the present day smooth long runways. Wheeler Field, in Hawaii, for example, was apparently little more than field covered with guava bushes (sadly lacking in bulldozing treatment). Accidents were not infrequent. Two of these accidents illustrate how primitive flying conditions were in those days. In February 1923, some cane stalks caught in the landing gear of a plane and cut the forward speed so much that the plane crashed. During this same month, an accident was caused by a plane crashing into a high tension wire stretched across the field. Until the wreckage and wire were removed, a nearby artillery drill field was used as a strip — something hardly conceivable today. Unlike the accidents of today, these old ones often did not result in serious injury. A plane could be destroyed and the pilot still walk from the wreckage in good condition. There naturally were fatal accidents and our squadron was no exception. One of the oddest and most touching accidents was the death of an enlisted man who was mortally burned while cleaning out a GI can.

The daily schedules smirked of a sameness symbolic of a peacetime army, though there were some notable flights, odd though they may seem in the light of today's events. One, for example, performed in 1923 to demonstrate the value of peacetime aviation was the sowing of 150 pounds of fig tree seeds in Hawaii's Ema Forest Reserve. At the time this was considered unusually dangerous. Planes from the 394th also escorted Kingsford-Smith's "Southern Cross" part way on its famous Pacific crossing, on a route similar to the one used today to go "down under."

Annual maneuvers were big events each year, requiring considerable practice and training. In this period the Squadron began its practice of flying *Alohas* to greet transports and celebrities. It made flights for greeting practically everybody from the Secretary of War, Patrick Early, to the King of Siam.

In 1928 the squadron began to get away from the DH-4's at which time some amphibians, OA-1's, came in. By 1931, type O-19 had been added to our equipment and the DH-4's disappeared at last. A great stride forward was made in 1936 when three planes of the bomber class, B-12's, were assigned to us. In spite of their being specifically bombers these planes were intended for observation work. Still later B-18's made their appearance on our field.

This change of equipment was an indication that there would be a change in the work our squadron was training to perform. Such a change followed. As early as 1931, part of this bombardment training was "diving" bombing, which, of course, antedated by many years the German's use of allegedly original *Stuka* tactics against their enemies in 1939 and 1940. During this period, however, observation work of the squadron greatly expanded. Our outfit was one of the forerunners of the present communications system found in operation. Technical training, in fine military style, went forward. Naturally the predominant business of handling routine work at the home field took care of most of the time alloted us. As we look on today's operations one can't help but crack a smile at some of the notations found in the expansive squadron history. In 1931, making reference to an inspection to be made by higher ups, the following is found:

Several barrels of paint were used in changing the color of the 42 buildings in the squadron area from a dingy red to a shiny green. Minor repairs were made where necessary and everything was placed in first class condition.

To make it even more comparable to similar happenings of today the inspectors never actually made an inspection but, of course, were pleased with what they saw. This particular phase of the army seems to have undergone no changes. Other laughable events today, which were serious business then, were the amazing cross-country hops in Hawaii, sometimes as much as 50 miles non-stop; reconnoitering missions 10 miles off shore for enemy vessels; sinking of the carrier *Lexington* in a mock battle during maneuvers; and lastly protecting the little group of islands from invasion by the enemy. (It shouldn't be necessary to add, also on maneuvers.)

With the outbreak of war in Europe, the squadron entered its most active period, a period marked by intensified training for imminent war and participation in it. The air corps expansion program was first felt in December 1939 just two months after we had moved from Luke Field to Hickam Field. At this time 95 percent of the original squadron had been promoted and several new members were added to the squadron roster. As the cloud of war became blacker in Europe the training program was further intensified. In May 1941 the first Boeing *Flying Fortresses*, B-17D's, to fly from the Mainland to Hawaii arrived and two of the *giant four-engine planes* were assigned to the squadron. At this time we proceeded to train as combat crews in the *Flying Fortress*. The B-18's were being used as a stepping stone between single-engine planes and the four-engined B-17. With these planes, the 394th became a part of the Hawaiian Air Force. The value of our squadron to it is confirmed by the 394th's winning of the *Bombing Goon* in 1941. This signified the best bombing record of the 5th Group.

At this point two pages of the squadron history appear in red as follows:

7 December 1941 — at 7:55 a.m. the first Jap[anese] bombs fell on Hickam Field and Pearl Harbor — at that time all members of the squadron were in their quarters. Immediately, all members reported to the hangars and participated in the dispersal of our aircraft. Prior to the attack, our planes were lined up in the apron in front of the hangars in regular peacetime order. Out of the four B-18's and the two B-17's in the squadron at the time none were damaged. However, during the second attack while all guns were being manned in the dispersed planes, one B-18 caught fire and burned to the ground, trapping one of our enlisted men in the nose turret. All planes were hit repeatedly by strafing planes including one B-17 which was put out of action for a period of weeks. The balance of the aircraft were made flyable by dint of all men from cooks to office help assisting in repairs that day. At the time of the first bombing the armament section was locked. The first members to arrive at the hangar procured a tug and battered the door down. They passed out guns to all personnel arriving, from .50 caliber machine guns to .45 caliber revolvers. Machine guns were mounted in hangar windows, squadron transportation, and even carried by hand. Alerts were held in all airplanes during the afternoon, and they were ready to take off in 30 minutes in case of renewal of attack. However, no renewal occurred after aircraft were recommissioned. Two men were killed in the attack and seven wounded. It is the tragedy of the squadron that at the moment of crisis it had no chance to use the skill in observation which it had acquired over a period of 20 years in the islands. The squadron went into operation immedi-ately after the attack of the 7th. We know today that the Jap[anese]s did not attack again, but the men of the squadron in 1941 expected them to return at any moment. The squadron historian wrote of the events of the next day. "We participated in reconnaissance; our object was to sight the Japanese fleet and to observe what further attack might be forthcoming. Boy, are we scared!

Immediately the squadron became a school squadron. It checked out first pilots in the B-18's and then qualified them as B-17 co-pilots. As each man qualified he was transferred to other squadrons and others came in. Navigation and bombardiering were also taught. All officers and enlisted men were eligible for this training. In the early part of 1942 additional B-17's were added and a pilot's course in this type airplane was set up.

One odd but interesting job was assigned to us in April 1942. Moana Loa, the active volcano of Hawaii, erupted. A crew was dispatched to be prepared to bomb the lava flow in order to protect the city.

On 26 May 1942 one of our planes was dispatched to Midway to assist our Navy in locating the Jap[anese] fleet. The mission was successful, the Imperial Fleet being located after the first attack on Midway. At this same time all of our B-17's, four in all, and crews were attached to other squadrons to complete a striking force to intercept the Jap[anese] fleet, believed to be headed for Hawaii.

The squadron's first actual bombing mission was performed on 7 June 1942, the target Wake Island. Four crews were at this time stationed at Midway for strikes and patrol missions. In July we were changed from a school squadron to a tactical unit and B-18's were transferred out except two which were kept for transition flights. Most of the missions that followed were matters of patrol and indirect help was provided forces moving into the Solomons by sending a secret photographic mission over the Marshall and Gilbert Islands as a feint.

In November 1942 the squadron acquired seven B-17E's and moved to Nandi Airdrome, Fiji Islands. At Fiji the prime activities were training for anticipated action in the Solomons campaign, flying almost daily search missions in protection of the islands, getting accustomed to that now famous army dish, "corn-willie," and making friends with the "Bulas."

The first real start against the Japanese after several months of intensive training was in January 1943. Although based at Fiji, our planes staged through Espirito Santos, New Hebrides and on to Guadalcanal. Ballale and Kahili, two Bougainville strongpoints, were the principal targets. From this time on, Zero interception, Japanese ack ack, and nightly air raids were daily events for our men in the air echelon. Routine patrols were still being flown from Fiji.

In May a detachment of men had been sent to Guadalcanal to set up camp for the balance of the squadron who was soon to follow. In July the squadron as a whole moved to Guadalcanal and started operations from Carney Field. This camp area was set up in the middle of the jungle on the banks of the muddy Malimbu River. Here the rugged jungle existence commenced in earnest and our men learned first hand the value of a good foxhole. Only a very few of those men who went through the early days at the *Canal* are still around but it won't take much begging to get them to tell of the heavy Jap[anese] air raids during June and July 1943.

In August 1943 we tried our hand at motherhood, inaugurating *Snoop* missions, referred to then as Col. Wright's project. All the B-17's were transferred to other squadrons and, B-24's replaced them. During this time, *Snoop* missions were carried

1 May 1944. Momote Airstrip, Los Negros Island, Admiralties. 394th Squadron, 5th Bomb Group (B-24s), 13th Air Force. Barney H. Clary crew after 5 missions. (l to r) Front row: SSgt. Salvatore Salato (radio-right waist gunner), SSgt. William Russell Bosley (engineer-top turret), Sgt. Rudalph Aguirre (nose turret-armorer), Sgt. Leland Rodgers (tail turret-assistant engineer), and Sgt. Daniel E. Zengerle (left waist gunner-assistant radio). Back row: 2nd Lt. Barney H. Clary (pilot), 2nd Lt. Hubert B. Walker (copilot), 2nd Lt. Arthur Keedy (navigator), 2nd Lt. William Zurivitza (bombardier), and SSgt. Ernest G. Moodie (ball turret-assistant armorer).

25 June 1944. Momote Airstrip, Los Negros Island, Admiralties. 394th Squadron, 5th Bomb Group (B-24s), 13th Air Force. Barney H. Clary crew (Mission 25) after 13 hours and 30 minutes in air on strike at Yap. Encountered Zeros (Japanese fighters), dropping aerial bombs, heavy and intense ack-ack damaging nose turret, number one engine nacelle and left rudder. Left waist gunner (Zengerle) shot down a Zero. (l to r) Front row: SSgt. William Russell Bosley (engineer-top turret), Sgt. Leland Rodgers (tail turret-assistant engineer), SSgt. Ernest G. Moodie (ball turret-assistant armorer), Sgt. Rudalph Aguirre (nose turret-armorer), Sgt. Daniel E. Zengerle (left waist gunner), and Sgt. unknown (group aerial photographer). Back row: 2nd Lt. William Zurivitza (bombardier), 2nd Lt. Hubert B. Walker (copilot), 2nd Lt. Barney H. Clary (pilot), 2nd Lt. Arthur Keedy (navigator), and SSgt. Salvatore Salato (radio-right waist gunner).

out for the first time on any war front. It is general knowledge now that the purpose of the *Snoop* mission was to seek out and destroy enemy shipping. Radar, the principal factor in this type of bombing, had never been used before by any other outfit. After performing several successful missions (one which resulted in sinking a sub and a destroyer and another against the *Tokyo Express* which sank one large transport and damaged three other ships) these *Snooper* planes were transferred from the squadron. The *Snoopers* then embarked on a long and colorful career of their own and daily carried on, after our careful and thorough tutelage, in unparalleled menace to Jap[anese] shipping.

In October 1943 we began the transition from our temporary status as a *Snooper* outfit back to the old status of a high altitude bombing organization.

In December of this same year we started the relentless pounding of Rabaul, and the adjacent airfields. Daily encounters with 50 to 75 hostile Jap[anese] planes were no rarity but fortunately we were at that time supported by our own friendly and superior fighters.

Early in March 1944 our air echelon moved to Munda Air Base on New Georgia, cutting the distance from the troublesome enemy targets by 300 miles.

On 30 March, we hit fanatically-defended Truk Islands in a daylight raid, and inaugurated a period of long over-water hops through the most miserable tropical weather imaginable. Nothing separated our base and the enemy strongholds but miles and miles of blue expanse, hostile fighters, and stinking weather. Our losses were staggering but nothing comparable to that suffered by the Nips. Forty to 50 enemy fighters were met by our unescorted planes daily but we kept up the attacks.

Early in April, to shorten the trip to Truk and to bring other enemy bastions within striking range we moved to newly acquired Los Negros Island in the Admiralties. When referring to it as *newly acquired*, we can't help but add the sinister note that Japanese were still there as we set up our camp and snipers bullets occasionally whizzed through the area. Guard duty was not simply a GI detail, it was on important necessary function.

From our new base, Momote Airstrip, Los Negros, we started out to liquidate Woleai Island and its triangular airfield. We hit this little island, again on unescorted overwater flights of 1,200 miles each, for eleven successive days and in that time, in conjunction with other planes from the 5th Group, practically tore the island from its moorings and won for the 5th Group our first presidential citation.

While we were accomplishing this feat, General MacArthur's forces sprang three surprise landings on New Guinea and were set for still another. We then spread out westward and pounded away at Biak Island for several days softening it up for another sucessful amphibious landing.

November 1944. Bill Blair in foxhole on Morotai Island. The Japanese made 82 air raids against Morotai from September 1944 through January 1945. There were 30 air raids in the month of November alone. The foxhole was to protect us not only from enemy bombs but also from falling shrapnel from our own .90mm anti-aircraft guns.

In June we performed our longest flight up to this time. Our squadron, leading the Group formation, made the first daylight attack against Yap Island, an overwater hop of 2,050 miles. We caught the Japanese with defensive pants down and smacked airplanes right and left, at least 15 being definitely destroyed and 25 others either destroyed or damaged. Continuing our strikes against Yap and Truk for the next few weeks, we were called on to help out another island-hopping event at Noemfoor. During this period our ground men set eyes on the first white woman seen since the days at Fiji. She was a Red Cross worker who gave a welcome feminine touch in handing out refreshments to returning crews. Another innovation was the rescue by submarine of one of our crews shot down in an attack against Yap.

In our destructive wake we worked ourselves out of targets and in August moved still farther westward to little Wakde Island, off the north shore of New Guinea, where we participated in the pre-invasion assaults against Palau and the Halmaheras. Operating from Wakde for less than 30 days we were off again, this time to Noemfoor, in Geelvink Bay, where the Philippines were brought within easy range.

From our Noemfoor base was staged the historic raids against the famed Balikpapan refineries and oil installations. These strikes shattered all existing records for heavy bombers, excluding the B-29's. The flights entailed a hop of 2,610 miles and better then 15 hours flying time. As a result of these raids at this southwest Pacific Ploesti, the 5th Group copped its second presidential citation.

Culminating an advance of several thousand miles we started hitting the Philippines in October 1944. We sought out the Japanese Fleet in the Mindanao Sea and found one of the Mikado's light cruisers which we promptly sent to the bottom.

At Noemfoor we experienced the first air raid since the Guadalcanal days, fortunately no damage was done. This raid was sort of an orientation raid for what awaited us at our next base.

Early in November 1944 we picked up and moved to Morotai, in the Moluccas, and then set about pounding everything the Japanese could muster in the Philippines, including his shipping. Off from Ormoc Bay, while the Leyte battle was in its hottest stages, planes of our squadron sank a 10,000 ton transport laden with Shinto troops who were attempting to reinforce Yamashito's dying forces. We made another stab at the Jap[anese]

Navy as it lay in its haven at Brunei Bay, off western Borneo and here damaged a Nip heavy cruiser. We roamed all over the Philippines but concentrated our attacks against the airfields in the Visayans. Just prior to the landing of our forces in Lingayen Gulf we plastered the airfields in and around Manila. We then concentrated our efforts in Manila Bay against historic Corregidor and the Cavite Island naval base.

As our airmen were doing battle all over this section of the world, the ground men at Morotai were not finding things peaceful and serene by any matter of means. *Washing Machine Charlie* was nightly making an appearance overhead with malicious intent. Our boys there logged many hours of foxhole time but fortunately in all of the many sleepless hours the hecklers caused only one man to come out of the battle with a purple heart.

Even the ruggedness of sweating out air raids was dwarfed by the extremely poor chow situation. "C" rations were the diet day in and out. Several days found us without sugar, coffee and flour. It has been recommended by squadron members that since each meal took on the proportions of a major campaign, a special "C" ration campaign ribbon should be presented to us.

After sealing the fate of the Jap[anese] on Cavite and Corregidor we diverted our attention momentarily to massive Borneo Island. While in the process of eliminating Jap[anese] holdings in Borneo we moved forward to our present base in the Visayans, arriving early in March 1945.

After more then two years of steady jungle existence, we finally moved into the Philippines and observed for the first time the fruits of our labors. The liberation of an en-slaved people and their open display of gratitude made the living difficulties of the past seem worthwhile and added impetus to the job remaining.

In spite of our changing bases we, during that first month, managed to shatter all records we had previously established, flying more sorties and missions than we had ever flown before and carrying the heaviest bomb load we had ever carried. The distance to our targets had been so considerably shortened that we stepped up the pace of our attacks to such an extent that it was not uncommon for us to fly two full scale missions a day.

Immediately following our move to the heart of the Philippines we proceeded to pound Zamboanga defenses until our ground troops took over. Next our attacks were moved north and relentlessly we bombed enemy troops, supplies and defenses on Cebu. We lent direct support to the landings made and then pounded the fleeing Nips as they retreated to the hills.

During this period we found another use for our planes. Our B-24's were converted into new type reconnaissance planes to spot enemy troop movement and installations. On numerous occasions we played the role of attack planes and roamed over the target areas at tree top level spitting 50 calibre bullets at every vunerable object that lay in our path. We covered landings on Panay Island and cratered Bongos Island just prior to another landing by our forces.

In April we devoted practically the entire month to supporting ground troops in Cebu, Negros, and Mindanao. Our targets for the most part were caves, ravines, and various strongly defended hill positions. Sending Japanese to honorable or any other kind of death was our prime object and

July 1944 in the Southwest Pacific, Los Negros Island, Admiralties, 394th Squadron, 5th Bomb Group, 13th Air Force. Lt. Virgil Blase's bomber crew. (l to r) Front row: Virgil Blase (pilot), Robert Neff (navigator), John Punch (bombardier), and Marvin Spiker (copilot). Back row: B.D. Flynn (nose gunner), G.W. Huebner (ball gunner), John Lawlis (waist gunner), Melvin Ballard (radio operator), Alex Framarin (flight engineer), and Donald Lighthill (tail gunner).

although no count can be made of how many met the fate we designed for them, we can be certain that it reached a high figure. During this month, we flew several sorties over Mindanao, giving the guerrilla forces an aerial hand and dug up strong points in the Davao Gulf area preceding another frog hop by General MacArthur's foot soldiers. We also kicked the teeth out of the Jolo Island intruders allowing our own men to take possesion of the island.

17 April 1945 was a momentous day in both squadron and Group history. On this day the 5th Bombardment Group (H) completed its 800th combat mission and our squadron had the honor of leading the formation on this epic raid. This we understand is a record for heavy bombardment groups, no other group in our vast Air Force having even approached that figure. We have since, of course, considerably extended this number of missions.

Several heavy assaults were directed against little Taraken Island in preparation for a successful landing made by our Australian and Netherland East Indies friends. Finishing this job we set about to render everything the Japanese had on western Borneo completely useless. The only diversion in the incessant pasting of Borneo objective was a long-armed reach into French Indo China, our deepest westward penetration.

Following our concentrated efforts on Western Borneo, the Aussie ground troops took over by their landing in the Brunei Bay area and closed another phase of the war to us. After completing this job we were called on to give a hand in knocking out everything worthwhile in the Balikpapon area on Borneo's southeastern coast. After hitting this area several days without letup, the Allied troops moved in, and we again waved farewell to a finished project.

This brings us up to the present date. Our future job (even if the writer knew what it is) is a censored matter. But it is logical, since we have been working the flanks until they no longer exist, that a portion of the battle for the Jap[anese] Homeland itself awaits us.

Compiled and written by Staff Sargeant Otis B. Chapman

HISTORY OF THE 23RD BOMBARDMENT SQUADRON

The 23rd Squadron insigné has been in use since 30 September 1931. Its originator is unknown. It is described as follows:

On a blue disk, a volcano in black silhouette with red lava flowing from the crater. Extending upwards therefrom and intermingled with clouds, futuristic, vari-colored rays from yellow to red; in front thereof fire dropped bombs, two on the dextra, three on the sinister side. The volcano represents the station as well as the destructive force of the bombardment units as represented by aerial bombs. The arrangement of the bombs alludes to the number of the Squadron.

1917-1919-World War I

On 16 June 1917, approximately one month after the 4th Aero Squadron was activated, the 19th Acro Squadron was formed. A week later, at Mitchell Field, Long Island, New York, the 19th Aero Squadron was redesignated as the 23rd Aero Squadron under the command of Captain Jack W. Heard.

In the early days, all aero squadrons were sections of the Signal Corps and officers were commissioned as Signal Corps Officers. This squadron was no exception; since it had been newly formed, it had a very small number of men and since the Air Corps had not proved itself at that time, flying duty seemed to be of secondary importance. At that time, men of this squadron had to perform a great deal of manual work. Because of this, the term "Pick and Shovel" was applied to this section of the Signal Corps.

As more and more men joined the squadron, the original "Pick and Shovel" men were relieved from their manual duties. Then only, did they find time to work on their Curtiss JN4s and R-4s which were housed in temporary canvas hangars along the edge of the field. S.O.P. consisted of lining up the airplanes, taking them apart, and then putting them together again. In addition, men were taught how to drive vehicles which were comparatively new to them-touring cars and trucks. Needless to say, in those days, driving these vehicles was quite an achievement. At the end of two months the men of the squadron had grasped the principles and mechanics of automobiles; in three months, those of aircraft.

The squadron moved to Hazelhurst Field, Long Island, arriving there 5 September 1917.

Here the squadron established an excellent reputation for efficiency which made it indispensable in the training of other men. Because of this reputation the 23rd was prevented from making an early departure for France. During this period men from the ranks of the 23rd Aero Squadron were selected as candidates for commissions, as instructors for various technical schools, and some trained men of the squadron formed cadres for units leaving for overseas duty. Thus the original men of the 23rd Squadron were scattered among many other units, and through these trained men for overseas units., the 23rd played an important part in laying the foundation of the Army Air Corps.

There were many changes in commanding officers. A special note should be made of Captain Andrew J. MacElroy, who assumed command on 23 November 1917. His leadership and handling of men welded them into one large family. The transfer of Captain MacElroy in February 1918 was a severe blow to the men of the squadron who had learned to love, respect, and obey him.

With a late winter in 1917, flying was discontinued. Consequently schools were opened, and everybody went through more training. Thereafter more men were transferred out and with the approach of spring, flying operations were continued.

Then came the joyous day of 6 July 1918 when this squadron boarded the SS *Ceramic* for an overseas trip. Morale was high. Men had been trained in JN-40, JUB, JND, DH-4, LFW, Caproni and Spad aircraft. In addition they had been trained on Hall-Scott, Thomas, Liberty, Hispano-Suiza, and Curtiss OX-2, and OX-5 engines. Other members of the squadron were proficient as transportation men and woodworkers.

Under the command of 2nd Lt. Ray D. Mills, S.R.C., A.S., the squadron landed in England in July 1918. Here the squadron was split into four sections for training with the Royal Air Force on RE-8s, DH-6s, DH-9s, Avros, and Pups aircraft with Gnome, Clerget, BHP, and LaRhone engines—motors as referred to in those days.

On 16 November 1918 the four sections were assembled as a Corps Observation Squadron and sent to France for action, but by this time, the war was over. Probably more than anything else, this squadron's reputation for excellent efficiency kept it from seeing action-it was held in England as a training cadre. Still many of its trained personnel were scattered throughout the many aerial units in actual combat.

Embarkation orders were received on 20 February 1919 and the squadron departed for the United States aboard the *USS Mexican*. Landing at Hoboken, New Jersey, the outfit moved to Garden City, New York where it was deactivated and its personnel mustered out of the service on 22 March 1919.

Peace Years to Pearl Harbor
1921 ReActivation

On 1 October 1921 orders were received at the Air Service Pilots School, March Field, California, activating the 23rd Squadron as a bombardment unit. Its assignment was to be foreign duty in the Territory of Hawaii. The nucleus of this squadron was composed of eleven officers, three flying cadets, and seventy-six enlisted men, all under the command of Captain A.F. Harold.

During its stay in the continental United States, the chief duty of the squadron was forest patrol for fire protection and training. The area covered was that section of Southern California covered by the National Forest Area.

1922-1930
First Years in Hawaii

On 21 March 1922 this squadron, under the command of 1st Lt. Harold Brand, A.S. departed from Crissey Field, San Francisco, aboard the U.S.A.T. *Buford*. Arriving in Honolulu, the squadron was sent to Luke Field on Ford Island, which was located in the center of Pearl Harbor, Oahu, T.H. This was to be the new home for the squadron. Here the 23rd Bombardment Squadron became part of the 5th Composite Group in the Honolulu Sector.

During the peacetime years that followed, right up to Pearl Harbor Day, the unit was engaged in training flying personnel and ground crews. As the type of airplanes changed, from Keystone LB-6s to B-5As to A-12s to B-18s to B-17s, training of flying and ground personnel changed. In addition, training was intensified as new types of equipment arrived.

Flying crews were trained in formation flying, high altitude bombing, gunnery, photo reconnaissance, cross country flying, and during later years, instrument flying.

Despite the great turnover in commanding officers and personnel of the squadron, the morale, pride, and efficiency of the unit was reported as *unexcelled*. Undoubtedly, the primary reason for this healthy condition was the keen competitive spirit that prevailed among the squadrons of the group.

During the entire period of its stay in Hawaii, the 23rd Squadron participated in all competitive sports and field meets. In October 1926, the athletes of the squadron finished the baseball season in a blaze of glory by winning their last game—it was their only win of the season. In track and field meets, however, the 23rd was far ahead, leading its nearest competitor by 19 points.

Many maneuvers were held during the peacetime years. They represented the climactic test for the training received by the personnel of each squadron. In all the maneuvers the 23rd Squadron made an excellent showing.

The eruption of Halemariman (House of Fire), an active volcano on the island of Hawaii on 20 November 1930, caused several Keystone LB-6s of this squadron to make a cross-country aerial flight to Hilo, Hawaii. The squadron's diary gives no reason as to the purpose of the flight.

1931

Beginning with April pilots were restricted to 12 hours flying time a month because of a shortage of funds. Two flying demonstrations were accomplished, however, toward the end of the year.

On 25 November 1931 in a demonstration of the power of aerial bombs, 100 pound and 300 pound bombs were successfully dropped from high altitudes by aircraft of this squadron.

In the same month individually loaded aircraft of the squadron flew as high as 16,000 feet in altitude tests-high indeed for 1931!

While the squadron was based at Luke Field two fires caused much property damage to the unit. The first was in June 1942, and destroyed the wooden barracks, mess hall and headquarters building in the squadron area. Mess equipment was totally destroyed and squadron furniture was reduced by 50 percent. Personal losses among the enlisted men included tailor-made uniforms to civilian clothing, and other personal possessions. Not until May 1932 was the total of damage repaired.

Scarcely a year later a second fire broke out in the hangar area, causing the loss of one plane in addition to the building. Seven other planes were dragged from the blazing hangar by 23rd personnel, heedless of possible personal injury.

One of the brighter spots of this period was the intersquadron baseball series in which the squadron successfully nosed out the 72nd Squadron for the championship. In addition to this trophy the volleyball championship was also taken by the 23rd Squadron.

Christmas Day was celebrated in the new mess hall with a Christmas banquet prepared in the new kitchen. Prior to this date the 23rd had been operating a joint mess with the 72nd Squadron.

1932

In January all activities were in preparation for the Grand joint Army-Navy Exercises. Since the 4th Observation Squadron was assigned the task of establishing outposts on other islands, the 23rd and 72nd Bombardment Squadrons shared the work of transporting men and equipment to these various outposts by air. With the arrival of these Joint Army and Navy Exercises the planes of the squadrons were shuttled from field to field in order to escape damage from theoretical enemy raiding parties.

After making two unsuccessful attempts to bomb the enemy's aircraft carriers, success was finally achieved with the bombing of the Saratoga which was 60 miles off shore. This carrier was considered out of action after being bombed. Several days later the squadron theoretically bombed and sank three enemy transports and successfully carried out two more bombing expeditions. While acting as pursuit aircraft, the squadron chased down five naval seaplanes. After 15 days of hard flying there were no casualties or injuries among the personnel and no damage to squadron aircraft.

November saw the squadron participate in an entirely new type of activity. This squadron supplied a camouflaged fully equipped bomber to fly in the MGNI motion picture *Hell Below*. In this same month the Territorial Forestry Division requested

NOSE ART

that a house be dropped on the most isolated part of the Koolau Mountain Range. By using ingenuity, M/Sgt. Davis and the Armament Section rigged up a device to drop the house in sections from the bomb bay of a B-5A. Despite low-hanging clouds and turbulent air which made the mission hazardous, the house was dropped without mishap.

1933

In February 1933, the squadron participated in an elaborate joint Army-Navy maneuver. The squadron simulated war conditions, hiding airplanes under brush and at the edges of the field. In four days of operations the squadron dropped approximately 36 tons of bombs.

The squadron track team defeated the 4th Squadron team by a comfortable margin of 13 points. The next month, April, saw the squadron win the Luke Field Track and Field Meet.

1934-1935

The squadron participated in a three-day field maneuver and communication problem in June 1935. The 23rd also participated with the 72nd Squadron in a very unusual aerial flight.

Upon the request of Dr. Jagger, volcanologist, and with permission of Wing Headquarters, the 23rd bombed a lava flow. The Mauna Loa Volcano on the island of Hawaii had started to erupt, pouring lava toward the city of Hilo. A flight of airplanes from the 23rd, commanded by Captain Ladd, dropped twenty 600 pound bombs on a spot, in the path of the lava flow, indicated by Dr. Jagger. Direct hits were scored and it is believed that these stopped the flow of lava two days later.

1936-1940

The date of 18 June 1936 saw the temporary rank policy in the Air Corps changed. Majors reverted back to captains, and captains became first lieutenants, much to the hurt of pride and pocketbooks.

The squadron in October 1936 again participated in another unusual mission. Upon request from the Forest Rangers, a Keystone bomber dropped 1200 pounds of wire on the slopes of Mauna Loa. The squadron first sergeant, flying as a crew member, made a perfect drop.

One of the most unusual squadron incidents occurred in November of 1938. Pfc. Fleigleman, mechanic and crew chief, *borrowed* an airplane to which he was assigned. His solo hop came to an abrupt halt when the airplane crashed five minutes after take-off. The plane was a complete wreck, but Pfc. Fleigleman was only slightly injured, and was able to walk away from the wreckage.

In 1940 enlisted men were trained as bombardiers in B-18s.

On 10 August 1940 Lt. Henry C. Goodman was presented with the Medal of the Brazilian Order of the Southern Cross. This medal was awarded to him by the Brazilian government for his part in a goodwill flight of seven Flying Fortresses to Rio de Janeiro from 6 November to 29 November 1939.

Flying activities for 1940 consisted of bombing, day and night navigation and gunnery missions, night transitional flying, instrument flying and participation in aerial maneuvers in which all aircraft were dressed up with camouflage paint for the first time.

1941 Pearl Harbor Year

The date of 5 February found 24 B-18 bombers taking off from Hickam Field to welcome Major General Short, the new commanding officer of the Hawaiian Islands. A perfect formation was flown with the 23rd Squadron in the lead.

Instruction during this Period covered communications, armament, ordnance and camera work. When this squadron received two of 21 B-17s which had arrived from the States in May, all personnel were pre-flighted in their armament and equipment.

16 June was Organization Day and it was celebrated as usual, with beer, good food and sports. By now the celebration had become an annual affair.

Aerial activities consisted of bombing, navigation, gunnery, transition, instrument and photographic missions. On 30 October and 18 November navigational missions were flown to Midway Island.

The squadron diary entry for 6 December 1941 reads as follows: *One flight to Hilo and return (no landing there), two instrument missions, and one flight to Hilo and return on 7 December 1941.*

The spirit and character of the old 23rd Aero Squadron carried right through to the night of 6 December 1941. Morale was high, pride in unit achievement was great, training and discipline were good. Then came the test—war!

HISTORY OF THE 31ST BOMBARDMENT SQUADRON (H)

The insignia of the 31st Squadron is a black triangle with the apex up, and skull and crossbones surmounting it. A white line surrounds the black triangle. Although the insignia was first placed on a 31st Squadron airplane by an aviator of the of the 31st Aero Squadron at Issoudon, France during World War I, it was not officially approved by the War Department until 10 September 1934.

1917 - 1919 – World War I

On June 26, 1917, twelve days after the 23rd Squadron was activated, the 31st Aero Squadron was organized at Kelly Field, Texas, under the command of first Lt. John E. Rossil. The personnel strength of the squadron was built around a nucleus of men from the First Company, "B" Provisional Battalion, Signal Corps, which had itself been activated the previous month.

A short time after activation the 31st Squadron received sealed orders and began training for overseas duty. All July was spent in drill and equipment checks necessary for preparation for an oversea move.

On 13 July 1917 a Captain Carl Spaatz assumed command of the squadron. This Captain Spaatz, who took the 31st Aero Squadron across the Atlantic in bleak World War I, became the General *Tooey* Spaatz, the poker-loving strategist under whose command the Allied Air Forces Europe pounded the Germans into oblivion.

The 31st left Kelly Field on 11 August for Fort Totten, New York, and shortly after arrival there took passage for England on the White Star liner *Baltic*. The 31st almost fell a prey to the vicious German submarine campaign, then at its height, when the *Baltic* was fired upon by a German craft in Saint George's channel; but the sub missed, and the 31st docked safely at Liverpool, England on 15 September 1917.

The Ordnance Section of the 31st Bombardment Squadron (H) on Guadalcanal, Solomon Islands during WWII in 1943.

Immediately after debarkation the entire squadron entrained for Southampton where part of the enlisted men were sent to various schools for instruction in machine gunnery and aircraft instruction. The balance of the squadron crossed the channel to LeHavre, France, in one of the famous sidewheelers, arriving 24 September. There the men were divided into three groups for training purposes, one group going to Issoudon, another to Paris and the third to Lyons. After three months of the best available instruction in aircraft maintenance the squadron reassembled at Issoudon in December of 1917, at which time first Lt. Edward Buford, Jr., assumed command. The 31st Squadron was one of the first eight squadrons to land in France, which gave the men ample opportunity to become acquainted with the people and customs.

On January 18, 1918 the squadron moved to Field 5, where they were assigned the task of maintaining 15 Meter Newports. These tricky Newports were considered one of the most difficult airplanes to maintain.

Here at Field Five the men of the squadron found it necessary to establish their own camp. In this connection the knowledge of the people and customs gained at Paris, Lyons and Issoudon served the squadron well. In addition to maintenance of aircraft squadron personnel built barracks, hangars, and other buildings. Ordinarily the double task would be difficult, but inclement weather made matters even worse. Despite all these handicaps Field Five and the 31st Aero Squadron reached 100 percent efficiency, a record which was maintained for the rest of the war. Credit was due the enlisted men for their hard work and the officers for their efficiency.

Although the 31st as a unit did not go into combat, some of its personnel had glorious war records. Captain Spaatz and Lieutenant Mumford both received Distinguished Service Crosses for daring forays against the Germans.

After a year and a half in France the 31st Squadron boarded ship 4 April 1919 and returned to the United States, where on 14 April 1919 the organization was deactivated at Mitchell Field.

1923

In April of 1923 the 31st Aero Squadron was reconstituted on the inactive list of the Regular Army as the 31st Bombardment Squadron.

1931-1937-Service in the U.S.

The 31st Bombardment Squadron was placed on the active list at March Field, California, in April 1931. Capt. Earl C. Harper assumed command of the squadron which had an enlisted strength of 132 men. The organization was equipped with what was then considered the ultimate in bombers —the Martin B-10. An intensive training program was completed at March Field by December of 1934, and the squadron then moved to Hamilton Field, California. From then until 1 February 1938 the activities of the 31st Bombardment Squadron were confined to the continental limits of the United States.

Before moving to Hamilton Field and as early as May 1934 the squadron worked closely with Army Air Corps mail operations. After moving to Hamilton Field the 31st was the only bombardment squadron on the west coast during 1935-1936. At the time the squadron was a part of the 7th Bombardment Group which was under the command of Colonel Clarence L. Tinker. These two years saw the entire personnel of the squadron complete all required training— bombing, aerial and ground gunnery, navigation and like activities. The unit also participated in the giant Army-Navy maneuvers and various other Group and Wing exercises, which extended as far east as Miami, Florida, and as far north as Medford, Oregon. July of 1936 saw the 31st begin a series of flights over the northwestern part of the United States. The purpose of these flights was to determine the value of civilian landing fields as emergency landing strips for military aircraft.

In early 1936 all pilots of the squadron completed training in a new type of bombing at Mather Field, California. Many difficulties were encountered in this new method. Cruising speed, high altitudes, and winds as high as 80 miles per hour created new problems. The air around Mather Field that May was rough; two bombardiers received black eyes from hitting their eyes against bombsights. There was serious consideration given to submission of an unsatisfactory report on the bombsight with a request that the Materiel Division supply a crash pad for such emergencies. During these practice bombings very efficient two-way radio contact was maintained at all times between aircraft in the bombing range pattern and the ground spotting tower. Findings of this program resulted in numerous improvements in over-all bombing technique.

The next month the squadron, flying from Hamilton Field, conducted its gunnery training on the range over the ocean just north of the Golden Gate. No serious difficulties were encountered during the firing on the gunnery course although machine gun jams and fog slowed up the schedule somewhat.

The squadron participated in all group and wing maneuvers of that year, these maneuvers covering virtually the entire United States. It became evident that the 31st was now a highly mobile unit, having gone through the practical experience of sustaining itself in the field, both as an individual unit and a subordinate unit of the 7th Bombardment Group.

During this period Lt. Carl A. Brandt was a member of the 31st Bombardment Squadron. Nineteen years later the squadron was a unit under Brigadier General Carl A. Brandt, Commanding General of the 13th Bomber Command of the 13th Air Force. Lt. Brandt was transferred from the outfit before it moved to Hawaii.

1938-1941-Hawaiian Service

On 1 February 1938 the squadron with thirteen B-18s, 180 enlisted men and 30 officers and their families, under the command of Major James F. Taylor, departed for Hickam Field, Oahu, T.H. The personnel of the organization boarded the United States Army Transport *Republic* on 1 February 1938. The B-18s, which the squadron had recently acquired, were shipped on the army transports *Meigs* and *Ludington*.

Arriving at Hickam Field on 8 February 1938, the squadron personnel were housed in tents on the hangar line, pending the completion of permanent quarters. The 31st was the first bombardment unit to be based at Hickam Field.

The arrival of the 31st Bombardment Squadron was welcomed by the remainder of Hawaii's air arm. The B-18s were entirely new to the territory, and their range and fire power added appreciably to the potency of the air arm as a striking force.

From 8 February 1938 until the time that the 31st left Hawaii for the South Pacific it was stationed at various times at Hickam, Luke and Bellows Fields, and Kipapa and Kualoa Airdromes.

31st Bombardment Squadron. (l to r) Front row: Lt. H. Simmons, Capt. M. Smith, Maj. E. Thurlow, Capt. C. Larsson, and Capt. P. Thompson. Back row: Capt. D. Asselin, Capt. D. Martin, Capt. E. Alexander, Lt. S Allred, and Capt. S. Berry.

1941-1945
World War II

(The following history of the 31st Bomb Squadron (H) through the World War II years was written by Squadron Historian Joanne Pfannenstiel Emerick. It was compiled from information located in the 31st Bomb Squadron Archives and from personal interviews with 31st Squadron and 5th Bomb Group personnel.)

Throughout the 1930s, Japan had been steadily moving through the Pacific rim nations of eastern Asia, coveting the oil, rubber, and other natural resources that she was sadly lacking. Calling her new empire "The Greater East Asia Co-Prosperity Sphere," the Japanese intended to extend their control from the homeland south to include Australia. The United States was fearful that Japanese success would eliminate American trade with Asia and indeed threaten the United States, with an attack possible on the West Coast. With tense negotiations taking place between Washington, DC and Tokyo, the 31st Bombardment Squadron (H) was put on alert in Hawaii. However, the entry into World War II caught the 31st, like most, by surprise.

The Japanese attack on Pearl Harbor, Hawaii, and nearby Hickam Field on 7 December 1941, began at 7:55 a.m. Japanese planes, launched from carriers several hundred miles north of Oahu, Hawaii, hit Pearl Harbor in two waves. Many of the 31st Squadron members, whose December Roster listed 27 officers, one aviation cadet, and 197 enlisted men, were either in the mess hall or the barracks when the attack began. Some took cover within the barracks, others ran outside and hid in manholes, under vehicles and behind trees. Many men grabbed their World War I gas masks and helmets and went to what they referred to as "the line" where the airplanes were kept. There were eight hangars in that location. When they arrived at the line, they could see that many of the planes had been shot up or destroyed. The first wave of the Japanese attack lasted until approximately 8:30 a.m.

Squadron men were attempting to put machine guns and ammunition in the few planes that survived when the second raid began at 8:54 a.m. The Japanese hit the air base, and one of the bombs hit the barracks in which the 31st bunked. It was a 3-story reinforced concrete barracks with a flat roof. The bomb that hit one wing had a delayed action fuse. The bomb went through the roof of the third floor, and it went through the floor

5th Bomb Group barracks. Photo taken 7 December 1941 at Hickam Field, Hawaii.

of the third floor and exploded on the second floor. After the Japanese dropped the bombs, they strafed groups of personnel before ending the second raid and returning to their carriers to begin the voyage back to Japan. The Americans were able to place only a few planes in the air. An unsuccessful search for the Japanese fleet followed, and fears of a Japanese invasion immediately surfaced. As 7 December drew to a close, 31st Squadron members were listed among the dead and wounded.

B-17s from the 31st and other squadrons began reconnaissance missions following the Pearl Harbor attack, flying out 700 miles, essentially searching for Japanese submarines, Japanese ships, etc. They found none.

31st Bombardment Squadron Medical Corps in Guadalcanal.

In February 1942, the 31st was assigned to the 7th Air Force and moved from Hickam Field on 23 May 1942, relocating at Kipapa Gulch on Oahu's central plateau. The move was in the interest of dispersion. If another attack occurred, the American forces would not be caught together, as they were at Pearl Harbor. Kipapa was a gully, and the wind was such that planes either had to take off over the Gulch or fly over the Gulch coming in. There were updrafts and downdrafts, and flight crews couldn't predict which would occur. They had to be observant because if they hit the downdraft hard, they'd fly right into the ground.

In the months following Pearl Harbor, the American forces anxiously awaited the next Japanese move. When American Intelligence deciphered the Japanese code, they learned that the Japanese, under Admiral Isoroku Yamamoto, wanted to take over Midway Island and from there possibly launch another attack on the Hawaiian Islands. An American patrol spotted Japanese transports steaming toward Midway. American warships were dispatched to intercept the Japanese while aircraft were sent to bomb the Japanese task force. Men and planes from the 5th Bomb Group, including the 31st Bomb Squadron, participated in this action. In a three-day battle lasting from 4 June 1942 to 6 June 1942, the Japanese were defeated.

After their defeat at Midway, Japan's easternmost base was tiny Wake Island, 1,300 miles southwest of Midway and due west of the Hawaiian Islands. Wake was also the westernmost outpost that US forces could reach by air. In June 1942, General Clarence Tinker led a small group of planes on a strike mission against Wake. On 7 June, General Tinker's plane was lost at sea. Flying on General Tinker's crew were five members of the 31st Bomb Squadron.

As the summer of 1942 progressed, US Intelligence needed to know how extensive the Japanese base on Wake Island was.

31st Bombardment Squadron engineering personnel. Photo taken at Los Negros.

It had been reported that two airplanes had been dispatched from Hawaii for photographic reconnaissance, but neither returned. Volunteers were needed for a third attempt. Major George Glober of the 31st Squadron and his crew volunteered and were selected for the mission. The mission, staging through Midway, would be over 16 hours in duration. It would be the longest reconnaissance mission on record. In the early morning hours of 31 July 1942, Major Glober's crew departed for Wake, flying through bad weather. Hail beat on the fuselage, and the plane was rocked by terrible turbulence. They broke out of the cloud cover and turbulence just 15 minutes from Wake. The crew made three runs on Wake, covering the island in 60 degree overlap. They photographed all of the gun positions, revetments, the anti-aircraft positions, and the personnel locations. Japanese fighters rose to fight the lone bomber, and a battle ensued for approximately 42 minutes. The Glober crew shot down six Japanese fighters but received bullet holes in their airplane. Major Glober, trying to escape the enemy, rose to 23,000 feet. He was indicating 350 knots on the indicator -- an unheard of feat for a B-17 at that time. One by one, the enemy planes were disposed of, and after a long, tense return flight, the crew landed safely at Midway.

By the summer of 1942, it became clear that the United States would embark on a "Europe First" policy. To the 31st and the rest of the 5th Bomb Group, that meant few supplies and even fewer planes.

On 7 August 1942, American forces landed in Tulagi Harbor, and on Florida and Guadalcanal in the Solomon Islands. The 31st Squadron and the 5th Bomb Group were readied to move into the South Pacific to help stop the forward advance of the Japanese in the Solomons. The 5th Bomb Group commander was Col. Brooke Allen. He would be put under the orders of Col. LaVerne Saunders for a short time when the 5th and 11th Groups were joined, but would again resume command of the 5th Group in February 1943.

The 31st Squadron moved to Kuoloa Point on the northeast shore of Oahu on 9 September 1942. The stay at Kuoloa was brief, for on 9 November 1942, personnel of the 31st Bomb Squadron boarded the *Peter H. Burnett* and sailed toward Espiritu Santo in the New Hebrides Islands, with a short stop being made

at Fiji en route. For many members of the Squadron, Espiritu Santo would be the last sign of civilization they would see for three years.

The 31st arrived at Peicoa Air Strip on Espiritu Santo 30 November 1942. For a short time, the 31st was a service squadron for the maintenance of aircraft. Guadalcanal was the base from which strikes against the Japanese were to be conducted, so advance units of the 31st landed on Guadalcanal 3 December, arriving in the midst of a Japanese air raid.

The 31st flew many search missions in the early days. On one such mission, two Squadron members were listed as "Missing in Action" over the South Pacific 1 December 1942. On 10 December 1942, the 31st lost its first man in combat. Carlyle (Moose) Coleman was killed when his plane was attacked by Japanese Zeroes. Two Squadron members were killed when their plane crashed in the New Hebrides 31 December 1942.

From Guadalcanal, US bombers struck the Japanese bases further up the Solomon chain. With this in mind, the remainder of the 31st arrived 17 January 1943, and established the first ongoing support base for the 31st Squadron as well as transients. The squadrons of the 11th and the 5th Groups that were temporarily stationed on other islands would fly in, fly missions out of Guadalcanal (code name Cactus) and then return to Espiritu Santo (code name Buttons). The Japanese still controlled the northern part of Guadalcanal, and there was danger from snipers. On Guadalcanal, the 31st camped near Henderson Field. The men dug foxholes for safety during Japanese air raids. They sat on coconut logs to watch movies at their outdoor theater. Air raids were frequent. During one raid, Japanese bombs dropped into the 31st bivouac area. One man was killed, while three mess halls, the Dispensary, Orderly Room and Operations tents were destroyed and the Intelligence Tent was damaged.

The 31st took care of both the aircraft and personnel of three bombardment groups on the Canal: their own 5th, the 11th and the 307th. They were the only heavy bombardment squadron with ground personnel on the island in early 1943. They lacked tools, parts and supplies but were highly commended for their work.

In early 1943, the 5th Bomb Group was assigned to the newly-formed 13th Army Air Force, and because they never camped near civilization, they were eventually named *The Jungle Air Force,* and were under joint Army-Navy control. The 5th Bomb Group Commander was Col. Brooke Allen and his executive officer was Lt. Col. Marion Unruh. At the end of February, 1943, the 11th Bombardment Group ceased activities as a combat unit. The original personnel of the 72nd Bomb Squadron were grounded and the 31st and 23rd Squadrons received their planes. New B-24s began arriving and in March, with both the air and ground echelons now at Guadalcanal, the 31st entered into air operations. Their 5th Bomb Group's mission was to neutralize Kahili and Buka Airfields on Bougainville in the Solomons. If successful, the Japanese strongholds at Rabaul and Truk would be rendered ineffective. The 31st Bomb Squadron was chosen to lead this series of air strikes.

Throughout the spring and summer of 1943, with tremendous support from the ground personnel, the 31st continued flying missions. The Squadron suffered casualties, however. On 10 June, First Lt. Richard Snoody and crew were listed as "Missing in Action" while on a mission to Kahili. First Lt. Gordon Hall and crew died 20 July, and the same fate befell First Lt. John Epple and crew on 25 July. Both crews perished in plane crashes in the New Hebrides. First Lt. A.B. Elkins and crew were listed as "Missing in Action" 28 July, after a water landing at Funa Futi. In August, while flying with Capt. William McKinley's crew, Stanley Smitty Zyskiewicz was killed while on a mission to Kahili. On 26 August, on another strike against Kahili McKinley's plane was hit again, resulting in the wounding of Owen Carr and the death of Harold Nerstad.

5th Bomb Group Commander Col. Marion Unruh and the "Pretty Prairie Special."

Life on Guadalcanal was primitive. The men lived in tents, walked in mud, and had their energy drained by daily rains, insects and disease. Fuse containers and gas drums were used for showers. Khakis were often wet, caked with mud and covered with mold. Washing Machine Charlie was a constant visitor. He was a lone Japanese bomber whose engine sound was reminiscent of a washing machine. Charlie's main objective seemed to be harassment of the Americans by keeping them awake and dropping an occasional bomb.

In the summer of 1943, the 31st also participated in missions that were flown against Japanese-held Munda Point on New Georgia Island which was located midway between Bougainville and Guadalcanal. The Japanese-controlled airstrip on Munda gave the enemy a much closer base from which to launch attacks on Guadalcanal. The Navy shelled the area south of the airstrip which was heavily defended. Thirty-first planes joined others from the Fifth Bomb Group to carpet bomb. The infantry followed, taking the airfield. The U. S. capture of Munda denied its airfield to the Japanese and allowed the United States to use it as a base of operations.

On 10 August 1943, Col. Marion Unruh took command of the 5th Bomb Group. Col. Unruh and his ten-man crew led 31st Squadron and other 5th Bomb Group planes in an attack on Rabaul on 30 December 1943. Over New Ireland Island, the Colonel's plane, *The Pretty Prairie Special,* was hit by Japanese Zeroes and crashed into the water. Two crewmen were never seen again. Natives in dugout canoes brought nine of the crew to shore on the southeast coast of New Ireland. Eventually, the Japanese captured the nine. Several of the men died of disease in Japanese prison camps. The rest were executed. Only Col. Unruh survived, spending the remainder of the war in a Japanese prison camp. Col. Joseph Reddoch took command of the 5th Bomb Group on 31 December 1943.

The 31st moved to Carney Field on Guadalcanal in late 1943. Again, the Squadron suffered casualties. Capt. Andrew Hughes and crew were listed as "Missing in Action" 4 December, after their plane crashed in the Chabai area of Bougainville.

By early 1944, the 31st Squadron was continuing to strike Rabaul. Rabaul was the heart of the Japanese defensive efforts in the Solomons and the Bismarck Archipelago. From Rabaul, Japanese planes could bomb Allied airfields and troops. Rabaul received planes and supplies through Truk from Japan.

From Carney Field, the 31st Squadron moved to Munda on New Georgia Island for a short stay, placing them closer to their targets of Rabaul and Bougainville. While flying out of Munda, the 31st suffered casualties on 5 March when a B-24 piloted by Capt. Lewis Haire was hit by ack-ack over New Britain Island. The plane burst into flames and disintegrated in midair. Three crewmen parachuted to safety and were picked up by a Navy PBY after hours in the water. A fourth crew member parachuted onto New Britain and was captured by the Japanese eight days later. The remaining seven crewmen were thought to have perished in the explosion.

On 20 April 1944, the 31st moved again. The new base was Momote Airdrome on Los Negros in the Admiralty Islands, the Bismarck Archipelago. This base brought the entire Caroline Island chain within the Americans' bombing range and enabled the US to aid General Douglas MacArthur's advance in New Guinea and Saipan. This was an important step in the island-hopping drive toward Japan. Tragedy struck the 31st while on Los Negros. First Lt. Leon Martin was piloting the Cisco Kid II as it attempted a take-off from Momote Airdrome. The plane, carrying a full bomb load, crashed into a Seabee camp. The entire crew perished, as did many Seabees. On 21 May 1944, Second Lt. Arthur

Belair and crew were listed as "Missing in Action" after a strike on Eten Island, Truk Atoll. The plane was last seen going into a steep bank before disappearing into the clouds.

At Los Negros, the 31st camped on the edge of a coconut plantation. They lived in tents, not having lumber of any kind. The latrine was a pit with a tarp over it and the shower was a 55-gallon steel drum, cut in half with holes bored in the bottom. Again, there was an outdoor theater and also a PX, another tent where the men could buy such items as toothpaste and chewing gum.

The 31st flew numerous missions out of Los Negros. Some of the most important were to Woleai in the Caroline Islands. Woleai was an important Japanese search plane and naval base, and a stepping stone for aircraft and supplies headed for the Japanese-held islands. In a series of 13 strikes, 5th Bomb Group B-24s dropped 140 tons of bombs on Woleai, destroying all facilities. For these efforts, the 5th Bomb Group was awarded a Presidential Unit Citation.

In April 1944, Col. Thomas Musgrave, Jr. took command of the 5th Bomb Group. He was wounded in the leg on his second combat flight. Col. Reddoch again took command. During May, the 31st Squadron concentrated on bombing Biak off the northern coast of New Guinea. These were pre-invasion air strikes to soften up Japanese defenses for the 28 May invasion by Allied Forces. It was 800 miles to the target from Momote: 10 hours, 10 minutes flight time.

Also in June, the 31st participated in the bombing of Yap Island which was one of a string of Japanese defenses leading to the Philippines. It was a 2,046-mile round trip all over open water. Flight time was 12 hours and 20 minutes.

The 13th Army Air Force transferred from joint Army-Navy control under Admiral William (Bull) Halsey to the command of U. S. Army General George Kenney in June 1944. Meanwhile, the 31st struck Noemfoor, New Guinea. The bombing raids were preliminary to the 2 July invasion by General MacArthur's ground forces.

By 1944, some 31st members in the ground echelon had been in the Pacific since the war began. The constant moves had worn them out. Many never had a rest leave, and saw no promise of getting home soon. Tokyo Rose played American music, and encouraged surrender. She called the men of the 5th Bomb Group "Blue-Tailed Devils."

On 21 August 1944, the 31st moved to Wakde, New Guinea Islands, Bismarck Archipelago. Wakde was one and one-half miles long and 3/4 of a mile wide. Camp was made in a compressed area between the runway, named Jap Strip, and the ocean. Tent pegs overlapped. Tents had no floors and the men lived on ground littered with rotten coconuts and tree stumps. From this base missions would be flown to neutralize the Japanese storehouses, arsenal and administrative departments in the Palau Islands, the last eastern barrier separating the US from the Philippines. On 15 August, Col. Thomas Musgrave returned to as-

5th Bomb Group Headquarters Staff, Col. Thomas Musgrave, Commanding.

In June 1944, 31st crews were bombing Truk. The Americans were planning an invasion of Saipan in the Mariannas, and air crews were to neutralize the Japanese striking force and repair facilities at Truk. Truk Atoll had four main centers of naval and army air might, and was called the largest and most formidable barrier facing the Allied advance.

The 31st Bomb Squadron suffered numerous casualties during the raids on Truk. Lt. E.L. Lynch was killed in action 7 June 1944, when hit in the chest and head by a 20mm shell on a strike over Eten Island, Truk Atoll. Three 31st members were listed as "Missing in Action" 17 June after they bailed out near the Hermit Islands while on a strike to Eten Island.

sume command of the 5th Bomb Group. He stressed the importance of the Palau mission, saying Palau must be knocked out so America's strategic plans in the area could go forth. The missions to Palau were successful.

Next, the 31st Squadron took part in attacks on the Halmahera Islands where the Japanese had airfields and excellent harbors. From there the Japanese could protect their oil and gasoline industries in Borneo. General MacArthur was planning an invasion after the missions were completed. His landing would put American forces within striking distance of the Philippines.

Thirty-first air crews and ground maintenance personnel moved to Noemfoor Island, off the northern coast of New Guinea 26 September 1944. The remainder of the 31st stayed at Wakde

From Noemfoor bombers were ordered to attack Balikpapan, Borneo, which was the most important source of aviation fuel and oil the Japanese had. General MacArthur said it was "the most strategically important Jap target in the Pacific."

The 31st Squadron and 5th Bomb Group Commander Thomas Musgrave led the first mission to Balikpapan on 30 September 1944. The mission took some crews 15 hours and 30 minutes, and some as long as 17 hours. The Pandansari Oil Refinery was the primary target. Alternate targets included processing buildings and tank storage facilities. The oil refinery was supplying over 35% of the fuel being used by the Japanese Air Forces in total. It was supplying 50% of the fuel being used in the Southwest Pacific by the Japanese forces and 65% of the aviation gases being used by the Japanese air forces in the Philippines. The flight was 2600 miles round trip. No formation of B-24 bombers had ever flown such a distance, and it exceeded the manufacturer's recommendations. The Balikpapan mission was successful. Photographic assessment of the raid showed 36 hits in the Pandansari refinery area, four hits on furnaces or pipe lines and the distillation units, three hits in the receiving tanks area, and two bomb patterns visible across the building and tank storage areas. The cost in men and planes was high, however. For this mission, the 5th Bomb Group received its second Presidential Unit Citation; the only one it ever received for a single mission. Other attacks on the same targets followed, and by the end of October 1944, 433 tons of bombs had been dropped on Balikpapan.

The 31st also participated in strikes against Japanese oil tank farms on Tarakan Island off the northeast coast of Borneo. The oil there was said to be so pure that it could be poured directly into the ships. The 31st bombed the main pumping stations. The success of the Tarakan missions was important because it stopped the supply of oil products the Japanese needed to defend the Philippines.

The Battle of Leyte Gulf was fought in the Philippines 24-26 October 1944. The 31st Squadron flew in support of General MacArthur's invasion of Leyte and assisted in the naval battle of Leyte Gulf. When American ground forces landed in the Philippines, the 31st's new missions were to knock out enemy airfields on the Negros Islands and keep them neutralized so the Japanese could launch no air attacks on advancing United States ground forces, and to keep a constant watch over shipping lanes in the Sulu Sea to prevent Japanese supplies and reinforcements from reaching the Philippines.

Intelligence reported that the Japanese were constructing a "defensive triangle" from the Halmahera Islands to the Palau Islands to Mindanao in the Philippines. Three Japanese armies and 80,000 troops were said to be holding the triangle. On 15 September 1944, U. S. forces invaded Morotai, the northernmost Halmahera Island, and within days an airfield was being constructed.

On 4 November 1944, the 31st Squadron moved to Pito Field, Morotai. Here the Squadron endured possibly the most intense Japanese bombing raids of the war. Between 15 September 1944, and 1 February 1945, the Japanese carried out 172 sorties and 82 air raids against Morotai. From Morotai the 31st bombed the Celebes Islands and Nichols Field in the Philippines, and hit Corregidor to knock out gun emplacements in advance of a US landing.

On 15 November 1944, remnants of the Japanese Leyte Gulf battle force were spotted in Brunei Bay on the northwest coast of Borneo. Thirty-firsters participated with the other 5th Bomb Group squadrons in the air strike against the fleet on 16 November. The flight time from Morotai to Brunei Bay was between seven and eight hours. The ack-ack was intense and nearly every 5th Bomb Group plane was hit. The Group succeeded in scattering the Japanese fleet.

Still based on Morotai, the 31st suffered another loss 10 January 1945, when Second Lt. Gerald Long and crew were listed as "Missing in Action" after their plane went down enroute to Morotai from a mission to Luzon, the Philippines. Eight Squadron members were killed when the C-47 in which they were passengers crashed on takeoff 7 March 1945. The C-47 had been carrying a jeep that had burst into flames when the plane crashed. Funeral services for Squadron members were held at the cemetery on Morotai. In early January, Col. Thomas Musgrave received orders to proceed to Washington for a new assignment. And Hq. XIII Bomber Comd. Special Order #6, par. 3 was issued which read as follows: "By direction of the President, announcement is made of the appointment of Maj. Albert W. James AC (1092), as Commanding Officer of the 5th Bombardment Group (Hv), APO 719, effective 7 January 1945." And almost at the same time Maj. James was alerted to move the Group to Samar Island in the Philippines as soon as possible.

Col. Albert W. James. Photo taken 6 July 1962.

The 31st air echelon moved to Aba Field, Samar, the Philippine Islands 13 March 1945. The rear echelon, which had been at Wakde since September, 1944, joined them and for the first time in seven months, the entire 31st Squadron was together. Morale rose. Men had complained about the food, especially C-Rations and Spam, but on Samar fresh meat, eggs, Coca-Cola and ice cream appeared and many men saw ice for the first time in two and one-half years!

The 31st lost another member on 14 March 1945. The Squadron sent a C-47 to pick up personnel on rest leave in Sydney, Australia. On the return to base, the crew was forced to ditch the aircraft off the coast of Australia. TSgt. Williams died as a result.

Second Lt. Cyril Reinstatler, 31st radar operator and bombardier, was listed as "Missing in Action" 9 April 1945. Squadron reports stated, "On 9 April 'Triple-threat,' as he was affectionately called by squadron buddies, flew with the 23rd Squadron on a 2-aircraft photographic reconnaissance of the Saigon, French Indochina, area. The aircraft were jumped by eight to ten fighters over Saigon and in the ensuing engagement, the crew with whom Lt. Reinstatler was flying, was forced to bail out. All but Lt. Reinstatler were recovered by a rescue Catalina and submarine. According to survivors, the parachute of the radar-bombardier did not fully open."

By mid-1945, the men of the ground echelon were drained and had begun to think they had been forgotten. Many had now been in the Pacific over three years and had seen more than their share of death and destruction. While the flight crews rotated back to the States with some regularity, the ground crews had to stay. They were the backbone of the Squadron. They were present on EVERY mission, for without THEM, no plane would have ever flown.

During the summer of 1945, the 31st joined 5th Bomb Group planes to bomb Japanese airfields in Borneo and the Celebes. On a 4 July mission, staged out of Morotai, 5th Bomb Group Commander Col. Isaac Haviland and his crew disappeared. Lt. Col. Albert James assumed permanent command of the 5th Bomb Group.

Beginning 1 August, strikes were flown against Formosa. The Americans were now on the doorstep of Japan. On 6 and 9 August 1945 atom bombs were dropped on Japanese cities. While Japan assessed the devastation, missions were still flown.

In September 1945, the Japanese formally surrendered. By this time, the 5th Bomb Group had flown over 1,000 combat missions and had traveled 7,200 miles to the Philippines. With the signing of the peace treaty in Tokyo Bay, the wartime activities of the 31st Bomb Squadron ended, with the Squadron departing for the United States from Samar, the Philippines in December 1945.

When the war ended, 5th Bomb Group Commander Col. Marion Unruh was released from a Japanese Prisoner-of-War camp. He undoubtedly echoed the sentiments of the men of the 31st Bombardment Squadron and the entire 5th Bomb Group when he addressed a Memorial Day crowd in his hometown, Pretty Prairie, Kansas.

"No doubt many of you thought, as I did, in the early days of the war, that we were fighting because the Japanese made a sneak attack on us at Pearl Harbor, or perhaps you thought that we were fighting Britain's war. Now -- that it's over - I think I know what was at stake. It was our freedom. A freedom that we have taken for granted and which we fail to appreciate until it is taken away. Believe me -- we fought for our families, our homes and our country. Unless you have faced our late enemies and been a victim of their vitriolic hatred, this is hard to believe. Nevertheless, we know it happened to the nations defeated by Germany and Japan. It is freedom from that for which we fought. Any man that would object and not fight for the freedom which we now have, does not, in my opinion, deserve to enjoy this freedom."

Memories

Lewis Hearron on Pre-war Hawaii: "We would arm the bombers with machine guns and ammunition and everybody carried side arms. They would run a patrol out 150 miles from the Hawaiian Islands and they checked each ship out that came within that area. We did practice blackout drills. You know they were conscious of danger, the potential anyway."

Mike LaRocca on Pre-war Hawaii: "We were always put on alert every once in a while. The talk was that they lost sight of the Japanese fleet so they would put everybody on alert. In fact, we were on alert the whole week before the war started. We had just come off alert the Saturday before, about noon time. I remember that vividly because I was playing baseball and they canceled the baseball season because we were on alert."

Max Baker on Pearl Harbor: "My first reaction was that the damn Navy was practicing even on Sunday. I said, 'Why are they shooting those guns on Sunday' I sat up in bed and looked out the window and saw a plane go by very low with a red ball on the side. So I jumped out of bed and put my coveralls on and

we went out of the barracks. There was a parking lot across the street and we got under the cars in the parking lot. I got to thinking that was not too safe a spot, that they would probably bomb and strafe those cars. So I said to this boy, 'Let's get out of here' and go over and stand against the reinforced concrete barracks which had a 3-foot lip that stuck out over the top of the windows. So we did. I really had exercised good judgment because it wasn't very long that they came down and they didn't bomb those cars but they strafed them with their 20mm and 7mm machine guns that they had on the front of their planes and they killed and wounded a lot of people there. We went over to the line. They came at this plane where we were working trying to load the bombs and ammunition. I got out of the plane because it was my feeling they were going to strafe the plane because we didn't have any guns that were in operation, so you couldn't return the fire. I got out of the plane and laid down on the runway facing the oncoming strafing plane and again had good luck and I was not hit by these machine gun bullets. And then, about that time, the second raid was over. The rest of the day it was just a matter of a lot of wonder and awe and discussion."

Ed Caton on Pearl Harbor: "There were 12 guys lying out on the concrete in the sun with blankets lying over them, and we thought they were dead. And I saw one of the blankets move, so I went over and pulled it off. The guy was still alive, so I got the aid men over to him, they rushed him to the hospital, and he did survive. We had a bomb go off in the corner of the barracks before I left and it killed 19 people there. One of 'em. was the First Sergeant of the 72nd Squadron, Frank Helms. He was stripped naked, and his body was all blue and of course, everybody thought he was dead. So the recovery crews just picked him up and threw him in the back of a quarter-ton truck and threw about six, seven or eight guys on top of him and took them to Tripler General which is where the morgue was. Three days later, when they went to identify the body, Frank had recovered enough of his faculties to blink his left eye. Two of my friends were there, and they recognized him and saw him blink his eye and one of them fainted. They got Frank up, and the medics got a hold of him and started treating him and he survived! He had a long, very fruitful life after that. I was outside the hanger when the last Japanese aircraft came down the main runway. He was firing his guns and so we fell flat on our faces and we were firing at him from the prone position. And then when I thought he had gone by, and to where he couldn't deflect toward us, I stood up and I'll be damned if there wasn't a rear gunner there. He tattooed the hangar wall behind me and those marks are still there today."

James [Jim] Carroll on 8 December 1941: "Things changed from a gentleman's army to a hardworking army on 8 December. Going to the flight line was almost risking your life. Where we used to go out to the airplane, crank up and fly, now when you approached the flight line there were two guards who challenged you and you laid your ID on the ground and backed off. One kept you covered with a Tommy gun and the other looked at your ID and once you were recognized, things went back to normal. The big planes, the B-17s, went out 700 miles, essentially searching for anything that was there: Japanese submarines, Japanese this, Japanese whatever—anybody who didn't belong there, and of course, we found nothing."

Glenn Guoan on Enlistment Following Pearl Harbor: "A lot of young guys got all enthused so I went down the next day to the recruiting office and the first thing they said was, Well, we want to take and get quite a few guys to go down on the bus, so we'll notify you when we can take you and then you can be sworn in.' I was 18, and the First Sergeant that we had here at the recruiting station in Bay City [Michigan], he said, 'I've go to have your parents' OK for you to go.' So Dad was a World War I veteran who served over there in the trenches, and he said, 'If you come home and tell me you went in the infantry, I'm going to kick your fanny clear across Michigan.' I was learning to fly at a local airport here before Pearl Harbor and I said, No, I'm going in the Air Force if I can get in,' which I did. I was fortunate to get in. I got sworn in 29 December 1941."

Mike LaRocca on Midway: "I remember at Kipapa Gulch I was standing by one of our airplanes and here comes a jeep with the combat crew for that airplane, and the commanding officer says to me, 'Get in the airplane!' I said, 'For what!' And he says, 'Get in the airplane!' So I got in the airplane and it took off, and as we're in the air I said to one of the crew members, 'Where are we going?' He says, 'We're going to Midway.' And that's when I knew the Battle of Midway was on. That's when I got scared. When he told me 'We're going to Midway!' and there were about 14 guys on the airplane and about eight parachutes; of course, a parachute wouldn't have done you any good anyway cause you were over the water. [LaRocca was sent to Midway because] they needed a ground crew to maintain the airplanes. We got the airplanes ready so they could fly out and see if they could find the Japanese fleet."

George Glober [pilot] on the Wake Reconnaissance Mission: "They asked for volunteers of two crews from each squadron. That was the 11th Group and the 5th Group, and those two groups had four squadrons each. So there was no trouble getting volunteers to try this. But I was the only squadron commander that volunteered himself. And, of course, each of my crew members volunteered independently and concurrently, so I sent in our name as one of the crews from the 31st and as you would expect, I was selected since I was the ranking man that volunteered to go."

Ed Caton [photographer] on the Wake Reconnaissance Mission: "We headed for home and about 15 hours and 40 minutes out, we should have been home and we weren't there. It was getting dark and George [Glober] spoke to every crew member personally and pointed out that a bullet had hit the compass and we'd been navigating with some pretty bad information on magnetic headings and we didn't know about it until the last hour. The navigator happened to notice the bullet was lodged there and he really couldn't correct anything because the sun had set and the stars hadn't come out yet. The radio operator was instructed to get on the emergency frequencies to ask someone to turn a light on at Midway to see if we could see them. They had a ground rule there that they were not supposed to turn lights on after dark because a submarine could range on them and fire into them which they DID do. But somebody in the Marine antiaircraft battalion turned on the search lights and we saw these three fingers sticking up in the sky and I'll never forget it! They were 90 degrees to our left so George just rocked it over. I was standing beside him when it happened and we just headed for the runway. George may not talk about it, but it was one hell of a feat of airmanship on his part and a lot of good luck for the rest of us."

Bob Holliday [gunner] on the Wake Reconnaissance Mission: "We were told the plans were to arrive at 12 noon Wake Island time, assuming that all the Japanese would be eating lunch or whatever. And that was a good idea because we went over the island exactly at noon and made a couple of passes taking pictures before any antiaircraft fire started to come up." [On our return to Midway] we went in and landed and just as we hit the runway we ran out of gas. The number one engine quit operating --fuel starvation-- and then the number two and then number three and then number four. They had to come and tow us to the bunker."

Nelson (Bill) Leever on the Guadalcanal Landing: "As we were getting there to Guadalcanal, to Henderson Field, there were some Japanese out there strafing this ship that we were on. I mean they were just strafing the hell out of it! So this old captain, he held that ship in as close as he could get without getting stuck and so then he says, Everybody off! Everybody off!' And boy, I'll tell you, we had these long duffel bags and you had everything with you; you had your rifle with you, you had your boots full of water because we came down these ropes stretched down the side of the ship and then we got into this little boat, I guess it held 40 or 50 people. It's one of those type of boats where you head onto shore and when the head of the boat hits the shore, you just put the gate down and everybody runs out. We got our butts pretty wet getting out. We ran into the water; it was above my waistline, pretty much up to my chest and so everything you had with you got soaked. We weighed about 200 pounds at that time. Yeah, that was a *wonderful* day, I'll tell you, on Guadalcanal that first day!"

William R. (Bob) Estes on the Guadalcanal Landing: "We had got on the beach and were waiting and some were still coming in, but they were trying to bring the equipment in and here they get the sound of an air raid and the ship has to take off otherwise it would be a sitting duck. All the guys get running and going through and the first they know, we'd run right through a mine field! Thank goodness it didn't work, none went off but it had been found because it had been marked. That's how we knew it was a mine field! We landed without even thinking, you know; the first thing you're thinking about is getting off the beach. You're heading for the trees for cover but we went right through a mine field. Of course, this was the first one—you learned after that!"

James (Jim) Carroll on the Death of Carlyle (Moose) Coleman: "Actually, Moose was a pilot, but he was flying in the copilot seat on the right side at that time. They were taking their first search out of Guadalcanal and they just ran into a swarm of Zeroes. They were attacked by about 25 Zeroes and the Zeroes shot out three of the four engines in the B-17 and they were limping home losing altitude and just barely got back in. Carlyle Coleman was killed on the last pass by the last Zero, and George [Glober] actually had to more or less move the now dead Carlyle Coleman so somebody else could sit there and help him manage the controls and the landing. It was a sad event. He [Coleman] was buried on Guadalcanal. We had a cemetery there and I visited his grave. The ground people liked him very much; he was very popular, an ideal commander. He got along with everybody -- the enlisted men, the top brass, everybody. They had arranged a monument to him. They put one of the propeller blades up for a headstone, a head blade and several bandoleers of 50 caliber ammunition strung across it. There was always a feeling among fly boys in those days, I guess there always is, that this can happen to somebody else, not me. Whatever happens, I can handle it. We felt the loss of Carlyle Coleman but we figured, 'Well, there but for the grace of God goes I,' and maybe tomorrow might be my turn. But in the meantime, I'll do my best."

William D. (Bill) Krimer on the 26 August 1943 Mission to Kahili Airdrome: "It was almost always the same target: Kahili Japanese Air Force Base on the southern tip of the island of Bougainville in the northern Solomons. That was actually also the southernmost point of Japanese advance in the South Pacific, barring Guadalcanal. We were attacked by Zeroes and we were in a running battle for a period of about 1/2 hour or so. Once we would get into a cloud bank, the pilot would warn us, 'Watch out when you get out of there -- they'll be right on top of us.' And that's precisely the way it was. I only remember that we had our hydraulic system shot out-shot out by a Japanese fighter, so hydraulic fluid leaked out and everything that would normally be handled by hydraulic controls, we had to do by hand, including lowering the landing gear, the nose gear, and the main landing gear, and pulling up the ball turret so we could land. It was Col. [Joseph] Reddoch and I that worked for about an hour pulling up-painfully pulling up that ball turret so we could land."

Donald MacAllister on the 26 August 1943 Mission to Kahili Airdrome: "We were leading the Squadron. When we came off the target, I dropped my bombs and when I caged my gyro and turned off my bomb site and closed the bomb bay doors, I was just starting to get up when I heard Carr say he was hit and he needed help. I didn't wait for anything. I just ran to the back. What hit them [Owen Carr and Harold Nerstad] in the waist was a 20 mm cannon. You know anything about a 20 mm shell? They turn into shrapnel. When they go through the side of an airplane they explode, just like a big hand grenade. Nerstad didn't look like he was hurt. I gave him first aid but he didn't look like he was hurt too bad. He had a wound somewhere on his leg and I put a tourniquet on it. But his back had a wound on it that I didn't see. It was not as big as a fingernail but it was right over his nerve center, his backbone. It severed his nerves. That's the last I saw Carr until I saw him at the hospital. The hospital was a terrible place in those days. It was a big series of tents. It was away from the field and it was next to a big road. It smelled bad. They didn't have any sewers. They didn't have anything. They did the best they could. But it was a depressing situation. At least to me, as I remember it."

Owen Carr on the 26 August 1943 Mission to Kabili Airdrome: "We cleared our guns and then they made the bomb runs and Don MacAllister salvoed the 40 100-lb. demolition bombs—they were painted yellow. I was watching them drop to the ground and they said, 'Here they come!' I was searching for them and I fired at what I hoped was a Zero. I got off a couple of rounds. I don't know if I hit him or not, and then that was just about the last thing that I did when I felt that horrible shock of that 20 mm cannon shell ripping my left leg apart. I didn't know what happened and I fell to the floor and [Harold] Nerstad, the left waist gunner had been hit also, and he was down but he was better than I was because he had the sense to call them and he said, 'You better send someone back. They got Carr and me.' Don MacAllister, he was supposed to be the first aid man, came back immediately and he took over both waist guns firing out of first one side and then the other. I remember very vividly the hot, empty 50 caliber shells popping out of the right waist gun and hitting me in the face and they were quite warm. I was pounding on Don, asking him for help. I should have just laid there, I guess. I was subsequently taken to the 20th Station-United States Army 20th Station hospital at Tenaru which was a few miles from Henderson Field. Members of the crew I remember coming and asking the doctor to do his best to save my leg but I really didn't care -- I wasn't a dancer or an athlete. All I really wanted to do was to get rid of the pain and I kept telling him [the doctor] to cut my leg off I had it in my mind that if they amputated my leg, in the same process they'd eliminate the pain." [For more details on this story, see Ulmer, "The Cisco Kid in World War II, in this volume.]

George Vickers on Life in the New Hebrides: "We hadn't had a decent meal for a long time. So, him [Donald MacAllister] being a Texas cowboy, we went and got a hold of an ordinance truck. It had a winch on it. We rode around the island and found about 15 or 20 head of cattle. This one was a young steer. He stood there and he was looking at us and it had to be at least 100 yards away. MacAllister had a carbine and he aimed at the booger and hit him right between the eyes, and he dropped like a log! So we got the truck over there and put him on a winch, hauled it

up and he gutted it first and then skinned it and we brought back a whole pile of beef back to the camp. We had beef for at least a week or so."

Ernie Ruiz on the Crash of *My Lovin' Dove*: [The B-17 *My Lovin' Dove* was on a search mission and as she passed near the Japanese-held island of Nauru, she was attacked by Zeroes.]

"I got hit in the leg when a 20 mm exploded in the cockpit. And I got shrapnel in my left leg and blood started pouring down my leg into my boot. I didn't realize that I was hit until I felt this squishing sound in my boot, and when I took it off I noticed that I had holes all over the left leg, but I was able to stop the blood all right. The pilot, Captain Classen, was hit in the mouth and he had blood coming out of his mouth, and some of the other fellows were hit. We radioed into Guadalcanal to give them our approximate position and just about that time we started losing our number three engine. We knew that we were not going to be able to get back to Guadalcanal. And then we prepared for a water landing. [They landed safely and evacuated the plane.] We had four in one raft and the other raft, we had five in it. The airplane sank with its tail in the air and it just slowly slid down and disappeared. We were kind of happy in a way that everybody was OK and we knew they had radioed in. We figured we'd only be out in the water a few hours or maybe a day at the most. Why, it turned out we were on the raft for 15 days. The first four days, we had sharks with us all the time. They were underneath the raft, they'd slide underneath and we could feel them, we could feel the fins as they came underneath these rubber rafts and we were afraid they were going to rip the raft so I'd fire at them with my .45 that I had, but after four days the .45 was rusted and we had to just throw it away. At times, we'd run into rain squalls and we would collect water into our canteens and we drank as much as we could, but then during the day it was so hot that we kind of rationed ourselves to two swallows of water a day per man. The funny part of it is that every time one of the men would tip the canteen up to take a drink of water, we'd watch his Adam's Apple to make sure it didn't go up more than once. Finally, we saw some seagulls flying around at a distance. Out of that whole flock of seagulls that was flyin' by, one of lem flew away from the bunch and came down and landed on our raft. And the boys kept saying, 'Get him! Get him!' And I said, 'I will! I will! I will!', you know, real quietly. Believe it or not, then that bird jumped from there and landed on the forehead of the guy laying right next to me. And I looked at that seagull when it was sitting up there perched, and it looked like a turkey sitting there. I reached over and I grabbed it and I handed it to the tail gunner who in civilian life was a butcher, and he cut it open and pulled all the feathers off and by the time he got all the feathers out, that thing was about the size of a canary. [After 15 days afloat, the crew reached a small island and were met by a group of islanders.] I was an Eagle Scout, so I got up and I was going to start my sign language and then one fellow who was in the front who apparently was the chief stepped forward and he put his hand out and he says, Hello!' in plain English. [The natives fed the crew and nursed them back to health.] I learned their language. They spoke Pigeon English, kind of a mix of their language and English, They say, 'Stop. You wait'em pass time. Me catch'em kai kai belong you.'Well, all that means is 'Wait there. I'll go get your food.'They would get a leaf off of a tree and would get some other bud and they'd stick it in their mouths and chew it. And their mouths would get just as red as anything, and I asked them why they did that. They said, 'All the same whiskey belong you. Head belong you, walkabout.' In other words, it made them dizzy! Anyway, I was on the island for 51 days! [Weeks after the crew had been declared missing in action and presumed dead, they were rescued.] The airplan landed in the lagoon and we were getting ready to leave. They didn't want me to leave, they wanted me to stay. And they said if I stayed, they'd give me a wife!"

Leon Rockwell on 5th Bomb Group (H) Commander Col. Marion Unruh: "I loved that Col. Unruh. I loved him. He was not only an excellent pilot but he was a graduate engineer and he was the one who was responsible for many modifications of the bombers down there including heavy Plexiglas windshields on the bomber to deflect bullets, the nose turret which they called the chin turret on the B-17 where it was just like the other automatic turrets on the plane, and other modifications with reinforcing in the back of the cockpits to deflect any bullets that would come in the back and hit the pilot. And he was brave. He never asked his men to fly any mission he wouldn't fly. One time he came in in a B-24 at night and one of the antiaircraft guns, our friendly guns on Guadalcanal, got jumpy and shot at him and they shot one of the hydraulic lines in the B-24 and he could not lower one of the main gears. He had the nose wheel and the other main gear and I watched him and it was the most beautiful landing! He only damaged the outside of the wing and one engine and propeller. That's how good a pilot he was! I saw the Navy do the same thing one time with a Navy B-24 and it tore it all to pieces."

Donald MacAllister on 5th Bomb Group (H) Commander Col. Marion Unruh: Col. Unruh was a man that wouldn't ask anybody to do something he wouldn't do. The first time I kind of worried about him was—I had 25 missions when he got there. When I had ten more missions, when I had 35 missions, Col. Unruh had 40 missions. He was flying every mission. He and his crew went on every mission that the Squadron flew. We talked over breakfast. I took the liberty to tell him one morning: 'Colonel, I'm not trying to tell you your business and I'm not trying to dig into your business, but you've got more missions than I have and I've been here twice as long as you have. I've flown a whole lot of missions I didn't have to fly, and you've flown a whole lot of missions you didn't have to fly.' I told him, 'There are a lot of things that could happen to you. You could have a mechanical failure, the weather can get you and the enemy can get you, and those three things could sure happen to anybody. And you can only dodge that black bean so many times. It'll come up and something real bad will happen to you. If you think the men don't respect you or the men think you're a coward, well, nobody dares to think you're a coward -you've proved you'll fly a mission. You've proved that you'll attack the airfields and the islands. You don't have anything to prove. You need to stay here and run your squadron. 'He said, Well, Lt., let me tell you, Sir, they can't shoot me down.'"

Bill Fallin on 5th Bomb Group (H) Commander Col. Marion Unruh: "We went on what somebody told me might have been the first daylight mission they had flown over there with B-24s. Col. [Marion] Unruh was leading the mission, and we were flying on his left wing, and we got in some clouds and we got hit by some Zeroes and we were wandering around in those clouds and we were following him and he turned kind of violently to the right and we stayed with him. I couldn't see so my copilot took over and we finally got out of it and came on home. Col. Unruh looked us up and he told me, 'That's as good a flying as I've ever seen on a B-24.' And I said, 'Well, it wasn't me. It was my copilot.' And he said, 'Well, you trained him, didn't you.' And I said, 'Yes, Sir, I did.' But, boy, I'll never forget that mission. I was never so scared in all my life!"

Marion Unruh on His Imprisonment in Japan: "On 25 February 1944, a Japanese named Watanabe came into my cell and started to question me regarding the organization to which I was attached and the locality from which I had come. He re-

marked that the U. S. was no good and made other remarks of a derogatory nature. I defended America stating that the Japanese seemed to want it pretty badly, whereupon he got very mad and said something which I could not understand. I shrugged my shoulders. He got very angry and picked up one of my flying boots which was outside of my cell and beat me on the head and knocked me down and kept hitting me while I was on the floor."

John Bauwens on the 5 March 1944 Raid on Rabaul: "We had just dropped the bombs and were turning away for our return. But unfortunately the antiaircraft hit right through our main gas tank, right in back of the pilot, right above the pilot's seat. So that's what caused the plane to explode. Well, when that missile exploded, immediately the whole aircraft was engulfed in flames and we didn't have much chance to do much of anything. There's a warning button on the pilot's panel that if you feel the aircraft's in danger, you push that button which gives signals to the crew to bail out. I was copilot at the time and I knew we were in trouble because the airplane was already turning over. I reached over to push that button and I never got it done because by that time the plane had exploded, just disintegrated. For myself, I was knocked unconscious. I came to while I was falling through the air. I oriented myself and opened my parachute and saw the other two parachutes close by, and, of course, pieces of the burning airplane were falling around us. So we landed in the water close to shore and I had to help them out because one had concussions and so forth so he was out of it and the other one had third degree burns all over his body, and I had a shrapnel hole in my leg. In fact, the Japanese did try to send boats out to pick us up but they couldn't locate us. Finally the Australian Air Force had a rescue outfit and they flew a Catalina PBY5 Rescue -- it lands on water -- and they finally located us and landed the plane and picked us up." [Bauwens and two crew members survived. Another crewman was captured by the Japanese. The remaining crewmen were killed in the explosion.]

Jim Berry Letter to John Bauwens Regarding the 5 March 1944 Raid on Rabaul: "Your pilot was a friend of mine, and I was sitting next to him at breakfast that morning. I recall that he asked, 'Jim, why are you so damned grumpy this morning?' and I answered, 'By God, I had to shave in cold water this morning.' I would not normally have remembered such a trivial conversation for so many years except that he died that day and that little bit of nonsense stuck in my memory. As I would reconstruct that mission, we approached the target at Rabaul in Javelin formation. After turning on the bombing run, the squadron leader and his two wing men continued directly toward the aiming point. Your pilot, a flight commander, was leading the second flight, and he led his flight to the right of the lead ship. I was flight commander of the third flight, and I led my flight to the left of the lead flight. The fourth flight followed behind the lead flight. The concept was saturation bombing of a wide area. Immediately following *bombs away*, we reformed into Javelin formation to concentrate our fire power against fighter interceptors. Almost immediately after I took my position behind you, a man came out your waist window. I jerked back on the wheel as it appeared that he was going into my propellers. Luckily, he went beneath the props as there was no way that I could have acted fast enough to have made any difference. [Tokyo Rose later announced that he had been captured.] Then my copilot shouted, 'That plane is on fire. Let's get the hell away from it.' At that moment I started a gentle climb, and your pilot, still in control, started a gentle descent toward the sea between the New Britain and New Ireland Islands. He never seemed to lose control, and the ship did not spin. Then there was a great ball of fire, and the wings folded straight up—wing tip to wing tip. Simultaneously, in the fireball, three parachutes blossomed."

Sid Ulmer on Life on Los Negros: "One thing I remember about Los Negros was when we moved from Guadalcanal to there. They put us in trucks and took us to the encampment and it had this horrible stench and I couldn't imagine what it was and we were sitting in the back of this open truck and I found out later it was a combination of dead Japanese bodies and rotting coconut palms and coconuts."

Rodger Rawleigh on the Crash of the Cisco Kid II: [Rawleigh's father, Walter, was a crew member of the Cisco Kid II] "They took off to make a bombing run, and witnesses said the plane rose about 150 feet in the air in a steep climb and the wing was low. The aircraft made a slow turn to the left and the nose dropped and the plane turned 180 degrees and crashed into a naval encampment off the runway. Then the plane's fuel caught fire and the aircraft's nine 500-pound bombs exploded. The crew was killed instantly as were 165 Seabees eating breakfast in the camp." [For more on this story, see Ulmer, "The Cisco Kid in World War II", in this volume.]

Jim Berry on Military Strategy in the Pacific: "We would soften it up and then the Navy would come in and they'd dive bomb it and shell it and then send the Marines in to seize the island. They'd land the Seabees and they'd build an airstrip. First we'd get notice that the airstrip was far enough along that we could make a belly landing on it and then a couple of days later, they'd say it's well enough finished that you can land with your wheels down in an emergency, and then about the next mission we flew, they'd say it's in good shape. It's ready to make any kind of a landing on."

John McNaughton on Family: "I got my first mail from overseas and my wife was pregnant and our son was born the last one in the year of '43. So I found that out about a month after he was born. I went to the Red Cross to check with them as soon as we got to New Guinea and heck, we'd stayed there a month. We'd moved up to the Mollucas and joined the Bomb Group and I got regular mail before I got confirmation from the Red Cross. Oh yes, anything like that is hard, but you've got a job to do and it's one of those things you can't reverse so you just have to take it in stride."

Manuel (Pete) Arniaz's Diary Entry Regarding a 21 May 1944 Mission to Truk: "Flight time: 9 1/2 hours. The crew was rather tense at the briefing, and no one got much of a night's sleep as evidenced by the red glow of cigarettes in our tents throughout the dark night. Take off from Momote was at 6:25 a.m. with 24 planes from our Fifth Group and 24 from the 307th Group. As we neared the Truk Atoll, most of the crew donned flak suits as protection. As the Atoll slid into view, the copilot spied a flock of Zero fighters waiting to pounce upon our formation. When the formation's guns began firing, it sounded like a state fair fireworks display. The flak became heavier and more accurate. Shortly after our bombs ripped into the target, the B-24 on our left began smoking from the number two engine. Suddenly it slipped under our ship, moved down and started what appeared to be a slow roll. Three men evacuated through the camera hatch. All three chutes bloomed immediately. Two Zeros dove in to strafe the ship and chutists. Our guns attempted to keep the fighters off the doomed men, but most likely the entire crew perished. "

Sid Ulmer on the First Mission to Balikpapan: "We believed we could fly it as far as the gas is concerned. But whether we could get back was another question. Most of us thought it was going to be worse than anything we'd encountered before and in the briefings we'd pick up clues that made us think about it. For example, when they kept emphasizing over and over all the plans for rescue, which they hadn't done before. This tells you that maybe they think they're going to need rescue more

than they had before and when they give you a dictionary of native words in case you get shot down—they hadn't done that before. I can tell you the 300 people in the briefing tent were not too comfortable with what they were hearing. Mostly it was dead silence which is a sign of fear. We took off right after midnight. The 31st Squadron and the 23rd were in the first section of 12 planes. We had to get all 24 planes off in 24 minutes, which we did. We were told that if a raid came while we were taking off to ignore it, and that if we got off and had difficulty before the other planes got off and had to turn back, not to come back and interfere with what was happening with the planes taking off but to simply bail out in the water and they'd come see if they could get us later. It was very important to get those planes off one right after the other, close together because they had to be at a rendezvous point over 1,000 miles away and they wanted them to assemble in formation within 24 minutes after getting there. The schedule was more than just a schedule; if not followed it could mean that you simply did not get back. We had to cross Halmahera, which was about 485 miles from Noemfoor. The Japs had a base there and we were afraid they had fighters there, but this was the middle of the night and they didn't know we were coming and by the time we were overhead, they couldn't get their fighters off in time. We went on down to the next piece of land, Celebes, where there were two Jap bases. They sent up 50 some fighters but as we approached there we ran into towering cumulus clouds. We had been flying at 8000 feet and when we hit the clouds, Musgrave [Colonel Thomas] took us up to, I think, about 14,000 feet to try to get out of it. The consequence of that was the Japs couldn't find us. About 30 Jap fighters, Zekes, Zeroes, and Tondys came at us pretty hard about five or ten miles before we got to the target. We got to the target and the ack-ack was the most intense we'd ever encountered. The target was socked in ten-ten; we couldn't see it. So we had a choice. We thought for a moment we could bomb where we saw a hole in the clouds close up and it would at least have some effect, but Musgrave said, "No, we've come a long way and made a lot of sacrifice. It's important. We're not gonna do that." So he started circling, waiting for an opening in the clouds until he could see the aiming point. He took us around and came in from a different direction. It took an hour and all that time the fighters were on us. When we were leaving the target we were being attacked fiercely and every gun on the plane was firing constantly except mine. I couldn't fire a single round because not a single Jap came within an angle that would permit me to fire. I was the tail gunner and all I could do was sit there while everybody else was firing, the Japs are diving, the flak is all around and I'm sitting there an observer. So I could pray and think. It's the only time I can ever remember looking down to see what kind of terrain I might fall into. And of course, it was all solid jungle and mountains and it would have been suicidal to go down any way in that kind of situation. But I can recall calling on my Maker to work his will, and hoping that it included my survival." [For further information about the planning and execution of the September 30, 1944 mission, see Ulmer, "Balikpapan: The 5th Bomb Group's Finest Hour", in this volume.]

Manuel (Pete) Arniaz's Diary Entry Regarding a Mission to Yap Island: "Our neighboring crew was picked up today adrift in life rafts. Seven of ten were found, four of those dead. They had bailed out upon running out of gas returning from Yap."

Walt Meibaum on Japanese Raids on Morotai: "Probably the scariest part was on Morotai with the Japanese bombing. They were right in Halmahera and bombing us time after time. In fact, I counted 44 air raid alerts in the first 30 days I was there. Sometimes they'd come over twice a night, three times a night, not always bombing; sometimes it was just an air raid alert. But anyway, you lost a lot of sleep because you were down in the fox hole during every air raid alert. We had a nice fox hole there. It was about four steps down to the ground and then about 8 steps underground into a left-hand turn. It was covered with several feet of metal and sand, so it was just an underground vault. The very first time it kind of scares you; you couldn't see anything, you didn't know what was going on."

Everett (Beach) Thurlow on- Japanese Raids on Morotai:
"We'd gotten by some way or another a big beer ration in this day and there were a number of people that were not exactly sober around. The Japanese would come over as a single airplane, circle the area out of range of the antiaircraft, seemingly just to keep us out of bed all night. Finally, after playing around a while, they'd come across the airdrome, drop a bomb and leave and then another one would come in a while later. The antiaircraft people we had there would just fill the sky with what we called ack-ack but they never could get the Japanese airplane. But this night the bomber came over and they had the search lights on it; we could see it at a very high altitude. We could see very clearly a shining Japanese Betty bomber making this run on Morotai. But the antiaircraft guns were not firing. We couldn't figure it out! We were all out there screaming, 'Shoot the bastard down! Shoot him down!' Then all at once we heard a whining engine, a very high-pitched propeller sound and what had occurred was that we'd gotten in a British Spitfire, I suppose it was Australian, and they had set him up there at an altitude higher than the Betty would be. And so when the Betty came in and the antiaircraft search lights were on him, the Spitfire just came over and with a stream of fire the Betty exploded and all of the metal and fire came on down on the beach in front of us. We're all out there cheering like it's a football game. That was always a vivid memory of mine."

Everett (Beach) Thurlow on the Mission to Brunei Bay:
"As we came into sight of Brunei Bay, we were dumbfounded because the bay was filled with ships! These huge ships had tremendous fire power, and we had been briefed to go over this target at 8000 feet which theoretically was too high for the low caliber guns and the high powered guns would be too low for them. As it turned out, we were at the fight altitude for both of them. We had 24 aircraft that went over that target. The lead

plane was just picked out of the air even before we got to the initial point and it was almost like flying instruments over that target with so much antiaircraft going off. The aircraft I was on managed to get over the target relatively in one piece - we had one engine shot out. We certainly disrupted their plans as to what they were doing, because those ships had to scurry to get out of that bay as fast as they could."

Paul Thompson on a June, 1945 Mission to Tarakan Island: "The Aussies [Australians] had got in a hole, they couldn't get the Japs off a ridge in front of them. They had tried everything, had all kinds of planes helping 'em so they called us in, and that's crazy, asking boys in a big heavy bomber to come in and bomb maybe 500 feet away. You had to bomb this hilltop, and, you know, it's scary because you're afraid you'll drop bombs on the Aussies. The Aussie boys would fire a flare into a section over there—it was all jungle down below, that's all you could see. But when they fired the flares, we synchronized on the flare. Well, we'd go maybe four or five seconds and the Japs would fire a flare back at the Aussies, and if you weren't on the ball, you might have thought the first one was wrong, and then you dropped short and you'd kill a bunch of Aussies. We dropped our bombs and right away they called the people down there on the radio and they said the results were good and thanked us and we went on home then."

Albert James on "Bomber Baron Airlines": "General Brandt, who was my immediate boss, suggested that I send some people down to the boneyard' on Biak which is in New Guinea and pick up four C-47s, one for each squadron, so that the guys could fly to Australia and pick up fresh food and so forth. We did that and we brought them back and practically made new airplanes out of them. We got rid of the olive drab paint and made them silver and put a blue stripe along the side and put a label on it, "Bomber Baron Airliner." We had four of those flying around the South Pacific and when people with these other organizations would see them, they say, 'Where did you get that? How do you get away with it.' It was real neat because the transport was a big morale builder for the squadrons."

William R. (Bob) Estes on the Medical Corps: We were the Squadron medics. One of the main things we did was having the crash duty at the airstrip but after they'd been wounded this

5th Bomb Group Operations, William J. Stuart, Jr. Commanding.

long, (they do for them in the plane what they can) the best thing we could do was to get them on a litter and get them to the hospital as soon as we could so they could have surgery. We could give first aid but by then, if they hadn't stopped bleeding, they wouldn't be there alive. This is why the man's own crewmen would do the first things for him and this is what it took. One of the planes came in and hadn't been able to get rid of their bomb load. I remember they hit a cross wind and this caused them to crash. When the plane crashed, one of the bombs went off. We [the medics] were trying to help the ones in the plane and get the injured out and the medical officer was standing up when one of the bombs went off and killed him. The rest of us were bent over doing things and we got saved but he was standing up at the time and it got him."

William R. [Bob] Estes on Length of Overseas Service for Ground Personnel: "I'll always remember this man's name, Neil Mauderer. He was a ground personnel but he was getting where he had to get out; he wanted to get home and it didn't look like we had any relief coming. They needed some gunners anyway and being in armament he had a chance to do this so he got into a combat crew. On one of his first missions, the plane went down and he never made it home. Chances are, if he'd have stayed on the ground, maybe he would have made it. He was so anxious to get home-you'd been there a long time! But you know, you sit and reminisce on some of these things and its hard. You had to be away so long. I was 38 months overseas and Wendell [Pfannenstiel] was just about 3 years. We were there to do a job and we did what we could do. None of us would have liked to have been there—we'd have rather been home somewhere but, it was one of the things you had to do!"

Albert James on the Disappearance of 5th Bomb Group Commander Isaac Haviland: We had heard by four or five o'clock in the afternoon that all the other craft had returned to Morotai minus the one in which Haviland was flying. And so we knew as of that moment that there was obviously some kind of problem. That same evening we received telegraphic information appointing me as no longer the acting commander but rather the commander of the 5th Bomb Group. I bugged General [Carl] Brandt, who was the commander, to let me fly out and take a look and see if I couldn't locate the wreckage scene which I assumed I could probably locate. But he would not approve it."

Lou Roffman on the Use of the Atom Bombs: "We had the war practically won, but Intelligence stated that if it hadn't have been done, at least one million American young men would have been killed on the invasion, and more than that of the Japanese. It ended the war and that was the primary factor of the whole thing."

William O. [Bill] Richardson on Missions Flown After the Atom Bombs: "We even flew after the two atomic bombs were dropped. We flew a mission each day after one of those bombs was dropped. For what reason, I don't know. We hit Formosa, which is now Taiwan. The only thing we knew was that there was some massive bomb that left a bunch of dirty material, radioactive material. We heard that nobody was going to be able to live there for — we heard anywhere from 100 years to 1,000 years. The day after they bombed Hiroshima we had a mission to Taiwan, which we flew. Then the day after they bombed Nagasaki we had another mission to Formosa, and eventually we flew one more mission. Those weren't 'ground zero' bombs. Those were detonated in the atmosphere at three or four thousand feet up because they could do the most damage and left a dirty trace and we figured out that the drift was to the south, southwest. We think now we flew through that drift."

Bill Fallin on the Importance of the 31st Bombardment Squadron (R): "I think the 13th Air Force was the forgotten air force, and that trickles down to the Group and to the Squadron. Because I don't think we got near the credit we should have gotten for what we did over there and we didn't get a lot of promotions and a lot of medals that some of the others got. We did the job we were sent over there to do, and we did it with due diligence and there was a camaraderie between all of us that we'd never had before and have probably never had since. Simply put, we did our job. We put a lot of Japs out of commission out there particularly when we were bombing Truk and Yap and places like that and spending 11 and 12 hours in the air and if they had not been stopped there, well, there's just no telling what would have happened."

Jim Berry on the Importance of the 31st Bombardment Squadron (H): "In terms of expertise and, just a great organization, I thought we were the best!"

HISTORY OF THE 72ND BOMBARDMENT SQUADRON

On 14 February 1924 the Secretary of War approved the insignia herein described for marking of aircraft of the 72nd Bombardment Squadron:

Two bolts of lightning appearing from behind a thundercloud, the bolts forming more or less vaguely the figures '7' and '2,' the lower end of the second bolt disappearing behind a second cloud. Black disc edge with white, white to gray clouds, white bolts.

1918-1919
World War I

The 72nd Bombardment Squadron is the youngest of all the 5th Bomb Group squadrons. Almost a year after the 4th Aero Squadron was founded, the 72nd Aero Squadron was activated. On 18 February 1918 the unit was activated at Rich Field, Waco, Texas, under the command of Lt. William Hensel, Jr. The personnel forming the squadron were from the 3rd Provisional Regiment, also stationed at Rich Field.

Five months later the squadron left for the Port of Embarkation, Garden City, Long Island, New York. Then under the command of Lt. George L. Twigg, the squadron boarded the *Matsonia* and departed for France on 14 August 1918. After an uneventful passage, the ship arrived at Brest, France, on 25 August 1918, where the squadron disembarked and proceeded to a rest camp in the city.

One week later the squadron moved to St. Maxient, where they were equipped for field service, and their designation was changed to Mobile Park Squadron No. 10. On 30 September 1918 the unit moved to Colombey-les-Belle, France, which was a large replacement camp for both aircraft and personnel. While pilots of the organization ferried planes to and from advanced bases, other squadron personnel were engaged in construction work.

After eight months of duty at this station the squadron boarded the *Julia Luckenback* and sailed from St. Nazaire, France, on 16 June 1919. Arriving in New York on June 28 1919, the unit took station at Hazelhurst Field.

The squadron, still designated as Mobile Park Squadron No. 10, was demobilized at Aviation Concentration Camp, Garden City on 10 July 1919. (Another source indicates that the squadron was demobilized at Hazelburst Field, Long Island, on 11 July 1919.)

72nd Bombardment Squadron at Biak, New Guinea. (l to r) Front row: William Wendt, John O'Brian, Pop Hommock, Earl Cockrell, Lou Brousseau, and George O'Brien. Back row: Walter Lund, Lockwood Scoggin, Elwood D. Storrs, Jr., and Ben Benesh.

1923-1930
ReActivation at Hawaii

On 7 February 1923 the War Department ordered that the old 72nd Aero Squadron become active as an organization at Luke Field, T.H. This organization was to be known as the 72nd Bombardment Squadron, Air Service. On 1 May 1923 the 72nd Bombardment Squadron was formed at Luke Field, Hawaii, from men transferred from Ross Field, California, and new placements. Capt. Ross G. Hoyt, Air Service, assumed command of the squadron.

In the years that followed, squadron activities were routine, consisting primarily of training flights and indoctrination of ground crews. Sports held the primary outside interest for the men. In these years morale of the men was high, and unit pride was developed through competitive squadron sports and like activities.

During the month of March 1926, Capt. C.V. Finter, A.C., commanding officer of the 72nd Bombardment Squadron, completed the first flight around the Hawaiian islands, visiting each island in the archipelago, and covering the entire group in one day. Total flying time was seven hours 30 minutes in a C.O.A.-1 Amphibian. At the time this sustained flight represented an astonishing achievement.

1930-1934

On 14 May 1930 three members of the 72nd Squadron became members of the Caterpillar Club. While flying a LB-SA airplane, the pilot lost control of the plane when the control cables jammed. One officer and two enlisted men jumped clear and pulled their rip cords. All parachutes opened, and they drifted down to the Pacific where they were later picked up. A fourth passenger, an enlisted man from the 4th Aero Squadron, was killed when he opened his parachute inside the ship. His body was never recovered. Two attempts were made by amphibian planes to rescue the three men, both failing because the amphibians AN-ere unable to take off in the rough sea. Naval vessels finally effected the rescue.

Two more men of the squadron joined the Caterpillar Club on 10 August 1931. An officer-pilot with his enlisted crew chief entered a dense cloud bank while flying over the Koolau Range of mountains as a member of a squadron formation. Sight of the other planes was lost, and suddenly the airplane was found by the pilot in an abnormal position. Unable to bring the plane under control, both men jumped and landed safely in the tree tops of Kawailea Gulch.

October of 1931 saw the squadron participating in Hawaiian Department maneuvers. The 72nd and 23rd Squadrons, combined under the leadership of Major Kisby simulated a night bombing attack on Pearl Harbor. Approaching from a point about ten miles offshore, the attacking bombers used as cover a layer of clouds at 4,000 to 6,000 feet. These clouds furnished sufficient cover to hide all but three bombers which were picked up by the antiaircraft defenses.

In February 1932 came the important Joint Army-Navy Maneuvers. This squadron in conjunction with the 23rd Squadron comprised the 5th Composite Group tactical units in these maneuvers. The squadron set up camp in the field and camouflaged its nine B-5A bombers. During these maneuvers the squadron participated in an attack on the (theoretical) enemy carriers, *Lexington* and *Saratoga*. After this attack both carriers were declared out of action, although the theoretical losses for the 5th Group were such that it was forced to proceed homeward. The flight home was marked by an actual loss for the *Fighting 72nd*. No sooner had the squadron assembled for the flight home than one engine of a B-5A "Panther" cut out completely; the *Panther* crashed into the sea. The pilot and his two crew members were unhurt and were immediately picked up by a destroyer of the U.S. Navy, theoretically an enemy. Later they were transferred to the *Saratoga* where they were held as "prisoners of war."

In succeeding missions the planes of both squadrons bombed enemy transports at night, shot down five enemy flying boats and bombed some additional transports. For these missions both squadrons were highly commended by General Wells. It is interesting to note that weather conditions were unfavorable during almost the entire period of maneuvers, and wind velocities up to 60 m.p.h. were recorded. Two parked aircraft were damaged by the high winds.

During similar maneuvers in 1933 the 72nd Squadron moved to Bellows Field. Once situated at this field, the squadron was alerted for action against the approaching enemy Black Fleet. Simulated attacks were made on the *Lexington* and the *Saratoga*. Both attacks were considered successful by the official referee. During these exercises the squadron participated in night maneuvers against searchlights. Only one plane was caught and held in the lights, and the success of the mission was unquestioned. Maneuvers ended on 9 February, the 72nd had functioned as only a well-trained, well-prepared unit could. Not a plane was idle at any time during the maneuvers because of engine or equipment failure.

Toward the end of 1933 the squadron experienced field training in aerial gunnery and tactical problems from Bellows Field.

The year 1934 saw the squadron establish again its camp at Bellows Field for purpose of participation in aerial gunnery training. After returning to Luke Field, the squadron participated in more Army-Navy maneuvers.

1935

On the morning of 12 January, the squadron, under command of Major John U. Hart, led an *Aloha* flight to welcome Major Asa N. Duncan, the new post commander who arrived on tile army transport *Republic*. During the year several more *Aloha* flights were made, one at the departure of Major Hart, and another in honor of the Secretary of War, Mr. Dern. The Secretary inspected the squadron on 1 October. Three days later the unit participated in a Hawaiian Departmental Review held at Schofield Barracks for Mr. Dern.

Two demonstrations were held for the Hawaiian Department in 1935. The first series was executed in February and March when food and supplies were dropped to ground troops located in an almost inaccessible part of Oahn Island. The second, a bombing demonstration, was held on 3 May. In a demonstration of aerial power one plane of the squadron dropped ten 100 pound bombs on designated targets. The final demonstration was a squadron salvo from 8,000 feet with 12 bombers participating. These demonstrations were a huge success.

An interesting note on the June maneuvers dealt with the squadron's adherence to field conditions and servicing of aircraft from 50 gallon drums and 5 gallon tins.

On Thanksgiving Day the squadron entertained officers and non-commissioned officers and their wives with a bountiful turkey dinner.

Near the year's end on 26 December, the squadron bombed lava flow from the active Mauna Loa volcano which threatened the Hilo city water supply. Thirty-three hours later the flow ceased.

October 1944 on Nooemfoor Island, New Guinea. 72nd Squadron, 5th Bomb Group, Terry Spivey's Crew. (l to r) Front row: Doug Myers (ball turret), Larry Flood (radio operator/top turret), John Shorkey (armorer/tailgunner), Robert Langlois (flight engineer/waist gunner), Carl Fraley (waist gunner), and Robert Latham (nose gunner). Back row: Terry Spivey (pilot), Bill Blair (copilot), Star Palmer (navigator), and Tom Golenia (bombardier).

1945. 72nd Squadron, 5th Bomb Group. (l to r) Front row: Bob Boeen, William Young, Leland Tate, Tom Palmer, Chuck Ross, and Loren Epley. Back row: Bill Mason, Bill Terberg, Ralph Henderson, and Bob Reeves.

1936-1940

The squadron Organization Day picnic on 1 May 1936 was marred by the death of an enlisted man. While riding the train from the picnic ground to the dock, the soldier fell under the wheels of the train, receiving fatal injuries.

A mid-air collision of two Keystone bombers on the night of 24 January 1936 caused the deaths of an officer and three enlisted men. Another officer and enlisted man saved themselves by parachuting.

In 1937 the squadron aircraft strength of Keystone B-4s and B-5s was augmented by B-12s. The highlight of the spring of 1931 occurred when a formation of Keystone bombers ran into bad weather while returning to Oahu from a training mission. When these planes finally landed on Luke Field after a great deal of hunting the *Small Rock*, there was enough gas left in the tanks to fill only a couple of tins.

One of the most perplexing problems of 1937 concerned the unique placement, by sex, of offspring born to members of the squadron. Much conjecture and genealogical thought was given to the disturbing fact that while personnel residing in Pearl City were almost invariably recipients of male offspring those residents of Luke Field were nearly universally blessed with the deadlier of the species. Some authorities believed there was something in the water of Pearl City.

The squadron won the efficiency rating for the group in 1937. The squadron guidon was decorated with a streamer at ceremonies held at Fort Schofter.

1938

On 25 to 30 of March, all squadrons at Luke Field participated in a Fleet Problem. The 23rd, 4th and 50th Squadrons were all attached to the 72nd, with the total unit comprising ten air-craft and three spares. The 31st Squadron of Hickam Field also participated in these maneuvers as a unit of the 5th Group.

Upon the completion of maneuvers personnel of this squadron moved to Hickam Field. Here on April 18 the 31st Squadron started a program to train the 72nd in B-18s. On 1 June a reorganization was accomplished with the squadron's strength being cut from 167 to 142 men. The arrival of five B-18s 9 June started a shakedown period in which pilots and crews became more familiar with their ships. They got so familiar they ran a ferry service in B-18s to Luke Field for chow. From 5 December to 15 December, the squadron participated in a demonstration of demolition bombings in which 100, 300, 600, 1100 and 2000 pound bombs were dropped.

During the year the squadron had a successful athletic program. They placed first in the inter-squadron swimming, track and volleyball games in the Gold League. A fine showing was made in other sports.

Again this squadron won the Group Efficiency Rating and had its guidon decorated with a streamer at Fort Schofter.

On 4 January 1939 the administrative section of the squadron moved to Hickam Field, with quarters and mess remaining at Burns Field. In March the air echelon moved to Burns Field, Hawaii, for the Departmental Maneuvers, and in May participated in the military exercises.

The end of February of 1940 saw the squadron comfortably situated in new barracks at Hickam Field. By June squadron strength had jumped to 202 enlisted men and officers under the command of Capt. Robert F. Travis.

1941

There were no entries in the squadron diary for 1941 up to 7 December, Pearl Harbor Day.

WAR STORIES

The audience for this book is principally those members of the Fifth Bombardment Group (H) Association and who are part of that history. One of the common activities at the biennial reunions of the Association is the retelling of war stories. It is therefore appropriate to include in this book a section of such stories. Furthermore the soul of the Group is its squadrons and the soul of the squadrons is men who brought them life. It is hoped that this collection of their stories will add a personal character to the book.

THE STORY OF MY BAIL-OUT

By Albert W. James, 2nd Lieutenant, U. S. Army Air Corps

4 April 1941. My flying school classmate, Lt. Jack Alston, had been visiting family in the Ogden area, and was in need of a ride back to Denver where he had left his BT-9. Jack was an instructor pilot at Randolph Field, and on his cross-country to Salt Lake, the previous week, he had encountered bad weather, and as a result had left his aircraft there and come the rest of the way by land transit.

I was due a cross-country of my own, and was able to obtain the use of our squadron A-17. Our bomb group, the 7th, had just recently moved from Hamilton Field, near San Francisco, to Salt Lake City. And our home was actually at Fort Douglas, a beautiful setting against the mountains on the east side of Salt Lake City. The commercial airport at Salt Lake City was almost totally taken over by our group and its array of B-17B's, C's and D's, and some B-18's and a smattering of other small types (of which our A-17 was one).

And so it was that Jack and I climbed into the A-17 and took off for Denver. It was a morning flight and we were forecast to have clear weather all the way. The A-17 was a strongly built aircraft, designed for low altitude "attack" work. As a result its engine was not supercharged for higher altitude flight. In fact the flight level for instrument work between Salt Lake and Denver was necessarily in excess of 14,000 feet since the mountain-tops went that high. However, in clear weather one could fly along the light line and make out very nicely at 8,000 feet. For those who may never have heard of a light line, since they have long since been removed, the light line was made up of a series of towers, each within reasonable sight of those on either side, from which a beacon would shine, emitting a coded signal for identification. A pilot could expect to always have one and perhaps two in sight at any one time, and thus be guided along the route. Of course the route selected was always that which enabled flight at the lowest reasonable altitude. Thus when going through hilly or mountainous terrain the route necessarily resulted in one wending his way around mountains and flying through valleys — a most pleasant and enjoyable experience in clear weather, but hazardous in low clouds and poor visibility.

The A-17 with its unsupercharged engines could barely manage to produce enough power to yield an airspeed of 100 to 105 mph at 8,000 feet, but since the weather was clear this was not a problem. The flight to Denver, although somewhat tedious (3:25 time logged) was completed without incident.

After bidding Jack good-by, eating a late lunch, getting the aircraft serviced with fuel and filing my flight plan for the return flight to Salt Lake, I was ready to take off. My clearance showed that I was to have clear weather all the way back to Salt Lake City. Not to my liking, I would be in darkness well before reaching my destination; however, since the forecast was CAVU all the way I gave it no thought. Ceiling and visibility unlimited is always a pleasant sound to a pilot about to embark on a flight.

The take-off at Denver's Lowery Field required a good portion of the rather long runway. The field elevation as I recall was approximately one mile, or something over 5,000 feet. This elevation of course had its effect on my unsupercharged engine and accounted for the longer take-off run. After becoming airborne the aircraft gradually regained the 8,000 feet cruising altitude, and we were off on our way back to Salt Lake airport. After a couple of hours darkness began to fall, and the light line beacons could more easily be picked out. It required very little course correction to follow the lights during this time, since the more mountainous portion of the trip was that portion just before getting into Salt Lake City. In due time I was able to identify the auxiliary landing field at Fort Bridger, and a little later the one at Green River. Both were outlined with lights and each had a green beacon in its light line tower. The enroute light line beacons were red, with the green signifying a landing facility.

Shortly after passing the Green River auxiliary field, I began to encounter wisps of clouds at my altitude of 8,000 feet. As I progressed the cloudiness became more pronounced. Darkness had set in and I was quickly becoming of the mind that I would soon be obliged to take some corrective action. The weather was not such that I could expect to continue under visual flight rules. I was aware that the radio beam for instrument was to my north. My plan of action was to increase altitude to at least 10,000 feet, turn to a northly heading, intercept the beam, then proceed east on the beam until reaching clear weather, then find and land at either Green River or Fort Bridger auxiliary field.

However, as I made my turn to the north (now on instruments) I noticed that the needle in the needle/ball instrument did not move. So I straightened up then tried a turn in the opposite direction — still no movement. Then I checked the vacuum, which seemed normal. But nevertheless I chose to cross-check it, so switched to the venturi vacuum. The gauge showed less, as to be expected, than the engine pump was delivering. So I switched back to the engine pump. Vacuum was not the problem. Obviously the flight instrument was faulty. I had known from the outset of the flight that the artificial horizon was not functional, but this was often to be expected in that era. So my useful instruments included airspeed, rate of climb, altimeter, compass and directional gyro, and of course, the ball without its needle.

I was able to worry the aircraft up to 10,000 feet, and also to intersect the beam, and to get myself headed in an easterly direction. It did not occur to me that in increasing altitude I had probably brought myself into more cloud cover than that which I had experienced at the lower altitude. Thus after flying for a time when I felt that I should have been in the clear, I was still on instruments. However, as I flew along, I began to see breaks in the clouds in that I could sometimes catch glimpses of lights on the ground. Since I was trying to locate one of the auxiliary fields I elected to take a look when one of the breaks occurred. After taking a look at one such break, I found myself in a spiral. I corrected by kicking top rudder and easing back on the stick then correcting back to the easterly heading of the beam. I made several attempts to locate myself and one of the auxiliaries. Each time I wound up in a spiral, always to the right. Each time the corrective procedure was the same. However, on the last such maneuver I was to make in that aircraft, I noticed that as I eased back on the stick the engine rpm increased!

I immediately concluded that I was beyond the verticle — that I was closer to being upside down than I was to being right side up. The A-17 was equipped with a two position propeller — a relatively flat pitch to be used for take-off and climbing, and a steeper pitch for cruising. With the increase in rpm, it was clear that the aircraft was heading more steeply down as I eased back on the stick. My immediate conclusion was that if I could not fly the aircraft on instruments while it was right side up, I sure as hell could not expect to fly it on instruments while it was upside down. With that I made preparation to bail out.

I immediately pulled the hatch back, unbuckled the seat belt, and started to roll out the left side of the cockpit. But as I looked back and saw the horizontal fin which stuck out some ten or twelve feet — I knew that if I rolled out I would surely be hit by the fin and perhaps be seriously injured. So I pulled back into the cockpit and then elected to dive for the left wingtip light. I had once put in a stint as a life guard and had been taught how to make a long and purposeful dive to get to someone in trouble quickly. Made such a dive for that little red light.

The feeling of being in space reminded me of being on the softest possible feather bed. I brought myself out of this reverie with the thought that I should pull the ripcord. Which I did, but I apparently did not pull it hard enough, since nothing happened. So I pulled it again. This time the entire ripcord cable and all came out. The chute popped open. My next thought was that the boys always like to kid around that the person that parachutes is always so excited that they lose the ripcord. So I carefully transferred it to my left hand and was so holding it when I suddenly hit the ground. With the darkness and the cloudiness, I had had no glimpse of the ground before striking it; fortunately I landed on soft ground but was so relaxed that I collapsed completely, with my head coming down and my left cheekbone near the eye striking the ripcord ring which I was so carefully holding, in my left hand. A black eye — my only injury.

When I left the aircraft, I neglected to pull the throttle back or cut the magnetos, so the aircraft kept flying for awhile. While floating in the chute, I heard the aircraft go through a couple of climb/dive sequences. At one point I thought it might hit me or at least catch my chute, it seemed to be close. As it turned out, the aircraft's wheels caught on the top of a ridge, the engine was immediately torn out and rolled to the bottom of the canyon, several hundred yards from the aircraft. The aircraft itself flipped over on its back and slid down the hill a short distance. The fuselage construction was so strong that it did not seem to be distorted or bent up at all. (A week later hiked up to see for myself.)

I had no way of knowing how close or far away the aircraft was from where I landed. After I picked myself up, I took stock of my situation. I knew only that I was somewhere in the Rockies, near the top of a ridge. My clothing consisted of a light flight suit over my pinks or greens trousers and shirt with French Shriner oxfords. I elected to carry my chute along. I had a pen light which afforded some help. But seeing anything was difficult. I landed about nine p.m. and hiked until about midnight. By then I had worked up considerable body heat and when I wrapped up in the chute, I was able to sleep for a while. I was awakened by being cold about five or six o'clock in the morning. Dawn was just breaking.

With daylight I discovered that there was a stream between the ridge I was on and an adjoining one. My direction of walking the night before was consistent with the direction the stream seemed to follow. I decided to follow the stream on the basis that it would sooner or later bring me to civilization. At first I thought that I would be able to walk beside the stream, but soon found that in places the slopes to the stream were so steep that I had to get down in the stream itself to walk. Before doing this I provided myself with two sapling staffs for two reasons. I could establish how deep the stream was before I took the next step and they were an excellent aid to keep balance. Somewhere, in my involvement with the stream I lost the ripcord. I had carefully placed it in a lower leg pocket. But the pocket had no closure and I may have lost my footing sufficiently to have permitted it to fall out. In any event it was no longer with me when I looked for it.

The ridges finally opened up enough to where I could walk along side instead of in the stream. The first sign of civilization I encountered was a trap with a porcupine doing his best to get loose. I elected to leave well enough alone and kept going. The next thing was a trappers abode with a pen for horses—but no occupants. Then I heard a train whistle, so I knew that I was going in the right direction. At least I could follow a train track until it brought me to civilization. Then the ground flattened out completely. Thus I could walk faster which I did. By about 8 a.m. I found myself at a paved highway. I immediately got out on it and started walking in a westerly direction. I had not gone more than a few hundred yards before a fellow came along in a Model A Ford, kind of looking as he drove along at a moderate speed. When he got to me he stopped and asked me if I was the pilot they all had been out looking for the night before. I allowed I must be. He took me back to his place which was a mile or two down the road in the direction I had chosen to walk. He owned and operated a small gas station/grocery store with his family's help. He called the highway patrol and reported my presence.

They were very nice people, and they invited me to share breakfast with them. I recall that the breakfast consisted of eggs and bacon, toast and probably home fries. When they passed the platter to me, I apparently helped myself to the entire fare. At least that is what I was told later. In any event they were fine people, and they said that the airbase people had been out the night before with several cars, trucks, ambulances, driving up and down the highway flashing lights up the mountainsides looking for any sight of me or the aircraft.

The place that I went down was known as *Devil's Slide*. It is just a few miles east of Ogden, Utah.

The tragic epilogue to all of this is that in the course of the following few days several individuals hiked up to see the remains of the aircraft. One poor soul died in the process of hiking there.

PROVING-UP THE FAMOUS FLYING FORTRESS (B-17E)

By Albert W. James, Col. USAF (Ret)

It was in the late summer of 1941 when I found myself on orders to Patterson Field in Ohio to participate in the Accelerated Service Testing of what was then considered to be our newest and most advanced heavy bomber. I was stationed at Geiger Field, near Spokane, Washington and was the C.O. of the 62nd

Squadron of the 39th Bomb Group (H). The 39th had recently been spun off from the 7th Bomb Group (H), then located at Salt Lake City.

The 7th and 39th were equipped with both B-17's and B-18's, though few in number. They were earlier versions lacking both self sealing fuel tanks and adequate gun positions amongst many other considerations. We knew from British experience that our aircraft were woefully inadequate for wartime combat. The new B-17E was to remedy these shortcomings. It was the job of those of us selected for this task to determine to what degree the new version would meet all of the criteria identified in its new performance envelope.

Enroute to Patterson Field by commercial airliner it was our luck to discover that one of the passengers aboard our DC-3 was Mrs. Eleanor Roosevelt. Since the aircraft was only about half full (having a total capacity of twenty-one passengers) we managed to engage Mrs. Roosevelt in conversation. I thought to see if we could derive any clues as to when or how we might enter the on-going war in Europe. I was aware of the recent order by President Roosevelt for the Air Corps to deploy a squadron of P-40's to Iceland, and with that question in mind I did ask Mrs. Roosevelt if she could shed any light on the meaning and possible impact of such an order. In response, certainly no wartime secrets were revealed, and I suspect that she probably was not privy to much, if not most, of what the President dealt with on a daily basis. My probe went nowhere.

Upon arrival at Patterson Field we discovered that the "Hotel-de-Gink" had been upgraded substantially. We were given quarters in the new operations building on the flight line, in lieu of the old wooden frame structure (a converted farmhouse) formerly located nearby. Over several days we were all put through an oxygen familiarization course, which included class instruction and time in a decompression chamber in which we endured simulated existence at 20,000, 30,000, and 40,000 feet altitude. We were enabled to actually experience the physiological effects on ones own body as the apparent altitude was increased. The hazards at the higher altitudes were also made eminently clear—death in seven minutes at 30,000 feet without oxygen.

There were five or six crews from various bases where B-17 Bomber Groups were located, available to fly the three new B-17E's sitting on the all grass field. We were each assigned a portion of the performance envelope to explore and validate—this included long range, bombing, gunnery, and high altitude performance and some others that I have probably forgotten. My crew was assigned the task of finding out how the aircraft would perform on a bombing mission at 30,000 feet. The mission was to last for four hours and we were to remain at 30,000 feet for the entire period.

My crew was composed of a copilot, an engineer and myself. My Form 5 shows my having made four or five flights for a total of about sixteen hours from 15 to 23 October 1941 in the B-17E. The initial flights were for familiarization with the aircraft, to come to know how the aircraft differed in its behavior from the B-17Bs, Cs and Ds we had previously flown. A marked difference was in the way one could three point the E compared to any that had gone before—the horizontal stabilizer and elevator no longer stalled out at the last moment, thus guaranteeing at least three landings for each single approach.

The day for our test flight finally arrived. Major Carl Brandt (later Major General) briefed us on what he expected us to do. We planned our flight over Michigan, Wisconsin, Minnesota, Iowa, Illinois, Indiana and back to Patterson Field near Dayton in Ohio. Our climb to 30,000 feet was routine and upon reaching our assigned altitude, leveled off and trimmed the aircraft for level flight at normal cruise power. Upon reaching our first

reporting point, a standard position report was made including our altitude. The response we got was that we must mean 3000 feet—despite our repeatedly correcting the recipient he apparently could not believe we were at 30,000 feet. This hassle was to be repeated at every reporting point thereafter. Obviously, in 1941, cruising along at 30,000 feet, making position reports from an unpressurized aircraft was unheard of—and unbelievable!

As we droned along, all of us constantly wearing oxygen masks, the aircraft purring contentedly, it seemed that nothing could go wrong. Our engineer was a dedicated individual who took it upon himself to move from one part of the aircraft to another to check things in all locations. He did so with a minimum of effort. Each time he moved from the nose to the tail or vice-versa he would stop briefly and check with the co-pilot and myself, and then be gone. After one of these visits when he had returned to the tail of the aircraft I felt called upon to check to make sure he was OK. I tried to raise him with a light signal and received no reply, so I tried the intercom and still no response. At this point, I told the copilot that we had to verify the engineers's condition, and he released his safety belt, removed his mask, and arose from his seat.

What was not to be expected, was the copilot's attempt to breathe in the rarified air. It was to be expected that he would have held his breath until he could grasp a walk-around bottle of oxygen, and use that until he could again replace his mask. This was the technique used by the engineer in his repeated travels from one end of the aircraft to the other. But such was not to be. After two gigantic attempts to breathe in the rarified atmosphere, the copilot had gotten only as far the upper turret structure, which is immediately behind the pilot/copilot seating arrangement—and there he collapsed in a state of unconsciousness. It occurred to me that I now had two problems rather than one!

My immediate reaction was to get oxygen to the copilot. Since the aircraft was flying on what we called Automatic Flight Control Equipment (AFCE), a form of auto-pilot, actually a part of the Norden Bomb-Sight system which enabled the bombardier to steer the aircraft on the bomb-run. I immediately released my own seat belt so that I could reach all the way across the cockpit and grasp the co-pilot's mask, at the same time rotating the oxygen control to a 100percent full-on flow of oxygen. Then by sliding almost all the way out of my seat—toward where the copilot now rested—I was able to hold the mask firmly on his face. He aroused in a few moments sufficiently so that I was able to get him back up in his seat, with his mask fastened in place and his seat belt fastened.

With still no word on the condition of the engineer, I reached up and hauled back on the throttles, bringing all four engines to a hasty idling intending to make an emergency descent to at least 10,000 feet. A descent of some 20,000 feet which no doubt would have subjected the aircraft to many unanticipated stresses. Suddenly the engineer appeared—the change in the throb of the engines sent a message to him like nothing else could!

With the knowledge that the engineer was OK, I elected to save the mission and immediately returned the throttles to full cruising power. Almost everything was now back to normal, except that the copilot kept picking up the microphone apparently believing that he needed to call someone. After two or three such attempts, I was able to convince him that he did not need to concern himself about making any reports. I was told later that it was not unusual for a person to be somewhat disoriented following a bout of anoxia.

After landing, Major Brandt asked me how the aircraft behaved, had we had any problems? My first reaction was to say no, then I remembered that the elevator trim tab had frozen up, a matter of minor consequence. Although we had been able to demonstrate that the aircraft had the ability to satisfactorily perform a bombing mission at 30,000 feet, it also became apparent that man's ability to perform at that elevation in an unpressurized aircraft was much more marginal. A momentary lapse almost did us in—now throw in enemy fighters and ack ack—how real could the effort be?

MAJOR GEORGE GLOBER'S MISSION TO WAKE ISLAND

In reply to your request of 17 June 1992, the following recollections are provided. You are aware that the events of fifty years ago are not remembered in the same detail as was furnished the post mission debriefer!

At the time of the mission under review I was a 22 year old Staff Sargent whose military specialty was aerial photography/ ground photographic technician with a secondary as an armament specialist. I was asked by my Section Chief to volunteer for a *classified special mission*. Shortly thereafter I met George Glober and his crew. The mission was identified as a *pre-strike reconmission* of the Japanese held Wake island. The U.S. Navy intended to conduct a Carrier strike against the facility but wanted hard evidence on which to base its plan.

During our preparations at Hickam, I heard from the operational people at 7th Air Force that two previous missions had been launched but were unsuccessful. The flight was a max-radius operation and being unescorted, depended solely upon its own

firepower for defense against the estimated many Japanese interceptors. With these considerations in mind H.Q. made available the resources of the Hawaiian Air Depot for modifications that the crew thought would enhance our survival. I don't recall all that was done but the entire crew working as a team came up with two pairs of forward firing 50 caliber guns to replace the standard single 30 cal. of the B-17E assigned to the mission. We also had them add two top firing 50s in the radio compartment manned by the assistant radio operator (the radio operator was our ball turret gunner). Oversize bomb-bay tanks were installed and while they could not be jettisoned in the air, at least we had additional fuel storage. Nobody had any ideas on the potential fire hazard due to combat damage so "Shorty " Inman, the engineer, suggested using the fuel first and when the tanks were emptied, to add the contents of a CO fire extinguisher. Shorty did that and luckily we had no hits there so we never found out if it was a good idea or not.

A vertical camera position to accommodate a K-17 (9x18 film size) was set up just aft of the waist guns, along with the standard grid view-finder.

While I was not a regular member of George Glober's crew, working together on the modifications gave us time to know each other, probably better than the average 8th Air Force crew members knew each other. After the mission, I believe I became a full-fledged crew member. I flew as a recon. photographer with 33 other crews and none came up to Globers standards.

We departed Hickam to land and refuel at Midway Island. The next day, with topped tanks and max ammunition load, we took off for the target island. As I recall the weather gradually deteriorated until it was a turbulent front. The rain and sometimes hail beat on the fuselage just about as violently as I had

(l to r) Front row: Claude Phillips, Maj. George Glober, Capt. Walker, Lt. Smith, and Sgt. Ed Caton. Back row: Sammy Sanford, Robin Fries, Bob Holliday, and Shorty Inman.

experienced. There was zero visibility and turbulence was extreme. Robin Fries, (waist gunner) and I had no seats and being in the waist position probably felt it worst. After what I recalled as being an hour of this rough ride we suddenly burst into clear sunlight and blue sky. The storm wall (and it looked like a wall) was behind us and in the distance was Wake. However just below and to our right was a Japanese wooden picket ship, so we knew then if the storm had provided cover for our approach, we were now uncovered.

The tail gunner, *Sandy* Samford, came back to man his position, Bob Holliday got into the Ball turret, Joe Lillis took over the radio guns and Shorty Inman got into the top turret.

I had two camera magazines, one on the camera and one wrapped up for warmth in the radio compartment. We had no camera lubricants that met cold weather specs, so I wanted some back-up in case the cold wind blowing through the camera hatch chilled the film advance gears and made my magazine unworkable. By now the gunners had all fired their check rounds and I decided to run through two exposures. Halfway through the manual winding procedure I knew the magazine gears had stiffened and I could lose my drive shaft. I discarded that magazine and retrieved the one I'd left forward. I put it on, pulled the slide and took my first picture of the skies just as Wake came into view in the viewfinder.

Just about then the tail gunner and ball turret started some serious firing. Then the nose guns and upper turret got into the action and finally the waist gunner cut loose. After that I was too busy to notice anything. I had one eye on the camera level bubble, and one on the view finder to maintain a 60l.- overlap and both hands holding the camera steady and winding film over as I tripped the shutter. George made three photo runs roughly west, north, and then east. He varied his attitude on each leg and I was glad he did because the flak showed in my viewfinder as heavy, tracking us, but below. It never did find our exact altitude that I know of. Perhaps the greenhouse crew had a better view? After the last photo I secured the camera equipment, removed the magazine and took it up into the radio compartment. There I took over as the starboard waist gunner, looking out the window for a target, I saw a "float type" aircraft below and too far away to shoot at. The forward guns were firing at aircraft coming in at our nose. At one point George lifted the right wing and a Japanese fighter aircraft slid by with a dead pilot, the entire canopy had been shot out as had the back part of his head and neck. George Glober flew that B-17 all over the sky, breaking up the Japanese passes. I really think he caused them to get in each others way, there seemed to be so many of them.

I remember we were briefed on a recovery plan in the event we were shot down. There was supposed to be an American submarine located ten miles off of Wake, a Destroyer 200 miles off and a Light Cruiser 500 miles out. Later I was also told the Submarine people followed the photo runs and the attacks providing confirmation of our kills. I also recall we flew over one of the Navy surface vessels. He was leaving station because after he used a signal light I saw the bow-wave grow increasingly larger and more prominent, George may be able to tell more about that event.

At one point I picked up a Japanese fighter approaching at about 4 o'clock low, I think George's flying put him in that position. He was firing at me but aiming too high. I opened fire with the waist gun and after a couple of short bursts which seemed to go right into the forward part of the aircraft, I fired a long burst for effect and he seemed to lose power, emitting increasing smoke and he went into a spin. While I did not see him hit the ocean I did follow his out of control aircraft for a long distance and then our maneuvers blocked my view and I lost con-

tact. From a close-up of about 400 yards his spin continued until he was no more than a few thousand feet above the ocean, and a long way from home. I saw no more fighters until after all guns had stopped firing.

Some 40 minutes after the fight started there was one single fighter at 10 o'clock high, flying our course and speed, but at an estimated 2000 yards range (beyond effective range). Then just as we were about to penetrate the cloud banks he started to slide into range but Glober pulled up in the clouds and in toward the fighter. My last impression was that even if he was firing, his shots were way behind and we had our cover.

The flight back was not as rough as coming in had been and the crew relaxed and talked to the nearest member. I was pretty exhausted but you must remember we didn't have oxygen masks. All those hours of flying had been done between 14,000 and 22,0000 feet.

As it started to grow dark it was clear that Midway Island wasn't where it should have been! Our Navigator was the best, but no one noticed a Japanese bullet had hit the compass and he was getting false readings. The radio operator had been signaling for lights on the island but being under black out conditions it didn't happen, until a Marine anti-aircraft battery member turned on three search lights. We saw those slender pencils of light and George turned to them making a straight-in landing. It was a textbook landing but in the landing roll I believe we ran out of gas, (ask George about that point). His log should also show the exact time of flight but I've remembered it as 15 hours 10 minutes, (maybe 16 hours 10 minutes).

The mission succeeded because of the prior modifications to meet anticipated problems of range and defense, the skills of Col. Glober as a pilot and leader and the teamwork among the aircrew members. Each knew his job to perfection and had respect and confidence in each other.

The film was developed while we were being debriefed and the first time I saw the pictures was three years later at the A.A.F. School of Applied Tactics. After the Navy strike the classification was lowered and they were used to illustrate certain classes in the intelligence course.

The debriefing produced more than one hundred crew recommendations for changes and modifications to the B-17E equipment. Most of which were improved upon by engineers and incorporated into the newer models.

DITCHING OF A B-17 OF THE 23RD BOMB SQUADRON

Major General Nathan Twining on Board

By T/Sgt. Harley Baird

Approaching Espiritu Santo was a bad storm and there wa a small mountain about 3,000 feet high near the airstrip; so wit bad weather and no radar aboard ship, we weren't very anxiou to get too close to that mountain. The pilot decided to go west o the mountain and circle until either the weather allowed us t come back in and land or we ran out of gas. About 10:30 o 11:00 that night we ran out of gas and he made a water landing He stalled it in from about 3,000 feet, did a very nice job o putting it in the water and was recommended for a medal by th General for the way he handled it.

Crew of Calamity Jane

When the plane hit the water everything was quiet, so the tail-gunner, who had been waiting in the waist, assumed we were in the water and went out the side window. As a matter of fact, when we hit the water the first time we bounced. We don't know how high we were in the air when Principe jumped out the window, but when we came down the second time he was about 150 yards behind us and screaming that his leg was broken, his arm was broken, and I knew that he couldn't swim; so I volunteered to go back and find him. It was raining hard, the wind was blowing, the waves were 18 to 20 feet. I asked the crew to keep talking, shout once in awhile, to where I could hear them and I went back and found Principe. He didn't have any broken bones but was badly bruised and I suspect he fell 30 or 40 feet while we were moving 90 mph. Just about anybody would have been bruised. Took a few minutes to find him and a few more minutes to get him back to the raft. I had been a swimming instructor at a Boys Camp in Maine before I joined the service. I learned to swim six weeks before camp opened so I could get the job. I was a strong swimmer but not a good swimmer. However I did a lot of swimming in Hawaii.

Anyway, seemed like an hour before we got back to the raft, though I'm sure it wasn't that long. They had tied two rafts together with twenty feet of line between them because if they had lashed them close together the high waves would have spilled people out. We could only figure out to get seven men in each raft, and since I was the most able-bodied swimmer I volunteered to stay in the water that night. I hung onto the life-line that went around the side of the raft. It was a long night. The water was quite flourescent—anytime a fish went through the water it would leave a ray of light in the water. About six in the

morning, a ray of light about two feet in diameter went by under me and tapped the bottom of my feet quite solidly and we found out how to get eight people in one raft. I can't remember whose lap I landed in, but when it got light enough to see an eight-or-ten foot shark was our guide for a few days. He didn't seen interested in us—a lot of small fish would collect under the raft. He'd wait till a school of them were up there, then he'd make a dash at them and whoever was sitting on the bottom of the raft would get bumped violently by the shark hitting the rubber floor.

We were in a rainstorm. We didn't have anything to make a sea-anchor of so we drifted with the storm. While we were out there—I can't remember our bombardier's name, I think it was Lamere? This fellow was a T/Sgt from the New Orleans area, Louisiana. He had a web belt with a pouch on it and he had two bottles of vitamin pills. He doled these out, and each of us got one pill a day. This was all we had to replace what we were losing. Now we didn't have any emergency rations because the fuselage broke right at the ball turret and the rations went down through the crack and we couldn't get them. During the rain we didn't think about saving water, so when the rain stopped we had very little. Any time a shower would come up, we'd quickly fill our canteens but we were still running short of water most every day. You know fifteen people drink a lot of water. So to keep from dehydrating too much we'd get in the sea, but with the shark there it made it pretty interesting. If he was on one side of the raft, somebody would take the little aluminum paddle and put it on the shark's nose and just hold him there while the people got into the water on the other side of the raft and lay there. He didn't seem to mind—he would just sort of watch what was going on. As I recall, about the evening of the fifth day he disap-

59

peared, so he wasn't with us when they found us. But he hung around, and he ate those little fish underneath the raft whenever there were enough for a good bite.

After three days the storm slacked up. The planes from our outfit were out searching for us during the storm but there was little chance of their finding us because, even down where we were, the visibility was no more than fifty yards, sometimes as much as one hundred yards, so planes never could have found us even if they'd flown right over us.

Anyway along about the fourth day on the raft, after it had cleared up, there were some seagulls flying around and someone suggested we shoot a gull.

Now bouncing around in a rubber raft and the gulls bouncing around in the air didn't make a very good target with a .45 caliber pistol. General Twining decided he'd like to take the first shot. He got a gull on his first try and we couldn't induce him to shoot again. He knew he had been lucky and he wouldn't try another shot. Anyway, the gull was divided up fifteen ways. I got a leg, some of the other guys didn't get such an appealing part, but that leg was about the tastiest bit of protein I'd had in a long time! It was pretty gamey and salty, but it was edible. I didn't throw it up but some of the other guys did.

I think it was about the fifth day Principe decided he was going to walk ashore. We had to physically restrain him until the Navy showed up.

When the storm had moved on to the west, our B-17's had finished their usual three-day search. But our C.O. decided he wasn't going to leave us out there, so he went to a native fisherman and asked where he thought we'd have drifted to by now. The fisherman pointed to the chart, and two days later they found us. So we were out there a total of six days. At the end of the sixth day, late in the afternoon, one of our B-17's spotted us. We fired our Very pistol (6) and they started circling. But they kept circling away from us. We thought there must be a boat over there that they were going to lead us to, but what had happened was that they had lost sight of us because, although the seas had abated a little bit, the waves were still running eight-to-ten feet. But at least they knew we were there. The next day they came back out and they had a couple of PBY's—from VP-23, incidentally, we were the 23rd Bombardment Squadron and they were VP-23 from the Navy. Landing in the rough seas, the PBY we got into had torn out about ten feet of its hull and was taking on water when we climbed aboard, but that didn't seem to worry the sailors a bit. They said, "Oh, we'll just bounce along until we get in the air." I said, "How about landing at the other end?" They said, "We'll land parallel to the beach in two or three feet of water and when we sink we'll be right on the beach." Losing a hull in rough seas wasn't new to the Navy; they expected it.

Our PBY did land parallel to the beach and in quite shallow water. The other PBY was undamaged so it landed out by the LES Curtis, which was an aircraft tender. Our PBY landed next to the beach, and the Pathé newsreel cameras were grinding away. The first my folks knew that I was involved was a couple of weeks later. They were watching the movies at the theatre at our county seat and the Pathe news came on between features and showed the PBY unloading and gave our names and home towns. By that time it was all over and they could see that everyone turned out alright. Anyway, they put us in a small boat and took us out to the Curtis, took us through their dispensary where the doctors looked us over. I had some salt water sores on my shins on both legs. They cleaned the wounds out best they could and taped some tubes to my legs to drain the sores. I was in the best shape of all the survivors—I'd gone from 190 pounds down to 160. The other fourteen on the plane, including Gen. Twining, were taken to the hospital on shore and were there anywhere

from two to five days, depending on the severity of their condition. (How about Principe, who wanted to walk ashore?) He recovered rapidly as soon as they got some food in him and some medical attention. I can't remember any more about that. We were all sent down to New Zealand about ten days later for R & R (rest and recuperation) and our pilot—and again I can't remember his name but Lee Benbrooks probably would—who was a schoolteacher from Arkansas, had always been after us to wear our flight coveralls instead of the cut-off khaki pants and a T-shirt because he said if we ever went down we'd suffer from exposure. But on that flight he was the only one wearing cut-off pants and T-shirt, and he did suffer very badly. The last three days after the storm went by and the sun was out, just lying in the water wasn't enough to protect you, so he was burned badly. On the flight down to New Zealand he started running a fever and they put him in the hospital where they discovered he had malaria. After a three-week stay in the hospital they decided he wasn't fit to return to combat, so they sent him back to the States. The word we got was that he retired from the service and went back to teaching school in Arkansas. He might have gone to a training base in the States, but no one saw or heard of him again so I suspect he did become a civilian.

UP THE SLOT TO BOUGANVILLE AND BACK BY AIR

The Slot (official name: New Georgia Island) is the body of water bounded by the Solomon Islands to the northeast and the New Georgia Group to the the Southwest. It was the route by sea and by air between Guadalcanal and Bouganville during the Battle for Guadcanal, and was used extensively by both sides in the conflict.

A B-17 type airplane under command of Major George Glober took off from Cactus at 0900 LCT and flew up the left side of the sector. Captain C. C. Colasum was in the pilot's seat.

At 0920 the airplane was over Russell Island. The guns were ordered tested and it was found that one top turret gun and one ball turret gun were out of commission. The observation here was negative. By this time an altitude of 3000 feet had been reached. A course was followed running 20 miles off the southeast shore of Now Georgia to Vella Lavella. Here the course was set directly toward Shortland Island and a gradual increase in altitude was begun. At 7°30'S, 156°10'E an airplane was observed off the left wing at a distance of approximately 10 miles, at a position of 7:00 to the B-17. Airplane was following the same course as B-17, direction being north at that time. Visibility was unlimited. This unidentified airplane continued in this same relative position until the B-17 turned onto a north westerly course in the vicinity of Shortland Island, but here the unidentified airplane continued its course to the north.

When an altitude of 18,000 feet was reached just south of Shortland, the number three engine began to throw oil, spreading it over the ball turret almost blanketing the gunner's vision Each time the ball turret switch was turned on, smoke was emitted which indicated the danger of fire.

Due to this engine trouble the airplane commander deemed it best not to go over the harbor at Shortland therefore setting his course some 30 miles southeast of the harbor to Faure Island This point 30 miles off Shortland was attained at 1100 LCT. No ships were observed in the area. Tonelei Harbor could not be observed.

At Fauro Island the course was changed to a southerly course which would bring the airplane over the center of Vella Lavella. A few miles inland from the northeasterly edge of Vella Lavolla, and about midway between the north and south shores, an area was observed under the trees which appeared as if there were grading being done. There was evidence of newly turned soil. This observation was made at about 1140 LCT. Sgt. Malloniz, bombardier, is most positive in this observation.

Shortly thereafter, when the airplane had reached a position from which observation was to be made of Beagle Channel, and the altitude was 10,000 feet, the left waist gunner (Frees) saw to the left at a distance, of about five miles, what he believed to be five Zeros. Upon immediate investigation eight Zeros were observed, four being at an altitude of 8,000 feet, and four at 12,000 feet, flying the same course as the B-17. The speed of the B-17 was at once increased and all planes held relative position about five minutes. The B-17 was now racing to get to cloud cover, there being clouds over the peaks on the islands. By holding the nose slightly down an indicated speed of 230 mph was attained. The Zeros were now closing in. One had detached itself taking up a position 1000 feet directly above the B-17 and holding this position. Said Zero began dropping bombs aimed at the B-17. Those bombs exploded at the level at which the B-17 was flying, however the deflection was off; sometimes exploding ahead and sometimes behind. As soon as one Zero would use up its bombs, its position was taken by another with the first returning to the fight with its comrades. The exact number of bombs dropped is not known, but a reasonable estimate would place it at between 20 and 30 bombs. None of these had any effect on the B-17 and no hits were scored, although one wing did go through the white smoke shortly after the bomb exploded. The description of the bombs used follows the same reports as given by other pilots. They burst giving off a large cloud of white smoke which spreads out in streamers. These streamers were usually pointed down.

During the time of this bombing, the ship was under heavy attack from the Zeros. The top turret/gunner gave most of his attention to the Zero that was in the bombing position, firing bursts when the Zero came overhead. The Zero would then fly into the sun and could not be seen until he again took up his position to bomb. This employment of the sun for cover was quite effective.

The Zeros first closed in and attacked in the vicinity of Gixe. These Zeros were of the new type with square wing tips, equipped with belly tanks which were dropped in a manner which would indicate they were aimed at the B-17. There is indication that dive bombing tactics were used. Some of these tanks came very close. All Zeros engaged were of this same type. Some of these were seen to have a marking of a black ball on the right wing and a red ball on the left wing.

The initial attack was made from below and in front on the left quarter. This being at the time the most vulnerable spot on the B-17. The bombardier raised his guns to the ceiling but this was not sufficient to get them on the target. The ball turret was covered with oil so that the gunner could not see clearly at the time. This turret was now being operated. The first attack was made by three Zeros in line coming in from the front left quarter and making individual passes at the same spot, one after another. This was followed by attacks made of groups of two and by single planes and in no particular order. The attack then became pell-nell with passes being made from all positions and without any seeming coordination. During all of this time the B-17 was being turned so that it would not present a steady target. Full speed was being maintained with the nose down and thus altitude was being lost. Major Glober knew that the ships'

climbing ability was impaired because of his number three engine and any attempt to avoid the attack by climbing would be futile. His purpose therefore was to fly as fast as possible and make use of the little cloud cover that was available over the peaks of New Georgia Island.

The running fight had by this time continued from Gixe to the vicinity of Munda Pointe. Here the Zeros were joined by at least seven more Zeros and possibly more. The circumstances made actual count impossible. From here on to the time the Zeros were lost in the clouds over Vangunu Island no member of the crew saw less than five at any time he was able to take a look.

Near the middle of the length of New Georgia, the pilot was successful in getting into some clouds ever the peaks. To use this cover it was necessary to come perilously close to the mountain tops. This is attested to by the bombardier who had doubts on several occasions as to whether the peaks would actually be cleared. The cloud cover afforded here was of short duration and upon breaking into the clear, it was seen that the Zeros were still overhead.

The attack was immediately pressed home again by the Zeros. The great numerical superiority allowed for attacks from all quarters. The Japanese pilots closed in and usually began firing when about 150 yards distant. All their fire was from 7.7 millimeter machine guns and no cannon fire was seen except by the tall gunner who reports two short bursts on the tail. This was in all probability due to the pilot's ability to maneuver the B-17 so as not to give them a target for a long enough time. The B-17 was now racing for the next cloud cover visible which was over the peaks on Vangunu Island. At this time the number one engine caught fire. This probably resulted from sustaining a hit on the oil line. The propeller ran away and the crankshaft began to describe a circle in the engine. Members of the crew could see molten metal dropping from it. Number 3 engine was still causing trouble and an attempt was made to feather. This caused a further loss of altitude and preparation was made for a water landing. The engines were brought under control and some altitude was regained. It must be remembered that each time cloud cover was had all the altitude that could possibly be gained was made.

By this time the B-17 was approaching the cloud cover over Vangunu Island. The mechanism on the tail gun had gone out of commission, and the tail gunner had adopted the expedient of manually loading the gun with one shell at a time and firing it at approaching Zeros. In this method he was able to hide from the attackers his real plight, and no attacks were pressed in a sustained manner on his position of the ship. Despite the fierceness of the attack, this crew was able to observe a Japanese submarine on the surface of the sea ten miles off Munda Point. This ship seemed to be at a standstill and did not appear to be in motion.

A short time before reaching the cover offered by the clouds over Vangunu, the last attack was made. This was a frontal attack. The Zero took up its position for the attack quite a distance ahead of the B-17 and closed in rapidly. The 7-7 guns began to fire some eight seconds before they were actually in range and the pilot rode this burst in. On this attack, Captain C.C. Coleman who had been piloting the ship was hit and killed.

Captain Coleman had shown the highest skill and daring to handling the damaged B-17 as pilot through the running battle which up to this time had been over 40 minutes in duration under continuous attack and bombing, and against great odds. Due to the condition of the ship he had been limited in his evasive tactics by the loss of power. The exercise of flying skill and clear thinking on the part of the pilots, kept this airplane in the air.

When the cloud bank over Vanguna was reached, Major Glober was able to make a 120 degree turn and stay under the clouds for about four minutes. Lieutenant Henans, the navigator assumed the duties of co-pilot and was of great aid to Major Glober in the handling of the damaged ship. On breaking into the clear there was no sign of Zeros and a straight course was followed to Cactus where the damaged ship was landed by Major Globor at 1415 LCT.

During the course of the battle at least five Zeros were certainly brought down. On one of these the bombardier saw the engine stop. The right gunner saw two go down out of control and smoking badly. The ball turret operator saw two hit the ground, of these he claims one; the tail gunner claims that he hit one that he saw go down, and the left waist gunner claims one but he did not see it crash. In addition the bombardier saw a portion of a wing tip shot off another but he could not tell definitely whether it went down or not. Additional Zeros were seen to sustain hits but conditions did not afford a opportunity to check on whether they fell.

The B-17 landed with two good engines. The aileron central had been damaged and there was half aileron control. The left flap was full of holes, and the left horizontal tail stabilizer had holes in it.

No casualties other than Captain Colman were suffered.

EMERGENCY LANDING

In August 1944, Thomas E. Thompson, a native of East St. Louis, Illinois, was a lieutenant with the 394th Squadron. His crew had just participated in a strike on Truk. Twenty minutes from the home base at Momote Strip, the crew discovered that the hydraulic system on their landing brakes had been severely damaged by enemy fire. The tower at Momote suggested moving the crew to the plane's tail, believing the additional weight would help hold the tail down as the plane came to a stop. Lt. Thompson agreed with their suggestion. His bombardier, Lt. Jim

Hope, of Topeka, Kansas, also had a brainstorm. They would use parachutes to aid the crippled plane in landing.

An account of this highly unusual landing appeared in the 5th Bombardment Group's *Tactical Bulletin* on 4 August 1944.

All of the crew, except the two engineers were sent to the rear, to stand as far forward in the waist as possible during approach and landing. QAC chutes were attached to two harnesses and the leg straps of these were buckled around the waist gun mount studs at the waist windows. This allowed the chute pack to completely clear the window before opening. It was agreed Pilot would ring the alarm bell for a signal to throw the chutes and open them after landing. This prevented anyone from prematurely opening the chutes while still airborne. A normal landing was made. On receiving the signal, two men went to the windows, threw out the chutes and pulled the rip cords. The rest proceeded to the rear of the cabin to help hold the tail down. One chute opened several seconds before the other, but according to the Pilot this caused only slight swerving. No tendency to 'weathervane' into the crosswind was noticed. Tail stayed down, dragging the wheel, and the chutes caused enough deceleration that crew members had to pull themselves along with their hands to get to the rear of the airplane. When he was sure she was under control, Lt. Thompson cut all engines (with idle cut off). When he had slowed to 40-50 mph he let the nose down and applied the one brake application he knew he had in the accumulators. He did not try to steer with the brakes but came to a halt with one application. A small swerve to the right was noticed here, but no damage resulted. The ship was considerably short of the tower when it came to rest.

B-24 Liberator around 1944.

In fact, Lt. Thompson's plane stopped shorter than any B-24, under normal conditions, has ever stopped on Momote.

George Thomas Folster, an NBC reporter, related the story in a broadcast from Gen. MacArthur's headquarters, and an account of the incident was picked up by the Associated Press. The story was printed in Lt. Thompson's hometown newspaper, the *St. Louis Globe Democrat*.

THE SAGA OF SQUIRRELY SHIRLEY

One of the 5th Bombardment Group's most recognizable airplanes was *Squirrely Shirley*, a B-24J assigned to 31st Squadron. Shirley was a lovely girl, dressed in a swimsuit and high heels. But it wasn't Shirley's good looks that made her so popular with the crews of the 31st, it was her long record of successful missions.

After Lt. Thompson's crew made their successful landing with the aid of parachutes, *Squirrely Shirley* had a similar experience. She landed at the Wama airstrip with parachutes rigged from the waist windows replacing the hydraulic brakes that had been damaged by enemy fire.

Ben Goldberg was a nose turret gunner with the 31st Squadron. An article (source unknown) provided by Lawrence W. Dismore, recounted Goldberg's thoughts on *Shirley*. "Everybody thought that would be the one to be in," Goldberg was quoted as saying. "The heck with that noise. It was held together with wire. That was the most rattly thing ..."

Despite her creaks and rattles, however, good old *Squirrely Shirley* managed to bring Goldberg and the rest of his crew home safely from their mission.

Some time in late July 1945, Brig. Gen. Thomas D. White, Deputy Commander of the 13th Air Force, located at Tacloban, in Leyte Gulf, elected to fly over to Samar and witness our early morning takeoff of the entire Group (twenty four aircraft) on another day's mission. He flew himself in a small puddle-jumper aircraft. He was met by the Group commander, Lt. Col. Albert James who escorted him to a good vantage point from which to observe the take-off procedure, explaining the 30 second take-off interval, and the formation reassembly procedure.

It took twelve minutes for the 24 aircraft to become airborne during which time Col. James had been regaling the General with the history of *Squirrely Shirley* and the fact that she had never aborted on a mission. *Shirley* still wore her olive drab paint, while all of the other aircraft wore the bright silver of the clean shiny aluminum. It was then that they saw *Shirley* on a close-in approach—a full load of gas and bombs. The crew chief had failed to see that the gas caps were tightly fastened—and one or more were losing gasoline. However the crew made short work of correcting the problem, and was airborne again in a few minutes. And the General was able to leave to return to Tacloban knowing that *Shirley* had not aborted.

ROGER FAKE'S DIARY

Roger M. Fake kept a record of each mission he flew from 28 May 1945, when he flew to the base at Guadalcanal until 4 February 1945, when he was released from combat duty. Fake flew a total of 595.83 hours.

Mission #13 to Yap Island, which took place on 16 July 1944, was a particularly unlucky one.

Vin flew as lead bombardier, with Capt. Robertson. We had a substitute bombardier who, luckily, had previous experience as a medic. We also had a cameraman along named Allison.

James Goldsberry and Allison were badly wounded. Goldsberry, after a stay in the hospital, returned to the United States. He also made sergeant (long overdue). He was replaced by Ray Slater who served as assistant engineer and waist gunner.

Just three days later, on 19 July, Fake and his crew again returned to Yap Island. And once again, their mission was a difficult one.

Our Squadron Commander, Capt. Longino, was shot down on this mission. We were intercepted after 'bombs away' and his plane was hit. One of his left wing tanks or a fuel line caught fire. It eventually spread to the bomb bay and soon the whole inside of the plane was on fire. We were flying on his right wing. He told me later that the fire burned his elevators and he couldn't control the plane any longer.

He bailed out and was picked up by a submarine after about an hour in the water. Most of his crew were also picked up later, but two men, who bailed out early, were never found. We stayed with him until he bailed out and we saw him in the water. We threw him a six-man liferaft but he didn't use it.

He was in his individual liferaft when they picked him up. The sub went first to the smoking B-24 and then followed their course backward to pick up the men one by one except for the two that bailed out early. It may have been a month before he returned to the squadron. The sub had to wait for a replacement before it could leave the area. He said he gave his gun and anything else he still had to the crew of the sub for souvenirs.

Perhaps the most difficult and dangerous mission that Fake flew on was the 30 September 1944, mission to Balikpapan, Borneo. The enemy put up fierce resistance, and several planes from the 5th Group were shot down. Many more suffered extensive damage. And the lives of several brave and honorable men were lost.

This was mission #22, our first strike against Balikpapan on the island of Borneo. The target was an oil refinery. Major Pierce was shot down flying with Captain Longino's original crew. This was our roughest mission. It was more than 2,500 miles over water after a night takeoff in an overloaded airplane. Forty-five Zekes attacked us upon arrival and stayed with us for what seemed like more than 30 minutes.

We stayed with another plane from our squadron until it was over the Celebes Islands losing altitude at less than 4,000 feet. We had no radio contact with it and left it to return to normal altitude so that we didn't lose two crews instead of one. I figured they could have bailed out over land in the Celebes, but we didn't see anyone leave the plane before we left them. We never heard any more of them or their fate. We could only communicate with them by hand signals...

Fake continued his account from notes made by Jerry, another member of his squadron.

Raid on Borneo — Target — Oil refineries at Balikpapan, Borneo. A more appropriate name would be the 'Bloody Battle of Balikpapan.' Moving up to Noemfoor, the rumor got around that a long range strike would be flown. Gross load was 69,000 pound. Three groups would participate. Led by the Bomber Barons 5th Bombardment Group followed by 'The Lone Rangers' 307th Bombardment Group and with the 5th Air Force attaching a group just for publicity's sake. The 90th Bombardment Group better known as 'Jolly Rogers' were it. First plane to take off was lead by Col. Musgrave, C/O of the 5th Group. Time was 0400 on the morning of 30 September 1944. The 31st Squadron led with the 23rd Squadron in trail. We were to hit the target in two squadron elements. Major Pierce led the second element flying with the 72nd Squadron and last but not least the 394th Squadron led by Lt. Bone. This trip was long and dreary but the rendezvous was accomplished although a trifle bit late and we turned on course for the target. I naturally was riding with the 394th in the #2 position.

The 72nd gradually widened the space between the two squadrons and at the target we found ourselves alone and with just five ships. A half-hour before the target a loner was spotted and he streaked back to his field to gather up his companions. About 40 fighters composed mostly of Zekes, Tonys, and Vals started to intercept about five minutes before the target. The target (an oil refinery) was covered by clouds so it necessitated two runs. Anti-aircraft fire was excellent. It was heavy, intense, and accurate. Our bombs were dropped through the clouds with the results unobserved.

Due to our squadrons being separated, the Japanese interceptors split up on the weaker looking formations. Our five-ship formation must have looked weak because we had 20 planes giving us their undivided attention. We had our hands full and they sure shot up our planes.

Both Lt. Bone and Lt. Whitman lost an engine. After the interception ceased, the formation slowly broke up. We tried to stay with Lt. Bone. He was steadily losing altitude. He then proceeded to lighten up his ship by tossing out flak suits, guns, ammunition, bomb bay tanks, and the lower ball turret. We had to leave them somewhere near the Celebes due to a gas shortage. Fortunately he made it to Sansapor off the northwest tip of New Guinea.

Lt. Whitman was not so fortunate. He said that he'd bail out over Major Island but he never reached it. Several days too late, they sent out a solitary search plane with nil results. He's probably still drifting in a rubber life raft somewhere between the Celebes and the Halmaheras.

"We proceeded back to our base at Noemfoor Island without further mishap. We suffered only minor damage. Lt. Woodard brought his ship back safely to our base although badly shot up. Lt. Russell's crew, also shot up and low on gas, crash landed on Morotai. Major Pierce, from Group, was shot down. Those that did bail out were strafed by

Japanese planes. A ship from the 23rd Squadron, although badly shot up, made it to a point where the Catalina (PBY5) was orbiting and the crew bailed out and were picked up.

Losses = three ships, plus numerous other craft shot up. The second raid was disastrous. The 307th Group had seven planes shot down and many other planes crash landed at other fields. Only four of their ships made it to this base. The 5th Group did not lose a ship, although several were damaged.

BOMBED BY FRIENDS

It wasn't just the enemy's defenses the Bomber Barons had to worry about, especially in bad weather, as Edward Scheffelin wrote in *Prepared for Enemy Fire, but Not Expecting Friendly Bombs.*

On a mission in 1944 to Rabaul, New Britain, near the island of New Guinea, the 5th Bombardment Group was flying above a solid overcast front at 20,000 feet when our B-24 lost an engine. Unable to maintain sufficient airspeed to fly with the formation at an altitude of 20,000 feet, our pilot Thomas Shearin descended to approximately 10,000 feet, below the solid overcast. We decided to go on at 10,000 feet and bomb the secondary target, a neturalized Japanese fighter base on the island of Bougainville in the Solomon Islands.

Once we found the airfield, I started my bomb run at 10,000 feet. As my bombs started to drop in train, anti-aircraft fire erupted from the airfield, but the shells were not exploding at our level. Instead, the tracers were ahead of us and disappearing into the solid overcast above us.

Then, off to the right side of our B-24 and very close to our plane, there appeared objects with American lettering, falling from the overcast and coming in our direction. As these objects kept getting closer, I realized that they were American bombs with American identification markings painted on the casings.

I abruptly finished my bomb run by salvoing the remaining bombs and Captain Shearin made the steepest and sharpest diving turn that he ever made in a B-24. As we were departing, I could see the bombs falling across the path of what had been my bomb run.

After arriving at our home base, we learned that the solid overcast front also covered the primary target; the group commander had decided to bomb the secondary target at 20,000 feet.

UP THE SLOT TO SHORTLAND HARBOR AGAIN

Jack B. McEwan, of the 394th Squadron, was flying co-pilot to Capt. Bill Ivey in Poison Ivey on a night bombing mission to a new airfield the Japanese were building on Balalle Island in Shortland Bay. A perfect mission is a thing of great beauty as McEwan described in his journal.

Unrich's crew.

Our squadron mission was of nine B-17s which flew in a V of V's and the attack was so planned and coordinated that we would arrive over the target area just at dusk. My buddy, Al Mobley, and his plane were on our left wing. We flew at 12,000 feet and our flight path took us over Shortland Harbor and where we saw just below us a Japanese light cruiser or destroyer getting up steam and trying to leave through a very narrow channel between reefs and small islands. It was a great temptation to drop our bombs on it as it was a perfect target, but our mission was to bomb the Balalle airfield, which we did. This island was quite small and the runway ran almost the length of the island.

It was a thrilling moment to see nine bombers with bomb bay doors open begin to release bomb after bomb in train. The planes rise a bit because of the loss of the heavy bomb load and we had to jockey a bit to compensate for it. All the time we expected to be jumped by Japanese Zero fighters from Kahili and the crew was on the outlook for them. However, the good Lord was with us and we were able to turn east into the darkening dusk, which made it difficult for them to see us. When we were about 70 miles away we could look back and see a dark plume of smoke climbing high into the last vestige of twilight. It was a perfect mission! Our formation and the spread of the 500 pound bombs resulted in our blanketing the target area.

We were all a happy lot on the approximately 300 mile flight back to Guadalcanal. What a sight for tired eyes it was when we could see the lights of our island blinking in the distance. After we had all landed, medicinal whisky was passed around to those who drank, and we sat in our tents and relived the mission with great exhilaration.

The crews who participated in the bombing strike on Balalle Island received a commendation from the Commanding General of the 13th Air Force.

COLONEL UNRUH SHOT DOWN

It was not only in the heat of battle that the men of the Fighting 5th showed their heart and courage, as Oscar C. Fitzhenry tells in his account of the search for the crew of the *Pretty Prairie*.

On a mission to Rabaul, Col. Unruh's plane was crippled by an enemy fighter attack. Eleven crew members bailed out, and nine of them were rescued by natives using dugouts. The plane, with Col. Unruh still at the controls, was last seen descending into the clouds over the southern tip of New Ireland.

Five crews volunteered to search for the crew in Japanese-held territory. Capt. Fitzhenry flew within 100 feet of a group of men on the beach. They dropped emergency kits to the men below and took photos for identification. They reported the information to COMAIRSOLS, expecting that a PBY Dumbo rescue mission would be quickly launched. The Dumbo's search, however, proved negative.

Nearly 50 years later, Fitzhenry relates, they learned what had happened to Col. Unruh and his surviving crewmembers. Through the diary and testimony of the widow of a surviving crewmember, an old newspaper interview with Col. Unruh and independent research, the true story was finally revealed.

"For several days, the crew was able to escape capture. On two occasions, they saw search rescue aircraft after Fitzhenry and Robertson's crews had located them, but they were unable to come out in the open for fear of capture. Most of the crew were captured within a few days after their bailout; Col. Unruh and Lt. Fessinger evaded capture for 16 days, but were finally found by the natives and turned over to the Japanese.

RESCUE IN THE PHILIPPINES

In November 1944, the crew of the *Li'l Joe Toddy* were shot down over Guimeras in the Panay Islands and rescued by a Philippine guerilla leader named Abelardo Javellana. Eighteen years later, Javellana and five of the B-24 crew members he had helped to rescue had a reunion in California. An Air Force news release dated 14 December 1962, describes how the reunion was arranged.

Through a query to the Air Force Times by an ex-Philippine guerilla leader of World War II, five former B-24 crew members who were shot down over the Philippines 18 years ago had a jubilant reunion in Hollywood today.

In September, Alberado Javellana wrote a letter to the Air Force Times requesting assistance in locating a group of airmen whom Javellana had assisted when two B-24s were shot down by the Japanese over Guimeras, P.I.

T/Sgt Dennis C. Jones, BSD, Norton Air Force Base, California, and Clyde R. Whitling, Standard Oil operator in Richmond, California, were the first to see the article in the Air Force Times and were put in touch with each other by contacting Javellana.

By coincidence, former 2nd Lt. John M. Wylder, another of the crew members, was visiting Norton Air Force Base in November 1962 as a sales representative for a sound equipment company, picked up the Norton 'NEWSCONE' and read an article which told of Sgt. Jones and Javellana's reunion through correspondence. Wylder picked up the telephone and contacted Jones. Wylder, who had been in contact with former S/Sgt. Harold A. Douglas and T/Sgt. Don P. Perri, was instrumental in getting the five men together.

Javellana, who picked up the five men after sighting the parachutes coming down over Guimeras, P.I. on 1 November 1944, still resides on the site where the B-24 crashed on the Island.

Crew of Lil Jo Toddy. (l to r) Front row: T/Sgt. Jones (engineer), S/Sgt. Daywalt (engineer), S/Sgt. Trotter (engineer), Sgt. Barrow (waist gunner), T/Sgt. Bigley (radio operator), and Sgt. Satterfield (tail gunner). Back row: Lt. Bolton (pilot), Lt. Riley (bombardier), Lt. Mossbury (navigator), and Lt. Christensen (copilot).

The five crew members remember Javellana as the only guy on the Philippines who had cartons of Lucky Strike cigarettes in the green wrappers.

COMMENDATION BY GENERAL HENRY (HAP) ARNOLD

The Fighting 5th, The Bomber Barons, by whatever name you call them, the men of the 5th Bombardment Group left their mark on history. They were pioneers in the art and science of military aviation. The significance of their acts of bravery and heroism have not diminished with time.

General Henry A. *Hap* Arnold, one of the great architects of the modern Air Force, one of the first to see the significant role that the airplane could play in war, as well as peace time, held the men of the 5th Bombardment Group in the highest regard. As the war came to a close, with a hard-won victory in hand, he saluted them with the following words:

The Jungle Air Force's Gallant Battle to clear the skies from New Hebrides, Solomons, Admiralties, New Guinea, Netherlands East Indies and Philippines to the Asiatic coast contributed greatly to our victory over the Japanese. All USAAF join me in heartiest congratulations to you for your illustrious achievements and fighting spirit, to which we so largely owe our Splendid Triumph.

IKE HAVILAND THE MAN

By Col. Albert W. James, *USAF (ret)*

I am afraid that I cannot add much to whatever you may already know about Ike Haviland's accident. Ike was an upper classman in Flying School, and had a very strong sense of winning-out regardless of the difficulties he encountered. As I recall, during primary flight training he could not keep from throwing-up every time he flew, yet he persisted and ultimately overcame this limitation. As a B-24 Instructor Pilot I was involved in checking Ike out in anti-submarine tactics at Langley Field when he came through in a group destined to go to Europe to combat the submarine menace in the English Channel /Bay of Biscay area. I did not encounter him again until he showed up at Morotai and was given the job of Bomber Command Operations (A-3). Ike told me the story of how, upon arriving in Hawaii, he discovered that there was a C-46 to be delivered to the Phillipines that apparently needed a pilot, so Ike arranged to fly it himself. That he had not been given a proper check-out was not a problem for him.

As Deputy Commander of the 5th Bombardment Group, I became Acting Group Commander when my boss, Col Thomas Musgrave left for a month's R and R in Australia. He returned in early December and immediately left for a state side assignment. In mid-1946 I had an opportunity to visit the Pentagon and looked up Col. Musgrave, and found him in the office of the Chief of Staff.

Almost immediately with my appointment as Commander of the Group upon Col. Musgrave's departure, I was given instructions to move the Group to the island of Samar in the Phillipines. I immediately visited the area and found that the 22nd Bombardment Group of the 5th Air Force had just vacated the area we were to take over. The 22nd had moved to Mindoro Island.

The new 13th Bomber Commander, Brig. General Carl A. Brandt, had told me exactly how I should have the Group Commander's tent arranged, in addition to a number of other things, such as going to the war-weary airplane dump on Biak Island and picking out a C-47 for each of the four squadrons, for fat-cat operations--which we promptly did.

As with all other moves, each squadron as well as the Group Headquarters squadron set about building, and or acquiring necessary buildings and equipment in addition to a Group Theater. We were fortunate in that there was a very large navy contigent already present on Samar. It did not take long for our units to acquire refrigerators, ice machines, and a multitude of other non-standard items unknown to regular Army organizations. Mess halls and club buildings were quickly created--with competition between units as to who had the best, biggest, or who was the first to achieve some goal! Our Group Theater took advantage of a hillside, coconut logs became seats, and a stage built at the bottom of the hill accommodated traveling USO Groups as well as a screen for movies.

Moratia Theater in 1944.

Operations were picked up without a hitch. With careful scheduling the day before mission had been prepared and departed from Morotai--with landing at Samar. And the next day's mission was scheduled with departure from Samar and, of course, landing at Samar. The Group table of organization provided a personnel complement of some three thousand men, of which approximately five hundred were officers, which included sixty-five ten man crews. Our aircraft inventory usually included sixty-five B-24's and the four C-47's, a B-25 and a Navy SBD.

Lt. Col. Haviland arrived in May or June and busied himself invoking such measures as occurred to him. One idea that he had apparently brought from U.K. was to have the crews when reporting for the daily mission briefing to be assembled into military marching units (from each squadron) and to be marched to the briefing tent, Although this was a more orderly method and assured timely and complete attendance for the briefing, since we had never before followed such a procedure it was met with some resistance. With less than full acceptance apparent, Ike elected to drop the requirement within a few weeks. Ike's arrival had, of course, changed my role. For he had been designated Group Commander, and thus he superceded my status of *Acting Commander*. My role now was that of Deputy Commander. Ike chose to qualify himself fully as Commander by flying on as many missions as possible, as quickly as possible. To accomplish this he would fly two or three times each week. He told me that he wanted to get in his quota of missions so that he could put in for a stateside assignment. It also seemed that his orders promoting him to full Colonel arrived almost as soon as he did. Nevertheless, I personally led the mission in support of the Tarakan, Borneo landing, staged through Morotai, and the Brunei, Borneo landing, staged through Palawan.

The mission on which Ike was lost was to southern Borneo--staged through Morotai. This would have resulted in their flying across Celebes, now called Suluwasi--where there are some mountains. None of the other, proabibly twenty-three, aircraft crews reported any problems or irregularities, no may-day calls, no enemy activity. The civilized world was made aware of the finding of the wreckage site as a result of a native of the Celebes finding Ike's flying class ring which contained Ike's initials (some twenty-five years after the fact.) I had asked Gen. Brandt's approval to make a survey flight at the time of the accident but he denied approval. I believed that I could locate the wreckage site, my beliefs were ultimately corroborated. A Marine pilot who had accompanied the Graves Registration Party that climbed the mountain to the wreckage site stated that the aircraft was obviously in full flight when it collided with the mountain. In the evening of the day in which Ike had failed to return (I believe it was the 4th of July) I received telegraphic orders appointing me Commander of the 5th Bomb Group--no more *Acting* status.

It is clear from the information that is available that Ike was a charger, a doer with a full steam ahead—damn the torpedos—attitude. He seemed to exude infinite personal confidence. He obviously set goals for himself and pursued them relentlessly. How does a man with these qualities take himself and nine other fine young men to their end—apparently so needlessly? The weather in that part of the world is seldom poor flying weather. Mountains often create their own cloud cover through the uplift action—invisible moisture becomes visible through cooling—thus clouds. The navigator may have miscalculated their position relative to the mountain. Ike may have been *resting his eyes* because of too little rest. The mountain may have been higher than that shown on the map. The speculation as to cause can go on endlessly. All we know for sure is that it happened, and there does not appear to be any extenuating circumstance or condition that brought it about.

THE BORNEO LOG

By Phil Corrin

16 November 1944 - Plane was shot down in North Borneo. Tom Coberly (pilot), Jerry Rosenthal (Co-pilot), and Fred Brennan (Navigator were killed in crash... never got out of plane. All men in waist bailed out fifteen minutes before crash - Tom Capin, Francis Harrington, John Nelson, and Philips. I was the last to leave plane. Dan Illerich landed 75 feet away. We contacted natives about four hours later and spent the night in small native village. Busar, Yakal's brother was first native we met.

17 November-Found Jim Knoch and Eddy Haviland who had been hit in face with plexiglass and received several broken ribs from chute jump. Moved to hut on top of hill in clearing. Have chutes to signal with. Will wait for friendly plane.

18 November-No sign of rescue. Natives very friendly, Food plentiful. Ed's eye little better - ribs same. When Ed can move we plan to travel river to coast.

19 November-Heard plane today but did not come in sight. Native wants to take message down river but we do not know whether to trust him or not. Ed little better.

20 November-B-24 passed over today but did not see us. What a discouraging sight! Spoke to native today who had a L.A. Evening News in his hat dated 15 February 1939.

21 November-Moved down to large river. Trying to get boat from natives so we can go to town natives call Long Berang which is three days travel from here.

22 November-Met District Official (Malayan man who speaks Dutch, Malay, Dayak, and a little English). He lives in Long Berang where he will take us tomorrow - one days' travel. We are in Dutch Borneo and not North Borneo as we thought. He has lived with American missionaries (Mr. Presswood and one other). We don't know if they are still at Long Berang or not...We have given him official papers telling him about us. He prepared excellent meal for us - broiled spareribs, rice fried in pork grease, boiled pork, coffee with sugar, etc. Living like kings!

23 November-William Ostania Wakahanap - District Official - decided not to take us to Long Berang because he was afraid some of his people could not be trusted with the Japs. However, we will move farther down river and his son Christian will cook for us. Food is delicious - pork fritters, fruit, fried rice, etc. If only G.I. chefs had recipes like this. We know everything is all right with the world when natives in Borneo hum *Come All Ye Faithful*, *Silent Night*, and *America*!

24 November-Traveled down river in canoe to Long Berang, village of about 200 people. William's house very nice. Had delicious meal with tables, chairs, tablecloth, plates, silverwear, and finger bowls! We were given clean clothes and ours were washed. Long Berang is on a tributary of the Sesajup River.

25 November-Fresh eggs for breakfast and chicken for dinner. Christian gave us haircuts and shaves. Spoke to man who is from Celebes (William and family from Celebes, too). He is minister of Christian Church here. He is member of the Christian and Missionary Alliance with headquarters in New York City. The missionaries who have been here are Presswood, Willfinger, Dickson, Jefferies, and Michaelson.

27 November-Moved from Long Berang today at 3 a.m., so people would not know where we had gone, back up the river to Peneragon Lagon's village - Native Chief friendly to the Allies. William gave us bottle of catsup, tea, coffee, sugar, salt, peanuts, rice, etc. Natives trapped a young deer on way up which we had for dinner.

28 November-Native brought note from the Japs in Long Berang telling us to surrender (Mr. Soldier: I am Japs. I think you did fulfill your mission. Your permissive and pistol gun give to this man, if consent and come to Long Berang. R. Iwasaki.) We headed back into the hills, immediately. Peneragon Lagon followed us and built us a leanto and will bring us food.

29 November-Moved to shack Peneragon and his tribe built hut which is closer to the village but well hidden. Have lived in eight places in two weeks.

30 November-Thanksgiving! For dinner - boiled rice, boiled root with sugar, pineapple, two K-ration dog biscuits, one-fourth bar of chocolate and one Camel cigarette a piece. We four have plenty to be thankful for.

4 December-B-24 passed over today but jungle here is too thick for us to signal. Have not seen Peneragon for five days. Running out of food. Hope someone turns up tomorrow.

5 December-Some of Peneragon's boys came and took us to another shelter next to a small stream where I think we will stay for quite a while. It is even better hidden than the last place. From what we can understand there has been a patrol of fifteen Japs looking for us.

8 December-Pearl Harbor Day! - Three years ago today, Perhaps it will be over this time next year.

10 December-Natives came this evening for the first time in four days. We had not eaten for the last two days and it seemed good to get some food in us once again. We understand that the Japs were on our trail and the natives were doing a little headhunting for our benefit.

12 December-Skeezix came this evening with some more rice, tobacco, and firewood. He told us to stay hidden and keep quiet as the Japs are still going up and down the river looking for us. He also said the Americans bombed Terakan again.

19 December-Two natives came today with pork, big bag of rice, bananas, sugarcane and ten ears of fresh corn. Delicious!

25 December-Christmas Day! Have not seen natives for six days. Christmas dinner - the last of our rice (half a pot), our last four squares of chocolate, and last four Camels that had mildewed but still seemed good.

26 December-Three natives came this morning with rice, root, sugarcane, bananas, coffee, sugar, salt, fresh fish, and tobacco.

30 December-Native came today with more rice. About noon we heard what sounded like bombing. The planes were evidently bombing Terakan again.

1 January 1945-Happy New Year! and it certainly will be a happy one for us and our families. Native came this afternoon with rice, bananas, roasted peanuts and tobacco.

2 January-*Alice The Goon* came this morning with rice and roasted wild pig rind and fat which you wouldn't feed your dog back home, but it tasted darn good out here!

4 January-Another B-24 passed over today evidently on a search mission.

5 January-*Fido* and his dogs came in today with a load of rice, tobacco, Coffee and sugar.

12 January-*Old Chris* came this morning with rice, pork rind, fat and meat. We had gone five days without food, and I've never been quite so glad to see any food in my life. Have been infested with body lice which make you scratch all the time. I could certainly use a good delousing outfit now.

14 January-*Old Chris*, *Charles Atlas* and one other native came this morning with rice, tobacco, salt, pepper, sugar cane, and firewood. *Atlas* is really a character - always has a grin on his face. Hope to see him again. He gave us all of his tobacco which was a green color.

16 January-*Herman, Sherman, and Vernon* brought some pork rind and fat this morning along with some salt, tobacco and bananas from Long Berang, but no rice! They said they hadn't been able to bring any because the Japs were around. *Skeezex* came later with some more firewood.

18 January-Two of the native boys came today with a little rice and some sugarcane, root, bananas, and fresh corn on the cob.

19 January-We were awakened this morning by *Herman* and another native boy. They told us that the three Japs on the river had been killed and that they were going to take us back to Peneragon's. We ate a hearty breakfast of rice, root, bananas, sugarcane - packed our belongings and said goodbye to *Polecat Gulch* and *Club Borneo* and started off. It was breath taking to reach the top of the first ridge where we could see for a great distance without having to look straight up. It's odd how you lose all conception of such things when you haven't seen them for a long time. As we walked along I couldn't help but wonder it this was the first step on our way back to the good old U.S.A. We could hear the drum beating and a lot of yelling as we approached Peneragon's. All the natives from miles around were there to greet us and we had to shake hands for about ten min-

utes. They immediately proceeded to show us where they had killed three Japs in the house. The massacre had evidently occurred this morning because the blood was still fresh on the floor and the fire was still smoldering down by the river where they had burned the bodies of the *Sons of Heaven*. We then ate some rice, sugarcane, bananas, pork, and some kind of fruit which tasted like a cross between a cucumber and a watermelon. They got the four chairs out for us and showed us the Japs souvenirs which they had salvaged - pistol, rifle, bayonet, money, gold teeth, cartridge box, pencil and clothes. The celebration then started - a pig was brought in and slaughtered and each native dipped his finger in the blood and touched his chest. They then did their tribal dances of victory and death to the beating of three big iron drums. Ten of the warriors then put on their best machetes, shook hands with us, and with their blow guns and darts took off down the river to kill five Japs at Long Berang...After they left the women formed a long line and did a dance around the house singing some native chant over and over. Peneragon then informed us that there are two more American airmen up the river. I wrote a note which will be taken to them, so we are looking forward to being joined by a couple more Yanks. As I sit here now the big feast is being prepared pork is being sliced - *kick-a-poo joy juice* has been prepared in a big jug and they have given us enough tobacco to last some months. Tasted the *joy juice* which surprisingly tastes like California Roma wine. Another meal - rice with pork gravy, boiled pork, and coffee-delicious! Tribal dances and women chanting continues. You drink the rice wine through a big straw and eat liver with it. In the evening one of the boys tried to tell us about the war. From what we could understand there are allied soldiers in Ambon, Celebes, Java and North Borneo! Can it be that our prayers and dreams are coming true? As the dancing and chanting continued two of the natives went down to the river where the Japs bodies had been cremated and brought back a couple of Jap skulls which were hung up over the fire. The men then formed a long line and did another dance to the beat of the drums. I'm a God fearing person but I was happy to sit in on the end of two so-called human beings who were members of a race of people who have brought so much suffering on so many people throughout the world. This indeed has been an interesting day and one I shall always remember. We are waiting for the return of the warriors from Long Berang and word from there to find out exactly what the score is. *Indigestion Joe*, with the horn hat came in last night with some of his village people. They brought another pig and lots of food so maybe another celebration is in the making. The *Butcher* was here, too, and he and *Joe* make a great pair. They both want us to come to their houses to live. The *Butcher* promised us each a wife if we would come to his. I gave *Joe* my lapel wings for his hat and he was very pleased. They told us that this village is Long Watoiel and the plane crashed at Long Kaseroeng. We find that *Peneragon* means village chief. *Joe* wants to go to America with us. The five Japs are dead! Some of the men returned with the No. 1 sons of the village who attended school in Long Berang, to tell us that three of the Japs had their heads cut off and two of them drowned. The people and food are really pouring into this place. Another pig and a young water buffalo Another celebration in the making. *Singing Sam* just told us that the Dutch flag is flying at Long Berang and the Rising Sun is down!

22 January-Some natives came up the river during the night to tell us that there are two more Japs at Long Berang. Peneragon wanted us to go down there and shoot them. We finally talked him out of it, so after I pinned my bombardier wings on his hat he took off with several other men for Long Berang. They took the Japanese rifle and their two muzzle loaders with them.

Peneragon returned this afternoon with William. There are supposed to be Allied forces at Brunei and William has given the word to all Dayak people to kill all the Japanese they see. Tomorrow we are returning to Long Berang where we will shoot any Japs who come up the river. William and Peneragon are going to make a five day trip to Los Santos to kill the six remaining Japanese in this territory. We will then be joined by several other Americans. The Japanese are leaving Terakan when they can and all we have to do is sweat the return of the Dutch or other Alllied forces. William moved all his family away from Long Berang except Christian. During the excitement Christian stole a machine gun from the Japanese and killed two of them himself.

23 January-Moved to Long Berang. Fried chicken for lunch. Fort Berang all set up with our pistols, Japanese machine gun, rifles, pistols, and mortar. They are having regular guard duty with the natives patroling all day and night. William left for Long Sempayan to kill the six remaining Japanese and bring the Americans down. A doctor and a young fellow (Edward Safri) came in from Malinau where they had been chased out by three Japanese. Some more Malayans came up from Malinau during the night. They had started out with three Japanese but killed them on the way. They had a boat load of Japanese supplies - two 100 pound sacks of rice, barrels of salt, sugar, fish, pork, towels, tobacco, cigarettes, several bottles of Jap saki, etc. We even have a mattress to sleep on here.

24 January-Have been given new clothes - shirts, pants, towels, handkerchiefs, *Chinaman* brought us tobacco and fresh eggs. Food is very good - peanuts, lemonade, fried bananas, tea, coffee, string beans, pumpkin, stewed chicken, etc. Wrote another note to one American airman up the river telling him to come here. Christian tells us that the American forces are spreading out in Sarawak from Brunei but I think it's all wishful thinking. Christian wants to learn English so he can come to America someday. Edward Safri ate lunch with us today. His father is Dutch and mother Javanese. His home is in Java. He came to Borneo in December 1941 — one month before the Japanese who forced him to work in a sawmill.

25 January-My turn to stand guard duty last night, but it isn't bad even though its raining when you can sit on a porch in a nice easy chair, smoke Japanese cigarettes at will, eat fried bananas and drink hot tea - a far cry from the interior guard duty I used to stand in Cadets. The hardest rain I've ever seen came during the night - river rose about 30 feet. Gave Christian an English lesson this morning from the Malay word sheet, Christian brought out a victrola and we played *Stars and Stripes Forever*, *Silent Night*, *When Irish Eyes are Smiling*, *Star Spangled Banner*, etc. This place will never cease to amaze me! Eggs fried sunny side up for breakfast. Christian's pancakes, and lemonade for mid-morning snack, and chicken soup and stewed chicken for lunch. Spent enjoyable evening with Edward Safri last night. He plays Hawaiian guitar and is very interested in music. He has learned American songs from Hollywood films he has seen and although he doesn't know what the words mean he can sing many of the old favorites. When we stopped singing he seemed rather sad and said it reminded him of his family and home in Java, but it reminded me of my family and home in America, too. Moley, the doctor, told us that Terakan was bombed this morning and there were Allied forces in the Malay States and Hong Kong. I only hope half of what they tell us is true.

26 January-Helped the Dayaks build a pillbox this morning in defense of the Japanese who might escape from the Cryan district. Had some fresh pineapple this afternoon from the bushes around Mr. Presswood's house across the river. There are many gardenia bushes there, too, which people back home would envy. We went through the house which is very nice - hardwood floors, glass windows, wiring for electric lights, etc. It was the scene for the end of two Japs and there is quite a bit of blood on the floors - a horrible sight. Goat meat for dinner with fried cucumber, rice and a delicious gravy. Edward visited us this evening and we had coffee and fresh roasted peanuts. He is a very interesting person. He came to Borneo as an explosive expert to work in the oil fields at Terakan. The Japanese forced him to work in the sawmill for 35 Japanese guilders a month. Rice was rationed to eight cups for ten days. Until he met us he was completely ignorant as to how the war was coming along as the Japanese told the people they were in Hawaii and the U.S. Edward says there is no more oil being pumped at Terakan since we bombed it and the people are living on casaba and mice. He asked us if the Americans would honor his Japanese invasion money. We said we didn't know but I'm afraid the answer is "no."

27 January-Native came from the northwest today with word that there are 170 Japs at Leombia on the North Borneo border where they were forced to go because of lack of food in North Borneo. 400 Dayaks are now gathering to go north and kill them. The woman from Sourabaya, Java, who name is Satoni, showed us a photo of Mr. Wilfinger. She is a nice woman. I'll never forget the second time we arrived at Long Berang. As I got out of the boat she came rushing up with a smile a mile wide on her face. At first I thought she was going to kiss me, but instead she gave me a hearty handshake and patted me on the back for several minutes, shouting "very good, very good" the only two words of English she knew I guess. She's waiting to go home just as we are. We had wild boar for lunch which had been boiled first then fried in some kind of egg batter - was it delicious! Christian made us some kind of fritters which tasted just about as good as anything we've had so far. We also had a drink made from green coconut milk, shredded coconut meat, and sugar. The girl who cooks for us, Benoom, baked us some sweet potatoes and fried them in egg batter - served them with coffee before bed.

28 January-Christian made some kind of dough, rolled it in a ball filling the center with chocolate and boiling them. After it was cooked they were rolled in grated coconut. If the food gets much better I won't want to go home. I wrote another note to one American up north and Christian took off to get him. I gave him my 45 automatic to carry with him and he was quite proud to be carrying an American weapon. He will be back in two days. Received word this afternoon that the six Japs at Long Sempayan are dead. Our friend R. Iwasaki was one of them One of the Chinamen brought us some eggs for breakfast and as he left he placed his hands on our shoulders and muttered some sort of blessing.

29 January-The warriors returned from Long Sempayan this morning with a couple of Jap, skulls and some more pistols and rifles. The natives told us that William went on to Cryan from Long Sempayan to get the other two Americans. Christian returned this evening because he had heard a false rumor that the Japs had come to Long Berang. He sent a native on to get the American he was after. Christian is mad at the Dayaks because they've been annoying us and won't stay out of the house. Christian doesn't think the Dayak girl cooks good and he says she's been stealing the food so from now on he will do the cooking.

30 January-Christian cooked us big chicken dinner which next to mother Hartman's, was the best I've ever had. He also got us a jug of wine made by the Chinaman and it was much

better than the Dayaks make. I got a haircut and a shave for the first time in over two months and I feel like a new man. Some Dayaks from other villages came in today for a celebration. They held their chanting parades throughout the afternoon. There was a goat and several pigs killed so I guess they had a big feast.

31 January-Christian left this morning to visit his mother who is staying some place up north until the excitement is over. He will be back in a couple of days. Peneragon and his warriors also departed this morning for Malinauto to welcome three more Japs who appeared there during the last few days. The village is very quiet now with most of the people gone. We spend our time now eating, sleeping, reading the five or six English books here, and swimming in the river I hope we will be able to leave soon because although it's been a valuable experience in a way, I feel that so much time is being wasted when you sit for hours at a time doing nothing.

1 February-William and Christian returned this afternoon and Tom Capin was with them and it was certainly good to see him! He has been living with some natives since he came down and was wearing a loin cloth, speaks the language, etc. He says John Nelson and Franny Harrington are up there some place but are afraid to come down. I'm going to write another note and William is going after them in a couple of days. We are going to stay here and shoot any Japs that may come this way. William is going to send a man to Brunei to see if there are really any Allies there and if there are perhaps we can join them. It will take us about a month to walk to Brunei. In a few days William is going to give the word to the Dayaks and they are going to carry this guerrilla war to Tarakan.

3 February-William says he will stay with us from now on - if he has to leave Long Berang then we will go too. I guess we were in great danger when William was gone last time. Those six Japs from Long Sempayan were only two hours away from here when they were killed. Several Saki or Mohammedans were also here while William was gone. They are scared of both sides now but were pro-Jap before the uprising started and they should have been killed. Mrs. Makahanap was crying because she couldn't be here to cook for us, William said. She also said to William "Americans dead, you dead. Americans alive, you alive." William had a pig killed for dinner today. We were telling him how good it was and he said when the Allies return that we'll really start to eat and that this is no good. That I want to see! William says we would have been executed if the Japs had ever got us, as they had done that to several fellows who came down near Tarakan.

6 February-There are supposedly ten Japs in the vicinity and so we are-standing guard duty all night, although with the system William has going - Dayaks on watch 24 hours a day for miles around - I can't see much use in it. He says it is good for the people's morale. The Mohammedans rounded up 30 of the native boys who ran away from the Jap school at Malinau, took them back there, and the three Japs down there killed them. Peneragon is on his way to do away with the Japs, and we are just waiting for some of the Mohammedans to show up here as they don't carry any weapons. Christian took us up in the attic of Mr. Presswood's house yesterday and we found many old Readers Digests, National Geographics, and Popular Mechanics. What a welcome sight! They sure help to pass the time.

7 February-Seventeen B-24s flew directly over us today. We tried to signal with our chutes and several mirrors, but I guess not one of the 170 men up there was looking down. As they flew on it was the most heartbreaking sight I ever saw! Tomorrow we are starting out on a two day trip to another village where we will stay until the Allies return to Tarakan or we can reach them some place else. Benoom, the native girl, is go-ing with us to do our cooking. William is afraid that if a lot of Japs come here the people will get frightened and we will have to defend ourselves. William will remain here to continue his rabble rousing.

9 February-William postponed the moving for a couple of days and we are leaving tomorrow. The Chinaman gave us a bottle of his liquor today and I think its darn near straight alcohol. I set a match to some of it to see if it would burn - almost, not quite. The natives had another big celebration today - killing a pig, dancing, chanting, etc. They are all drunk this evening. They raised the Dutch flag and when the hangover wears off they'll be on the warpath again. We had duck and pudding for dinner today.

10 February-Hiked to another village - straight up and down all the way. Three girls came with us to do the cooking. William's brother-in-law, *Uncle Looie*, is here and he says another B-24 was shot down eight days from here, so I wrote another note asking the guys to join us. He also says there are definitely Allied forces at Miri. William says Franny and John will join us here in two days. William will decide then if it will be necessary for us to move further up. I don't see how the Japs could find us here or why they would even want to make the hike. Natives bring us lots of gifts - bananas, chickens, cucumbers, and other Borneo fruits. My native name is *Yo-Kong* meaning pig trap.

13 February-Hiked to another village in the middle of a large rice field - largest I've seen so far. Yakal and Benoom and the other two girls will stay with us. William left for Cryan to organize natives. If he is near any Allied forces he will give them a note I wrote telling them we are here.

14 February-Hiked on to our destination - a nice clean little hut in another rice field. It is a Christian Chief's house. His name is Sadi and he is chief of the village of Bang Giau. They killed a wild boar on the way and we had it for dinner. The natives tell us that Franny and John won't be here because the guy they're staying with has been intercepting all the notes we've sent them. He evidently doesn't want them to leave his place.

18 February-Sunday - Attended Church today! Since this is a last out-post, the people gather every Sunday to hold their worship services. *One Eye* gave the sermon - several prayers were said and songs were sung. They prayed for us asking God to make us like them. They also asked God to make my stomach well. They are afraid that they won't go to Heaven because they've been killing Japs, so they asked God to forgive them for that. Some of their most prized possessions are the little picture cards with Bible stories on them (like we used to get in Sunday School) that Mr. Presswood has given them. These people have carried on for three years without the missionaries which is enough proof to me that their land may be occupied but that they will never be conquered. Sadi's wife made us some pop-corn yesterday and today we had another kind of root, sliced up and fried in deep fat, and salted - which tastes very much like Ritz Crackers. I've also eaten roasted grasshopper, which tastes like crabmeat or lobster. We have tree mushrooms quite often, too.

1 March-Balang, one of Sadi's men, brought us a note from Franny and John. They said that a copilot from a Navy B-24 had joined them and was taking them to a safer place where there are more Allied airmen. The Navy pilot was shot down 13 January and he said the Philippines were in our hands then and that the Allies were near Berlin.

9 March-William came this evening with four Dutch soldiers from the Celebes. They fought the Japs in 1941, but were captured shortly after and were put in a prison camp at Kuching. They escaped from the Japs a few weeks ago and are now anxious to join Allied Forces so they can fight the Japs again. The

prison camp they were in was run by a Jap Colonel who was supposedly a Christian. They said that most of the prisoners were killed - many of them tortured to death by having lighted cigarettes placed in their eyes, nose, and ears and then having their arms and legs chopped off. There are supposed to be Allied forces in West Borneo but William thinks it will be better to wait here until they invade Tarakan as there are too many Japs on the trail and in the jungles. These Dutch soldiers are regular guys - know several American songs and are full of horseplay like the American soldier.

12 March-William and the soldiers left this morning. William is going to get five American airmen and bring them here. I wrote a note to them and we hope John and Franny are among them. The four Dutch soldiers are going out after Japs. I also wrote a note for them introducing them to Allied forces if they should contact any.

14 March-A native came this morning with a note from Franny and John. They had started out for West Borneo but their guides deserted them and they had to come back. There are four men from a Navy B-24 with them now. The other five men from the same plane took off for North Borneo but the Japs captured them and they were killed. The rest of the guys will be in Long Sampayan tomorrow and William will be there to meet them. I wrote another note last night and we hope either that one or the one that William will give them will convince them to come here. I guess the Navy fellow told them the great news which they passed on to us - that my team USC beat Tennessee by a large score in the Rose Bowl game this year. How I would have liked to have seen that. Army beat Navy also. We were out of tobacco for a few days and when the natives heard about it they started bringing it in so fast that we have enough to open a smoke shop now.

20 March-*Uncle Looie* arrived this morning with another note from Fanny and John. They have at last decided to join us. The day after tomorrow we are leaving here (Bang Biau) to go to the village of Pa Silau where William will take them. There is a bigger house there and it is a little farther back in the interior. Two of the Navy fellows are with Franny and John and I guess the other two will be here later. The people here don't want us to move - guess they'll really be broken up when we leave for good, but that day can't come too soon for me.

March-Left today for Pa Silau. Seemed as if the trail were straight up all the way. Stayed all night in an old hut on top of a mountain where it is really cold. There were even a few pine trees around.

23 March-My birthday! I thought we would be out of Borneo by now. Would sure like to have a piece of that chocolate cake grandmother sent me this time last year. Arrived at Pa Silau and it was swell to see Franny and John again. The two Navy fellows are Lt. J.G. Bob Graham from Rosemont, Pennsylvania and Jim Shepherd from Kansas City, Missouri. *Mamma*, Mrs. Makahanap, is here and she cooks some delicious foods for us. I'm glad we can be together at last and hope we'll be able to leave soon.

1 April-Easter Sunday! - Sadi from Bang Bieu brought us the magazines and the rest of our clothes today. He says that the Japs have all left Malinau and Tarakan! If only it's true we may be able to leave soon. William is going to send Peneragon down to check up on it. *Mama* made us one of her gelatin puddings with the sauce today - delicious as usual. It seems as if the days are getting longer and longer - if only help will come soon.

3 April-William Monahan, the man from the Celebes who took care of Franny and John, and several other natives all came in this afternoon with word that seven white men and one interpreter have either landed a plane or bailed out four days from here for the purpose of organizing the natives into guerrilla bands

to fight the Japs. They say planes are dropping them supplies and they have a radio! I wrote them a note and William will take it to them. If only it's true this time and not another rumor!!

9 April-William returned today with great news. He brought a note from Major Tom Harrisson of the Australian Reconnaisance Corps. He is here to organize the natives and *Help Us To Get Out*! He sent some medical supplies, tobacco, gum, etc. Dan and I are leaving tomorrow to meet him at Wy-agong. William killed a goat for dinner and we had a big feast. In the evening *Mama* made us some fried bananas and hot chocolate that never had any that tasted better.

10 April-Dan, Tom, and I left today with William, *Uncle Looie* and Christian to meet the Major. We spent the night at Palamamoot, one of the cleanest villages I've seen. They fried a chicken for us and gave us lots of sugarcane.

11 April-Walked to Long Sempayan on the Pacryan River this morning. It is very much like Long Berang being the headquarters for the Cryan District. They were holding school led by another man from the Celebes when we arrived. Long Berang is on the Pa Cynaya River. It was their music hour in which they sang songs in four-part harmony. They also have an orchestra with flutes, drums and long bamboo sections for the base notes and it all sounds pretty good. Had some limeade made with sugarcane juice, chicken, string beans, squash for dinner. Sgtoni, the woman from Sourabaya, is here.

12 April-Walked to Long Braun. Before we left, William made a speech to the school children telling them that the white men were returning and were going to kill all the Japs. Long Braun is quite a nice place - on a grassy hill. There are 10 cows here - how I'd like to have a nice steak! All the people are out picking rice so the place looks like a ghost town. The people here are no good - very friendly to the Japs.

13 April-Finally arrived at Wy-agong - what a trail. It's been raining all day and this place is just one, big mud hole. We've got a nice house to stay in, though, and the Major should be here tomorrow. William has been out *kidnapping* chickens for us. We now have five, so I guess we won't go hungry. Had some small tomatoes today and some wild raspberries - all we needed was sugar and cream. Twenty-three natives came with us.

15 April-The Major couldn't make it over because some more men and supplies are coming in but he sent Warrant Officer Rod Cusack and a note over asking us to come there. He wants Dan and Tom to work on the radio and discuss plans for getting out with me. Cusack is a very nice fellow - from Brisbane in Queensland, Australia. The Major is an Englishman. We are leaving tomorrow for the Major's guerrilla headquarters in Sarawak. Cusack brought us some coffee, sugar, dried prunes, tobacco, peanut butter and some real Scotch whiskey!

17 April-Walked to Pa Melada - William, Christian and several natives were with us.

18 April-Walked ten and a half hours to Belawit today and saw flat ground for the first time in a long while. Belawit is situated in a large valley full of rice fields. Stayed at Mr. Aris Doemat's house - the Malayan missionary from the Celebes whom we had met before at Long Berang. He had the native school orchestra play *America* for us. The Aussies claim it's "God Save The King" but we always maintain it was *America*.

19 April-Walked about two hours down the valley to another large village. We walked through the rice fields and in many places the mud was up to our knees. The people here are different than those on the other side. They speak with a different accent and use a few different words. Some of them wear heavy rings in their ears and it pulls them down below the shoulders. Dan and I played chess all afternoon with a set the natives carved out for us.

20 April-Walked to Pa-trapp today and Cusack caught up with us in the evening, The natives here are very different from the people we've known before. Very big people - wear bones and rings in their ears - drink a lot of rice wine and smoke constantly.

21 April-Arrived at the Major's headquarters today at Baree. Major Harrisson is a swell guy - tells us that the Australians are due to invade Tarakan in a week and the Americans are going to hit Brunei. We received all the latest war news and the shock that President Roosevelt is dead. The Australian doctor is giving us medicine for the itch and we've got chocolate, cigarettes, jam, cookies, peanut butter and a bottle of Scotch that the Major gave us.

22 April-The Major is dividing the outfit up into five platoons. I'm in charge of #4 with eight rifles, five hand grenades, and ten blow guns. William received word from the Chinese doctor at Malinau that the Japs are threatening to come back to Long Berang so he's leaving tomorrow with several guns for there. Cusack will follow the day after with ammunition. I'm going over in about four days with the Major and Capt. Edmonds. I had a nice talk this evening with Major Harrisson and he told me all about his life which has been most interesting. Before the war he was a scientist and has written several books and traveled all over the world doing scientific study for Oxford University. For a year he lived on an island in the New Hebrides with savages who still eat human flesh. He has marks all over his body in evidence that the natives there have initiated him into their very secret tribal rituals. Doug Fairbanks, Sr. once tried to make a film of it but Harrisson got fed up with Hollywood publicity and walked out.

29 April-Liberator came today and dropped ten storpedoes full of guns and ammunition. I'm leaving tomorrow for Long Berang with twenty .303 rifles. The Major will come later. Received the news that the Aussies have landed at Tarakan. Stayed all night at the native longhouse in the valley. Had some borak, rice wine with the natives. The wine they make here is a lot better than that at Long Berang. They pray before drinking and always hold your glass while you drink.

30 April-Walked today to Pa-Trapp with Capt. Rick Edmads who is going to the Truson River in North Sarawak to kill Japs. He's a swell guy and truly a soldier of fortune - born in India, lived in New Zealand and enlisted in the Australian army. He plans to make the army his career as it has been in his family for generations.

1 May-Arrived at Mr. Doemat's house at Belawit. Had delicious dinner of fried chicken and fresh beef. He had his orchestra play for Rick and me—*America, Silent Night,* and *Nearer My God To Thee.*

2 May-Rick left this morning for Truson. I went on to Pa Wylieya. Am getting the itch quite badly now and the leech bites have made my feet very sore. Had a lot of fun talking to people this evening. I finally got across to them that the Jap invasion money is no good and one guy offered me his to roll my cigarettes in. I gave them some medicine - many people being sick with boils, dysentery, fever, etc. I guess they're my friends forever now.

3 May-Walked to Pa Oamong - very difficult to get enough carriers with so many people sick. The poor carriers I do have are way overloaded.

4 May-Made it to Long Moleda getting women, children and anybody not sick to carry. On the trail the natives saw a big bird (the great hornbill) and asked me to kill it. I took a shot at it with one of the .303s and luckily I hit it! - couldn't have been a better shot if the thing had been sitting on the end of a barrel. The bird was all black except for white tail feathers and a yellow throat - had a six foot wing spread and curved beak about 12 inches long It was about as big as a turkey and had a lot of meat on it. The natives cooked it for lunch and it tasted quite a bit like chicken liver being very red meat.

5 May-Walked to Long Bruan but feet are getting very sore and swollen now.

6 May-Walked to Long Sempayan today and stayed at the school teacher's house. Had a sulap built and cached some goods there as instructed by the Major. They have a regular church building here and I attended services this evening. The school band surprised me by playing *Pack Up Your Troubles in Your Old Kit Bag.* My feet are very swollen and sore - can hardly walk.

7 May-Sent guns on to Long Berang. Stayed at Long Sempayan as my feet are very bad.

8 May-Stayed another day - am going to try to leave tomorrow. Between the itch, a case of dysentery, my feet and a cold - feel great! The Malayans tell me that the swelling in my feet is known as beri-beri.

13 May-Finally left today for Long Berang - one of the school teachers is with me. All the guys at Pa Silau moved down to Long Berang a couple of days ago. Stayed all night at an old deserted hut. Am not feeling well but will be glad to reach Long Berang, because of the dysentery at Long Sempayan.

15 May-Arrived at Long Berang safely - my walking days are over, I hope! All the guys are here and it was good to see them again. The Major has not yet arrived. Received word today that Malinau was bombed by three B-25s and most of the Japs were killed and the rest took off into the jungle. One of the B-25s was shot down and another flew too low and crashed into the jungle - all men killed. When the Major arrives and gives the word we should be on our way to Tarakan and home! Today makes a half a year that we've been in Borneo.

19 May-Received a note from the Major today and he is still at Bareo awaiting another drop before he can leave for Long Berang. He sent word that the war in Europe ended 0001 hours May 9, 1945. He also said that the Aussies at Tarakan had not yet moved to the mainland so we would have to be patient a while longer.

29 May-The Japs are all gone from Malinau and it is now safe for us to go to Tarakan if only the Major would come! Have not heard from him for ten days. We had a big feast today - William killed a cow and we had real steaks for dinner, and plenty of rice wine to feel happy on - what else is there to do in this place? It seems so long and now that we know we can get out it seems longer.

1 June-Eight more Aussies have landed at Belawit and one of them, Warrant Officer Hurst arrived here today with more guns and ammo. The Major sent a note saying he would be here by June 8. He is sending a radio ahead. He also said that he had contacted the 13th Air Force and he hoped they would drop us some supplies. He asked Cusack to write and tell him where a Catalina could land to pick us up. Malinau is the best place.

7 June-Cusack received a note from the Major stating that Jim Robbins (one of the Navy fellows from Omak, Washington) and I are to leave for Belawit immediately. We don't know for sure but think the Major is having a plane land there somehow and perhaps we'll get out. Six more days of walking - may it be the last.

8 June-Left Long Berang this morning with Jim and Robby. The people gave us lots of gifts and almost everyone was in tears when we left. Stayed at Pa Silau tonight.

10 June-Walked to Palamamoot and had good meal of pig and chicken. People very good to us and all want us to stay here. They all cried when we left.

12 June-Arrived Long Bruan and saw the stuff the 13th Air Force dropped us - was sadly disappointed - few boxes of K rations and only six packs of cigarettes and seven pairs of shoes all the same size which didn't fit any of us. Hurrah for the Americans! Met the Malayan school teacher, Thomas E. and he told us that Harmes, the other Navy man, has already been flown out from Belawit and the rest of the fellows have left Long Berang for Belawit, too.

14 June-Arrived Belawit! The natives have built an airstrip out of bamboo which is about 400 feet long and 30 feet wide. Small Austercrafts will land here and evacuate us one by one.

23 June-Was flown to Labuan Island in Brunei Bay.

1 July 1945 We arrived at Morotai Island to report back from our mission of 16 November 1944 and to complete our 8th mission.

BRUNO'S DIARY: STATESIDE TO SOUTH PACIFIC TO STATESIDE

Anthony V. Bruno was an Engineer on a B-24 Liberator Bomber with the 23rd Bombardment Squadron of the 13th Air Force from 23 October 1944 until 13 June 1945. Following are selected excerpts from a diary of his overseas experiences:

28 September 1944 -Left States from Hamilton Field, California at 10 p.m. We flew over.

29 September-Arrived Hickam Field in Hawaii. Stayed there about three hours. Went to town (Honolulu).

30 September-We were in Tarawa at 8 p.m. then took off for Guadalcanal and then to Nadzab, New Guinea.

1 October-Arrived Nadzab at 10 a.m. Kept busy all day moving around.

2 October-Reported in to Far Eastern Air Force Headquarters.

3 October-Started our training which consisted of gunnery and jungle schools.

19 October-Pulled our first mission today over Wuyaik AD. Dropped eight 1,000 pound bombs. Took off on three engines. No ack-ack or interception.

21 October-Moved to Noemfoor Island to be assigned to our outfit.

22 October-Reported to Air Force Headquarters on Noemfoor.

23 October-Received our assignment to 13th Air Force, 5th Bombardment Group, 23rd Bomb Squadron.

27 October-Outfit moved to Morotai this morning. Before we set up our tent we were given orders to dig our foxhole.

30 October-We have been on this island two days and they are still battling the enemy up the road about five miles.

31 October-Set up the orderly room tent today. Had another air raid tonight. We've had an air raid every night since moving up here on Morotai - not much damage done.

1 November-The Squadron flew its first mission from this island today. Had another air raid tonight. Made Sgt. today.

3 November-Our squadron and the other squadron flew today. Our squadron lost three air planes today over the Philippines. Had an air raid tonight.

4 November-Our group flew another mission today. All went well. We still haven't flown. Another air raid tonight.

5 November-Was questioned today about engineering. Passed everything O.K. Had an air-raid again tonight.

6 November-Reinforced our fox hole. Air raid tonight. Suffered light losses, four planes.

7 November-Flew our first mission with our outfit. Attacked by twelve zeros shot down four. Lost two B-24s from our squadron. Had air raid before take off.

11 November-Mission: Negros Island. Hit A/D. Number 3 engine cut out then we got it back. No fighters or ack-ack. Had top cover. Lost no ships.

16 November-Mission Shipping off Borneo. Lost five of our six ships. We got shot up by flack but made it home - the only ones from our squadron.

18 November-We got six new airplanes in our squadron today. We got a new one because they had to junk our other one. Dick Finch was getting his leg treated.

21 November-Mission: Lumbia A/D on Mindanao. No ack-ack, no enemy fighters. All came back O.K.

24 November-Mission: Alicante A/D Negros Island. Two zeros attacked but our P-47s shot both down. All came in O.K. Made S/Sgt.

26 November-Mission: Talisay A/D Negros Island. Dropped eight 1,000 pound bombs and destroyed this A/D. No opposition whatsoever.

27 November-Air raid destroyed eight B-24s. Seven enemy bombers came over - three went back. Since we moved to Morotai Island we have had air raids every night with the exception of two or three. It was raining those few nights otherwise we would have had air raids then too. Sure was annoying getting up in the middle of the night and spending four or five hours in foxhole. They didn't do much damage, except one or two times. They were called *nuisance* raids. I got more foxhole time in this month than flying time. That's war for you, I guess.

1 December-Mission: Fiabica A/D Negros. A few zeros attacked but were turned off by our fire. All came back O.K.

3 December-Mission: Munda A/D Celebes. Landed in Neumfoor. Attacked by Zeros but our 38s took care of them. Stayed in Noemfoor.

5 December-Mission: (from Neumfoor) Halmshanns - eight miles from Morotai. We were supposed to hit an A/D up in the Philippines. It was socked in so we came back and hit one at Malmahaias.

6 December-Two planes cracked up on take-off from Neumfoor yesterday. It was raining.

8 December-Mission: Tapul A/D on Panay Island. Dropped eight 1,000 pound bombs on the strip. No interception or ack-ack

11 December-Mission: Panay Island. A few Zeros attacked Our 38s took care of them.

14 December-Mission: Carolina A/D Negros Island. Saw our P-47s knock down Zeros. We encountered both fighters and ack-ack. No one was shot up.

17 December-Mission: Jolo A/D Jolo Island. No interception or ack-ack. Excellent bombing. Knocked out this A/D.

21 December-Mission: Bacolod A/D Negros Island Dropped twelve 500 pound bombs. Excellent bombing. No interceptions or ack-ack.

24 December-Mission: Kndot A/D Borneo Island. No interceptions or ack-ack. All came back O.K.

25 December-Christmas. Got up at 10 a.m. Went to dinner and had turkey. Attended Mass last night after mission.

27 December-Mission: San Jose A/D Panay Island. Knocked out this A/D. No interception and no ack-ack.

31 December-Played the 394th Squadron in softball. We won 9 to 2. In the month of December we had air raids about 20 nights out of 31. This wasn't as bad as last month. It sure is annoying as hell though. It's getting so we don't even get out of bed after we hear the alert go off. Sure wish I were home now

6 January 1945-Mission: Nicholas A/D Luzon Island near Manila. Awakened at 12:45 a.m. and took off at 3 a.m. We encountered heavy ack-ack.

8 January-Mission: Nicholas A/D Luzon Island. Plenty of ack-ack. We got holed again but nothing serious. 307th Squadron lost one plane.

11 January-Mission: San Jose, Luzon Island. Went after personnel. This aided our boys who made a landing up there. Ack-ack was accurate.

15 January-Mission: Jesselton A/D Borneo. Encountered a few fighters but drove them off. All came back O.K.

18 January-Informed we are leaving for Sydney tomorrow.

17 February-Returned to Morotai from Sydney, Australia this morning.

19 February-Mission: Misa A/D Borneo. No fighters or ack-ack. Last mission flown from Morotai.

21 February-Took off from Morotai to move to Samar Island in Philippines.

26 February-Mission: Japanese personnel on Mindanao. Had good bomb hits.

2 March-Mission Sandakan A/D North Borneo. No fighters or ack-ack.

6 March-Went after Jap personnel on Mindanao. No interception or ack-ack.

9 March-Mission: Zamboango Town in Mindanao. One of our ships blew up in air over target.

15 March-Mission: Lahing A/D on Mindanao. Bombed at 4,000 feet lowest we have bombed. Bad weather. No interception or ack-ack.

18 March-Mission: Alicanti A/D Negros Island. No fighters or ack-ack.

22 March-Cebu - Target #15. No fighters or ack-ack.

23 March-Cebu - Target #17. We led squadron again. Good bombing 100percent on target.

30 March-Mission: Bangao Town, Bangao Island. We led the squadron. Good bombing.

6 April-Mission: Japanese personnel on Cebu Island. Aiding our boys to overtake Cebu Island. Good bombing.

8 April-Mission: Japanese personnel on Cebu Island to aid troops.

9 April-Mission: Same as yesterday. Japanese personnel on Cebu.

16 April-Today is my birthday. Was supposed to fly but it was cancelled.

17 April-Mission: Cebu Island. Recon. mission. Landed on Cebu. Had trouble. Stayed all night.

18 April-Still on Cebu waiting for part to be flown in.

19 April-The starter came today. Installed it and took off at noon for base.

21 April-Mission: Recon. on Cebu Island. Guided fighters and other attackers into target.

24 April-Mission: Miri Town in Borneo. Good bombing. Started numerous fires in warehouses and supply dumps.

30 April-Received a Christmas package today.

2 May-Mission: Recon. to Mindanao. Photographed the whole west, south and east coast. I flew as Inst. Engineer on the crew.

3 May-The rest of the crew is flying today with our ex-copilot (now Pilot). McDowell is grounded.

9 May-Mission: Mindanao. Bombing enemy installations. Excellent bombing results. No interception.

12 May-Mission: Labuan A/D North Borneo. Excellent bombing. No fighters or ack-ack.

15 May-Mission: Mira A/D North Borneo. Good bombing. No interception. Bad weather over and back.

22 May-Mission: Bitulnu Supply area - Borneo. Good bombing. No interception or ack-ack. LAST MISSION. Total combat hours: 419.45.

28 May-Started work in operations office. Will work there until my orders come.

12 June-Heard today that our orders are out and we will be leaving tomorrow.

13 June-Left Samar for the U.S.

DISASTER AT BALIKPAPAN

By: Bill S. Schmidke

Glad you called. I would like to keep in touch with you and Gigi, also Jonesy. I wrote to him a couple of times, but he only answered once then stopped. Hope he is still alive. We would be doing pretty good with four of us old tent mates still around. Of the nine men who were on that last Balikpapan mission with me, only three of us are alive. Elvin Comstock is in Stuart, Florida. I haven't heard from him in quite a while. Maybe I should drop him a note and see if he is still alive! Theron Borup, our tail gunner, is a Morman Missionary and lives in St. George, Utah. Six of us came out of that ordeal alive and well. I was the only one hit — shrapnel wound above my right eye, but not real bad, just bled a lot. Tom Farley (top gun), Jim Menzie (Ball Gun) and Jim Elder (Bombardier) have died since. I was flying extra that day, on Major Pierce's crew, Menzie and Borup were really the only guys I was really acquainted with. I flew a number of missions with Pierce, but didn't really buddy around with the Major. I believe that was why I was assigned to his crew that day, because of the missions I flew with him. I was assigned to the nose gun that day; I went down to the strip the night before and was checking my turret out. It was a new ship, still silver electric turret, which had me thinking. I had never operated one before. Roy Surface from Belgrade, Montana was assigned to the waist; he came down to the strip also. On his regular crew he was the regular nose gunner. He asked me to swap guns for that mission, so I said OK. Most of my missions were in the nose. What I didn't like about that position was that the bombardier had to open the doors to let me out and I never trusted the bombardier (I flew with a lot of different ones). Flying in a strange (electric) turret and someone else's bombardier just didn't sit right with me, so I didn't hesitate when Roy asked to swap. We didn't tell Pierce; we just traded. I always felt funny about that. I knew Pierce wanted me in the nose. Oh well, that's fate especially when that Jap *Jack* came in at about two o'clock, and the nose guns jammed. One gun jammed, and the other was out of ammo. That was really a battle, flak was bursting all around us and the Jap fighters were attacking right through their own flak which was very unusual. I guess they were getting desperate. I was in the left waist and Comstock was in the right. Everyone was firing. I counted 15 fighters high at 11 o'clock, just sitting up there trying to draw our fire; they were just out of range. I just threw a few tracers at them to let them know I was aware. Comstock on the right side was firing merrily away. I took a glance out his window, and there was a Jap fighter — I believe it was a Raven, just sitting about three or four hundred yards at about three o'clock looking over at us. Commie was firing at him, and you could see tracers bouncing off his ship. I don't know why the guy sat there or why he didn't go down. I guess he had a lot of armor on him. Then the Bombardier, Elder, starting hollering here he comes, here he comes etc. Surface yelling his guns are out, then boom. My headset flew off, and everything turned blue. I could smell powder, and my waist window got bigger. I thought a 20 mm hit the corner of it. Menzie came up out of the ball, and Borup came barreling out of the tail looking really scared. The tail was vibrating real bad; I was more or less stunned. I thought I was sweating, took off my oxygen mask and wiped my arm across my face. That's when I knew I was hit; I had blood all over me. Farley (Top gun) opened the door from the bombays and asked for a raft. I reached around and gave him one; he left. Commie told us that Pierce said for us to hold our position and that we were going to bail out over our rendevous point. We had two engines (Number 3 and 4) out. One was burning, and the other windmilling. So we just waited; I helped Menzie put his harness on, strapped on his chute and got a 1-man raft for him. Everything got real quiet; no Jap planes around us; no flak. I had my harness on, so I put on my chute and went to put on my raft, but couldn't find one. The other two, Commie and Theron, were all hooked up, so I told them I was going up front to get a raft. Menzie had assured me that I wasn't hurt bad. I started up through the bomb bays which were partially open. I couldn't make it through the racks with all my stuff on, so I walked around them. I had my chute under my arm, got to the front, looked under the flight deck, and didn't see anything there. So I looked on the flightdeck, under the Nav table, under the radio table, then in the cockpit. It was then I realized; no one was there. The plane was on auto, and everyone in the front had gone out! Believe me, Charley, that was really a moment of truth. There were still three guys back in the waist, and there I was up front, with that B-24 dipping to the right and burning with two engines gone and no pilot! I can't remember just how I got back to the waist, but I did. When I told them Menzie and Borup went out the rear bomb bays, but Comstock wouldn't believe me. I didn't want to go before him without a raft. Finally I convinced him, and he went out the camera hatch with me right after him. I had my hand on my ripcord when I went out, and my head hit the edge of the door. The next thing I knew I looked up and there was my chute above me, the ripcord in my hand and a Jap fighter coming right at me. He didn't fire. Below me was another chute. Off at about 12 o'clock our plane just dropped into the ocean and blew up. I was trying to loosen my harness, but I couldn't. I thought sure that they would come back and strafe. I was going to drop if they did. There were about five fighters buzzing around the B-24, and they never came back at me. I hit the water, and my chute fell away from me real nice. I inflated my Mae West, but it wouldn't hold me up because of my heated suit. I took the suit off and dropped my shoes. In the meantime, I realized that was a real mistake because my feet got burned pretty bad by the sun. Anyway, here I am floating around in Makassar Straits with no raft and blood all over me. It was real choppy, so I guess that's what kept the sharks away. I imagine I floated for about 45 minutes to an hour before I spotted Comstock and got in his raft. This was about 10 or 11 in the morning, and we floated together for a couple of hours and came across Borup. We tied our rafts together. Then about five or six o'clock we saw a big Jap hospital ship. It was real close but didn't see us. The Sub (Mingo) was actually tracking it and thinking about sinking it. But decided not to. They were looking for us all the time. When it got dark, we thought we saw something big slither past us. We didn't want to take any chances; we had a light that would work! The next morning we saw something way off to the south of us; it was Menzi. He came paddling up to us as unconcerned as if he was out for a boat ride; he still had his pipe and hat and holes in his raft. He kept blowing it up all night and stuffing his shirt in the holes because he couldn't swim! About two o'clock in the afternoon we spotted Farley off to the north of us. Right after that came across Capt. Elder. He was

real sick because he swallowed a lot of salt water. Then we tied our rafts together and waited. Farley and Elder told us what happened. Farley pulled a long delayed jump, and the Japs never did see him. Jim Elder pulled his ripcord real fast and hung up high. The Japs didn't see him right away. The other four pulled medium jumps, and the Jap fighters thoroughly strafed them — according to Farley. Then they spotted Elder high above them and strafed him. They missed but hit his chute, and he started falling real fast. They made another pass at him and missed again. He hit the water hard, and the Zekes made a pass at him and missed! He played dead, and they left. Us guys in the back figured that this was why they didn't shoot at us. We had a long fight with them, and then they expended a lot of gas and ammo strafing. Then I decided to go up front and get a life raft — otherwise we would have gone down with the ship. I actually watched the plane hit the water, and the Jap fighters diving around it. They were probably taking pictures for the newsreels in Tokyo! Everyone (of us six) came through fairly well; I was the only one actually hit and it was minor but messy. Elder was very sick from swallowing so much salt water; he threw up the whole three days we were out there. The water was rough and choppy the whole time. It was real hot in the daytime and real cold at night. We were wet always and thirsty. All we had was a halfpint of water and a couple Kraft carmels. We were really glad when it rained the third day early in the morning. We caught the rain in our drift anchors and silk escape maps. The second day was fairly uneventful except for the Jap patrol planes and the high waves. The planes were up pretty high, and I don't think they were looking for anything in the water. We saw a couple native sail boats off in the distance, but they were too far away to see us.

The next day (third) started off pretty exciting. It was the second raid, and the 307th went in first. One of their planes was hit and dropped out of formation. The Japs were giving it problems, and when our group caught up, they dropped down and covered them until they got out of range and bailed out over the rendevous point (Celebes). We threw out our sea marker (dye) hoping they would see it. They did, but the Sub still couldn't find us. They knew the exact location of the 307th plane. In the meantime this Jap boat came toward us from the north and stopped for some reason about 500 yards off and just sat there. We sweated that out for almost an hour and a sea gull kept circling our rafts then flying over and doing the same thing to the Jap boat. Still they didn't see us. Then the boat got up steam and took off for the south. Just about when the sun was going down, we heard loud explosions to the south of us and saw a lot of smoke on the horizon. Then we saw something dark heading east out of that melee, and we figured it was a sub. We flashed our light (which was still working), but it turned and headed south. We were really disheartened. We then spent a cold, wet night. The next morning about 10 a.m. we saw this boat coming at us, and for a while, we thought they were Japs until we saw the white boats and the flag on the Sub. What a feeling. They were headed north to pick that 307th crew that went down the day before. They had practically given up on us.

There is more to this story. I'll write about it another time. We were on the Sub 11 days. They took us to their base in Perth, and we stayed at the King George Hotel with them for 12 days. We lived like royalty with great food, girls, and everything. Then we flew around Australia to the 85th Sta. Hospital in Brisbane. We were there for about three weeks, and then we went to Townsville by train. They put us in a transient camp and told us to stay put until they provided transport to our outfit. In the meantime Menzie ran across Capt. Dougherty who told us to get our things and meet him at the strip. He was returning from rest leave. How's that for an adventure!

While we were at the 85th Sta.Hospital in Australia we were with a group of Philippino Guerillas who had been evacuated for security. They were part white, and the Japs put out death warrants on them. What a great time we had talking to them. There were also a couple American soldiers who had escaped from the Death March and a couple of German priests who were actually our prisoners. They were actually German citizens who were missionaries. They ate, slept, and played right with us. They just couldn't leave the hospital, but I don't think they wanted to. The food was the best they had ever seen for a long time. Actually there were three of them, two priests and one *Brother*. The brother was a missionary of a Leper Colony. When the Japs found out it was a Leper Colony, they left. Right after that our B-25s sent in a strike, and the brother was wounded real bad. We found that out and sent in a PT Boat and brought him out. He was still not recovered when I left the Hospital. He was about 60 years old at the time.

Well, Charley, you tired of reading? Guess when I get started, I just don't stop. I'm really interested in that mission where those guys were picked up by the head hunters. Right after I came home, our newspaper had their story in a series for a whole week. I should have kept it, but didn't. I've been trying to find it in our library, but have had no success. If you would send it to me I would be forever grateful. That was some adventure. I'd like to show it to my children and grandchildren (all 12 of them). The guys who had our escape papers were killed, so if we had made land, we would have been in real trouble. Well Charley, write when you can and tell Gigi I said hello, and you write if you can.

LAST FLIGHT OF 'LIL JO TODDY'

By John Wylder

Just what did happen to the plane and crew of that famous B-24 Bomber *Lil Jo Toddy* (All A — No Body) on that ill-fated mission to bomb the Alicante Airdrome at the northern tip of Negros Island, P.I. of 1 November 1944? Well, I can tell you, as I was the Bombardier on that mission, Lt. John M. Wylder. On 31 October 1944, the Lt. Martin Roth crew boarded a C-47 transport airplane on Noemfoor Island, New Guinea and were flown to Moratai Island with our tent and all of our gear to our new base of operations. Arriving at around 1600, we landed at the airfield and began the usual long drawn out wait for transportation to our 23rd Bombardment Squadron location. It has always seemed odd to me that an aircrew had a big heavy bomber to fly around in and get shot at, but the only time we could ever feel sure of getting a ride on the ground was when we were going to fly a mission, in which we were picked up at our tent and driven to our assigned airplane, otherwise we walked, unless we could bum a ride.

We were finally picked up and driven to the 23rd Bombardment Squadron and assigned a place to pitch our tent. We dropped off our gear beside the road and were taken to the mess hall for dinner, which was probably Spam. During dinner, our crew and six other crews who made it up from Noemfoor that day were informed that we would be flying early next morning to bomb supplies at Alicante Airdrome on what was to be a milk-run, getting in an easy mission before our much needed rest leave in Sydney, Australia. This would be our 18th mission. Having no place to sleep, we slept on benches in the mess hall.

We were picked up at around 0430 and taken to the plane *Lil Jo Toddy*. We took off at 0700 and proceeded to our rendez-vous point at a little island named Basilan, just south of the big island of Mindanao, P.I. We circled around for perhaps a half hour and were informed that the other twenty-one B-24 Bombers from our 5th Bombardment Group had been rained out and wouldn't make this mission, so we proceeded to our target without them. After all, it was only a milk-run to bomb supplies. It seemed that the Japanese would fly to the western Philippines from China, land, refuel, load up with bombs and ammo, then proceed to bomb the MacArthur landing in Leyte Gulf and take off for their home base. When our fighters and bombers went looking for them they couldn't be found. I remember our Navigator, Lt. Albert Klein informing me over the intercom that we were at the southern end of Negros Island, P.I. and headed north to our target. Our pilot, Lt. Martin Roth, liked to have the navigator up with him, hence he wasn't up in front with the bombardier, which was the normal location on a B-24. About this time our gunners had taken their normal combat positions and were checking their guns. S/Sgt. Dennis Jones, in the front turret, couldn't get the outside door behind him on his turret closed, so I had to use a hammer and a screwdriver to bang it shut behind him.

It was a beautiful day, and while flying along the west coast of Negros Island, I saw the first concrete paved road since Honolulu. It was a short flight and was like flying from San Diego to Santa Barbara. Upon arriving at our destination at an altitude of 18,000 feet, we couldn't see our target due to the cloud cover, so our flight of seven planes circled around and dropped down to 17,000 feet. On our bombing run, all hell broke loose. There were about 20 Japanese Zeros, Tonys, etc., fighter planes already in the sky, with a large number of their planes on the runway taking off. During the first pass at our plane from above, our number 3 engine was shot out. It began smoking with oil streaming over the wing and running away. Marty immediately feathered the prop. At the same time, I felt like my heart was in my mouth and a cold sweat covered me, even though the temperature was freezing. I went back to the bombsight to finish the bombing run, dropping forty 100 pound bombs at fifty feet apart. That stopped most of the movement on the ground. On the bomb run, I saw several Zeros coming up underneath our plane, one of them shooting off three of the four posts which held the ball turret to the plane, stalling out under the turret. S/Sgt. Hal Douglas shot him in the face with two .50 caliber guns. Hal then climbed out of the turret, which tore loose from our plane. By this time, our pilot moved our plane forward and under the plane ahead to protect us from further attack. Then the plane ahead, flown by Lt. Sanders, was rammed down the cockpit by a Zero and only two fliers, both waist gunners, S/Sgt. Clyde Whitling and S/Sgt. Don Mix survived. The seventh plane in our flight, which was in the slot to the left and rear of us, flown by Lt. Pinks, was hit and spun into the sea with no one getting out. At the same time, in the rear turret of our plane, S/Sgt. Nicholas Mascetta was shooting down a Zero making a headon approach.

Never before had the Japanese fighter pilots ever made headon attacks at the ball or rear turrets as they were almost sure of being shot down. We found out later that these Japanese fliers were suicide pilots and were on their way to ram into the ships landing at Leyte. They weren't going to live anyway and just picked on our flight first, as we were an easy target. Meanwhile, S/Sgt. Jones was having a turkey shoot with his front turret. I started shooting three .30 caliber guns, one through the astradome, and one out each side window, firing over one thousand rounds. A .30 caliber machine gun fires much faster than a .50 caliber does. I would fire one gun until it got hot and quit, then grab another gun and do the same. There were plenty of moving targets, so I was kept very busy shooting. One by one,

June 1943. The Martin Roth crew of the Lil Jo Toddy. (l to r) Front row: Martin Roth, Harry Elgee, Al Klein, and John Wylder. Back row: Dennis Jones, Don Perri, Harold Douglas, Nick Mascetta, Don Kabisch, and Brad Galbraith.

all of our engines were shot out and our plane caught fire, the crew in the back jumping out to avoid the heat. I saw a Zero shoot out our number four engine from about 50 feet away, coming up from the rear so close that I could see the pilot's face. About that time, S/Sgt. Jones somehow got the rear door to his turret open and said that we should bail out. I was trying to reach the other members of our crew by intercom, which had ceased to operate since the wiring must have been shot out. S/Sgt. Jones and I observed that no one else was firing except the two of us. The first attack must have shot out the top turret besides having shot out the number three engine.

After shedding my flack suit and attaching my chest chute to my harness, I tried to hook on my one-man life raft, which was filled with survival supplies, to one of the lower rings on my parachute harness. The plane went into a violent dive and the "G" forces kept me from attaching it. With all of my strength, I got it within six inches from attaching it to the ring, so I dropped the raft and then proceeded to pull the two red handles attached to the nose wheel hinge pins, but only one side came loose. With the extra strength that God gives one in a survival crisis, I tore the other side loose and proceeded to try and bail out through the open doors. The force of the wind was so fierce (over 300 mph) that my feet blew back up so that I had to grasp both sides of the opening to jump. It then felt like a giant had picked me up and was violently throwing me backward for the first few seconds. As I began my free fall, there wasn't any sensation of falling. My whole life didn't pass in front of me, but I did think that my family would never know how our crew had done the best job they could. We had inflicted a mighty blow to our enemy, for which we were all trained. No pilot could have done a better job than Lt. Martin Roth in trying to protect our crew from harm. With all four engines shot out, a B-24 has the glid-

ing angle of a brick. I delayed pulling my ripcord too soon and becoming a target, until I was about 500 feet above the water. The chute opened with a violent jerk and then the water slapped me in the face as I went under for a few feet and then popped back up like a cork. I knew upon checking my two CO_2 cylinders on my Mae West that one was empty, but that wouldn't be a problem because this mission was only to be a milk-run. As soon as I hit the water, all of my cigarettes, my pipe and tobacco floated away as if my life-blood was suddenly leaving me. However, all of the survival training came back to me like hearing a tape recording of what to do. First, get out of your parachute, be calm, and keep on all of your clothing and shoes, as you will need them. Don't fight anything in the water. Suddenly, something grabbed the calf of my leg with a firm grip and then my natural reflexes took over. To hell with not fighting back anything in the water! Whatever it was, took off as I flailed in the water. The next problem was to get more air into my Mae West life jacket, as my nose was just barely out of the water. Loosening the air valve on one side and upon hearing a hissing sound, closing it and trying the other side and hearing another hissing sound, and then closing that valve. Just imagine trying to blow up a balloon with all of your clothes on and your nose just barely out of water, and see how you make out. Instant failure!

Now the reality of just how lonely the life of a flier is set in. If you were in the Army or Navy, at least you wouldn't be all alone. If you were on the ground or on the seas you would have a lot of other buddies alongside you, but now I was out here floating over 7,000 miles from home and all alone. When we were in Hollywood, pretty girls would whistle at fliers in our uniforms pinned with wings as we walked down the boulevard. Shortly after cursing my fate, I saw something floating on the water a long distance from me. Although I didn't know it at the time, it was my nose gunner S/Sgt. Dennis Jones who got out with his life raft. Every time he turned it over to the top side (yellow) those damned Jap fliers would take off over our heads from Bacolod Airfield and then he would have to turn it over to the blue side (the bottom) to keep from being straffed. It must have been several hours before he came along side of me, the two of us getting into the one-man life raft. Shortly thereafter, a flight of P-38 fighters straffed the airfield and that was the last of the Japanese flights. Jones and I tried paddling towards the safe side, away from the airfield, but we didn't know at the time, that a ten knot current made our efforts hopeless. I asked Jonesy if he was afraid of sharks. With a white face, he said that he wasn't. We also did not know at the time that this was the worse shark infested area in the Western Pacific. Sharks were all around us. It was sort of like being Daniel in the lion's den when God closed the lions' mouths. This day he closed the sharks' mouths. One of the sharks was so big that we thought it was a sub coming to rescue us.

A little later we saw an outrigger coming in our direction with what appeared to us as two civilians wearing short sleeved shirts and short pants. They stopped paddling and one of the men stood up and looked our way. I hollered out "Americano!" and they began paddling over to us. I had two knives and gave one to Jones, and told him to holler out anything if he thought that they weren't friendly, then to grab the nearest one to him and do away with him, while I did the same to the one up front with me. Although that would probably be like trying to do away with a crocodile, as they were a lot stronger than we were. The first man, who was smiling, placed me in the front of him, and S/Sgt. Jones in the back, in front of the other man. We were both on the floor of the canoe as they started to paddle away from Bacolod. Not a word was spoken and they just paddled awhile and then rested. I asked Jones if he knew what language they spoke and he said, "I think a little Spanish." All I knew was "senorita si taco, enchilada," which wasn't much use. I pointed towards Bacolod and said "Japanese?" He nodded in the affirmative and then I pointed to several other locations and got the same answer. I then pointed in the direction to where they were taking us, and he shook his head from side to side, meaning no. I asked Jones what he thought of these two. He said that the one up front with me looked OK, but the one back with him was very questionable, as he had the meanest face and wore a Japanese aviator's helmet. Salvador Lopez spoke out in English and said to me, "Sir, I have only been to the fourth grade, but then I get you on shore, some of the people there have been to Stanford and they speak English." I told Jones that I didn't know whether or not they spoke English at Stanford, but we would soon find out.

A little later, we were greeted by a sailboat with a crew who told us that they had seen us bail out and had prayed they would find us. We sent them out to look for other members of our crew while Salvador Lopez and his companion paddled us to shore to Guimeras Island. Before we had gotten out of the canoe, several hundred men, women and children were wading out to greet us, saying "Happy New Life." We asked where the Japanese soldiers were in the area. They told us that they were four kilometers over the hill. Then I asked them where we should hide, because we were worth ten thousand dollars dead or alive and that they would be killed if they helped American fliers. One of the Filipino elders said that if we had come half way around the world to save their country, the least they could do was die for us. What a statement!

Naturally, we wanted to live and be protected, and perhaps return home someday, but we couldn't truthfully feel that our two lives were worth a whole village of men, women and chil-dren being wiped out to save us. "We will all die before we let you get captured" they said -- and they meant it. They asked us if we were hungry, which we were, and they then made us a tremendous omelette with chopped onions and rice. I asked Jones what he thought our buddies back at Moratai were eating.

After eating fresh eggs for a change and resting for a while, we were taken to a large coconut grove that had been ripped apart by *Lil' Jo Toddy*, with engines, turrets, wings and tails strewn between the knocked down trees. What a mess! The plane was still smoldering. We didn't look for bodies, but found what was left of the IFF and took off before the Japs came to investigate. At dinner we were fed rice and barbecued chicken, which tasted great, even without the normal seasonings that we Americans are accustomed to. We learned to eat off banana tree leaves and with our fingers. But as we were hungry, we found out how to shovel the food even without first washing our hands. That was a real luxury when we could wash up.

Shortly after dinner, the sun set and everything went dark. There were no city lights to reflect from the sky, just darkness. We were taken upstairs of a little stilted bamboo palm leaf house and we had a coconut oil lamp for a small amount of light. Soon a guerrilla captain arrived, and as he hadn't eaten, he asked us if we'd like some more food. As he ate his dinner, we joined him. I was eating something that tasted pretty good, but I didn't know what it was until I got closer to the little lamp. I then figured out that it was a barbecued part of a chicken's intestine. After gulping a bit, I remarked to Jones it wasn't half bad. From then on, we didn't look too close at what we were fed. We were their guests and were most thankful for what we were fed. We had steamed brown rice three times a day, and sometimes rice cookies which were good and were fed fairly well for about the first two weeks.

Later that night, after we were almost asleep on straw floor mats, we were aroused by one of the guards outside, telling us that some more of our crew had arrived, which we were very excited about. They weren't from our crew. In fact, we didn't even know them, but we were happy to meet other members of the 23rd Bombardment Squadron. They were S/Sgt. Clyde Whitling and S/Sgt. Don Mix of the Lt. Sanders crew who had bailed out after a Jap fighter dove his plane into the cockpit of their plane. The next day we were still on the island of Guimeras for most of the day, meeting many people before taking a sail boat across Guimeras Strait, hidden out of sight below deck while we could see the Japanese soldiers on the beach as we went by on our way to a place near Iloilo City. We were met by Captain Gollez, known to the Japs as the *Terror of Panay*. To us he was a mild mannered soldier who wore a cowboy hat and eyeglasses. Of course, we weren't looking down the other end of his automatic rifle as an enemy. We had dinner with him. People (cooks, teachers, businessmen, etc.) were coming to meet us from Iloilo to find out what was going on in the outside world. Later that night we were aroused from sleep at about 0130 and told to leave as there was a compound of around 15,000 Japanese soldiers a few kilometers away. For our safety, we took off to the hills before someone told them that American fliers were in the area.

After several days, we arrived at Col. Chavez headquarters and met Ensign Bill Shackelford, who had proceeded us after crash landing and burning his plane. He had a few medical supplies and a yellow plastic cover, which was good for waving at planes who never seemed to notice. We were informed privately by some of the Filipinos that Shackelford didn't like rice, which was almost a sin to them. Col. Chavez was one of the first Filipinos to attend West Point. After spending about four days with Col. Chavez and his most gracious wife, we were sent on north

Above photos: January 1945. Binalbagan Sugar Refinery. Negros Island, P.I. This sugar refinery had been converted to alcohol production to fuel enemy war machines and aircraft. Main plant ablaze from bomb hits. The bottom photo was taken approximately 10 minutes after the top photo.

to Kalibo. We were given chickens, rice, sugar, homemade rice cookies, and fruit, which was carried by our guerrilla soldiers. As we said our goodbyes, thanks and salutations, departing down the path through the jungle, there were tears in our eyes; sort of like leaving your favorite aunt and uncle. After coming out of the jungle, we were walking on the perimeter mounds of the endless rice paddies with a guerrilla soldier walking in front of me with his automatic rifle cocked, set on fire and full automatic — slung over his shoulder and pointed directly at me. If I moved over to the other side, the rifle barrel always seemed to be pointing at me. S/Sgt. Mix, who had a good sense of humor, got quite a laugh about it until it happened to him. I sure hoped he would never stumble. Meanwhile, we were protected by other guerrilla soldiers fanned out on each flank. The guerrilla soldiers never had their guns on safety, which sometimes gave us an uneasy feeling with the way that they handled them, but after all, they were only kids and so were we.

During our travels on the Island of Panay, we spent most of the time on foot with a few boat trips. When we reached our final destination, we figured that we had walked about 150 miles over a period of some 20 days. Quite often we stopped to get something cool to drink. Often we were given a dipper made of half a coconut shell with a handle of bamboo, fastened to the shell with rattan. Everybody in the village drank out of the same dipper — not very sanitary — but we were so hot and thirsty, we could not refuse to drink. We were their guests and this was what was provided, so we drank gladly. However, we never drank to the bottom, as usually there would be something floating in the water, so we would throw the rest out and dip in for some more water. It often seemed to us that the Filipinos retained water like camels, for they were seldom thirsty. Our limit on coconut milk was one a day, or we would get diarrhea.

On one particular day, we were so hot and sweaty that we asked our guerrilla guides where we could get a bath to cool off. We were informed that in the next town there was a river in which we could bathe. Upon our arrival, the mayor, his family and all other public officials in the area, plus the whole town turned out. We asked to bathe first before getting introduced to everyone, as it would take a long time. We were taken by a canoe across the river, which was at least a good city block wide, to a sand bar. We proceeded to disrobe, and with our backs to the town folks who lined the shore, started to take our bath. It was very important that you took good care of the lousy soap made by the Japanese and colored orange to look like the popular Lifebuoy soap, as one bar would only do for two people before the whole bar disintegrated. Without any warning, suddenly the townspeople had gotten over to the other side of the river and we were being introduced to the mayor, his family, other officials, and the rest of the people while we were stark naked. The Filipinos weren't immoral, but just didn't worry about being modest. Many times we would be bathing in a river or creek, stark naked, and women would come down and start washing their clothes only ten feet away. As for going to a restroom, there weren't any, so one would watch out for the people who were always around just watching us all day and night, as we were the first white people they had seen in three years. No movie star ever signed more autographs than S/Sgt. Jones, S/Sgt. Clyde Whitling, S/Sgt. Don Mix and I. All of the time we were going north from place to place, we didn't always know why or our intended destination. The thought of being worth $10,000 dead or alive, we sometimes wondered if someone would turn us in for the money. After attending a court marshal of Captain Tomboken, accused of being a collaborator with the Japanese, we realized that anyone turning us in would be sought and killed by the guerrilla soldiers without mercy. This eased our minds.

When you are behind enemy lines, you are your own finance officer and can write checks of any amount to purchase your needs: food, guns, ammo, hire soldiers to help fight if necessary, purchase a boat, truck, car, or animal for transportation, or any other need. Just sign your name, rank, and serial number. Our Filipino helpers wouldn't take a dime for all of the help that they rendered to us. In fact, they even gave us Filipino *emergency money* to spend. After two days, we walked northwest to a place called Libertad. On the way we met a famous guerrilla leader named Col. Peralta as he made his way to another encounter with the Japs. Upon arriving at Libertad we met a number of Navy and Marine fliers and eight Filipino fliers from Luzon. They flew P-36 airplanes, which had only two .30 caliber machine guns for armament. When they ran out of ammunition they used their propellers to saw off the tails of the Zeros. How is that for flying? I guess that if you are trying to save your country, and the enemy was on your shores, you would go to extremes for survival.

At Libertad we were living in an area devoid of food, even in peacetime. Some of the Navy fliers would go out looking for any chickens and ask to purchase them. On being refused sale, they would shoot one and then negotiate its purchase. The farmers were mad, but we were hungry. About all we had to eat was brown rice and a piece of fish or chicken about the size of a silver dollar. Not much to eat for us young fliers, so we lost a lot of weight. Wish I could lose some weight now — but not under those conditions.

On Thanksgiving Day we were given the calf of a water buffalo to barbecue. Cut up in steaks, the meat looked good when you placed it on the grill, but when it was cooked it was as tough as a truck tire. Perhaps even tougher, as you couldn't even chew it. However, the thought was good and we were thankful for being alive, Americans and prayed for the Philippines, our country, victory over our enemies, and a safe return to the USA and our families.

On November 24, S/Sgt. Jones and I were awakened by a Navy flier at about 0500 with the news that a Japanese patrol boat was traveling along the shore. We could hear the rumble of the diesel engine as we were living in a stilted grass house only about 250 feet from the shore. After grabbing our shoes, we vaulted down the ladder and took off to the schoolhouse where the other fliers were living. In a short time, we engaged the enemy and victory was on our side as S/Sgt. Jones got a direct hit on a gasoline drum on the deck, causing a terrific explosion. Later the bell was taken from the boat and hung up at the school house.

Before eating breakfast early one morning, S/Sgt. Jones and I were discussing just what we would tell the relatives of our missing crewmembers, that is if we ever got home, when we were alerted by the ringing of the bell. One of the Navy fliers came running over to tell us that some members of our crew had just arrived. We were shocked but overjoyed to see S/Sgt. Nicholas Mascetta, S/Sgt. Harold Douglas, and T/Sgt. Don Perri. We had figured they were all dead. They knew that Jones and I were alive, but were always about a week behind us on our journey.

Libertad was also called Halsey's Harbor as US submarines came in with supplies every now and then, making this area secret and known only to a few guerrilla leaders. The local Filipinos in the area had to stay there and could not leave so as to protect the secrecy of the place. A coast watcher, with a radio transmitter and located in the hills, contacted the Army and Navy headquarters concerned with rescue operations. Each day they wanted to know the conditions of the men, serial numbers, birthplaces, and other vital information to ascertain our identity. We were informed that after an elaborate placement of signals, which could be seen through the periscope, that a sub would surface just as the sun went down at sunset.

We were taken aboard a large sailboat; 17 American fliers, eight Filipino fliers, and two Filipino civilians who needed medical help. Just as the sun set, up came that gray looking sub -- what a welcome sight! After being identified by the submariners, we were taken aboard the *USS Hake* (SS 256). We were in the harbor for only about 45 minutes as they unloaded supplies for the guerillas and then we were underway. "Take her down!" the command was shouted. We then dove down about 150 feet as glasses, dishes, and cups slid across the table, but not onto the floor because there is a raised edge to prevent that from happening.

The next day we were depth charged by Jap destroyers coming out from their base at Tawi Tawi. It was a little unnerving, to say the least, as we maneuvered to escape from being sunk. After that encounter, we stayed submerged for several hours and came up on top at night to recharge the batteries. We were always on top unless being attacked. Next day we were in the Macassar Straits, a small Mediterranean sea, with the Philippines at the north end, Java at the southern end, and between Borneo and the Celebes. No place to get caught if you don't want to get sunk. The British lost two battleships in these waters, The Prince of Wales and the Repulse. We were submerged to scope depth (85 feet) just off Balikpapan at 1200 when we heard "Now Hear This! ... Chow down refugees". Our friendly greeting as guests and not members of the crew.

I was in the forward torpedo room washing my hands for lunch when all of a sudden a Jap plane dropped a bomb on us while the officer at the periscope was making a visual sweep, but looking in the wrong direction to see the approaching plane. Lights went on and off, coffee cups shattered on the steel deck, cork fell from the ceiling, and the command was shouted, "Take her down and check for leaks!" I was stunned, but had the presence of mind to look into the mirror in front of me to see what one looks like under these extreme emotional circumstances. I can tell you that the color drains out of your face and your lips turn a grayish white. Now my Bombardier mind took over. If the enemy put an "X" on the chart and made circles of maximum distance each day, and for several days they would return and finish trying to sink the sub. Fortunately, we were not damaged and only lost the starboard antenna and were still under way.

Upon approaching the Lombok Straits in Java, we were submerged for sixteen hours and thirty-five minutes, coming up to surface at night. It was darker than the inside of a cat, thank God. We made a surface run at flank speed (the pedal to the metal), 28 knots and a four knot current in our favor, making a one and a half hour run on the surface running through a mine field. Everything was fine for the first 45 minutes when two Japanese patrol boats began converging on us, one on each side. Thank God we did not fire a shot, nor did they. We saw them on radar, but they didn't see us. We came out into the Indian Ocean where we could dive and maneuver for safety. The reason we were on top in the Lombok Straits was that the water was too shallow to be underneath.

Now we were heading southward to Perth, Australia through some really rough seas with 35 foot waves coming across the sub at one o'clock. Sometimes I was on top on the backside and when the sub rolled over 25 degrees, the crew would look back to see if I was still aboard.

Upon arriving at Perth Harbor, the Admiral came aboard by a pilot boat, bringing fresh milk for the crew. I never did like milk that much except with a piece of double chocolate cake, but others didn't share my feeling, since they loved milk. After being introduced to all of us refugees, he made the statement, "I guess that you fly boys will tell your buddies not to bomb any subs; just let the Navy know where they are and we will take care of them".

USS HAKE

By John M. Wylder, 2nd Lt., 23rd Squadron

To Whom it may concern:

Know ye, that the above named John Wylder, did, on a certain date, in a certain area, while hedgehopping and flathatting about in the *wild blue yonder*, in a flying machine, well knowing said machine to be of an unsafe and dangerous nature, allow himself to be most ignominiously and thoroughly shot down by the enemy, thus bathing in the ocean, being out of uniform the while; nor was it even yet Saturday night. Thus with feathers wet and wings temporarily disabled, he did so lower himself from the usual high plane occupied by *Airdales*, to use such lowly means of transportation as the sailboat, the dugout, the horse, and even in times of extreme stress and under the utmost duress, his own two feet in order to reach a certain heaven, where he did hide in the bush and upon the ground licking his wounds and soothing his injured vanity, while awaiting rescue.

Brother *Birdman* being neither of the nature nor in the vicinity to save the above clipped fowl, word was sent to the gallent men of the submarine service, in particular, to the men of the Mighty *USS Hake*, of the sad plight of their allies the aviators. Undaunted by the untold dangers of their mission the Men and Officers of the *Hake* rushed boldly to the rescue. After many great hardships and untold narrow escapes, too numerous to here mention, the *Hake* succeeded in effecting the safe recovery of this aforesaid *Zoom-boy*.

The above mentioned aviator, in return for his being plucked from the *very jaws of death*, did, then and there, commence, during transit to a great and friendly port, heckling his saviors in a most unseamanlike manner, by Lording it over all the good and true submariners, eating all the available chow onboard, using the softest sacks at all times of the day and night, and in many other ways, known only to those who fly, making himself generally obnoxious to all hands. Not until the generous members of the *Hake* had allowed their uninvited guest to share a terrific shellacking with bombs, by enemy airdales bent on the destruction of the aforesaid gallant Submarine, did this *Birdman* come down from the overhead, where he had been hovering for days and allow himself to associate with the mighty undersea men even, at times, suffering himself to say a few haughty words to his saviors. Nor, would he admit, even after having been checked out for 36 hours of submerged time, that the airplane is just a passing fancy and is certainly not here to stay.

Be it recorded, however; that the above named *Fly-Fly*, did, though unwillingly, serve, after a fashion, on board a submarine of *Uncle Sammy's Underwater Fleet*, namely the *USS Hake* (SS-256), in enemy controlled waters, from 5 December 1944 to 16 December 1944 inclusive, and did acquit himself well; that is as well as one might expect a clipped sparrow to acquit himself if forced to live in a sardine can emersed in a fish bowl.

The attention of all other aviators, with little or no submarine time to their credit, is directed to the foregoing facts and to the further statement that this particular *Birdman*, undaunted by the dangers of the deep, did dive bravely to 150 feet, and did cross under the equator at said depth. Furthermore, be it known that *all* aviators, regardless of rank and/or station will be expected to show at all times, when in the presence of the foregoing *Airdale*, the correct amount of deference to one of such priveledged character, and to uncover and bow deeply from the waist when spoken to by this much enlightened *Zoomie*.

THE CISCO KID IN WORLD WAR II

By S. Sidney Ulmer

Introduction

The first combat zone in which I served during WWII was Guadalcanal. I was a B-24 tail gunner assigned to the 31st Bombardment Squadron in the 5th Bomb Group, 13th Air Force. The first B-24 in which I flew after reaching Guadalcanal in May 1944, was The Cisco Kid, (Consolidated B-24D, Serial Number 42-40174).[1]

Because of my first encounter with The Cisco Kid, I have a natural interest in that plane and those who flew her. In May 1996, I attended a reunion of The 31st Bomb Squadron Association in Topeka, Kansas. There I met Jim Berry and Owen Carr, both of whom had flown in the Kid from Guadalcanal in 1943. Conversations with Jim, Owen, and other 31st veterans led to the discovery of several stories that I retell in the following pages. These stories focus primarily on the experiences of several B-24 crew members whose lives, for a while, were entwined with the life of The Cisco Kid.

The Original Cisco Kid

The original Cisco Kid was purchased by the United States government in 1942 for $297,627.00. The first pilot assigned to the plane was Jim Berry of Cisco, Texas.[2] The crew consisted of Leon Martin, copilot; Jethro W. Mock, Navigator; John (Ace) Hayes, Bombardier; Bill Kellums, Engineer and Waist Gunner; John Gilb, Radio Operator and Waist Gunner; Walter Rawleigh, Assistant Engineer and Top Turret Gunner; Owen Carr, Assistant Radio Operator and Nose Gunner; (later replaced by Alvin Stanley) Willis Butler, Ball Gunner; and Alden Campbell, Tail Gunner.

At the end of February 1943, the Berry crew completed their Third Phase B-24 Combat Crew Training at Clovis Army Air Base, Clovis, New Mexico. At that point, each enlisted man was given an additional stripe (from Sergeant to Staff Sergeant and from Staff Sergeant to Technical Sergeant). In early March, the crew was ordered to Topeka, Kansas, to pick up a B-24 (which later became the original Cisco Kid) and take it overseas. At that time, all crews were given seven days delay enroute orders to report to Topeka Army Air Base. However, the state of public transportation in 1943 was such that it was almost impossible for many of the men to travel to their homes for a brief visit and then get to Topeka on time. Yet it would be the last opportunity they would have before going overseas. Thus, many crews agreed among themselves not to arrive at Topeka on the appointed day — even though they knew it would cost them their stripes. Even some officers failed to report on time — possibly costing them some forfeiture of pay.

When a crewmember suggested to Jim Berry that they all agree to arrive late, Berry said: "Don't tell me about it, it will be a conspiracy. I'll see you when I get there." All but one of the enlisted men then arrived three days late. For their tardiness they were "busted" to privates. The one exception who had arrived on time was Bill Kellams.[3] So with the exception of Kellams, Berry left for the Pacific theater with a bunch of well-trained buck privates.

Considering all this more than fifty years later, the decisions of these men seem eminently rational. As it turned out, many of them saw their loved ones for the last time when they ignored their orders and showed up late in Topeka. One member of the Berry crew in violation of his orders was Alden Campbell, the tail gunner on the Cisco Kid. It would have been impossible for him to go from Clovis, New Mexico to his home in Maine and back to Topeka in only seven days. Campbell died in April 1944 when his plane crashed on take off from Los Negros in the Admiralty Islands. Other men, of course, returned physically or mentally altered. One must assume that they never regretted the judgments they made to visit family and friends in violation of their orders.

Jim Berry, from the small Texas town of Cisco, was a vital cog in all that happened to him and his crew while serving in the South Pacific in 1943-44. The qualities he possessed as a person and as a professional airman were, in my judgment, rarely matched by other personnel I encountered while serving in the same theater in 1944-45.

As a person, Jim was very solicitous of the needs and welfare of his crew. Al Stanley says that once, when coming off a mission to Bougainville, a large number of Zeros jumped Berry and his boys. Since bombs had already been dropped, Berry went off course in order to take advantage of cloud cover — thereby losing the Japs. When being debriefed back on Guadalcanal, General Matheny asked Berry: "Why did you turn away from the zeros and fly into that front. Why did you not stay on course and fight those Zeros?"[4] Berry replied: "Gentlemen, if you want to fly these missions, you ought to get a crew and go up there and fly them. I'm not needlessly going to put my men in a position to be killed." Jim does not recall this event, but it is so like the salutary qualities he exhibited in so many other instances that I am inclined to credit it.

Berry was also quite a wit. For example he says that while overseas and living in the jungles that served as encampment areas for the USAAF, he had two pairs of brogans. He would alternate them every other day since " ... if you wore one pair two days, the other pair would start to grow and the pair you wore would start to stink." He was also quite low key. Rarely excited. Took a lot to tick him off. For example, Berry flew combat with a gunner who would not fire his guns. When in combat, this gunner would sit at the radio table. The crew usually had an extra man aboard (photographer, radar man, intelligence officer or Squadron Navigator). This freed someone to fire the waist guns. Yet this *gunner* was allowed to remain on the crew throughout Berry's missions.

Al Stanley reports that he only saw Berry show irritation once in 44 missions. Jim recalls the occasion this way: On a mission to Rabaul

> ...Jap fighters came in about a thousand feet above us at 12 o'clock, and they all dropped phosphorus bombs that exploded some three hundred feet above us. White streamers of burning phosphorous fanned out like Fourth of July fireworks. Those chunks of burning phosphorous were intended to burn holes through our planes. Bomber Command devised a plan to discourage the little yellow bastards from continuing that pursuit. We would all go in abreast with all our nose guns and the top turret guns blazing. On that run Rawleigh, in the top turret, was firing straight ahead with muzzle blasts about a foot above my head. The vibration shook dust all over the flight deck, and the panel lights shook loose and dangled by their wires.[5] Stanley, in the nose turret was firing short bursts just like in gunnery school, where upon I shouted into the intercom: "Stanley, G... D... it, burn out those friggin

gun barrels. They've got plenty more where those came from." After that day, we never encountered any more phosphorous bombs.

Jim was equally impressive as a pilot and navigator. Since Jim was the son of a pilot who owned and flew a Travelair bi-plane powered by a World War I OX5, some of his flying skills may have been inherited. Yet, he had special qualities, as reflected in one decision he made while in training. A portion of pilot training time on the ground was spent flying on instruments in a Link Trainer. When actually flying the B-24, however, trainee pilots were forbidden to fly on instruments. A possible reason is that the Air Force, or its instructor pilots, wished to minimize the loss of planes and aircrews prior to going overseas. Recognizing the importance of instrument flying skills, Jim, in spite of the rules, flew on instruments every chance he got while aloft. Thus, he avoided the anxiety reported by some pilots who flew in a pitch black sky for the first time when they flew their B-24s from the States to Hawaii.[6] While overseas and flying with the 7th Air Force, Jim remembers a mission to Nahru with a night takeoff over water. It was so dark that visibility was zero, necessitating an instrument takeoff. The first plane off went into the drink. The second got off without difficulty. The third crashed into the ocean. While such incidents are unfortunate, they were not all that rare in the Pacific while I was overseas in 1944-45. Indeed, I know of one case in which a pilot in a night takeoff lifted off the runway, raised his landing gear and crashed back into the runway. The possible causes of so many crashes in night takeoffs are several.

As Jim Berry has pointed out, lack of instrument practice flying the B-24s in state-side training would be one possibility. For example, an inadequately trained pilot may fail to maintain the proper ratio between air speed and rate of climb on takeoff. Avoiding a stall by maintaining air speed is drummed into pilot trainees with so much intensity that paranoia sometimes results.

Taking off over water in pitch-black darkness may cause a pilot with inadequate instrument training to panic the first time he encounters such conditions. Concern about air speed may cause him to lower the nose of the plane in order to maintain or increase air speed. Yet, if he lowers it too much a crash is inevitable. In short, fear of stalling may cause an over compensation in rate of climb. Either error is likely to be deadly. Further complicating the picture was the common practice in the 31st Bomb Squadron of overloading bombers with extra gasoline. This was necessary in order to fly the distances required to reach many of our targets. Unfortunately, a pilot had no systematic way of knowing what the stall speed might be for the overloaded B-24 he might be flying on a given night. These long distances also meant that most takeoffs were very early and very often in the dark. So the problem was not insignificant. As for the B-24 that took off and crashed into the runway, one may surmise that the pilot raised the landing gear to reduce drag so that the air speed would pick up sooner; he then dropped the nose and ploughed back into the runway.

Because of his foresight in training, Jim Berry was, in the modern vernacular, not instrumentally challenged. That was one of many reasons why his crew loved and respected him. The crew considered him the best pilot in the 31st Squadron and often reported members of other crews wishing they had Jim Berry for their pilot.

As for navigational skills, the following story is quite revealing. Once Jim was flying from Hawaii with a navigator who made a wrong turn while looking for Johnston Atoll in the Pacific. The result was that he was then going away from the island. Jim quickly suspected error. He asked the Navigator "Where

the hell is that island?" The Navigator replied: "Jim, have confidence in me." But Jim was tuned to a dot-dash station of Johnston. He noticed that the farther they flew on the new heading the weaker the signals became. He had been taught in Link training that such an event meant one was going away from one's intended destination. But rather than make a big scene out of it he flipped off the automatic pilot, and did a 180 degree turn to resume the original course. The strength of the signal then increased. The Copilot said: "Sure hope to hell you know what you're doing." Jim replied: "I do too." But, of course, he knew exactly what he was doing. He eventually was able to contact Johnston Atoll, got the proper heading and made it in without further difficulty. The navigator knew what was happening but made no response. Once on the ground, Berry told this navigator to "Get as far back in the tail as you can get. I can take us back to Hawaii." Unlike the outbound trip, Jim had a beam back to Hawaii. So the return trip was navigationally uneventful.[7]

Prior to going overseas, Berry's crew could not have known all there was to know about Jim Berry. But they had certainly seen enough to know they liked what they saw!

Topeka To Guadalcanal
Acquiring Nose Art

Before leaving Topeka, Owen Carr and other enlisted members of Berry's crew decided to put some nose art on the plane to honor their pilot. They chose a figure of a Mexican cowboy in an enormous sombrero hat straddling a large bomb. A collection was taken, a ground crew mechanic-artist was located and the deed was done. Right beneath the painting, they put the words: The Cisco Kid. Jim Berry had a conversation with the man painting the Mexican cowboy on the plane and learned that he had been involved in doing the advertising for The Cisco Kid movie.

As it turned out, Jim was never all that fond of the painting. Today, Owen doesn't blame him. After all, the painting is not all that flattering to the Kid and it bears no resemblance to Caesar Romero who played The Cisco Kid so strikingly on the screen. At the same time, if *The Cisco Kid* implied to the Japanese who would later encounter him some of the qualities attributed to the Kid by O. Henry — the message would seem quite apt.

Given Jim's lack of fondness for the painting, one can't be too surprised to learn that he proceeded to paint (with yellow chalk) the words *Royal Texas Air Force* to the left of *The Cisco Kid*. There they remained until the matter came to the attention of some General, whose name cannot be remembered. He ordered the slogan removed. I suppose he didn't want the luck of the Alamo to contaminate the war effort of the U. S. in the Pacific Theater.

Goodbye Topeka

After leaving Topeka, Jim was ordered to take The Cisco Kid and its crew to McClellan Field in Sacramento, California. On the way, Owen Carr came up to the flight deck and said to Berry, "Any way we can go to Denver to see my mother?" Berry said "No" and Carr went on back in the plane. Jim then said to his engineer, Bill Kellums, "Find something wrong with the son-of-a-bitch." Kellums replied, "The number three engine is heating up a bit. Maybe we better go into Denver and fix it." So the Kid put down at Lowery Field in Denver and Carr got to visit his mother one last time before going overseas. He and the crew had a jolly time in Denver that night.

The next stop was Kingman, Arizona where Jim visited his brother — a pilot stationed there. Later that day, the Kid finally reached McClellan Field. After a few days in a hotel, during which time radio and other equipment were installed, Berry and his crew flew to Hamilton Field, outside of San Francisco. After one day at Hamilton — at 2300 hours on 5 April 1943. The Cisco Kid took off for Hickam Field, Hawaii. The trip took 14 hours and covered 2200 miles.

On the approach to Hickam a mistake caused the Kid to come in at John Rogers Airport, a civilian airport adjacent to Hickham. These two fields have since been merged to form Honolulu International Airport. Before it could take off from Rogers the Kid needed refueling. Since this was a civilian airport the U. S. Army Air Force, presumably, had to foot the bill. I am not aware that the crew had to reimburse Uncle Sam — but given the Army's propensity to collect for any lost or damaged GI issue, who knows?

The Hawaiian Period

While at Hickam, the Hawaiian Air Depot made several modifications in the Kid. These changes had been requested for all B-24s coming into the Pacific Theater by Lt. Colonel Marion D. Unruh, who later became C.O. of the 5th Bombardment Group. They consisted of installing a Sperry lower ball turret just forward of the waist windows, removing the tail turret and putting it in the nose, and placing a twin-fifties, hand held stinger in the open tail. By the time I reached the South Pacific in May 1944, all B-24s came with ball, tail, and nose turrets factory installed. But the desirability of nose and ball turrets was first determined by the airmen who were engaged daily in actual combat.

After modification the Kid and its crew were attached to the 7th Air Force at Kahuka Point on the other side of Oahu. From there the crew flew sea searches of ten to eleven hours; 800 miles out, then cross over for 150 miles, then back to Kahuka to complete the triangle. The purpose: to look for enemy submarines. Altitude for these searches was 500 feet. One word describes them: boring! Jim Berry would break the monotony by watching the flying fishes "...to see how high they would flop." Jim says: "It was a hard way to make a living."

During this period, Carr was sent to the Hickam Field Radio School, not surprisingly since he was the Assistant Radio Operator-Gunner on his crew. Owen remembers flying, on occasion, down to Hilo on Hawaii to pick up fresh vegetables. Having served a year in the Pacific in 1944-45 without fresh vegetables, I can easily understand why this particular memory has stuck with him so long.

Espiritu Santo

Since, after four or five weeks, The Cisco Kid and its crew were assigned to the 5th Bombardment Group (H), Owen did not get to complete his radio training. It was on to Espiritu Santo in the New Hebrides. Flying searches resumed. One day Owen volunteered to substitute for a sick gunner on another crew. Right before take-off, he was told he could not go because his own crew might need him that day. He had just started back to his bivouac area when he heard a loud thud! The B-24 in which he had volunteered to fly had crashed on take-off.

Owen and other members of his crew attended the funeral of nine airmen, including the pilot killed in the crash — John F. Epple. After the crash, Jim Berry told Owen: "Junior, (a name Owen picked up because he was only 18), you're dipped in s____!"

In spite of occasional tragedy, this bunch of privates believed in having their fun. While on Espiritu Santo, the Berry crew had a white female dog named Malfunction. One night the crew decided to have a *Big Push*. This involved everyone drawing a case of beer and putting it all in a tent. The floor of the tent

was two feet off the ground, thus requiring one to climb several steps to enter. Malfunction got so drunk that, after going outside to relieve herself, she could not get back up the steps, thereby living up to her name. The crew's condition was probably not much better since the party was still going on a 0300. At that point the word came that the crew would be flying a sea search before dawn. Jim Berry, at that very moment, was " ... as full of that Australian beer as [he] ... could get." But on two to three hours sleep Berry and his boys did their duty. The reader may guess in what condition!

Al Stanley Joins the Crew

It was on Espiritu Santo that Al Stanley joined the Berry crew. Stanley tells the story this way: He had been in the Pacific prior to the arrival of The Cisco Kid. He had been flying in B-17s in the 72nd Bombardment Squadron. At one point new crews began to arrive with more stripes than Stanley possessed. He was a Corporal while they were Staff and Technical Sergeants. Seeking equity, he requested promotion to the rank of the new crews. When his request was turned down, he was so ticked off he refused to continue flying.[8] In response, he was *busted* to buck private and assigned every dirty detail his officers could find. One of these was the so-called Mosquito Patrol. This consisted of spraying kerosene in various water puddles and other jungle sites scattered around the island. As for effectiveness, Stanley compares it to *pissing in the ocean*.

Another assignment was permanent KP in the Officer's Mess, a job he got by transferring from the 72nd Squadron to the Headquarters Squadron. In that job he thought he could begin to get his stripes back and eventually get the rank enjoyed by the combat crews without, as he put it, "Getting my butt shot off." While on this duty, the main cook in the Officer's Mess became ill. Stanley took over as temporary substitute. The officers liked his cooking so well that they gave him the job as cook. This job had some hidden advantages. For one, Stanley got to eat as the Officers did — in his words — *high off the hog* — fresh eggs, and chicken every Sunday instead of dehydrated eggs, Spam, Vienna sausages, stew, and C rations. In addition, he could hide food until late at night when he would invite some of his buddies from the 72nd over for an *officer's feast*. This was at a time when food for enlisted men on Espiritu Santo was quite deficient. It was "not uncommon for men at Espiritu Santo to enter the mess halls, look at the food, and walk out."[9] Even when the enlisted men's food was palatable, Owen Carr says that "...one had to battle the flies to see who would get the most." But, in any event, Stanley's *good deal* was not to last.

One night he went to the *Snake Ranch*, which was a clearing in a field with a few tables. Airmen and others would gather there to drink beer and shoot the bull. After drinking a few beers, Stanley says, one could then go back to his tent, take his *raisin jack* out of its hiding place (usually a fox hole) and drink to his heart's content. Or, if no raisin jack was available, get some deicer fluid and cut it with grapefruit juice. Either way the job would get done.

On this particular evening, Stanley sat at a table next to a bunch of guys who were complaining loudly about their misfortune. Prior to getting into combat, one of their original crewmembers, Assistant Radio Operator-gunner Owen Carr, had left the crew. They were anxious to start bombing and shooting down Japs — champing at the bit, so to speak. After a few beers and listening to the complaints, Stanley volunteered his services. Necessary approvals were obtained and he became the Assistant Radio Operator-gunner on The Cisco Kid in the 31st Bombardment Squadron.

Guadalcanal

In August, Berry's crew moved on to Guadalcanal in the Solomons. Shortly thereafter, Stanley H. Zyskiewicz (*Smitty*), of Captain William McKinley's crew, was killed instantly when hit by a 20 mm canon shell over Kahili Airdrome on Bougainville. After attending the funeral, Owen was assigned to the McKinley crew to replace Smitty as Radio Operator-Gunner on *Thumper*, the plane assigned to that crew.

The Bougainville Strikes

Owen Carr flew his first combat mission on Thumper on August 24. The target was Kahili Airdrome on Bougainville. However, weather prevented Thumper from reaching Kahili and bombs were dropped on Rekata Bay, the secondary target. While a few shots from Jap anti-aircraft gunners came up, (not too close) no fighter interception appeared.

On August 26, the Berry crew was not slated to fly but the McKinley crew was scheduled to strike Kahili Airdrome again. This would be Carr's second combat bombing mission. The Commanding Officer of the 31st Bombardment Squadron, Colonel Joseph C. Reddoch Jr., decided to go along — using The Cisco Kid. He had been checked out earlier in the Kid by Jim Berry. The Bombardier on the McKinley crew was Donald B. MacAllister who was already gaining a reputation for hitting the targets assigned him. That may account for Reddoch's decision to ride with McKinley and his boys.

Carr and Nerstad Hit

Although major fighter cover had been expected, only four Corsairs and three New Zealand P-40s went along. Reddoch's plane took the lead, dropping forty 100 pound demolition bombs on the target. Then all hell broke loose with 75 Zeros in screaming dives all around the formation. They came with a vengeance! After getting off only a few rounds, Carr was hit in the leg by a 20 mm shell from the wing cannon of a Zero. The shell exploded on contact with the Liberator, taking off a large chunk of the fuselage. He felt, he says, "... as if my left leg was being torn to shreds." That is about what was happening. As he fell to the floor, the other waist gunner, Harold Nerstad called over the intercom: "You better send someone back. They got Carr and me."

Don MacAllister Responds

MacAllister, the Bombardier, was also the first aid member of the crew. In response to Nerstad's call, he came back immediately. He could not begin first aid right away as he had to take over the waist guns to fend off the Japs who were still attacking as if there were no tomorrow. Turning from one waist gun to another, MacAllister kept the waist fifties hot. And Carr was feeling the heat as the hot, empty 50-caliber shell casings from the right gun kept hitting him in the face. While MacAllister shot at Japs, he kept feeling Carr pulling on his leg and begging for morphine, a Hobson's choice to be sure; damned if you do and damned if you don't! As soon as possible, MacAllister turned to see about his wounded comrades. He proceeded to place a tourniquet on Carr and to give morphine — 1/4 grain syrettes — three before getting back to base, the last plane to land at Henderson Field on Guadalcanal.

Don also had the presence of mind to pin the three empty vials to Carr's electrically heated suit so the medics would know how much morphine had been administered. According to the medics at Henderson, this was critical information since, in their judgment, one more vial would have been fatal.

While Don was placing the tourniquet on Carr, Nerstad was lying with his back to Carr. Nerstad had gone down saying he had no feeling in his legs and couldn't move. Don examined Nerstad but could find no damage. After return to base, it was discovered that the nose fuse of a 20 mm shell had severed Nerstad's spine. Since nothing could be done for him on Guadalcanal, he was sent by hospital ship to New Zealand. Unfortunately, he did not survive and was buried in New Zealand. Eventually, his body was disinterred and returned to the United States.

Before landing, MacAllister tore open a parachute to make cushions for his wounded buddies in the event of a crash landing. As it happened they did not crash. The hydraulic system, along with the mechanism for raising the Sperry ball turret, was shot out over Kahili. Since a Liberator cannot land with the ball turret in the down position, this presented a quandary. The landing gear had to be cranked down and the ball turret up-both by hand.

The gear presented no major problem but the ball turret was another story. Gravity helped in the first case but was a significant enemy in the second. Don MacAllister, Bill Krimer, the tail gunner, and Colonel Reddoch had to work for a considerable length of time before the task was accomplished. On landing, Carr was lifted out through a waist window. Though out of his head by this time, he still remembers Jim Berry standing beside the plane as the medics removed him and rushed him to the 20th station tent hospital.

Carr in Surgery

The hospital was in a very rough setting — but fairly well equipped with the essential medical items. As for the operating room, Owen has described it this way:

The operating room of the hospital was a Quonset hut with a concrete floor in the front portion and a tile floor in the rear where surgery was performed. The temperature in the hut was 98 degrees Fahrenheit and a large pedestal fan was circulating the air. I remained in the operating room for 48 hours. During the first 24 hours I was given four pints of whole blood and six pints of plasma, and they continued pumping blood and plasma into me for about a week. My red blood count was at the very dangerous level of about one-half million. I was truly on the brink.

But, he goes on, I was extremely fortunate in having an excellent surgeon, Major Patrick J. Nagle, work on me. Members of my crew were asking the doctor to try and save my leg while I was screaming at him to 'cut the damn thing off'. In my condition I falsely believed that by cutting off the leg they would also cut off the horrible pain. Anyway, they had no choice as dry gangrene was moving up from my toes at about two inches per hour. I remember clearly Major Nagle pulling the lamp cord over my table, staring down at my leg, and saying to another doctor, "We better get to work on this man." The next thing I remember was a sharp instrument cutting into my thigh. I screamed and sat straight up. After that, I remember nothing until I woke up in a tent ward. I told the attendants that I had to get back to my squadron and started to get up. They pushed my shoulders down.

The leg had been removed at or near the hip joint.

One *essential* item the hospital did not have was good food. But it mattered little for at that time Carr had no appetite. His weight proceeded to drop from 120 pounds to a mere 90. At one point, medics offered Owen whiskey to improve his appetite, but he couldn't drink it. So a couple of the ward boys got a windfall, but not before arguing over who should get the ration. Another time, a Chaplain, who visited regularly, asked Owen what he would like to eat. The answer: "fruit cocktail." But, of course, he might as well have asked for a ten course meal prepared by the finest chef in Paris. Fruit cocktail would have been a real luxury in that place at that time. Yet, it was obtained, eventually, from an aircraft carrier. A kindness Carr has never forgotten.

Recuperating in the Tent Ward

The floor of the tent in which Owen recuperated was concrete poured over coconut logs. Beneath the floor was a dugout bomb shelter for the patients in the ward--three at this time. And air raids they had — several while Carr was in the tent. The Japs were quite fond of night strikes. When they came, the ward boys would move the patients into the dugout which was lit by two or three candles so patient care could be given if needed. Carr hated the dugout and having to be moved into it, but he recognized the necessity.

While recuperating in the tent ward, Owen received two more memorable visits: an unnamed Non-Commissioned Officer and Eleanor Roosevelt, the first lady of the United States. The NCO came bearing a gift one day before Owen's 19th birthday. Carr describes it this way:

> [He] ... brought me a very small, cheap cardboard box and asked that I sign for it, which I barely managed to do. The NCO then left. Inside the small box was a small piece of colored cloth and a piece of cheap, painted metal. On the outside of the box was a sticker with the words Purple Heart printed on it. I guess it was some sort of birthday present.

Obviously, this is not the way Hollywood portrays the presentation of Purple Hearts. But it does remind one that war is hell behind the scenes as well as up front and on camera. A different kind of hell but just as personal.

On 17 September 1943, Carr received a visit from Eleanor Roosevelt, who came through on a B-24 with a large entourage. All facilities on Guadalcanal at that time were quite primitive. How primitive is well illustrated by Billy Wilson, the 31st Operations Officer. Since there was no flush toliet on Guadalcanal, an aircraft was sent to New Caledonia to procure one. On return to Guadalcanal, the toliet was plumbed into a Quonset hut serviced by two oil drums fastened to a coconut tree. Wilson also was ordered to stand down an aircraft with a select crew as a backup for the first lady's B-24. So, a plane and crew that might have flown a mission with the 31st that day sat on the ground during the first lady's visit.

In visiting Guadalcanal in 1943, the first lady took considerable risk. Yet Owen's memory is not about the first lady's courage. It is about a story she told him, in good faith, undoubtedly, to cheer him up — i.e., the old story of a young man she had met who had one leg but was *a wonderful dancer*. Owen says that practically everyone he has met has a similar story — one he has heard ... *at least ten thousand times*. And, one might guess, not with approbation!

The first lady's visit also had ramifications for the Berry crew. They were scheduled that day to fly a strike to Buka in the Solomons escorted by P-38's. At the last minute, however, the P-38's were diverted to escort Mrs. Roosevelt into Guadalcanal. So the Berry crew had to do without. Over Buka, Berry and his boys ran into a hell of a fight. Worse, the Jap fighters could fly from Buka to Bougainville and refuel for the return trip. That made it tough on the bombers since the battle was quite extended.

One of Carr's tent mates in the hospital tent was Donald Owens Harrison, whom everyone called Owens. He was brought to the 20th Station Hospital from Carney Field two days after Carr arrived. Owens had taken a 7.7 mm bullet in the abdomen from a zero, after an attack on Kahili Airdrome--all after he had already shot down two Zeros. He was a tail gunner on Homer Faucett's crew in the 372nd Bombardment Squadron of the 307th Bombardment Group. The 307th, flying out of Carney Field, frequently accompanied the 5th Bombardment Group on its strikes. On this particular day (August 30, 1943) the strike on Kahili was led by the 5th Bombardment Group and the 31st Bombardment Squadron, with the 307th in trail.

Shortly after Owens Harrison arrived in the ward, he was in extremely serious condition-moaning and groaning in the bed across from Owen Carr. Carr was also moaning and groaning, which led Harrison to complain to the doctor: "Major Nagle, that man over there is mocking me and making fun of me." Nagle replied: "No he isn't, son. He's just as bad off as you are." This began a friendship between the two Owens that continues as this is written. They were both on the U. S. Navy Hospital Ship, Solace, and in the Army's 39th General Hospital in Auckland, New Zealand. Carr preceded Harrison to the States by quite a spell since Harrison's condition was too serious to permit him to make the journey at that time.

Another episode Carr remembers concerned a Red Cross Field Representative who visited the tent ward once or twice a week. Carr says: "He was perhaps middle-aged and he offered the usual basic necessities such as toilet articles, stationary, playing cards, etc. (I think about the only thing I could use was chewing gum). Anyway, he had an old, small, portable wind-up victrola and a few old records which he would gladly play for us. We really didn't feel much like listening to the music which wasn't all that good, but we listened because we felt sorry for the poor fellow who was trying his best to do a good job under very adverse conditions with very limited logistical support."

As for the mission that led to such a catastrophe for Carr and Nerstad, it was quite successful. McKinley's crew shot down several Zeros, Bill Krimer getting two of them.[10] While Owen was recuperating from his operation in the 39th Army Hospital in Auckland, New Zealand, a flight surgeon informed him that aerial photographs of the raid on Kahili Airdrome "showed a path of destruction that looked as if a bulldozer had driven through the bivouac area of the Airdrome." Given that knowledge, and after visiting Nerstad's grave in Auckland, Owen could justifiably feel that his mission had been accomplished.

The Kid Limps Home

After The Cisco Kid landed on 26 August, all shot up, with no hydraulic system, Jim Berry taxied it off the runway. The Kid was damaged so severely on this and subsequent missions that in December 1943, it was sent to its back base for extensive repair. Eventually, after many months of work, the Kid returned to action and was available for my crew, with Pat Earhart as pilot, to fly in May 1944. Although able to fly combat missions after its ordeal, the Cisco Kid was in pretty bad shape. Jim Berry said it never functioned as well as it had originally. He told the McKinley crew it was very nice of them to return it to him in such *fine* shape. One of my crew members referred to it as *a pile of junk*. Nevertheless, the Kid survived the War and ended up on the scrap junk heap in Brisbane, Australia.

Guadalcanal Revisited

In 1992, Carr returned to Gaudalcanal and found the remains of the 20th Station Hospital. He was able to take pictures of the concrete and tile floors and some rusting steel girders. The site was then occupied by a Marist Fathers church and school but a small plaque identified the place as the onetime site of a U.S. Army Hospital.

More Memorable Adventures
Heckling the Nips

Subsequent to the use of The Cisco Kid by the McKinley crew on the 26 August mission to Bougainvile, the Berry crew flew a number of harassing raids on the same island. These "Heckler" strikes were flown from Munda. They were missions designed to keep the Nips up all night. They were not flown in The Cisco Kid. The Berry crew and three others flew two especially equipped B-24s on a rotating basis.

Under cover of darkness, two planes would alternate flying over the Jap's sleeping areas, drop a bomb or two and depart. After circling at sea for awhile, and taking a snort or two, each would return and repeat the process. Each plane would bomb three times each night for a total of six raids. The bombs were fragmentation bombs with aerial burst fuses. If all went according to plan, they would go off in nineteen seconds about 200 feet above the ground. Mission planners thought that this would get the Nip's attention and possibly enhance the fear of God that might be lurking in the back of their minds. The effect of all this is described in the book Zero by one of its Japanese authors who was on Bougainville at the time:

He reports that every night the sirens would scream, and they would hear the bombers approaching. Then the bombs would begin to hit and great explosions would bang against their eardrums and shake the airfield. After the bombers left, the ground crews would go back to work—continuing what seemed endless days characterized only by work, exhastion and ceaseless enemy attacks.[11]

Courage in the Crew

Walter R. Rawleigh began his service in the Army Air Force in 1942 as a pilot trainee. On 19 May 1942, after drinking too much, taking a plane up, hedge-hopping, hitting a tree, and crashing — he washed out of the pilot training program. He then spent eight weeks in the hospital with a broken leg and collarbone. Upon his return to active duty he was sent to gunnery school at Las Vegas and eventually became a top turret gunner on Jim Berry's crew.

Although known as a *fun-loving guy*, Rawleigh was quite conscientious in discharging his responsibilities as a member of the Berry crew. For example, when picking up The Cisco Kid in Topeka, Rawleigh went out in freezing weather and washed the outside of the plane with gasoline. (It's hard to believe that his responsibilities as Top Turret Gunner included any such obligation.) Still beyond the call of duty, Rawleigh checked out as a Bombardier. Ace Hayes taught him the ropes and Berry tells us that Rawleigh "...became a respectable Bombardier." On at least one mission, Berry went without Hayes and Rawleigh dropped the bombs. Not bad when one considers that some Bombardiers "Can't find their ass and hit it with two hands."[12]

Rawleigh was also a courageous member of the Berry crew — as exemplified by his behavior in responding to a crash on Munda, New Georgia. The Berry crew was sitting on the runway waiting to lift off. Another bomb laden Liberator, while attempting to take off, crashed into a truck. It then blew a tire and ground-looped to the left with the left prop plowing the ground. It finally ended up in a taxiway where it burst into flames. All but one of the crew escaped. Although one should not be in the bomb bay on takeoff, it is thought that the crewmember who lost his life was hit by a falling bomb within the plane.

The Berry crew was adjacent to the burning aircraft. Though the plane was burning slowly, Jim Berry assumed that when the fire reached significant proportions, the bombs on board would explode. Therefore, he and his crew debarked and moved about 100 yards behind an embankment. Shortly thereafter, two of the bombs exploded. There was imminent danger that others would do likewise, and the burning plane threatened to destroy another B-24 parked nearby. At that point, the Operations Officer, Bill Fallin, said to Rawleigh: "Let's save that plane." He and Rawleigh then got on board the parked aircraft, started it, and moved it to safety. Thus Rawleigh risked his own life to save valuable government property.

Another close call for Rawleigh and the Berry crew occurred on a mission to Bougainville. On that occasion, Berry and his crew were carrying forty 100 pound bombs — twenty in the front bomb bay and twenty in the rear. All were armed with time fuses which were set to detonate the bombs nineteen seconds after leaving the bomb shackles. At one point, Jim was advised that in dropping the bombs, one had hung briefly on the shackle and dropped into the bomb bay springing the bomb bay doors. The wire that ran through the front and rear arming vanes were fastened to the shackle. The wire stayed on the shackle when the bomb fell, and the arming vanes — taking wind through the sprung bomb bay doors — spun off the bomb, thereby arming it. At that point the nineteen-second clock began to run.

Having bombs hang up or fall into the bomb bay was familiar to those flying combat missions in B-24s. But, normally, they would not explode until the arming pin struck an object with some force. Usually when a bomb would hang up or drop into the bomb bay, Jim would have one or more crewmembers check it out, pick up the errant bomb and drop it by hand. When carrying time fused bombs, however, Jim always had one crewmember stand in each bomb bay so that no time would be lost in taking remedial action in the event of mishap.

In the present instance the nineteen seconds were ticking away and there was little time to rectify the situation. Willis Butler, the Armorer and ball turret gunner, was standing in the bomb bay. He moved quickly, kicking the bomb bay doors until the bomb jostled loose and fell from the plane. The rear bomb bay doors failed to open further and it was contrary to standing orders to land with timefused bombs on board.

Subsequently, Ace Hayes, (whom Berry describes as the best Bombardier in the 31st at that time) reinserted the pins in the remaining bombs in the back bomb bay so they would not go off accidentally. Then, in pitch dark, he, Butler, Rawleigh, and Kellums, moved them to the front bomb bay in "piss ant fashion". Each of 19 bombs was then tossed out one by one. This was a tricky maneuver since it involved carrying 100 pound bombs along a seventeen foot, ten inch wide catwalk with the bomb bay doors open. Heavy clothing and other gear usually worn by air crewmen further complicated the matter. For example, on his missions, Walter Rawleigh normally carried a 38 pistol in addition to a 45 in his shoulder harness. He also wore a leather jacket, a Mae West, a flak suit, a steel helmet, an ear phone, and an oxygen mask. Given all the heavy clothing and other gear normally worn by air crewmen aloft, and the fact that they were working in the dark — one can have nothing but admiration for the guts displayed by these members of the Berry crew. (Parenthetically, I never liked to walk the catwalk with the bomb bay doors open with both hands free, much less carrying a 100 pound bomb.) After this experience, Jim recommended that the bomb bay doors be left open if bombs remained in the bomb bay for the trip back to base.[13]

He also recommended decorations for Butler and the others for their involvement in the errant bomb mishap. After all, quick and courageous action here probably saved the lives of his crew, not to mention the courage displayed in moving and dropping the remaining bombs. Unfortunately, his superiors would give it no thought. Such recommendation, after all, required approval by the Navy. The 13th Air Force was not Navy — though it was, in that time and place, under naval command (COMAIRSOL) and Admiral *Bull* Halsey.[14]

The Cisco Kid II

Prior to the return of the original Cisco Kid, to combat action, a second B-24 was named The Cisco Kid II.[15] The new Kid was assigned to Jim Berry in February 1944. Though having the same name as the original B-24D — it was a B-24J which, in Jim's mind was inferior to its namesake. Indeed, he considered B-24Js to be inferior to the D models. The J took more runway to lift off and, according to Jim, was "...always trouble every time you went up."

In March 1944, Jim Berry and Al Stanley returned to the states. As for those not departing, Berry waked them all, shook hands with them, and said good-bye. The remaining crewmembers had not compiled enough missions to qualify for return at that time. The requisite number of missions was determined by a point system. Crewmembers who volunteered to substitute on short-handed crews compiled points faster than those who did not avail themselves of this option.[16] After Berry's departure, the remaining crewmembers and two replacements made up a new crew headed by Leon Martin, Berry's original Co-Pilot. Thus, seven of the Berry crew members, including TSG Walter R. Rawleigh, were still flying with the Martin crew.[17]

On 18 April 1944, Lt. Martin, TSG Rawleigh and the other members of the Cisco Kid II crew were directed to fly to their new base on Los Negros in the Admiralty Islands. On the way, the Kid and five other Liberators dropped 27,000 pounds of bombs on Woleai, 690 miles from Los Negros. The next day, they returned to Woleai with five more B-24s and, bombing from an altitude of 11,500 feet, scattered 22,500 pounds on the taxi strip and in the building area. During the entire campaign against Woleai, the Martin crew, and other gunners in the 5th Group, shot down 25 Japanese aircraft and damaged a number of other planes on the ground.

The Kid's Luck Runs Out

Although success had characterized the earlier efforts of the Martin crew, Woleai was yet to exact a price. A pendulum always swings two ways; and the see-saw of combat is little different. At this point The Cisco Kid II was about to ride that see-saw on its downward stroke. On 20 April 1944 Lt. Martin and his crew were once again directed to fly a strike to Woleai in The Cisco Kid II. (s/n 42-73307)[18] At this time, a new replacement crew had just joined the 31st Squadron, and some of them were anxious to fly a combat strike. Consequently, Hayes, Mock, and Kellums yielded to the desires of three of them and relinquished their positions.

Walter Rawleigh's son, Chief Master Sergeant Rodger A. Rawleigh, currently stationed at March Air Force Base in California, tells the rest of the story this way:

Piloted by Martin, who at this point had accumulated only 162.65 hours as a first pilot and 835.05 total hours in B-24s, the Kid took off second in formation from Los Negros. At 3,000 feet down the runway, the #1 engine began to backfire and throw off smoke in spurts from the #1 exhaust. After an additional 1,000 feet, #1 prop started to windmill, the plane now skidding sideways. It now appeared that Martin forcefully pulled the plane off the ground. Rising 150 feet into the air in a steep climb, with the left wing quite low, the plane took a slow turn to the left. The nose dropped and after making a 180 degree turn from its starting position, the plane plowed into the ground.

Upon crashing, the gasoline caught fire. Two seconds later the nine 500 pound bombs on board exploded. It was later learned that the plane had gone down in a naval encampment containing a mess hall. A large number of Seabees were having breakfast. It was to be the last meal for over 100 of them! None of the ten crew members of the Kid survived.

At this point, only one plane was in the air. Takeoff for all remaining planes was aborted. The one plane still airborne, the first to takeoff, now proceeded on to Woleai and dropped its nine bombs-walking them across a taxiway and one end of a runway. One Betty on the ground burned and exploded; another was destroyed. The crew also observed five fires and a large explosion in a supply area.

So, in the final analysis, of the ten members of the Berry crew who flew all or most of their combat missions from Guadalcanal in The Cisco Kid, five did not survive the war. For Rawleigh, in death, on 20 April 1944, was joined by Leon Martin, John Gilb, Willis Butler, and Alden Campbell — all of whom, with Rawleigh, last saw their loved ones when they violated their orders on the way to Topeka.

Bad Luck Bombers or Bad Luck Crews?

Given the exposition so far, how should this question be answered? It is true that the failure of all members of Berry's crew to accumulate *points* at the same rate accounted for five of them being in the wrong place at the wrong time. And some of this may be attributed to luck. One may also concede the congruities in the fact that Radioman Owen Carr and the Radioman he replaced both suffered a terrible tragedy over Bougainville when hit by 20 mm. cannon from attacking Zeros. And some will undoubtedly see a role for luck here. But one should not be tempted to conclude that The Cisco Kid was a bad luck omen any more than was *Thumper*, the plane in which Smitty was flying on his tragic day. Nor that the crews that flew with the Kid were bad luck crews. As Owen Carr has expressed it: "...It wasn't luck, it wasn't the crew, and it wasn't the airplane. It was simply the situation! That's all."

During the War in the South Pacific, many B-24 Liberators and the lives they carried were lost. Many to enemy fighters, others to bad and unpredictable weather. Some failed to make it home because of the distances they were forced to fly, some because of mechanical malfunction, and some because of pilot or navigational error. It was not uncommon to have Jap air raids during take-off, sometimes resulting in Liberators blowing up on the runway as they waited for clearance.[19]

At the same time, it is quite clear, that luck played a role, as it always does, in the lives of The Cisco Kid's crewmen — and particularly in the lives of Owen Carr, Walter Rawleigh and the other crewmen who lost their lives with Rawleigh. First off, the makeup of crews prior to going overseas is best described as a random process. And then there is the question of who will be riding in which *flying boxcar* on any given day. The assignment of planes to crews on any particular mission was often the luck of the draw. For in the South Pacific Theater one could not realistically expect the luxury afforded European crews — i.e., to fly in the same plane on every mission.

Europe had first call on supplies and equipment. As a result, we not only had to cannibalize some Liberators to keep others flying, we frequently had to struggle to keep enough B-24s going to make up a Squadron or Group. This shortage of flyable aircraft forced us, on occasion, to put a crew on a plane that might have been assigned to someone else. Neither the wishes of crews nor sentimentality were allowed to interfere with this process. We had no choice. Thus, in forty-four combat missions in 1944-45, I flew in eighteen different Liberators; in no single one more than four times. So, who would be flying in the Kid on a particular strike was pretty much a lottery choice. Or the whim of an Operations Officer.

If Owen Carr had not been an Assistant Radio Operator (with five weeks in radio school at Hickam Field), he would not have been called on to replace *Smitty*. If Berry had not completed his missions before Martin, then Martin, with his small number of first pilot hours in B-24s, would not have been first pilot in the Kid II on the mission that ended in disaster for so many. Finally, if Martin, Gilb, Butler, Rawleigh, and Campbell had flown every flight with Jim Berry while overseas, they all would have returned home safely with him.

Yet, having said all this, the men who flew in The Cisco Kid, (I or II) were no more nor less lucky than hundreds, perhaps thousands, of other crews who flew missions in B-24s during World War II. For any of us could write a volume on the *what ifs* in life that may have contributed to our failures. But one who would play that game, in all fairness, would have to consider the instances in which luck led to better outcomes, as in Owen's narrow escape on Espiritu, Rawleigh's good fortune in escaping injury from the burning plane, and Butler's adeptness in freeing the ticking bomb over Bougainville, as well as the superb timing of Hayes, Mock, and Kellums in giving up their seats for the April 20 mission to Woleai. So It's a fruitless exercise, to be sure.

What we can do is admire and take pride in the courage of those who flew B-24s in the South Pacific in World War II--and particularly the remarkable devotion to duty and each other exemplified by such airmen as Jim Berry, Willis Butler, Owen Carr, Bill Krimer, Don MacAllister, Walter Rawleigh and the crews with which they served.[20]

Notes

[Editorial Note: Unless otherwise indicated, the quotations used in this paper are taken from letters to the author, personal conversations, or taped interviews made by the parties quoted.]

[1] The Cisco Kid first appeared as the main character in O. Henry's short story, "The Caballero's Way." The Kid is pictured in O. Henry's opening paragraph as an Anglo "...who had killed six men in more or less fair scrimmages; had murdered twice as many (mostly Mexicans), and had winged a larger number whom he modestly forbore to count. .... He killed for the love of it — because he was quick tempered — to avoid arrest — for his own amusement — for any reason that came to his mind would suf-

fice." Mexicans he killed just "...to see them kick." O. Henry, <u>Heart of the West</u> Doubleday, Page, & Co., NY, 1919, pp. 187, 189

[2] The Cisco Kid was supposedly from Cisco, Texas though O. Henry nowhere so states. In The Caballero's Way. He gives the Kid's habitat as anywhere between the Frio and the Rio Grande. Today, Cisco is a city of about 4,000 people, located adjacent to Interstate Highway 20, 105 miles west of the Fort Worth/Dallas metropolitan area and 46 miles east of Abilene, Texas.. Cisco, founded in 1881, was named after John Cisco, an easterner who helped finance the Texas Central Railroad. 0. Henry came to Texas in 1882 and lived on a ranch, working as a cowboy, for several years. He was in the state when gunmen, rustlers, comanches, and assorted desperadoes could make life nasty, brutal, and short. So his characterization of the Kid may not have been an excessive extrapolation from some of the nefarious characters circulating in the state at that time.

[3] When the members of another crew arrived late and were "busted"! The only crew member reporting back on time ripped the telephone off the wall so he could get busted too. And was!

[4] Al Stanley reports that Zeros were so thick, you could walk wing-tip to wing-tip on them.

[5] Rawleigh had an eight mm movie camera which he attached to his turret and took all kinds of movies. It is not known what happened to the film. It is possible they were confiscated by Squadron Intelligence after his death.

[6] John Boeman, Morotai, Sunflower University Press, Manhattan, Kansas, 1981, p. 50.

[7] Boeman tells a related story about a Navigator with whom he once flew. The base was Morotai, the target Borneo. As they cleared the runway the navigator gave a heading of zero nine zero. "Oh! Oh! I thought. Do we have a navigator, or just a guy who draws lines? 'Better check that heading Navigator.' I yelled back above the cockpit noise. 'What you have given me has a better chance of getting us to South America than Borneo,' then started turning west. 'Make that two seven zero,' he came up and told me, 'I read my Wheems Plotter backwards." While this may seem humorous at this point in time, it was no joking matter when taking off from Morotai. Because of mountains on Halmahera, an adjacent island, pilots taking off from Morotai had to make a right turn and fly out the strait between the two islands or risk running into a 4,000 foot mountain. Boeman reports at least one instance when such an accident occurred. (pp. 230,121)

[8] While in the service, Stanley was often in trouble with military authorities. He was quite independent and had a strong sense of what was just and unjust. As a consequence, he "...went up and down in rank as often as a fireman climbs a ladder." Stanley left Guadalcanal with Berry to return to the states. They were ferrying back home with a stop in Hawaii. While there, Stanley got drunk and couldn't be found when time came to takeoff for San Francisco. Berry, when informed, said: "Put him on a boat and ship him home." So Stanley came home on a Norwegian ship. He was then hospitalized for two months in Miami, later becoming a Radio Operator Instructor. Yet, in spite of everything, Stanley got on famously with Jim Berry and always expressed great affection and admiration for him. All this suggests that Jim was quite easy going; didn't worry much about rank; just loved to fly.

[9] Cravens and Cate, Vol. IV, p. 271.

[10] It is possible that other crew members got a Zero or two but officially claimed none. I do not know McKinley's policy but Jim Berry's policy was not to allow his crew to claim any kills of Jap planes in combat. His reason: when a number of B-24s is attacked by a number of enemy fighters, with any number of gunners from any number of Liberators shooting at the enemy, it is usually impossible to tell who got what. To avoid argument at debriefing, and the hard feelings that might result

Berry simply had his crew forego any claims. A fringe benefit of such a policy is that gunners, while in combat, would devote all their attention to the job at hand rather than being distracted trying to see if a possible enemy kill actually crashed into the ground or the ocean-information debriefers often wanted in order to credit the kill. An exception to Berry's policy on claiming kills occurred only once when another crew claimed its Ball Gunner and Berry's Nose Gunner (Al Stanley) got a kill. When Berry was asked by intelligence officers whether that was correct, he said: "yes."

[11] Masatake Okumiya and Jiro Horikoshi, Zero, Bantam Books, NY, 1956, p. 246. This comment triggers a flood of memories for me. While stationed on Morotai in the Moluccas in late 1944, I experienced a number of night raids by Japanese bombers. They were coming from the island of Halmahera ten miles across the bay. Between September 15 and February 1 there were 172 sorties and 82 air raids. (W. F. Craven and J. L. Cate, eds., The Army Air Force in World War II, Vol. 5, U.S.A.F.) Office of History, Washington, DC, 1983, p. 315. The Japs were using twin engine Bettys. They would come over one at a time, always at night, usually between 2300 and dawn. The sirens would sound, we would jump off our folding cots into a fox-hole, pray that no Nip bomb found our particular hole, pray even harder that the shrapnel from our exploding anti-aircraft shells did not find us, and wait for the all-clear signal. Then out of the hole, back into bed, hoping to get some sleep before arising for a mission the next morning. Since our missions usually took from ten to seventeen hours, this meant rising at anywhere from 0330 to 0430 for pre-flight briefing, breakfast, and a 0600 lift-off. The Bettys would come several times each night, sometimes as many as eight times. After jumping in and out of the foxhole all night, it is a wonder we did not take a forty-five and shoot the poor enlisted man whose job was to stick his head in your tent at some ungodly hour and yell. "Time to get up. Everybody up, briefing in thirty minutes. Lets go!" The result of all this: We often began a mission day in an abnormal state of fatigue. Did the Japs learn the effectiveness of such tactics from us at Bougainville? We cannot know for sure. But I can testify that they practiced the art exceedingly well. On one occasion, I spotted a snake curled up in the hole while bombs were falling all around us. Afraid to get out of the hole, I cowered in the corner until the all- clear sounded. Such was life on Morotai.

[12] Boeman, p. 181.

[13] On one occasion, a plane carrying time fused bombs disappeared for no apparent reason. Jim surmises that a bomb might have fallen into the bomb bay doors and exploded in the plane.

[14] Chief Rodger Rawleigh, Walter Rawleigh's son, later sought a Distinguished Flying Cross medal to be awarded posthumously.

[15] I have not been able to ascertain the nose art on the Cisco Kid II. But it was not the Mexican Cowboy with the big sombrero that graced the side of aircraft 42-40174.

[16] Other influential factors were more unpredictable. Floyd Streeper tells this story: Our crew started breaking up in September [1944] and I got an assignment on a C-47 to fly a fat cat run to Sydney. As was the practice any whiskey brought back from Sydney sold for $50.00 a bottle. The operations clerk asked me to bring him two bottles. When I returned, I took the two bottles to him and he asked 'how much?' When I told him $100.00 he cussed me out and said he had put me on that flight. I held out and he paid but he said he would get even. It started the very next day. He had me flying transition flights almost every day, but no combat. His thinking was to keep me from getting rotation points for missions and combat hours. At that point I felt like he

had me cornered. However, neither of us remembered that non-combat flying hours earned rotation points. A rotation list had just come out prior to my Australian flight. One month later and countless hours of transition time, the new list came out. To my amazement I had jumped two men on the list, due to all that transition time. I went into operations and told the still glowering clerk Thanks. He said 'for what?' I then told him that because of all the flying I had jumped two places on the list. After he checked the list, he put me back on combat status. This was just in time to make that joyride to Balikpapan. After two missions, however, I was placed on DNIC (duty not involving combat) and then just pulled ground duty awaiting orders home. (From 5th Bombardment Group (H) Association Newsletter January 7, 1996)

[17] Berry had forty-four missions but the total number one flew was not predetermined. In the period 1944-1945, when I was overseas, crewmembers flew forty to fifty missions. I flew forty-four.

[18] Woleai was a critical target for the 31st Bombardment Squadron. It was especially important as a base for staging of Japanese tactical aircraft between Japan and the vital naval base at Truk. The damage done to Woleai by 5th Bombardment Group bombers flying from Los Negros led to a Presidential Unit Citation--for a job "well done." This was one of only two such citations ever accorded the 5th Group. The other was for the September 30, 1944, mission to Balikpapan, Borneo. Two of my 44 missions were flown to Woleai. I also flew the September 30 strike on Balikpapan.

[19] On a mission to Balikpapan, Borneo (30 September 1944), Cortesi reports (p. 101) that "...More than 50 crew members aboard the Group planes were killed and another 50 wounded, not counting those who had been lost on the downed Bomber Baron B-24s." He also reports the loss of three planes, with ten men rescued and twenty lost. (Pp. 100-101) This gives totals of at least 71 dead and 50 wounded, or 121 casualties. There were twenty-three 5th Group planes over the target carrying 230 men. Thus if these figures are accurate, the mortality rate was 31 percent (71/230) and the casualty rate 53 percent (121/230).

[20] Though my name is on this paper as author, I am heavily indebted to a number of people that supplied the stories retold above. Especially I want to thank Jim Berry, Owen Carr, Al Stanley and Walter Rawleigh's son, Rodger Rawleigh, for their contributions. Without them there would have been no paper. I also wish to thank Jacqueline Berry for her editorial assistance. The Owen Carr story, as retold in this paper, has appeared previously in Tail Winds, the newsletter of the 31st Bombardment (H) Squadron Association.

BALIKPAPAN
THE FIFTH BOMB GROUP'S SHINING HOUR
30 SEPTEMBER 1944

By S. Sidney Ulmer

Introduction

"The Wild Man of Borneo" was a concept I had heard on the playgrounds of South Carolina where I grew up. It pretty much exhausted my knowledge of that jungle island as I departed for combat in the Southwest Pacific in April 1944. I was a tail gunner on a B-24 crew of ten headed by Pilot Pat Earhart. Other officers on the crew were Charles Bauserman, copilot;

Harold Page, Bombardier; and Howard Thompson, Navigator. The nose turret gunner was Hildrey Pollard. Top turret was the responsibility of Hubert Warnock. Stuart Clemmer and James Shine held forth at the waist guns with David Hopson in the ball turret.

As a tail gunner, I fully anticipated that some anxious moments lay in my future. I did not know, however, that I would one day be looking down on mountains, mud flats and mangrove swamps — a Borneo occupied by native headhunters and wild men of a somewhat different stripe.[1] Equally cannibalistic in a figurative sense, and, on occasion, cannibalistic in a literal sense,[2] these particular wild men spoke Japanese. The date was 30 September 1944 and the place was Balikpapan, Borneo.

As the major source of fuel for the Japanese in the Pacific Theater, Balikpapan was a choice target. Captured from the Dutch earlier, the oil and gasoline refineries there were annually producing over 7,000,000[3] barrels of oil and high octane gasoline. They supplied over 35 percent of all fuel needs for the Japanese armed forces.[4] In the Western Pacific theater, that figure reached 50 percent.[5] And in the Philippines, 65 percent of the aviation fuel used by the Japanese Air Force came from Balikpapan.[6] As a consequence, Balikpapan was frequently referred to as "The Ploesti of the Pacific." The reference was to the successful strikes on oil refineries in Ploesti, Rumania in 1943, by B-24s flying from Italy.

In support of the upcoming invasion of the Philippines, MacArthur thought it vitally important to damage or destroy the Balikpapan refineries — using heavy bombers. Doing so would severely diminish the ability of the Japs to project fighter/bomber aircraft and naval warships in the imminent battles for Leyte, where MacArthur finally honored his pledge to return to the Philippines. However, while his logic was impeccable, accomplishing the task would not be easy.

Initially the idea was to use B-29s. Unfortunately, MacArthur had no such planes under his command. The 20th Bomb Group in China and the 21st Group in the Pacific did possess such planes; but General Hap Arnold, CinC of USAAF, rebuffed MacArthur's attempt to use them. Subsequently, he decided to go with B-24s.[7]

Necessary Command Decisions

MacArthur's air Commanders now had their own decisions to make. From the 13th Air Force, they chose two heavy bomb groups, the 5th (The Bomber Barons) and the 307th (The Long Rangers). The 90th Bombardment Group, (The Jolly Rogers) of the 5th Air Force, was added to complete the task force planned for the mission. General George Kenney, MacArthur's CinC of Far Eastern Air Forces decided that the mission would be primarily a 13th Air Force show,[8] with the 90th Bomb Group in a support role. Then General St. Clair Street, Commanding General of the 13th Air Force chose the 5th Group to lead the strike. And since the 31st Squadron led the Group it led the mission. Colonel Musgrave's 5th Group Liberators would fly in two sections of 12 planes, with the 31st and 23rd Squadrons in the first section and the 72nd and 394th in the second in that order.[9]

Assessing the Dangers Inherent in the Mission

Complicating the use of B-24s was big distance. The load to be carried was almost 70,000 pounds or 12,000 over the gross weight specified by the manufacturer. The scheduled load was greater than had ever been carried in the Southwest Pacific-even over shorter distances. Balikpapan was over 1300 miles from Noemfoor in the Schouten Islands, the nearest base from which U.S. bombers could be launched.[10] A round trip would be 300 miles beyond the maximum range set by the manufacturer, Consolidated Aircraft. Not only had the Ploesti raids entailed flights of only 1,000 miles to target, the distances to Balikpapan meant that, unlike Ploesti, no fighter cover would be possible.

Furthermore, the entire route would be over water, except for tiny slices of land in Ceram, the Celebes, and the Moluccas. On the Ploesti raid, by contrast, the flight over territory in friendly hands allowed 23 B-24s (13 percent of the total planes on the flight) to land in Cyprus, Sicily, or Malta. The route would also be entirely over enemy held territory with major Jap fighter bases all along the way. And it would require flying most of the night to get there. Night flying alone posed a problem since some of the pilots had not flown at night since leaving the states. So practice for pilots was set up.

In general these practices went well. But one Squadron in the 307th Group had unusually bad luck. To reduce the personnel and aircraft involved, three pilots and one engineer would go up in one plane and the pilots would take turns landing. One night, with clouds at 80 to 100 feet, a pilot leveled off too high, flew the entire length of the runway — making no attempt to pull up and crashed into the sea killing all aboard. The next day the nosewheel washed ashore.[11]

The threat of fighter attack diminished if the Americans had the advantage of surprise. MacArthur told his Commanders on 20 September 1944, that the Japanese fully expect an invasion of the Philippines. At the same time, he thought we could take them by surprise at Balikpapan.[12] But this was either wishful thinking or an attempt to boost morale. General Soemu Anami, CinC of Japanese forces in the area, had his own intelligence sources. On 18 September, he told his Commanders that the enemy intends to invade the Philippines. Further, he said that it would be naive to think the Americans had no intention to bomb the oil complex.[13]

On 20 September 1944, General Kenney told his Group Commanders that the Japs did not have many planes on the fields between Sansapor, New Guinea, and Balikpapan. If you keep a tight formation and if you keep your gunners alert, he went on, you should not have much difficulty going to and returning from Balikpapan. He thought the Japs had no combat planes on Balikpapan itself. Boredom, he said, will likely be your biggest problem, given the long flight. At the briefing of the 5th Group, on 29 September, however, our Commander, Tom Musgrave, indicated otherwise. Yet, he was optimistic that if we held a tight formation, interceptors would be discouraged.[14]

Those of us in the briefing tent that night appreciated that tight formations were less likely to attract fighter attacks than loose formations. And God help any stragglers. But as the briefing unfolded on 29 September, a silence, the like of which I had never experienced, was palpable. It slowly descended over the 300 crewmen in the tent until a whisper could be heard from one side to the other. Eventually, questions followed — at first haltingly and then with an anxiety, not panicky, but clearly reflecting an appropriate appreciation of the arduous task that lay ahead.

Some suggested that our loss of bombers would be low, as compared to those over Ploesti (32.9 percent).[15] The reason: the B-24s over Ploesti went over the target at altitudes as low as 20 feet whereas we would be flying at 9,000-14,000 feet. However, the briefing officers constant and detailed references to plans for rescuing downed crews undercut the argument. Passing out dictionaries of native words, in case the Japs shot us down along the way or over the Borneo jungles, did nothing to allay our concerns.[16] One could infer that our officers expected substantial losses.

I drew the inference and, apparently, not alone since Tom Musgrave was later recorded as saying: "We were scared to death when first informed of the mission."[17] Our briefer's frequent use of the word *feasible* in describing the mission did little to calm the waters. *Feasible* after all, is a rather ambiguous word. During my service in the Pacific theater, I saw many of my colleagues lost on perfectly *feasible* missions.

Seasoned aircrew members, whose senses had been razor sharpened by their earlier combat experiences, declined to accept these low estimates. I know for a fact that most other crewmembers, as I, thought the losses would be considerably higher than any suffered on earlier strikes. And some undoubtedly shared the feeling of a tail gunner seated next to me who whispered under his breath: "Lord, prepare to receive thy servant". I was more optimistic than that, though hindsight tells me I was naive; I was also 21 years old at the time! I learned later that while General Kenney was always gung-ho to hit Balikpapan

with a daylight raid by B-24s, General Ennis Whitehead, CinC of the 5th Air Force, had his doubts,"...fearing losses would prove prohibitive."[18]

In any event, the Japanese did anticipate the mission and took special steps to blunt any success we might have. Specifically, they planned to station at least 120 fighter planes at Balikpapan.

Other plans called for 50 fighters and 20 fighterbombers at Manado in the Celebes. Additional assignments were 50 fighters and 30 fighter-bombers at Kudat, Borneo, 20 fighters and 20 fighterbombers split between Ambon, Ceram and Babo, New Guinea, and 50 fighters and 30 fighter-bombers at Kendari in the Celebes. At Bitjoli, Halmahera, (about 400 miles from Noemfoor) an additional 20 fighters and 20 fighter-bombers were to be stationed. The fighter-bombers specialized not only in direct attack on bomber formations but, on occasion, showered our Liberators with phosphorus bombs.[19]

The *Pat Earhart* crew. (l to r) Front row: Charles Bauserman (copilot), Pat Earhart (pilot), Howard Thompson (navigator), Harold Page (bombardier), unknown (substituting for Hildrey Pollard, nose gunner). Back row: Hubert Warnock (engineer and top turet gunner), David Hopson (ball turet), James Shine (waist gunner), stuart Clemmer (radioman and waist gunner), Sid Ulmer (tail gunner).

In addition, the Japanese planned to defend Balikpapan with their newest and deadliest anti-aircraft guns.[20] With these guns came the 246th Battalion of anti-aircraft gunners — men who had performed with distinction in the Solomons, on New Britain, and in the Philippines. These gunners, according to their Commanders, were 'the best' in Japanese service.[21]

Assessing the Capabilities of B-24s to Fly the Mission

MacArthur's choice of B-24 bombers for the Balikpapan strike was an easy choice given his options. But it was a choice that posed a number of difficulties. B-24s have their limits. The mission order called for half the normal ammunition, 40 percent of the normal bomb load,[22] and 700 extra gallons of gasoline. Even after removing everything not absolutely necessary from the planes, (bomb hoists, extra bomb shackles, radio frequency tuning meters, tool kits, and assorted personal equipment)[23] gross weight would be 13,000 pounds greater than recommended for this type of plane.[24]

Whether the planes could lift off the runway with such a load and fly the necessary distances with the gasoline supplied was open to question. Proper power settings were critical to obtaining maximum mileage. The B-24's center of gravity was also considered. Various factory-determined settings were useless given the weight, instrument flying all night, and other conditions of the proposed flight.

Flying a B-24 is not a mechanical job. The mileage obtained from aviation gasoline will vary from pilot to pilot since some are more adept than others in handling the controls. The center of gravity could not be constant since as gas was burned and ammunition used, that center shifted. The B-24 is more sensitive than some planes to such shifting. (That is why landing under even ideal conditions requires that the ten members of the crew be positioned in particular parts of the plane on touchdown.)

After exhaustive consideration, the planners provided detailed directions, which varied by the hour of flight. A specific place in the plane was determined for each man's parachute, flak vest, emergency ration belt, medicine kit, helmet, and canteen. The designated speed was 150 mph. Explicit power settings — which varied for take-off, rate of climb, cruising, approach to target, break away, descent and cruise home — were adopted. And the crew members were directed to redistribute themselves in the plane depending on the hour into the trip.[25] All this was printed and circulated to each crew scheduled to fly the mission. Since no such mission had been flown before, however, mission planners conducted an experiment to test the hypothesis of feasibility.

Six *average* crews were chosen and six aircraft, employing all the specifications adopted earlier, sent out to fly a distance equal to the 2600 mile round trip to Balikpapan. Each plane carried a surplus of 400 gallons of gasoline, beyond that considered necessary for the actual strike. If successful on this *trial run*, Commanders could then say to the aircrews: "We know it can be done. We have flown the distance with the load and in accordance with our specifications and all planes returned safely to base." Of course, MacArthur and his Commanders had concluded as early as September 20 that the mission was feasible. And it was going to be flown no matter what the experiment might show — on the assumption that at least enough planes would reach the target to do significant damage to the Balikpapan refineries.

This is not to say that our Commanders had no concern for losses. Yet, acceptable loss in a combat situation is always married to the significance of the object to be accomplished. Clearly, in this particular case, our Commanders were willing to take substantial losses to damage or destroy this particular target.

In the event, each experimental plane flew the trial course and returned without mishap. As for the surplus gasoline, only one plane consumed any of it and that one burned only 25 gallons. So, logistically, one could argue that the mission was feasible. Yet, hindsight suggests that the experiment did not resolve all questions. It did not allow for variation in weather conditions, or the jockeying while in formation that might be necessary, nor time spent circling the target or dropping bombs on an alternative target. Nor the extent to which actual combat, along the route and over Balikpapan, would impact fuel consumption.

Combat conditions could easily force the bombers to fly at other than circumscribed altitudes. Moreover, while B-24s burn, on average, about 200 gallons of gasoline an hour, individual planes can vary as much as 40 gallons an hour one way or the other. We could not know that the particular B-24s on the mission would meet the *average* specifications? Given variation in the ability of pilots to get the maximum mileage from their fuel, planners attempted to assign the best pilots to the *gas hog* B-24s. Obviously there was a lot of subjectivity involved in the whole process.

Finally, one may recall that the center of gravity on the six experimental bombers was a continuous variable governed by the successive redistribution of men and equipment over the entire 2,600 mile flight. How could one be sure that under the conditions of the actual flight, which might involve combat at more than one point along the way, the crews on the actual mission would be able to duplicate all the moves made by the experimental crews. The short of it is that the six experimental airplanes and crews, and the continuous decisions they made, did not constitute in any scientific sense a reliable or representative sample. As a prime example of that proposition — in the deed itself, several B-24s in the 5th Group did run short of gas and did not make it back to base.

Yet, in the final analysis, the experiment was better than nothing. Criticism, written in the comfort of my study 52 years later, in no way detracts from the importance of the experiment in boosting and sustaining the morale of the men chosen for this particular endeavor.

Lift-Off

After chopping off Palm trees at the end of the runway to improve clearance, ambulances and medics were assembled on the flight line in the event of mishap. Then at 030 hours on 30 September 1944, 24 B-24s of the 5th Bombardment Group lifted off from Noemfoor for their flight into the unknown, the beginning of "... the longest daylight mass formation bombing missions ever flown by B-24 aircraft." [26]

My Pilot, Pat Earhart, has described his feeling this way. "I remember we took off in the dead of night into what I considered a black hole. No horizon of any kind and we had to rely on instruments and my instrument training was about nil. Guess it wasn't considered too necessary in those days more like a necessary evil. ...I remember that that 'black hole' ahead of us was real scary. Jesus Christ, or someone, must have been with us that night to assist us into the night sky. But after sweating out the night take-off, our day had just begun."

Each plane was scheduled to lift off exactly 60 seconds after the one preceding it. As each cleared the runway, it headed for the rendezvous point (RP) 1,035 miles away. Delay in takeoff would add up to unacceptable gas consumption since planes would have to circle endlessly over the RP. Pilots who encountered trouble after take-off were not to return to base until all planes on the mission had departed. In case any plane had an emergency, after take-off but before all B-24s had cleared the runway, pilots were instructed to bail out, let the plane crash, and await rescue by PBYs or other means.

Though Jap air raids on Noemfoor were not infrequent, all pilots were directed to ignore any that might occur during take-off.[28] As it turned out, the first twenty four B-24s (Fifth Bomb Group) got off in exactly 24 minutes — each one using up all but about 100 feet of the 7,900 foot runway.

While one 5th Group Liberator later turned back, 23 reached the rendezvous point. That point was 220 miles from target but only 40 miles from a major Jap air base. The journey to the RP was a major challenge for our navigators. They had to navigate for 1,035 miles to a given point over enemy held territory. The first section of 12 planes was allotted just 24 minutes to assemble in formation and start for the target. That meant they had to arrive at the RP within 24 minutes of each other. At the RP, the first section assembled in formation in only 13 minutes.[29] This meant that 12 individual Navigators had flown over 1,000 miles in the dark, all reaching the RP within 13 minutes of each other; a remarkable navigational feat, to say the least.

Along the Way

While the Presidential Unit Citation describes the Balikpapan mission as a daylight flight, we flew half the mission in the dark. This was both good news and bad news. The bad news is that instrument flying burns gas. The good news, ostensibly, is that Jap interceptors would find it more difficult to locate and attack the bombers at night.

Discovered Over Halmahera and the Celebes

In actuality, the Japanese radar on Halmahera, 845 miles from Balikpapan, picked us up as we flew over. But it was in the middle of the night, their pilots were asleep; their Zeros, Tonys and Oscars sitting cold on the ground. So they were not able to get up in time to bother us. However, they immediately notified their bases at Kendari and Manado that we were on the way. Two hours later, as we approached the Celebes, 30 Jap fighters rose from Kendari and 24 Oscars and Tonys scrambled from Manado.[30]

We had flown at 8,500 feet but rose to 14,000 when we reached the Celebes because of towering cumulus cloud cover. Since we were at that time within a couple of hours of Balikpapan, Colonel Musgrave thought that our target, the Pandansari oil and gas refineries, would be obscured. But these clouds had a silver lining. When radar on the bombers picked up the 54 Jap fighters, Musgrave took the Liberators down to

14 October 1944. 5th Bomb Group strikes oil refinery, Balikpapan, Borneo. 2,600 mile round trip from Noemfoor Island, New Guinea. Bombing altitude 19,000 feet.

14 October 1944. 5th Bomb Group strikes oil refinery, Balikpapan, Borneo. 2,600 mile round trip from Noemfoor Island, New Guinea. Bombing altitude 19,000 feet. Balikpapan was sometimes referred to as the "Ploesti of the Pacific."

8,000 feet, deep in the cloud banks, and continued westward on radar. We learned later that the Jap Commanders knew exactly what we were doing but they could not find us or feared the attempt under prevailing conditions. Some of the flight Commanders of both fighter squadrons reported to their superiors that the Americans were hiding in the clouds. They thought it too perilous to engage us in the cloud banks, fearing that they might run into each other. So they adopted a *better safe than sorry* policy.[31]

Would it have mattered had there been no clouds? Seems very likely. On the second Balikpapan strike on 3 October 1944, 48 fighters from these same bases attacked 44 B-24s and downed two. One of the two was from the 5th Group. A phosphorous bomb exploded right against it, setting off an intense fire that seared eight crewmen to death instantly. The Japs strafed two others in their chutes, killing both. Four other B-24s turned back because of severe damage.

Corteri reports that a total of 40 men were killed or wounded in this attack. Yet, it could have been worse. Another squadron of 23 Zeros arrived too late to get into the fray.[32] All this suggests the critical significance of the cloud cover over the Celebes on 30 September. Our luck held and we passed on without loss

at this point. As we shall see, these same clouds impaired a heavy cost before we were back on the ground at Noemfoor.

Picked Up By Spotter Planes

So on we went. At 250 miles from Balikpapan, we picked up two enemy reconnaissance planes that escorted us on in to our target. While it is true that the Japs at Balikpapan already knew that we were on the way, the spotter planes were able to track our number and altitude all the way to the target. Thus, when we got there, they were ready and waiting. While they had not brought all their defensive plans to fruition, they had secured an additional 70 fighters from one crack naval fighter Group and the lead echelon from a second.[33]

The Japs got, and appropriately stationed, additional anti-aircraft guns. They knew we were without fighter escort and when we would arrive-to the minute. They estimated that we were about 60 in number. The actual number for all three groups was 69. They estimated that we would come in from the west at 13,000 to 15,000 feet.[34] But the four squadrons of the 5th Group were a little lower than that, making the bomb run at an average of 12,750 feet.

Our First Setback Encountered

We arrived at the Makassar Strait, which separates Borneo from the Celebes, at 0920 hours. Then, a huge letdown! Ten/Tenth cloud cover socked in the target. We could see nothing but white. Presumably, the same cloud build-up that had been so welcome over the Celebes now threatened to punish us for our earlier good fortune. It seemed as if dame fortune, or mother nature, wanted some balance in her account book.

Musgrave Decides to Wait for an Opening

As usual, there were alternate targets assigned and we could have simply peeled off, hit those targets and headed home. As we got closer, a tiny hole appeared in the clouds and we thought for an instant that we could use that opening to drop our bombs. It was not to be, as the hole quickly closed. Should we drop anyway or divert to the alternates? The decision was up to Musgrave. Even with the hole in the clouds closed, we knew it's approximate location--which gave a glimpse of the target. It would have been possible to drop in that general vicinity, be assured of doing some damage, and scat for home.

Musgrave dismissed both these possibilities. We had come too far and with much sacrifice to abort at this point. He ordered his bombardier to hold his bombs and took the 5th Group in a wide circle to the East to come on to the target from a different angle. This gave the Nip anti-aircraft gunners on the ground what they undoubtedly considered the opportunity of a lifetime. And since we had no fighter cover, the Jap pilots must have been jumping with glee. They were later to learn, howver, that even without fighter cover and 1,300 miles from home, we were no pushover.

At the same time, we were burning precious fuel that may be needed to get back to home base at Noemfoor. So the air crews were undoubtedly disappointed to hear Musgrave's order.[35] In any event, we continued to circle for an hour, until we could see exactly what we had been assigned to hit. Only then did we drop our bombs. Such a delay meant that the enemy fighter pilots had time to land, refuel, and come at us again. All the while we were in the flak zone and additional excitement was in the offing.

Jumped by Jap Fighters

First we were jumped by 30 fighters — ten Zeros, ten Oscars, and ten Tonys. The first section of 12 aircraft got jumped first. We were in a javelin step-down formation — i.e., echelons of three planes in the shape of an inverted V. The second echelon in each squadron was lower than the first.[36] The Japs mounted a determined and sustained attack. Though we had seen aggressive enemy pilots before — these took the prize for their eagerness. In number it was like some giant gatling gun spewing zeros in our direction without letup. But there were reasons for their determined attacks.

Under threats of punishment if they disobeyed orders, the Nip pilots made a "maximum effort" to get,the B-24s before they could do much damage to the Balikpapan refineries. Anti-aircraft guns were set for an altitude of 13,000 feet while the enemy fighters patrolled at 16,000 feet.[37] The fighter pilots had orders to attack in single plane dives[38] with each plane close behind the one preceding it. The advantage of this arrangement was that our gunners could not follow the first diving fighter all the way in for others were close on his tail. If we stayed too long with the first one, those following had a good chance of getting us first.

Sitting in the tail of aircraft #613, I was fully occupied; all my attention focussed on the Jap fighters screaming by and around us. Usually, all but the most reckless Japs avoided straight in attacks on the tail of a B-24. For while it gives him a golden opportunity to shoot you down, his chances are no better than that of the tail gunner to do the same to him. But in this instance, I got several tail-end passes, in apparent violation of their orders but well within my range — and I in theirs.

Many more dove past us from other angles--some very close, within 25 feet. Some straight on at the nose. We could see their oxygen masks! While all this was going on, the flak was close, thick, and loud — "...heavier, more intense, and more accurate than any... ever encountered at the enemy bases of Rabaul, Truk, or Palau," possibly because they were throwing up 120-mm shells from newly acquired guns.[39] While, normally, the Nip pilots stayed clear of the area in which their anti-aircraft shells were exploding, here they flew right into and through it in their determination to shoot us down.

On they came, vertical and dangerous slashes right through our formations, their guns blazing; all this in a hail storm of anti-aircraft shells and phosphorous bombs bursting all around us. The long spidery tentacles shooting out from the bombs-burning, like acid, through whatever they touched-were interspersed with big chunks of steel given direction by other *human* beings on the ground.

When the flak was too close, a plane got holed or downed. When not quite close enough, the smaller fragments would pepper our plane with a sound indistinguishable from hail on a tin roof, the concussion sometimes rocking the ship like a baby's cradle, sometimes pitching it like a canoe in a storm. Thus, even when not penetrated, we were somewhat humbled; sharply reminded that the Japs had our range — in and of itself enough to make one sweat — and anxiously await the next burst!

The noise of all this, along with that coming from our fifties, was greater than I had encountered before, probably because there was more of it. I wondered, at one point, if God could hear my prayers above the racket. But that came later. Now all my senses were telling me that the Nips were trying their best to end what, in my mind, was too short a stay on God's green earth. Every now and then a Nip fighter went down, sometimes clearly from our guns. Other times without apparent cause. Sometimes exploding in a dramatic display of fireworks. A few of the pilots bailed out but most did not. For, in general, the Nips used no chutes. It was against their religion to be taken prisoner and jumping without a chute meant instant death. Yet General Kenney reports seeing one jump in the Philippines when his Zero caught fire while strafing one of our air fields. The Jap pilot hit flat on the steel plank surface of the airdrome about a hundred feet from where Kenny was standing. He said it was not a pretty sight.[40]

On earlier missions we sometimes had the luxury of watching Jap fighters go into the ocean or the ground. We needed to see such things in order to get credit for kills. Not this time. No time! Generally, while one would not think the show worth the price of the ticket — what happened over Balikpapan was one hell of a show!

While this show was going on, we began to take damage. The Japs seemed to concentrate on the lead section, and, particularly, on the lead plane with Tom Musgrave, our Group Commander, on board. That plane also carried the lead bombardier. So the attack on the lead plane was furious. Musgrave's plane immediately caught big hits, 10 to 12 inch holes from 20 mm hits in the wings and the fuselage, and a 7.7 mm round crashed into Musgrave's window.[41]

On we went. As for the Nips, (shorthand for Nipponese or People of the Sun) they were taking some licks! An Oscar lost its tail and plunged like a dead bird into Balikpapan Bay. A Zero burst into flames, did a fiery Roman Candle loop and crashed to earth. Others rolled over and headed down with no apparent damage. As for me, though none of this was routine, it was only later, upon reflection, that I fully appreciated the drama that unfolded before we even dropped our bombs that day.

As for Musgrave's decision to wait for an opening in the clouds, it earned appropriate accolades in the words of The Presidential Unit Citation awarded to the 5th Group for this mission:

> *Although the primary target had been obscured by cloud cover, the 5th Bomb Group, ignoring the less perilous alternative of hitting the secondary target, circled until the aiming point cleared, then made a precision run. During the circling maneuvers, anti-aircraft fire badly damaged fifteen of the [23] bombers, four of which were later finished off by enemy fighters, but they continued to drop their bombs with devastating effect.*

In my plane, AC 613, our Bombardier, Harold Page, certainly contributed to that *devastation*. Earhart says that Page could drop a bomb down a smokestack. He had proven himself as about the best *bomb aimer* in the Squadron. ...and he could make that Norden Bombsight stand up and take notice ... We circled the target hoping the clouds would go away. All of a sudden the target appeared and Page said: "I've got it' or words to that effect."[42] And down went our load!

Heading for Home

Once bombs were away, we rose to 20,000 feet and got the heck out of there. As it turned out, this period was the most difficult for me.

The Japs in Hot Pursuit

On earlier missions, Nip fighters would occasionally follow us away from the target briefly. And I remember one episode coming off of Yap with several damaged Liberators when the Japs followed with alacrity for 20 to 30 minutes. One was in tight formation right next to my tail position. He initially took a hit in the top of the fuselage where his life raft was stored. A six-foot flame sprang forth immediately. Then I saw a crewman trying to put it out. But the Japs spotted the fire as soon as I and then, as was their practice, gang-attacked — one after the other. All this so close to me I could see the fighter pilots faces.

I had many shots, several close in, at the attacking fighters. But I failed to halt the carnage, or be sure I got any *kills*, and watched the Liberator descend slowly into the drink. I still remember vividly the exact moment that ship touched the water. For 50 years afterward I felt some guilt for not being able to prevent this loss or at least make the Nips pay some price for their evil. It is only in the past two years that I have been able to shake such feelings — for I now believe I did the best I could under the circumstances. The lost crew occupied a tent adjacent to mine on Los Negros in the Admiralty Islands. I shall never forget the truck that came around several minutes later to collect the belongings of my lost friends nor the way I felt at that precise moment. And the fact that the clothes of missing airmen were later recycled to other crewmen was a constant reminder of such events. But, to pick up our tale again, we now encountered a new ball game.

With 15 of our 23 planes seriously damaged, the Nips smelled blood. They attacked for another hour, going out from Balikpapan 240 miles in the process. The 5th Group bombers downed on the mission went down during this phase of the operation. One, a lead ship, got hit and nose-dived into Balikpapan Bay. No one got out. Another plane on that mission, piloted by First Lieutenant Oliver L. Adair, got hits on an inboard engine, a wing, the tail, and the fuselage. Hough and Arnold starkly describe what followed.

A blaze 50 feet long spurted from the tail. A waist gunner had his gun shot out of his hands. The gun was damaged but was hand-held and fired anyway using a parachute to protect against the hot barrel. A lot of praying took place. Before returning home, it was necessary to toss the ball and top turrets overboard to save fuel. Holes in the gas tanks were plugged with rags, pencils, and pieces of a wax candle.[43]

Yet, Noemfoor, the home base, was not to be reached. An emergency landing at Morotai (400 miles from base) was ordered. The landing was successful, in the sense that any landing one survives is *successful*. But due to a broken brake line, the plane plowed through palm trees — a stump hitting one crewmember in the leg. The nose wheel gave way and shot into the plane hitting the same crewmember in the other leg. Yet all members of the crew escaped major injury as the plane nosed up into a sandbank.

But, to return to my story, leaving the target was the most difficult time for me. While I had been quite busy while circling and over the target, and believed I had one kill and one probable, now I was left with nothing to do. For although the 5th Group was continuously under attack for over an hour, with over 70 passes, and although my plane endured pass after pass by zeros, Tonys and Oscars throughout that entire period, none of the passes were from an angle which allowed me to fire my fifties.

I like to think that the *heads up* we tail gunner's gave them earlier now encouraged them to try some different angles of approach. In any event, I now sat feeling quite isolated — as every gun on No. 613 fired nonstop, incessantly, for the entire time.

Sitting in that tail and being an observer rather than a participant in the action going on all around me was almost intolerable. I not only had time to think, which is usually not the case in combat, I also had time to pray; a luxury denied me earlier. It was the only time I can remember looking down on Jap held territory to see just what kind of terrain we might have to fall into. Not promising since all I saw was mountainous jungle, thickly covered with a deceivingly soft and inviting vegetation. No terra firma in sight anywhere. But I was not deceived! I knew full well that water or jungle, a fatal welcome was likely for most who tempted either hostile environment.

I now called on my Maker to work his will, at the same time expressing the hope that his plans included my survival, my heart beating so hard and with so much noise that I expected it to rip open my rib cage at any moment.[44]

Clearly, fear was a passenger, a first class passenger, on this journey through Pacific skies that turned out to be not so pacific. But he was a constant companion to those flying combat missions in the Southwest Pacific (Could it be otherwise when we are all cowards at heart?) At the same time, fear is often accompanied by another passenger — courage. While the former may fly without the latter, the reverse is never the case. For where there is no fear, there is no courage.

The presence of fear in combat, in and of itself, is not a very debilitating presence. Combat soldiers manage to function effectively in spite of any emotions that might be present. That is the goal of training and discipline. And although we did have some people who could not stand the stress and experience mental breakdowns, (I knew of three on one crew) such cases were relatively rare.[45]

Given a choice, I would much rather have never seen a Jap fighter in an attack mode on this or any other mission. Yet, if my plane is going to be under attack, give me a part of the action!

Losses and Accomplishments

While the 5th Bombardment Group lost three of its 23 Liberators at Balikpapan, the 307th Group lost none and the 90th Group only one. That is the price we paid for being first over the target. But, be that as it may, it is not the whole story. It does not take into account the number of casualties suffered by the 5th Group. Of the 19 Liberators that finally escaped from Balikpapan, 11 were badly damaged, and five did not make it back to our base at Noemfoor.[46]

I have not been able to confirm these figures, but Cortesi reports that the casualty rate[47] for the 5th Group was 53% and the death rate 31%.[48]

By contrast, the 307th Group lost no planes and had serious damage to only two. Not a single man in their planes was killed or wounded. Part of this discrepancy is due to the fact that, being first over the target, we initially caught the brunt of the attack. But perhaps there was more to it than that. The Commander of the 307th Group, Colonel Bob Burnham, said later: 'We were goddamned lucky compared to the other Group (the 5th). We got intercepted by 20 or 30 planes but, apparently, they got a little squeamish after their clash with the 5th Bombbardment Group gunners.[49]

The 90th Group — coming in last — lost one plane but all crew members were rescued.[50] Had the 5th Group, emulating the 90th Group, opted for the alternate targets described by the Presidential Unit Citation as "less perilous," our good fortune might have matched theirs. Boeman reports that while stationed on Morotai in 1945, he frequently heard airmen argue about the relative merits of the 13th and 5th Air Forces. Indeed, on one occasion he even witnessed a fist fight over who had the roughest time over Balikpapan.[51]

A mere tail gunner, such as I, can take no credit for the decision to hang in there until our target cleared. That was Musgrave's decision. And though the airmen in the 5th Group all got Air Medals for their *gallantry and skill.*[52] It was Colonel Musgrave's courageous decision that gave us the chance to confront the challenge.

The Japanese losses were considerably less than ours if measured in manpower. Their fighter planes carried a single pilot while each of our Liberators carried ten men. We claimed 11 kills or probables but we had many more casualties on this mission. At the same time we imposed serious damage on the major assigned targets. The Unit Citation described it this way: "Photographic assessment of the damage showed 36 hits on the Pandansari refinery area, four hits on furnaces or pipelines and the installation units, three hits on the adjacent receiving tanks area, and two bomb patterns visible across the building and tank storage areas. The success of this unusually long and daring mission definitely proved the vulnerability of this Japanese refining center to daylight raids by land based heavy bombers and resulted in a disruption in the flow of oil and gasoline which had an immediate effect on the enemy's tactical operators.[53]

After three more strikes, not a single building of the 100 plus in the Balikpapan oil complex still stood. While our Commanders estimated a six months delay before the Japs could start producing significant amounts of gas and oil, the complex remained devastated for the rest of the war. It is probable that the Japs thought repair useless. After all, we had established beyond a shadow of a doubt that we could return and repeat our bombing successes anytime we chose. The Japs did have producing oil fields and refineries at Brunei on the North coast of Borneo. So some fuel was shipped over to Balikpapan or directly from Brunei to other Japanese units. But it was not enough.

General Street, in a 1945 interview with reporters, said: 'They talk a lot about Ploesti but the efforts against the Balikpapan refineries made the conquest of the Philippines a hell of a lot easier and certainly shortened the war in the Pacific.' And after the conflict ended in 1945, the Commander of Japanese Escort Squadron 103 said: 'We could only give flyers 30 hours of flight instruction because the destruction of the Balikpapan oil complex had drastically cut our training fuel allotments. Of 750 training planes, we only had gasoline rations for 180 of them. So, by the spring of 1945, we had nothing but raw, inexperienced pilots to fight the Americans and we did not even have many of these. So defeat became inevitable.[54] Of course *defeat* was a forgone conclusion from 7 December 1941. The Japanese Commander in Chief at Pearl Harbor, Admiral Isoroku Yamamoto, had recognized as much even prior to the war when he reminded his compatriots that the United States was a sleeping giant--vulnerable when slumbering but a monster when aroused.[55] So we are reminded once again that wars are not always fought by rational men making rational decisions.

Over the Celebes Again

Coming back over the Celebes, we feared that the cloud cover that had protected us so effectively inbound might have dissipated. As we feared, Jap fighters from Manado and Kendari were waiting for us for a second time. And we were now much less able to defend ourselves. But, just as before, we encountered billowing cloud banks one to two miles deep. So we took cover and pressed on, avoiding any contact with the Nip fighters searching for us.

Halmahera One More Time

As we passed over the Molucca sea that separates the Celebes from the Halmaheras, Musgrave scanned his hostile environment. He feared that the interceptors from Bitjoli might jump his damaged planes and the exhausted and decimated crews they carried. There would be no surprise this time. After Balikpapan, every Jap Commander in the theater knew where we were, our precise heading, and the approximate time we would be within the range of enemy bases.

Thinking quickly, Musgrave radioed FEAF headquarters on Noemfoor: "We're in tough shape. We've got a lot of cripples coming home. If we get jumped over the Halmaheras, half of us might not get home. Can we have some fighter cover?" The immediate response from FEAF: "You got it Colonel."[56] General Streett, with admirable foresight, had a squadron of P-47s waiting at Cape Sansapor for just such an emergency. The base was contacted and 22 P-47s from the 49th Fighter Group, 9th Squadron, raced westward to meet us.

Just as we hit the west coast of Halmahera, someone yelled: "bandits!" But a second look revealed they were the P-47s. Were they needed? Absolutely, for just about the same time 20 interceptors from Bitjoli appeared on the horizon. A dogfight quickly ensued--and not to the Japs advantage. The boys of the 9th shot three Nips out of the sky[57] before we could say "Thank God for the 9th Squadron!" Four others were damaged, at which point the Japs turned a fast tail back to their base. Reluctantly, the Squadron leader of the 9th gave up the chase and the squadron, as was its duty, formed around the 5th Group to escort us home. So our luck held again.

Noemfoor at Last

On to Kornasoren strip on Noemfoor where the Bomber Barons landed one by one, the first ones attracting three salvos of anti-aircraft fire until recognized as "friendlies." Of nineteen Liberators safely past the Celebes on the return flight, 11 were severely damaged. Three of the planes made emergency landings on Sansapor, two on Morotai[58] — on unfinished Wama strip — right across the bay from Halmahera and the large Jap base at Bitjoli.

One was aircraft 092 (Squirrely Shirley), from the 31st Squadron. Over Balikpapan she had picked up 11 holes from anti-aircraft fire and damage to her wings and nose turret from Zero attacks. And she was so short on gas that making it back to Noemfoor was out of the question. So she became the first Liberator to land on Morotai. Unfortunately, the invasion of Morotai had occurred exactly two weeks earlier — not enough time to complete construction of the air strip. The completed portion was just too short for a normal B-24 landing. So the crew released parachutes out of each waist window, she hit the ragged runway, and managed to come to a stop just before she reached the end.[59]

The crew members of another 5th Group plane (394th Squadron) were seriously wounded for the first time in making a crash landing on the unfinished Wama strip. The first night there, they had a Jap air raid. That crew did not get back to Noemfoor until 8 October. And their troubles were not over. They were scheduled for the 18 October Strike on Balikpapan but developed some major problems after take-off and had to return to base. 'Twas not easy. They had a heck of a time making it after dumping gas and bombs and sweating out maintaining altitude for six hours!

As for our AC, # 613, we knew, given our original distances and all the *unexpected flying around* we had done, that getting back to Noemfoor might be a problem. Sure enough, while several hundred miles out from Noemfoor, but past Morotai, we began to fear that we would run out of fuel before making land. At that point, Earhart had a lengthy discussion with Hubert Warnock, the Flight Engineer, in whose judgment he had great confidence. When Warnock suggested that Earhart lean the fuel to the engines to the verge of backfiring, it was quickly done. But, even with that adjustment, we calculated a little later that a dip in the salty brine was a little too probable. So Earhart then shut down engines # 1 and # 4.[60] As for the rest of the crew, we did our part by jettisoning the bomb bay tank, flak suits, ammunition, and other items — finally landing with 100 gallons of gas — enough to fly for 30 minutes if 613 was burning gas at the average of 200 gallons per hour. If burning more than that, a water bath was that much closer.[61] Given that we were in the air for 15:30 hours, that was cutting it too close for comfort — in my book! But we did make it back to Noemfoor.

Of the twenty-four 5th Group Liberators that lifted off from Noemfoor on 30 September, only 14 were able to make it back to the strip from which they had departed 15 to 17 hours earlier. Of these 14, some bellied in. Some plowed off the strip with coral chips, dirt, and vegetation flying in all directions. Two came in with feathered props.[62]

Hough and Arnold set the scene quite well:

On the ground at Noemfoor, ground personnel, flight crews which had not flown the mission, and assorted others packed the area around the air strip. As the planes from the strike descended, it was all too clear that many were riddled with holes, parts of tails, wings, and turrets all shot up. It was an emotional moment and it led the 5th Group Operations Officer to burst into tears. But he was not ashamed of it.[63]

So the only strike for which the 5th Group earned a Presidential Unit Citation — this nightmare — was over. But only for this day. A difficult time now ensued for the medics who had the job of removing the dead and wounded from the planes and moving the crewmen who were seriously wounded to the hospital. A depressing experience also for the ground crews who had to clean up the blood and guts that littered the interiors of the Liberators. On only a slightly more protracted basis, repairs had to be made fairly quickly since the Bomber Barons would soon fly four more missions to Balikpapan to finish what they started. But none of that was of concern at that moment to the totally sapped crewmen who survived the strike.

While not looking forward to the debriefing that was inevitable, all recognized its importance as they straggled into the briefing tent. The usual whiskey ration was offered. Some took the ration; some gave theirs away. I did the latter — as I had done and continued to do on all my missions. We gave the interrogators what they wanted and departed.

It was now about 5:00 p.m.— 17 hours since takeoff and twice that many since my head had seen a pillow. So I went back to my tent to get a little rest before chow. However, there was to be no chow for me at all that day. I did not rise again until the next morning, after a very fitful night. Just as exhausted as I had been on retiring but glad to be alive, no matter what my condition.

Notes

[1] John Boeman, Morotai, Sunflower University Press, Manhattan, KS, 1981, p.111.

[2] On another island, Noemfoor, the tent area of the 31st Bomb Squadron was right in front of a former Japanese encampment area. Meat racks were still standing in the area. Starving Jap soldiers, who had been "forced" into cannibalism in order to survive, used the platforms for processing the bodies of Australian soldiers and airmen .... In captured Jap documents, a Lt. Sakamoto is quoted as saying: 'The taste is said to be good' Pete Arnaiz, APO-719, Somewhere, S. Pacific, (ND) p. 14. To give this episode perspective, it may be noted that on several earlier occasions, Japs had been caught stealing food from garbage cans on Biak. (Boeman. p. 99). And while I was stationed on Morotai, hungry Japanese soldiers, in stolen GI clothing, were caught in our chow lines. Not that the food was all that good — but these episodes do show that hunger and starvation was a threat for Nips caught on the islands MacArthur bypassed or which he had cut off by his island-hopping strategy. So the animalistic behavior of the Japs on Noemfoor was simply the culmination of a process driven by hunger. History teaches that extreme hunger can and, sometimes does, lead to cannibalism. The Japs were no exceptions to such a generalization.

[3] From the Presidential Unit Citation awarded to the Fifth Bomb Group for the September 30, 1944 mission. Reprinted in The History of the Fifth Bomb Group, Hillsborough House, Raleigh, NC (1946)

[4] D. Hough and E. Arnold, Big Distances, Duell, Sloan, Pearce, NY (1945) p. 153

[5] Lawrence Cortesi, The Deadly Skies, Kensington Publishers, NY (1982), p. 71

[6] Ibid., p. 55

[7] Geoffrey Peret, Winged Victory, Random House, New York, (1993) p. 438

[8] Cortesi, p.13. The 13th Air Force was activated on January 13, 1943. It was designated the 13th for a particular reason.. General George C. Kenney initially commanded all allied air forces in the Southwest Pacific. Instead of mixing Americans and Australians, Kenney decided he would like to have an American air force. He so informed General Hap Arnold, CinC of USSAF, requesting the number five, one of his two favorite numbers. The other was 13, the number of his flat in Lennon's Hotel in Brisbane, Australia, where MacArthur was also quartered. When informed that the number five was already taken by the 5th Air Force, the new Air Force became the 13th. (Geoffrey Perret, Winged Victory, Random House, NY, 1993, p. 169)

[9] Field Order #153 identified the 31st as the lead squadron on the mission.

[10] We had moved up to Noemfoor only days before from Wakde. The move was accomplished using B-24s only. The rubber bomb bay tanks were removed and replaced with wooden racks. Everything the 31st owned--tents, duffel bags, weapons, etc. — were loaded and away we went. At the time I thought. "Now I know what the members of a traveling circus have to go through, even though they traveled in trains instead of planes." After landing, the planes were unloaded and returned to Wakde to pick up the bomb bay tanks.

[11] Sam Britt Jr., The Long Rangers — A Diary of the 307th Bombardment Group (H), The Reprint Company, Spartanburg, SC (1990), p. 134

[12] Cortesi. p.18

[13] Cortesi, p.14

[14] Ibid..

[15] S. Birdsall, Log of the Liberators, Doubleday and Co., Inc., Garden City, NY (1973), pp. 18, 35. cf. Perret, p. 499 at fn. 52, and generally pp. 216- 218, and Philip Ardery, Bomber Pilot, University of Kentucky Press, Lexington, Ky. (1978) p. 109. In interpreting these loss figures, a distinction must be made between the number of bombers taking off and the number reaching the target. While 176 took off, 11 aborted and did not fly the mission. The 32.9 percentage is based on 164 bombers flying the mission, with 54 lost, on August 1, 1943. However, it is unclear whether this loss figure includes eight which landed in Turkey. Birdsall, p.35 reports that of 53 bombers lost, 45 were scattered along the way with eight crews being interned in Turkey. If 45 bombers were lost, the percentage reduces to 27.2 percent. Perret (p. 217) puts the loss at 73 but, presumably, that figure includes those planes that aborted and those that landed in Turkey.

[16] Hough and Arnold, p. 159

[17] Air Force Magazine, 1944, p.58

[18] Perret, p. 439. What is prohibitive in any given situation is an interesting question. It must always be related to the importance of the target. In the case of the Ploesti raid on August 1, 1943, Commanders anticipated a loss of 50 percent (Perret, p. 217) and actually lost 27.2 to 32.9 percent of the Liberators that made it to target.. It would be interesting to know exactly what our Commanders thought our losses would be over Balikpapan and what loss they would have been willing to take to accomplish this mission.

[19] Cortesi, p. 65. Phosphorous bombs, in fact, downed at least one of the B- 24s shot down over Balikpapan., Birdsall, p. 197

[20] Hough and Arnold, p. 153

[21] Cortesi, p. 31

[22] Cortesi, P. 73

[23] Hough and Arnold, p. 153

[24] Presidential Unit Citation

[25] Hough and Arnold, p. 155

[26] Presidential Unit Citation

[27] Letter to author from Pat Earhart, dated July 1, 1997.

[28] Hough and Arnold, p. 157-158

[29] Hough and Arnold, p.160

[30] Cortesi, p. 87

[31] Cortesi, pp. 87-88

[32] Cortesi, pp. 127-128

[33] Ibid., p. 89-90

[34] Ibid., 92

[35] A former Squadron Commander of the 31st Bomb Squadron informs me that in such situations he always gave the order to bomb the alternate target and head for home. The distances being flown in the Southwest Pacific were simply too great to take chances on running out of gas--or taking damage which would prevent a safe return to home base. One can only surmise that Musgrave's courage coupled with the importance of this particular target to the overall war effort, was sufficient to overcome any doubts he might have had about his decision.

[36] Hough and Arnold, p. 157. This kind of formation made for nice concentration of the bomb pattern. But it was not as safe for bomber crews as the box or diamond formation that was adopted for the second and later Balikpapan strikes.

[37] Cortesi, p. 92

[38] Cortesi, p. 93

[39] Presidential Unit Citation. See James F. Sunderman, Editor, World War II in the Air, The Pacific Bramhall House, New York, (1961), p. 168.

[40] Sunderman, p. 201.

[41] Cortesi, pp. 95-96

[42] Letter to author dated July 1, 1997

[43] Hough and Arnold, pp. 163-64

[44] I later learned that my prayer was simply one of many. For example, the copilot on Adairs ship was heard on the intercom begging God to get him out of there.

45 Perret reports one case in which a P-40 pilot, after witnessing the crash and death of a buddy, jumped in his plane, flew straight up, then nosed over into a steep whistling dive which ended only when he met the ground. In this way he joined his recently departed friend. In other cases, gunners have been known to jump from planes while airborne to avoid any more combat missions. (Perret, pp. 408-409)

[46] Cortesi, p. 107

[47] Casualty rate refers to these killed and wounded

[48] Cortesi, p. 101

[49] Cortesi, pp. 109-110 (Three Japs were shot down by the gunners on Musgrave's crew alone.

[50] On approaching the Celebes on the return flight, the 90th Bombardment Group was attacked by 30 to 40 interceptors resulting in considerable casualties. Apparently, the cloud cover that had protected the 5th Group inbound and outbound was not available to the 90th Group on the return trip. Thus doth fortune play a role in the lives of men.

[51] Boeman, p. 99

[52] Presidential Unit Citation

[53] Ibid

[54] Cortesi, p. 224

[55] Thomas J.Cutler, The Battle of Leyte Gulf — 23-26 October 1944, Harper-Collins, New York, 1994, p. 14. Yamamoto, while still serving as Commander in Chief of all Japanese Naval forces, was shot down and killed by 13th Air Force P-38's on April 18, 1943. He was aboard a "Betty" flying from Rabaul to Bougainville to inspect Japanese naval forces. Since we had earlier broken the codes the Japanese used to communicate throughout the Pacific, we learned of this flight far enough in advance to send a welcoming committee of P-38's. While

Yamamoto was escorted by nine Jap fighter planes, they were no match for our sixteen P-38's. And the guns on Yamamoto's Betty had less range than the guns on the P-38s. Catching the formation 15 minutes from Bougainville, black smoke soon boiled up from the dense jungle below. Yamamoto was dead-along with two other Jap Commanders who were aboard. Masatake Okumiya and Jiro Horikoshi, Zero, Bantam Books, New York, 1991, pp. 210-211

[56] Cortesi, p. 103

[57] Cortesi, p. 104

[58] In this paper, I have used Cortesi's report that five of the nineteen planes surviving Balikpapan did not make it back to Noemfoor. But if Hough and Arnold are correct , Adair's plane would make it three on Morotai and three on Sansapor for a total of six.

[59] "Shirley" went on to become probably the most famous of all the Liberators flown by the 5th Group during the War. She successfully completed over 100 combat missions, two of which involved making her bomb run on three engines.. Though often holed by enemy action, no crewmember flying her ever suffered combat injury. Her missions averaged over ten hours each, mostly over water and in all kinds of severe weather. But she always returned. Her mission included the roughest targets ever hit by the 5th Group — Balikpapan and Brunei Bay, as well as targets on Yap, Woleai, Palau, Truk, Biak, Halmaheras, Ceram, Borneo, Negros Island in the Philippines, Nichols and Nielson Fields near Manila, Corregidor, and Cavite. Given her record, there is little wonder that air crews loved her and were always pleased at the opportunity to fly her.

Though my records are incomplete, I have established two dates when I flew with "Shirley." July 14, 1944 on a 12 hour and 30 minute strike on Yap and September 15 on a nine hour and 15 minute mission to Halmahera. The latter was in support of the invasion of Morotai which occurred on that very day. Morotai was ten miles from Halmahera, a major Jap base with 40,000 Jap troops and several major air bases. It was essential that we prevent any major use of the air strips on Halmahera to launch fighter planes. While we were not able to completely stop such activity, we certainly made the Nips pay a price. I have had Shirley's name painted on the fuselage of a currently operational and combat- configured B-24 touring under the auspices of the Collings Foundation. While some may not appreciate the sentiment, those of us who flew her and know of her successes will have no doubt she deserves this honor. (See Press Release from 13th Air Force, Morotai, 1945 for additional details about Squirrely Shirley.)

[60] See Letter from Pat Earhart to author, July 1, 1997

[61] See Letter from Harold Page to author, June 7, 1994.

[62] Cortesi, p. 104

[63] Hough and Arnold, p. 166

Acknowledgements: The account of the Balikpapan strike presented in this paper relies heavily on the author's recollections as a Tail Gunner on that mission, recollections drawn upon over fifty years after the event. Heavy use has also been made of two previously published accounts of the same event: Donald Hough and Elliott Arnold, Big Distance, Duell, Sloan and Pearce, NY, (1945) and Lawrence Cortesi, The Deadly Skies, Kensington Publishers, NY (1982). While none of these authors were present on the mission, their accounts, compiled from various sources, have buttressed and supported my memories and have supplied additional facts either never known to me or simply forgotten with the passage of half a century. Readers may wish to consult either or both sources for additional details.

Excerpts from The Deadly Skies are reprinted by permission from The Deadly Skies, by Lawrence Cortesi, Copyright " 1987 by Lawrence Cortesi. Published by Kensington Publishing Corp., NY

The excerpt from Winged Victory is reprinted by permission from Winged Victory, by Geoffrey Perret, Copyright " 1993 by Geoffrey Perret. Published by Random House, Inc., NY

The excerpt from Morotai, is reprinted by permission from Morotai by John Boeman, Copyright " 1981 by John Boeman. Published by The Sunflower Press, Manhattan, KS

DOWN IN THE PHILIPPINES

By Bob Mahanes

31 October 1944: Here, down on Noemfoor (Dutch New Guinea), we had heard that the Japanese were bombing our positions up on Morotai five to six times each night but never in the daytime. So, when my crew packed aboard *Lil Jo Toddy* (all ass and no body), our modified B-24D, tail turret field-modified into the nose, we were excited and ready to go. We were all expecting anything the Japanese might try. We had heard that the airstrip on Morotai was not yet fully secured. Nevertheless, we departed Noemfoor 1300 hours 31 October 1944 with ten crew members and gear, and also a load of canned milk.

Our arrival on Morotai was without major event. We unloaded our gear, loaded onto a 6x6 truck and were driven to our tent area, a newly-bulldozed smooth stretch of light cream-colored coral. As our tent was already erected, we settled-in in a very short time, got our mosquito netting arranged properly, and had a shot of Australian White Horse Scotch (we had not been long returned from Rest Leave in Sydney, hence, still had a good supply of nerve medicine, Scotch).

Our social hour was interrupted by a corporal who drove a beat-up Jeep to our tent and informed me to have my men have their chow and be at the Squadron briefing tent by 1900 hours. As I was crew chief, it was part of my job to see that my crew knew about and arrived at the proper place at the proper time.

We had chow such as it was. Transparent, dehydrated potatoes, bright red Australian corned beef, and synthetic lemonade (battery acid, we called it), but we did have real, freshly-baked bread (unusual for such a forward-based unit). We ate as much as we could stomach, dipped our mess kits into the three half-drums of scalding-hot boiling water, and headed back to our tent.

Bill Gillispie, our tail turret gunner, and John Davies, our former nose turret gunner, said they needed just a little sip of Scotch to kill the battery acid taste still in their mouths. Frank Brown, first engineer, and Al Desmarais, his assistant, were discussing the brand new B-24J that had been promised us. Johnny Duarte, my assistant radio operator, and I had settled in on plans to paint a new leading lady on our new bird if we really did get one (B24-J). We were thinking about a *Lil Jo Toddy II* . Our navigator, Carlos C. Page, had liked the one that Johnny Duarte and I had painted for the 31st Squadron. It was called *Blue Jay*. It was copied from a picture of an 8th AAF B-17, but had no title that we could read. Johnny and I changed the color of the gal's dress because we had plenty of bright blue paint, but didn't have the bright orange to match the B-17 picture, so we just gave the title *Blue Jay* ourselves; it stuck.

Our train of thought was abruptly shattered by the sudden screeching of Jeep brakes just outside our tent. We all loaded on the Jeep and the driver took us to the briefing tent. Here we met our officer, John Emig, first pilot, and bombardier, Eugene Nagle. Our former copilot, Larry Toole, had transferred from 23rd Squadron to 31st Squadron as 1st pilot and instructor for new incoming pilots. Our former navigator, C. C. Page, had been an astronomy major in an Ohio college and had now become a Group Navigator.

I had been offered a radio spot with 5th Group as I had left Stateside Tonopah, NV, with a 100% E Rating, but with 20 missions behind me, I felt comfortable staying with the crew that I had trained and fought with. All of this is to say that we had a new copilot, and navigator whom I had never met and wouldn't even see until we boarded our B-24 for our next strike. It would be #25 for me. I was becoming a *short-timer*. Most crews with 25 long-hour missions got to go back Stateside ...those with 25 missions and short-hour time got another R&R in Australia. I believe the replacement copilot was a Lt. Harris, and the navigator, a Lt. Thomas.

As I sat in the briefing tent, it occurred to me that here I am, not on Morotai a full 10 hours, and now I'm being briefed on the first land-based bomber strike back into the Philipines, Alicanti airdrome in Northern Negros, right in the middle of the Versian Isles. I was reminded of General MacArthur's admonition, "I shall return." We met our brand new B-24J on a Morotai airstrip in the dark on 1 November 1944, pre-flighted and made ready with six other crews of the 23rd Squadron, 5th Bomb Group (H), 13th Army Air Force, for our first strike into MacArthur's old domain, the Philipines. The 25th mission for me. For some reason I mumbled to myself, "twenty-four and one half."

As I mentioned before, Johnny Davies had been our nose Turret gunner. At the time, I was manning a single 50 cal. hand-operated gun from the right waist window, a new position for me. I had previously operated a single 50 out of the left waist window, getting two confirmed kills in one month over the Jap base at Yap Island. Because of our plane's position to the right and just aft of the lead plane, this new position gave a much greater visibility for on-coming Jap fighters. Because of this, Johnny Duarte wanted to try this position. Johnny Davies would take Johnny Duarte's place at the left waist gun, and I would go up in the new Emerson nose turret (I had done the same on a strike on the Balikpapan oil refinery on Borneo).

We were now nearing our initial point where the squadron would form up into a tighter formation in preparation for our bomb run. In a tight formation, the bombing pattern is more concentrated, and the gunners are better able to provide protective fire cover.

We were about 12,000 feet altitude and were encountering about 90% heavy cumulus cloud cover, and only about 25 minutes away from the target area, and we were wondering if our target, Alicanti Airdrome, would be visible. The cloud cover was so heavy that I could not see all of our squadron formation as I looked out while leaving my radio operator's station on the way to my battle station in the nose turret. In a B-24, this is a crawl-space beneath the copilot.

On the way down, I met our substitute navigator in the passageway. We nodded and gave each other a thumbs-up signal (this was the only time I saw his face or spoke to him.) I met Lt. *Gene* Nagel, our bombardier, in the nose compartment, gave him my chest chute, and he stored it in its proper place. We had the few usual words, gave each other a thumbs-up, and he helped me into the Emerson nose gun turret through two sets of doors, one on the turret and another on the airplane, both of a sliding configuration more easily operated by the bombardier in the nose compartment than by someone in the nose turret.

As I have mentioned previously, today our bomber was a new B-24 Model J, and the nose turret was a new, more spacious Emerson Turret. It was covered by a single, half capsule, clear plastic covering with no metal reinforcement at all such as the old smaller consolidated A-5 turret had. I could get a much better view of incoming enemy fighters from the new model. I buckled up, checked my guns and gun sights, rotated the turret through extremes, both zenith and azimuth. Everything seemed to be in perfect working order. I called into the intercom "Nose turret to pilot, in place O.K., and ready... over." My answer was simply, "O.K., nose turret." After a short pause, the other gunners started reporting in. First, Bill Gillisie, tail turret; then Johnny Duarte, right waist; John Davies, left waist; Frank (Brownie), ball turret; and last, Al Desmarais, upper turret; all in place, O.K. and ready.

We were now only about 15 minutes from our target at about 12,500 feet in heavy clouds, about 90%, with occasional breaks. Normally, by this time the bombardier has control of the bomber, but this time we passed close to our target without any visible sighting. Then the formation made a 180 degree turn and took up a heading of about 220 degree. From my vantage point, I could see the airdrome, and so I notified our first pilot, Lt. John Emig. Minutes later, the whole formation made several abrupt changes in flight pattern. These changes did not concern me now, for I had turned full attention to the lookout for Jap interceptors, those fast little Zeros, the Zekes, and the chopped-wing Nates. Now, the B-24 was on a straight and level path — the bomb run.

I heard Gene Nagel's *Bombs Away* just about the same time 500 pounders had begun to emerge from the bombay of Lt. D.D. Campbell's plane just ahead and to the left.

When the sharp, accelerated, descending breakaway turned to the left, I had already braced myself for the slight *G* changes that accompanied this manuever. We were now headed for the straits between Negros and Panay. Over the water the clouds were becoming thinner, and I was able to see more and more open water. We were ten minutes out of target, and as I looked to the right, I thought I could see the outline of Panay beneath the thinning clouds.

My concern with the geography abruptly changed to an intense concern about numerous black specks in the clouds about two o'clock high in front of me. I pulled my amber-colored aviation goggles down over my eyes. This is it, Jap fighters, more than I had ever seen before, here seven, there ten, a whole string after that, and here another group, just as many, coming toward us from about eleven o'clock high. I yelled into my intercom, "Bandits eleven and two o'clock high." The only reply I got was from Brownie, our ball turret belly gunner, with a crisp, emphatic "Where?" I did a "Say again," and noted that we were over water and almost completely out of the clouds. The Jap planes were coming in real close now, passing over and around in an ever tightening circle. Al Desmarais, in the top turret, yelled into the intercom, "Bandits diving in from six o'clock high." I heard the chatter of his twin 50's, followed by the same from Bill Gillisie's twin 50's tail turret. Gillisie reported that number seven bomber of our formation was hit and one engine was smoking but still in formation. Now, the Zeros were diving three in succession with guns blazing; then our formation number seven bomber (last one in formation) was hit again, two engines on fire, plane is losing altitude, rolling over on wounded side, parachutes popping out, one, two, three, four, five, six, seven chutes were open, lost sight of bomber; three more Zeros dove in. This time on the number six bomber, same for number five. Now they were coming through our formation close enough for us to see the Jap pilots. "Flamed one yellow-bellied bastard," yelled Gillisie. I glanced down and to the right of my turret. "There it goes...a Nate on fire headed toward the ocean in a trail of smoke."

Now they were attacking frontal—three came right into my range. I was as excited as hell, which one should I try for, one was on top of me blazing away, but no hits, now he was gone. The second one was on me; I fired away. But I was too late; he hit my turret, I was O.K., but the turret plexiglas was damaged. He was gone; number three was in my sights; I was firing, got a hit, saw the canopy of Zeke shatter. Blam! Blam! I was hit with 20 mm cannon, my plexiglas dome peeled off. I was sitting unprotected in the wind. Here came three more Zeros. My guns would move, but would not fire. I kept moving the guns toward my attackers, squeezed the trigger, but no fire. He opened up on me and hit the thick glass sight shield. I was O.K., but he hit the pilot. "Two engines on fire," I heard Desmarais say, I felt something wet under my goggles. I felt my face with my left hand—blood. My whole arm was bloody, but I felt no pain only a burning sensation momentarily in my left foot. I felt like I was sitting on a loose, cushion spring, left cheek of my buttock, but no real pain. I looked out in front of me just in time to see a Nate Kamikaze dive into the number three bomber where, by now, we had fallen back behind. The Jap prop was still windmilling through the air and would surely hit our left wing. John Emig was able to raise the wing just enough to let it pass under. I saw that number two was afire and out of control; I did not see any chute come out. I brought my injured turret back to a neutral, forward position just in time to hear the abandon ship bell ring. I reached over my shoulder to open my escape door. I didn't have to though because Gene Nagel beat me to it. The wind pushed me partially through, but somehow the turret was energized, and rotated enough to catch both of my feet across my toes. I was stuck, and my feet hurt like hell. Nagle gave me a terrific jerk, freeing my feet. I was able to stand up just in time for him to buckle on my chest chute. Then came the long, continuous ringing bell — Bail Out! Bail Out!

Gene had our escape hatch open (the nosewheel door). It closed, he pulled the control lever, blood-colored hydraulic fluid sprayed all over, but the nosewheel door did open up again. Nagel motioned to me, Are you O.K.? I nodded yes, and motioned for him to jump. He did, and immediately opened his chute. By now, the bomber was losing stability, and I was thrown sideways as I stepped out into the slipstream.

I had the red D-ring that opened the chute in my hand. I counted to ten rather rapidly and pulled. I waited for the jerk of the parachute opening; there was nothing. I looked again in my hand, there was the red D-ring. My chute wasn't open, and I could tell by the air rushing by that I was gaining speed toward the ocean. I threw away the D-ring, grabbed the flap of my parachute and tugged as hard as I could. Seconds later, I welcomed the jerk on my chute harness as the big, white canopy blossomed above me.

I had fallen several thousand feet free-fall before the parachute opened, and now I was well below the Zeros that continued their rat-a-tat of the 7.7mm machine guns and the bang bang, bang of the slower, but more deadly fire of the 20mm cannon.

I heard Brownie's voice, "Gee whiz ... Damn!" As I looked to locate him, my eyes fixed upon a human arm falling by, followed by a tumbling headless human torso, and a little later, an empty, collapsed parachute. My God, I thought, it must have been Eugene Nagle. I didn't have much time to dwell on these thoughts as a Zero whizzed past me and was now making a 180 degree turn back toward me. Here the little yellow bastard with his machine guns opened up on me. I raised my feet and put my hands over my face. The Zero flamed by. As he did, I went limp, faking dead as though I had been hit. He circled me once, then left. It had worked! I remained in my *dead* posture until I could no longer see the Jap plane.

Again, I heard Brownie's voice above me but recognized it as only some Brooklynese cheer. I was nearing the ocean in my descent. I knew that I must release my parachute soon so that the canopy would not come down over me in the water and possibly drown me. I estimate I was maybe 200 feet or more above the ocean when I released my parachute. I fell for a long time. I hit the water hard enough that my inflated life preserver was ripped off.

I went down, down, down into a misty azure-colored world. I couldn't tell which way was up. My heavy, electrically-heated flying oversuit restricted my movements, and my Mae West didn't work. I swam this way and reverse. I was drinking gallons of salty Pacific water, and my lungs were about to explode. I couldn't find the surface. I began to think, "Am I going to die in this kingdom of Neptune?" Hell, no! I remembered my seat pack, life raft. If I could find the inflator ball and pull, the raft would inflate and pull me to the surface. Why didn't I think of this sooner? There was the red, wooden inflator ball now in my hand. I pulled and heard the CO2 rushing into my raft as it sped me toward the ocean's surface. I literally was lifted out of the water with a rapid ascent. My aching lungs gasped the welcome fresh air as I reached out to secure myself to the raft. My heart was pounding, and my stomach was cramping and churning. I leaned over the side of the raft and emptied back into the Pacific all that I had drunk plus what food I had in my stomach. Now I felt better.

I climbed into the life raft and collapsed. I was about to get into a comfortable position to rest and collect my wits. My heated flying oversuit was waterlogged and heavy. I started getting out of it when I heard Jap machine gun fire in the distance. I forced myself to quickly shed my cumbersome suit and cast it out of the raft. I heard the machine gun fire again; this time much closer than before. I could now see the Jap planes strafing my crew mates in the water, and now one was headed directly toward me.

I flipped my yellow and blue life raft upside down so that its blue bottom was now exposed. This was done to make a less visible target for my enemy. I was just a little late executing this defensive maneuver. The Jap Zero sent a string of rapid fire bullets across my raft. I dove as deep as I could and put my hands on top of my head in a defensive gesture. When the firing ceased, I slowly surfaced under the overturned raft. Again, I had escaped the attack. When I could no longer hear the sound of machine guns, I came out from under my raft. The Jap planes were nowhere in sight. I flipped my raft rightside up again. However, something was wrong. It was deflating; the machine gun fire had hit the raft. Two holes were visible. With my life jacket gone and holes in the raft, the only thing I could think to do at the moment was to stick a finger into each hole. This I did, P.D.Q.

With the Jap planes gone and floating along with my fingers keeping the raft partially inflated, I decided to just rest for awhile and think out my next move. As it turned out, it was a bowel movement. Now that my stomach cramps were gone, my thoughts of survival began to flow again. I tore my handkerchief into two pieces, rolled each half up tightly, and twisted each half into a bullet hole. I then re-inflated my raft by blowing into the mouth inflator tube that was attached to the raft. I would have to repeat this from time to time in order to maintain proper inflation.

Now, sitting upright in my repaired raft, I could hear a voice calling in the not-too-far distance. I recognized it —Brooklynese. It could be no one but *Brownie*, Frank Brown, our engineer. I paddled toward him, and in about two hours, I had joined him. He too, had been a target of the strafing, but neither he nor his raft had been hit.

It was now near sunset when I joined up with Brownie. He had witnessed the Japs brutal strafing of *Gene* Nagle and dismemberment of his body. Brownie also thought that he had seen another raft being strafed, and he pointed in the direction. We tied our rafts together and paddled to see if we could find another survivor. I guess in about a half hour we spotted the third raft, and about the same time, we heard the drone of a multi-engined airplane. It was low on the water when it came into view—a U. S. Navy PB4Y-2, the Navy version of the B-24, easily recognized by the big ball-shaped nose turret. Golly! Our spirits got a big boost; we paddled harder and shortly came upon Johnny Duarte, assistant-radio operator. He told us the strafers had missed him but had killed and destroyed the raft of someone near him. He did not know who it might be.

By now, only the glow of the setting sun allowed us to follow the low, circling orbit of the Navy plane. As it passed over us, a small parachute with mini-buoy was tossed out. It landed within 50 feet of our now tied-together rafts. We retrieved the buoy as the plane continued its low orbit.

There was a note which read, "Eight survivors, get together, go to large raft at orange smoke signal, some wounded. Will notify your location." Signed, VPB 104.

We watched the Navy drop a large inflatable raft, and then the bright orange smoke signal. As it was now almost dark, the Navy had done all it could. They made a final pass over the three of us and disappeared in the darkness to the south. I felt a profound sadness to hear the fading drones of its engines. All three of us tried to get a fix in our minds on the location of the orange smoke signal. We paddled about two more hours in its direction and decided to rest and try for some sleep. Johnny Duarte had not been hit, and he volunteered to stand first night watch. The sea was now fairly calm, and the moon was full, darting in and out of those puffy, tropical cumulus clouds. Even in the tropics, the sea air is cool at night. I had begun to feel a chill. I inflated my raft again, and pulled my blue and yellow tarp close around me. Although my toes were hurting and my left foot was beginning to swell, I felt it better to leave my shoes on for the warmth provided. Soon, I was in a fitful sleep. Brownie took the second watch around 2200 hours (10 p.m.). I heard Johnny and Brownie discussing the luminous visions they had seen on the water's surface, and occasionally, a luminous streak would leave the water and sail for twenty or thirty feet, then splash with a mini-explosion back into the sea.

2 November 1944: Brownie aroused me at 0200 hours to take the watch. Johnny was sleeping. He simply raised his head and asked, "You O.K.?" I nodded yes, and he went back to sleep. During the next four hours, I watched phosphorescent flying things go whizzing by leaving a glowing trail. Finally, one landed squarely in my lap. It surprised and startled me, causing me to let out a stiffled, "Oh!" which caused both Brownie and Johnny to raise their heads and say in unison, "What's up?" I had determined that the flying ghost was only a flying fish, native of tropical seas. I quickly helped it back into the sea and told the other guys, "It's only a fish." They resumed their sleep. My feet felt awfully tight in my shoes, and below my left ankle I could feel a hole in the side of my shoe. Painfully, I removed the left shoe, felt my ankle, something hard under the skin near the sole of my foot. I felt something hard and metallic—a bullet. All my toes were badly swollen. I remember now that I caught them in the turret exit door. Nagle had pulled me loose. So I hung my feet over the raft into the sea water; they felt better.

After a few minutes, I got up enough nerve to try to remove the bullet from my ankle. With my pocket knife, I eased the Jap 7.7 out; it didn't hurt as much as I thought it would. I felt better now and decided to remove my right shoe also only to find that

all my toes on that foot were also badly swollen. Both feet went over the raft into the water. My buttocks and head now began to hurt as the pain in my feet subsided.

At about 0430 hours the eastern sky began to show signs of sunrise. First, a grayish pink, then an orange glow, followed by brilliantly emerging sun...first, just a peep, then soon, a glorious ascent into the clear morning sky, a beautiful sight even in such precarious circumstances. I took a moment just to admire it.

As the sun rose, it cast its golden slick on the quiet Pacific to the east of me. I shaded my eyes with my hand as I looked eastward. I wasn't sure at first, but then, again and again, I stared eastward. Yes! There really was something afloat way over yonder. I aroused Brownie and Johnny, "Look, can you see?"as I pointed eastward. It was Johnny who confirmed my sighting. "Yes! It is, and there is some movement, also." It must be some of the other downed crew members. The Controller of the seas and wind was kind to us during the night. Now, we could easily close the gap between us and our buddies. By midmorning, we were close enough to see a big raft with five people aboard.

By ten-thirty we were greeting each other. In the big raft were John Emig, first pilot; Al Desmarais, second Engineer; Bill Gillisie, Tail Gunner; John Davies, Waist Gunner, and our substitute navigator, Harris or Thomas(?). Of the five, John Emig was the most extensively wounded, having multiple wounds about the body but none in vital areas. Bill Gillisie had an unexploded Jap 20mm shell in his right thigh. It had entered above the knee and penetrated about five inches up into the thigh. John Davies' hands were both badly hurt. Somehow, the skin of the palms of both hands had been pulled away, leaving him in a very painful condition.

Al Desmarais showed no outward signs of wounds, but his mind was out of this world, he was in profound shock. When I spoke to him, he could only stare at me with no voice or emotion. The navigator also seemed to be in mild shock, but he was able to tell me that Emig needed help.

There was a medical kit on board the large raft, but no one had been able, or did not know how, to properly use its contents. Nevertheless, as a pre-war, pre-med student, I was looked upon as the Medic in charge, now. A quick survey of the medical kit revealed morphine injectables, sulfa powder, bandages (some were water soaked, but still clean), an oily ointment for sunburn, aspirin, ammonia inhalants, insect repellant, iodine crushable swabs, tourniquet, scissors, a five inch set of tweezers, and a bottle of eye wash with eye cup. I guessed this was enough to relieve some of the discomfort of my crew; so I started first with John Emig. I thought it best to first relieve the pain with morphine, thus I gave Emig, Gillisie, and Davies each a shot. It proved to be effective rather quickly.

Moving about in a six-man life raft afloat with injured people was not an easy task, but by the time the morphine had put Emig into a world of euphoria, I was able to manipulate myself into position to clean his wounds and apply sulfanilamide powder. The same was done for Gillisie. Right or wrong, I dabbed some of the sunburn oil on Davies skinned palms. He said it made them feel better. Al Desmarias's eyes were glassy and fixed on some distant point. I really didn't know what to do for him. I found water in a can (in the emergency kit). I slapped Al sharply on the cheek, he spoke "Hey! Stop!" This was what I hoped would happen. I offered him some water; he drank some, then started talking. He said that his top turret had been hit at the same time our pilot was shot. He asked me if John Emig was dead. I replied, "No, but is badly hurt."

The Sulu Sea was calm, and the golden glassy sheen, caused by the bright sunshine, soon caused great discomfort to our eyes. We knew that we were in for an extra hot tropical day; thus we all faced away from the sun and splashed sea water on each other in an effort to keep comfortable.

As the wounded lay in the big raft, the rest of us stayed mainly in our one-man rafts which were each tied to the main raft. Conversation was at a minimum for most of the day. We surveyed our rations that came with the eight-man raft.

Eight cans of water and two small cans of peanuts was all of the food items that were not lost. However, I had some prunes (sent to me from the states by my wife). I usually put several in my shirt pocket before I went on a strike. I opened two of the cans of water, and each of the eight of us took a swallow. We kept the cans for future use. During the rest of the day, we just tried to keep as comfortable as possible and alert for the sound of aircraft. Nightfall brought a much-welcomed relief from the scorching sun, to be followed by a fitful sleep interrupted from time-to-time by a groan or painful yell from the wounded.

3 November 1944: That big ole bright orange sun came up out of the east horizon in full glory again. After tending the wounded, we had an indepth council meeting to determine our situation and what would be our best move to assure survival. We had determined that Lt. Nagle was lost in his parachute by strafing, and our navigator had been killed in his life raft by strafing Jap Zero's. Thus the remaining eight crew had to settle on a plan. After a short discussion, it was decided that Johnny Duarte, who was not wounded, and I would leave the group in our one-man rafts and paddle north, hoping to get back into the Southern Philippines to secure help. We left about 1000 hours that morning, and with the sun to our right (East), we started our effort to make landfall in the Philippines. By noon we were well out of sight of our comrades. We would paddle about 30 minutes and then rest for 15 minutes. By nightfall we were both exhausted. We did have the good fortune to have a torrential rainfall every afternoon, at which time we caught rainwater in our tarps, drank all we could, and filled our empty water cans (beer can size).

I gave Johnny two of the prunes that I had in my shirt pocket, and we each enjoyed one for our daily meal. That night there was a clear, full moon with scattered clouds. We both slept soundly.

4 November 1944: Morning skies were dark, and the wind was making whitecaps by 0900 hours. By 1000 hours, we knew that we were in for one of those tropical storms. We tightened the ropes between our two rafts and also tied ourselves to the rafts. A half hour later, we were riding great swells with a strong wind out of the south to our backs. We were headed north at a pretty good speed. By 1030 hours, we were being tossed about by the storm, waves and wallows twenty feet apart. Our rafts rolled over and over in the pounding spray, but we stayed together with our rafts.

By noon the wind was calming down, and we began to see blue skies again. This day we did not catch rainwater, and we lost our little water cans in the storm, but we were alive.

5 November 1944: There in the eastern sky, now all rosy and orange, came that big bright sun again. A little breeze from the south helped us along with our constant paddling. By mid-morning we could see a mass of floating kelp (orange-yellow sea weed). As we approached closer, we sighted what appeared to be a floating pole or upright channel marker. This gave us hope; for if it was a channel marker, we must be getting closer to land. Our hopes were dashed as we got closer. We could now see that it was a submarine periscope; the sub was protected from aerial view by the dense floating kelp. We paddled on and pretended not to notice the movement of the periscope. It was a Jap submarine, but it did not surface or move at all (we were not worth the risk of surfacing). We were glad to get over the hori-

zon and leave the sub behind, out of sight. It rained again that afternoon, and we drank as much as we could hold. It was as good as an ice cream soda.

6 November 1944: During the last night, my left buttock had begun to hurt awfully bad. I could feel something hard under the skin but couldn't move it. By this time the under skin of my left arm had become sore from rubbing against the raft while paddling. The same had happened to Johnny's right arm, so we decided to exchange rafts. In the exchange Johnny noted that the left side of my pants was bloody. I told him about the hard object that I had felt. The next thing I knew I was lying across my raft with my pants down and buttock shining in the sun. Johnny was easing a Jap bullet out with his pocket knife. You! It hurt, but I had to chuckle at the thought of what was happening. My new surgeon. After the operation, I thanked him, and I felt better.

Later we saw shark fins in the distance. As we paddled north the fins came closer. We now noted that many fish also had come up to our raft and were following us quite closely. The approach of the sharks (two of them) gave us quite a bit of concern. They came within 20 feet of our raft and circled several times. I wondered if they were interested in us or the fish congregating about our raft. As the closest shark turned toward the raft, I put the muzzle of my .45 into the water and fired. Both the shark and the fish about our raft scattered. We saw no more of the sharks, but soon the small fish were back with us. We saw dolphins later that same day. It rained and we had water again.

7 November 1944: It was clear again this morning. My butt felt quite a bit better, thanks to Dr. Johnny. At 1030 hours, we heard a multi-engined aircraft. As we scanned the sky to the south, we could see a formation of B-24's. They are in and out of the clouds. We saw only three squadrons of seven planes, but could hear the roar of a fourth squadron. Johnny and I both wondered if it was our 5th Group or maybe the 307th. We also hoped that they would see us and report our position. We felt a bit sad as the drone of those Pratt-Whitneys faded away.

We tried to catch some of the fish that were touching the sides of the rafts. We could catch them, but we were not able to hold them. I was getting weak, and they were so slippery that it was impossible to hold them. I hoped that I would feel better tomorrow. Maybe I would catch one. It was nightfall, and there was still a little wind from the south. I was beginning to feel chilly. With the sunburn, salt crust and yellow skin coloring from many doses of Atabrine, I looked really dark skinned. My auburn hair was now bleached blond from the sun and salt water. I was dehydrated somewhat and beginning to tire more quickly when paddling, but we had to keep going. Today we saw birds that didn't look like sea birds. We figured that we must be nearing land.

It didn't rain on us today. I was dreaming of a strawberry ice cream soda along with other pleasant thoughts. Johnny and I took time resting. Nodding, we were both saying prayers during this time. When I got a little blue and despondent, Johnny would cheer me up, and I would try to do the same for him. We were both determined to survive, and so far things seemed to be going fairly well. We both felt that the sight of land birds was a good sign. We paddled into the night until we were both exhausted.

8 November 1944: We were surprised, in the distant north, there seemed to be a land mass on the horizon. Small, yes, but it was certainly no cloud. As the sun climbed higher into the clear morning sky, we shaded our eyes with our hand and strained to be sure what we saw is not a mirage. No! It was not a mirage. A high peak standing still. Now it was partially hidden by a wandering low flying cloud, but wait, there it was again. That same

solid peak. "Johnny, do you see it?" "I'm not sure. I believe it is, but I'm not sure." We paddled harder than ever. Now we could detect some green color. Yes. It was an island. By noon we could see a clear outline of a high peak with a cliff facing the south and east and a gentle sloping to the west. By mid-afternoon we could see that the western slope ends in a wide beach. To the east, below the cliff, seemed to be a rocky surf. We paddled so feverishly that we were both exhausted. We both decided to rest for awhile.

Our thoughts began to wonder out loud. "We could make it today?" "Yes!" "How about Japs?" "Not sure." "Wait until dark to go in?" "No." "Beginning to feel a current in water that may take us away from the island. Let's go in at sunset when sun glare is brighter on the water." "Yes! That's a good plan. Stay out a few miles. Lay flat in raft and go in at sunset." We both agreed. We laid flat in our rafts and pulled our tarps (blue side up) over us. We raised it just enough to keep sight of the island. What a wonderful feeling. We rested about two hours. The low tropical sun had spread a wide golden paintbrush on the sea between our little rafts and the island. We eased to an upright sitting position and slowly began to paddle toward the wide white coral beach.

Once the sun was on the horizon, it quickly sank out of sight leaving only a rosy pink glow in the sky. This was happening now, and as we paddled in closer toward the beach, we could feel an increase in the water current around the island. We could feel ourselves being pulled toward the rocky shoreline beneath the cliff. We paddled harder and harder to stay away, but our strength was waning, and the current was getting stronger. We were being pulled into the rocks. We held off with paddles, then our feet and pushed and shoved through the treacherous rocks until we could touch the coral bottom with our paddles. We pushed toward the smooth coral beach. Finally the rafts drug bottom on the beach; the tide pushed us in a little more. Solid ground at last. We tried to get out and stand up, but our legs would not hold us up. We crawled hands and knees ashore, pulling our rafts behind us.

Once on high ground, we crawled into the brush, flipped our rafts upside down and crawled upon them. After a prayer of thanks, we both fell into a deep sleep. High on dry land we both still had the sensation of sea motion as we slept.

9 November 1944: Just before daybreak we were awakened by the crow of a rooster...that's right, a rooster. Right away we knew that the island was inhabited, but by whom? Friend or foe? With a good night sleep behind us, we were able to stand up on both legs and walk about slowly at first and later in an almost normal manner. I guess proper circulation had returned to our half-numb legs.

There were coconuts hanging about ten feet above us, but neither of us had the strength to knock one down with stone or stick. We just sat down again to plan our next move.

We could see that there was a trail in the underbrush leading away from the beach. With our .45s in one hand, we followed the trail on hands and knees. It also led us to the sound of the crowing rooster. The trail opened on a native village. There we saw an old man dressed only in loin cloth, squatting and feeding chickens. Not knowing what else to do, I boldly stepped out of the brush pointing my .45 directly at the old man and said loudly, "I'm American."

This scared the old man so badly that he fell backwards flat on his back. It took him a few seconds to regain his composure, and when he did, he exclaimed in a loud voice "Bueno Cano, Bueno Cano!" This I knew to be "Good American," for he began to smile, then cry as he called his grandchildren out of the bamboo house. The old man began mumbling in a mixture of broken English and Spanish. At this my companion, Johnny Duarte, began speaking to him in Spanish. The old man told us that we were the first Americans he had seen since the Japanese occupation. He called the *Jap Harpon*. He said *Harpon* had raped his daughters and made a house servant of his wife. So when an opportunity came, he took his family and grandchildren away from the main island of Negros and had brought them to the tiny islet of Unison.

Yes, there had been five Japs on this island of Unison. There was a lookout post high upon the cliff, but the Japs had deserted their post three days before we arrived. They had feared that the big American bombers would see their exposed lookout and bomb them.

He wondered why the *Harpon* patrol boat had not seen us as they departed and went south. I remembered now that must have been one of the days that we saw the flight of B-24s pop over our life raft. The Japs, too, must have seen them and kept their patrol boats out of sight.

Soon the children brought their school teacher to us. He was a young Filipino who was about 22 years of age and a second Lt. in the Filipino Scouts Army (We would call him a guerilla fighter). He introduced himself in perfect English as Lt. Carlos Rameriz, but insisted that we call him Carls.

Carls noted our physical condition and ordered raw eggs and fresh coconut milk for us to eat, then he ordered four teen-age girls to fix hot water for us to bathe.

Our shower had only two sides of bamboo thatch, L-shaped with a metal bucket with holes punched in its bottom hanging above. The girls poured warm fresh water into the overhead bucket while each of us took turns standing in the nude under it. We were supplied with a new cake of Palmolive soap. We soaped up to a good lather that washed us clean of the encrusted salt that the Pacific Ocean had bestowed the last eight days .

The girls stood by giggling as they repeatedly filled shower bucket. When we were finished, they gently patted palm oil on our sunburned face and arms, then fixed us beds in the abandoned Jap lookout post. We slept until dusk, then we were fed a meal of fried fish and rice. Man, this really did taste good.

After the shower we were given white short pants and shirts and a straw hat. Our uniforms were washed, dried and put in a small basket (we kept our dog tags). In this white dress outfit Carls told us that we could pass (at a distance from the Japs) as farm managers, as we were as dark skinned as any one else on the island. Carls said that the Jap patrol boat was due to come to the island the next afternoon, so we should leave by sailboat the next morning for the large island of Negros.

10 November 1944: From Kalliling to Base Camp. Johnny Duarte and I had slept in a large fish basket that had been hoisted high, some 20 feet or more from the earth floor of the village warehouse. Although the whole warehouse reeked with the very pungent odor of dried fish, our particular basket was new and had not been used to hold fish, thus the odor was not too oppressive. We were both awake when we heard voices in the doorway below us.

Second Lt. Carls Ramerez was directing his friends (and ours) to gently manipulate the ropes that would lower our sleeping quarters to the floor of the warehouse. This completed, Carls led us to an elevated bamboo dwelling on the outskirts of the village. Here, we had a breakfast of boiled prawns (similar to our Louisiana Tiger shrimp) and brown rice with a sauce made of frajioles negros (black beans), and a cold orangeade drink made from very tasty fruit no larger than a golf ball. The meal was both satisfying and delicious. A prawn is of the shrimp family, but in the live state, before boiling, they are almost transparent. They are highly prized in the Phillipine Islands (P.I.).

After finishing our meal, our sunburn and wounds were again treated. Palm oil was copiously applied to our sunburned faces, necks and arms; it had a soothing quality that felt good. My left foot wound was washed with warm sea water, swabbed with an iodine swab, then a loose bandage, over which I placed my freshly washed brown socks. (I had lost my shoes when my raft was overturned at sea).

Lt. Carls asked me if I had ever seen a *Hapon* (Japanese) pilot close up, and I responded that only the Kamikaze pilots that shot us down came so close that I could see their faces. I wondered why this question was asked of me. Carls noted the puzzled look on my face; then he said, "Today you will see them close up."

With our stomachs satisfied and other physical needs attended to, we set out on foot through the carefully guarded mountain trails. It was a slow and painful walk for me because my left foot had begun to swell after about 3 hours walking up these mountain trails. My bodyguard, a young Filipine lad of about 15 or 16 years, said that we would be stopping to rest pretty soon. This I was glad to hear.

About 10:30 a.m., as we entered a clearing in the jungle, we were met by two rifle-carrying Filipino scouts who greeted us quite warmly with the Versian greeting, *My aya ung bien*, literally meaning *Good morning*, or *Hope you are well*. And, of course, our reply was a smiling and curtly spoken *Sa Lamot* (one word, but pronounced as two) which, in my simple interpretation, means *Same to you*.

They spoke privately with Lt. Carls briefly, then shaking their heads in approval they beckoned Johnny and me to follow them. They took us about a kilometer into the jungle until we came onto another heavily guarded clearing. We could see several thatch buildings around the perimeter and a small building in the center surrounded by a heavy wire fence interwoven with barbed wire. We were about to see the Hapon pilots face to face.

I had expected to see small-statured men with squinted, fiery eyes, with a defiant scowl. To my great surprise, the two captured Jap pilots were about my size, five feet, ten inches, one of medium build. They were not defiant at all, but rather had faces stricken with fear. I remembered the strafing my parachuting crew had suffered on 1 November, and muttered aloud to Johnny, Eduardo and the big Filipino scout who accompanied us to the prisoners, "Kill the bastards."

Eduardo (or "Big Ed" as I called him) said that they had been captured that same day when they ditched their *Zero* fighter planes near the shore line of S. Negros. I was still wearing my .45 automatic in my shoulder holster when Big Ed told us about the capture. I remembered Gene Nagle's body being shot to pieces, and his collapsed parachute plunging into the Pacific. I pulled my gun from the holster. As I did, both Japs fell to their knees. As I hesitated, Big Ed tapped me on the shoulder and shaking his head in a negative motion said, "Captain, you don't have to...we will do it." I was both relieved and surprised. I had been addressed as a Captain, yet he saw by my sleeve stripes that I was a Tech Sergeant. This elated me. He had complimented me highly and had also kept me and my anger from executing a prisoner of war. (I later learned that the Filipino scouts referred to all flying personnel as Captain). I holstered my .45, turned and walked away from the prison compound.

Big Ed followed me and pointed to my feet and questioned, "What size?" He had to repeat his question before it dawned on me what he meant. Finally, I said, "91/2 C," but my foot was swollen and my normal size may not fit. "Maybe a 10." He nodded as we walked to one of the other buildings. It was

here that we stayed to rest and to have a lunch of rice cakes with black beans and tropical fruit marinated in coconut milk and brown sugar. The fruits were mango, red banana, copra, guava, and wild, red berries the size of a cherry that they called passion fruit.

After the noon meal, we took a little siesta which was not uncommon in the tropics. I had elevated my injured left foot, and by the end of my rest period, the swelling of the ankle had subsided considerably. I felt little or no discomfort after the rest.

By 1330 hours, Lt. Carls said that we must leave to be able to get to our next destination by night fall. This would be where we would stay for several days. As I was preparing myself to leave, Big Ed appeared in the doorway sporting a broad smile that displayed a mouthful of perfectly shaped, glistening, white teeth. He looked very proud of himself as he approached me, holding in front of him a large pair of Jap flying boots. Still grinning, he said, "Capt'n! These should fit just fine." He was exactly right. I slipped my feet into the soft leather boots. The left foot was a little tight, but it gave my ankle some much needed support. We said goodbye to our host and departed up the mountain trail. My young bodyguard bid me farewell and good luck, and he headed back to his family and friend at Kalliling. Big Ed was to be my permanent bodyguard from now on.

Most Filipinos that I had met were smaller than I, but Eduardo Arroz, my Big Ed, was a good inch-and-a-half taller. He seemed very pleased to be my personal bodyguard, and I was delighted to have it so. Johnny Duarte was shorter but well built and had assigned to him, as his personal bodyguard, a young scout just about his equal in age and size. Because Johnny was quite fluent in Spanish, he and his new friend, Luis Escondido, kept up a lively conversation in Spanish. I had taken Spanish in high school and for two years in college and could get the gist of this conversation, but could nod only a "Si" occasionally.

Our progress up the trail was good; the Jap boots helped me enormously. When we did come upon some minor obstruction or small ravine, Big Ed was always there with a strong, helping hand. The air in the mountains was a little cooler than it was down in the coastal flatlands. This made our travel less difficult; thus, by dark, we had passed the last guardpost to our destination, the headquarters of the Island of Negros Allied Military Commander, Col. Ferdinand Abcede, a West Point graduate who had escaped the Japs at Bataan. We received a grand welcome from the colonel and his staff. We had the evening meal of roasted monkey meat (I didn't know it at the time), with brown rice and black beans; our drink was water in which chinco bark had been soaked. It was in essence quinine water. Before retiring we were served as a night cap a native beer, fermented sap of the coconut palm known (the beer) as Tebe or Tuba, depending on the locality you are in.

11 November 1944: It was the 24th anniversary of my birthday. The sun was up and bright, but as we were on the occidental (west) side of the mountains we could not see it, yet. The camp had a subdued military character. The buildings were in proper rows that were as neat and clean as a pin; however, vegetation was so placed that few, if any, of the buildings are visible to aircraft passing overhead. Springs higher above bring fresh, cool water through bamboo pipes to several terra cotta holding tanks conveniently placed between the mess facility on one side and the shower and laundry facility on the other. The latrines are on the other side of the compound below the barracks area. Above the barracks was a separate shower joined by six smaller buildings. I was to learn later that this was the quarters of the ladies-of-the-camp. (Even the ladies from Gen. Hooker's Civil War cadre had other jobs to fulfill.)

Johnny and I were assigned quarters closer to the ladies than to the general barracks but away from, and to the west side, of the compound. I later learned they were transient quarters for message runners and wounded personnel not requiring constant medical care. It was airy, cool and very clean; both of our bunks had new mosquito nets, a kapok-filled pillow, and tancolored military sheets. There was not an inner spring mattresses, but never the less, it was comfortable.

Big Ed summoned us to mess call after we had an excellant. shower with lukewarm, fresh water heated the previous day in tanks exposed to the sun and plenty of Palmolive soap—yes, the same green soap we used back in the States. It was made in the city of Bacalad, Negros, P.I., before the Japs came, but the whole inventory of the finished product had been spirited away before the invaders knew about it. Our breakfast consisted of fresh fried eggs, fried baby squid, brown rice and fried sweet yam slices. The fried baby squid was new to me; however, it was fried crisp like breakfast bacon and seasoned with sea salt, and freshly ground white pepper (which grows wild abundantly in P.I.) and it was quite tasty, actually really good. There was coffee available, but it was made with the quinine water and, to me, the plain quinine water went down easier. We were told to drink some quinine water each day, a medicinal for malaria. We did.

Col. Ferdinand Abcede received us graciously after breakfast. He himself had just returned to his command post that morning from a trip to the oriental (east) side of Negros. He had brought with him a distinguished guest in the person of Admiral Raul Intengan, a Fillipino honor graduate of the U.S. Naval Academy at Annapolis. The Admiral was a tall, handsome man, some six feet plus, with an easy smile and deportment of authority that fell naturally upon him. He was quite a contrast to Col. Abcede who was barely over five feet, two inches. The two seemed to be the best of friends, and through our conversation, I learned that Admiral Intengan had assisted in making arrangements for the MacArthur escape by P.T. boat to Mindanao, and by B-17 to Australia. Col Abcede had asked the Admiral to join him, and the Admiral was glad to do so.

We spent most of the morning exchanging stories about the war. I was surprised to learn that a U.S. invasion of P.I. had already begun on Leyte, P.I., and that Ol' Mac himself had already made good his famous promise, "I shall return." Both the Col and the Admiral were surprised that B-24 bombers had struck the oil fields and refinery at Balikpappan on Northern Borneo. Both were amazed that the B-24 could stay in the air so long and still carry a punishing bomb load. Neither had seen a B-24 or even a picture; thus, it left quite an opening for me to do a bit of bragging. They took it gladly.

When Big Ed introduced me to Col. Abcede this morning, he did so by calling me Cap'n Mahanes. He also told the Col. that today, 11 November 1944, was my twenty-fourth birthday. Well, the Col. saw the stripes on my sleeves, and he knew I was not a captain. He also knew that I was the first American flyer to come into his command, and it was my birthday. He stood his full five feet two, and said firmly, in an authoritative manner and with a twinkle in his eye, "Cap'n Boop (his way of saying Bob), this is a good day to have a birthday party, so today we are having one for you." I really was stunned, and thanked the Col. as best I could. I turned and glanced at Admiral Intengen. He smiled back, and said, "I have some real English gin...I'll break it out." At this, the Col. replied, "and I have some special Vermouth I brought down from Manilla, and I needed an excuse to open it."

We passed most of the rest of the afternoon discussing the progress of the war. They seemed to know very little of the Allied progress in Europe, and neither Johnny nor I could tell them any real late news. We did note that new B-24 Bombers were steadily replacing the older ones, and they didn't have camouflage paint on the new planes. The Admiral said that Allied subs had placed many agents with two-way radios on many of the islands and that he had received such a set from the island of Panay, and had brought it here with him, but didn't know how to set it up or operate it. Both Johnny and I had had some previous radio experience before coming into the military, thus we both were very anxious to see what kind of radio the Admiral had. He promised to let us have a *look-see* in the morning.

Our evening meal was a special one. We had fried chicken, fried and baked fish, boiled prawns in a spicy, hot sauce, and, of course, brown rice followed by a real cake coated with grated coconut. It was a real birthday party. After the meal was finished, we sat and discussed the situation at hand on Leyte and Cebu now that U.S. troops had come ashore and were making rapid progress. We decided that a program of harassment of the Jap forces by cutting their supply lines would be the best action to help the U.S. forces. We decided to deny the Japs any food supplies they might try to take from the Philippines. Now came the final toast. Col. Abcede passed each a double shot of his Vermouth; we raised our glasses. They wished me a *Happy Birthday*, then wished a rapid and total defeat of the enemy...it was down the hatch with the Vermouth. It was hot and strong. I staggered as I swallowed. I tried to recover but soon saw that I could not. Big Ed, standing close by, saw what was happening and shoved a cup full of quinine water into my hand. I gulped it down and made a partial recovery—enough to thank everyone and excuse myself. Big Ed, as usual, was at my side. He guided me across a moonlit terrace to my quarters and saw that I made it safely to my bunk. I got sick during the night but made it outside on my own. After clearing my stomach, I slept soundly the rest of the night.

The next two days, Johnny and I worked with the Admiral's radio. It was a Halicrafter H200 model, 200 watt output transmitter. The power unit was a two-man, hand-cranked type generator without peak suppressors, thus, the voltage output was governed only by the speed of the cranking team. We got the receiver set up fairly easily and listened to many different frequencies; most of them CW (Morse code). A lot of the signals were Jap junk and occasionally, a Dutch plain language transmission. Very little seemed to make any sense to us. Tokyo Rose came in clear and strong and told us we were losing the war in Europe and the Pacific, but she did play some good American music. We told the Admiral that a transmitting antenna would have to be erected before we could send any messages. This had to be delayed because the troops were busy harassing the *Hapon*.

Most of my time the next several days was spent talking to the Scouts in small groups — talking mainly about the progress the Army Air Force had made since coming up from Guadalcanal. How we had cut off supplies and left stranded many Jap bases as we bypassed them. I spoke of our constant strikes on the Jap supply bases. First on Truk and, after its neutralization, on to the Jap-mandated island of Yap. The Japs had been there since World War I.

Most every day we could either see or hear the ever-larger flights of B-24's passing overhead on their way North to strike more Jap installations. Occasionally we would witness aerial dogfights between the Navy's Gruman 74F's and the Jap Zeros and Nates (clipped-wing Jap Navy version of Zeros). Most of the dogfights ended with the Jap, Zeros falling to the earth in flames, however, once in a while we did see an F4F hightail it from the battle zone. We hoped they made it back to their Flat Top or some friendly field on Leyte or Cebu.

As my foot was getting better each day, I began to walk the trails out of camp with Big Ed. We saw many people who had fled the coastal towns and cities for the safe sanctuary of the mountains. The *Hapon* had long ago found the mountains were no place for them. Big Ed knew many of these people and we did visit with many of them. Some of the people had taken pictures of the bodies of downed Jap, fliers; some of the pictures were of Jap families back home in Japan, some were of American fliers being beheaded by Samurai officers; some were pictures taken in China and some in the Philippines. Many of these families gave me the pictures to show to the outside world. Some, I did show and some, so terrible, I did not show until after I was back home on U.S. soil.

It was on one of these family visits that I met an unusual Chinese lady and also literally lost my shirt. Big Ed insisted that I attend a local cock-fight. Now, these fights usually took place on Saturday afternoon, just outside a village, usually only three-or-four families who had moved up from the coastal towns to a place with a good freshwater spring close-by. Well, there, was no village close to the military compound of Col. Ferdinand Abcede, so the Colonel authorized a clearing with proper facilities to be constructed a half kilometer away. There was a square, bound-off area no larger than 12x12 feet; this was the actual cock-fighting area. Around this were several rows of logs placed as seats for the spectators. Behind these seats, at one end, were a number of pens or chicken-holding boxes in which the cocks were held until it came their turn to perform in the ring.

Betting on the fights was always a highlight of the occasion. Big Ed explained that if a person had run out of money or whatever he had in collateral goods, he could bet the shirt off his back. This proved to be my misfortune as I was encouraged to take part in the fun. I looked over the cocks and picked out the largest and most ferocious looking rooster, and because I had no money nor collateral, bet my shirt. Big Ed looked at me, shook his head, and smiled. This caused me a little concern. Soon, it came time for my chosen rooster to enter the fighting ring. He was opposed by a fiesty little bird about two-thirds his size. Before the owners put their roosters in the arena, they would rub their head feathers backwards and blow hot breath onto their heads to irritate them and make them more beligerent. Well, the fight didn't last long. Both birds charged each other several times, feathers and loud squawks filled the air, then suddenly, my chosen bird just took off and flew out of the arena. He had lost the fight and I had lost my shirt literally. The biggest laugh and applause came as I removed my shirt and gave it to the little rooster's owner.

It was at these small gatherings that Johnny Duarte and I heard many stories of the atrocities committed by the occupying Japanese. Most of these stories came from the elderly who spoke in both Spanish and English. As Johnny spoke Spanish fluently, he was able to fill me in on the parts that I didn't quite understand. Both of us knew that we were hearing first-hand important information, and we discussed it with Col. Abcede. The Colonel gave us some tips on gathering this information as we traveled from settlement to settlement. The first rule was to write nothing down while in the presence of the villagers, but write their stories out in detail only after returning to home base. The reason for this was two-fold. First, the villagers would not talk if they saw you taking notes. These notes could fall into Japanese hands and cause reprisal raids, and secondly, if the notes were caught on us by Japs, we would be shot as spies.

Back to the cockfights. This lasted an hour and a half after I had lost my shirt. They joked among themselves about the "Cano" (American) who lost his shirt, and by the time we returned to base camp, Col. Abcede greeted me slyly with, "Sargeant, I be-

lieve you are out of uniform." I could only grin and say, "Colonel, you are exactly right."

By 1 December 1944, Johnny and I had made many visits to the outlying villages, always accompanied by Big Ed and usually ten native scouts. We were gathering as much information as possible about Jap positions, strength, weak areas, as we could to pass on to our people. It was on one of these trips that I received word that a Chinese merchant would like to meet the "Cano" who lost his shirt. I was not totally surprised to hear this, as I had been told that many such families had fled their homelands in China when the Japs invaded.

3 December 1944: We left base camp early this morning, headed North along a much traveled trail which was kind of a main highway (foot trail) that the guerillas used in their numerous raids on Jap, supply lines. We were going to see the Chinese merchant. Sun Li Kao who was tall, thin-framed, light skinned and flashed a broad smile as he extended his hand to me. He welcomed us in perfect English and invited us in to his home. His home was actually a real, wooden building with real floors and glass windows. It had been, before the war, a weather station operated by a U.S. agency. As we had arrived around-noon, Sun Li had a meal prepared and waiting for us. The usual chicken soup with rice followed by a stir-fry type of dish consisting of red meat and native vegetables (bamboo shoots, different kinds of root vegetables). For the first time on the island, we were served with real chinaware dishes and chopsticks, instead of on parts of GI mess kits and banana leaves.

During our meal with Sun Li there were no women present. Only to refill our cup with hot tea did a female appear, and this was an elderly lady. Our conversation was devoted almost entirely to the Japanese situation on Negros. Their food sources (the Japs) were becoming a real problem. As the Jap food supply dwindled, they became more and more demanding upon the native population for food supplies. They had begun taking additional rations from the natives' already short supply of rice and sugar. These items were being stockpiled in abandoned fish warehouses on the west coast. Sun Li was in no way officially connected with the U.S. or Philippine military, but he hated the Japs for good reason and proved to be a great source of information concerning Jap movement on Negros. He had personally watched from a distance the stockpiling of two of these warehouses. He knew what and how much each had inside. He knew the number of both day and night guards and the hour and routine of their change of watch. This was not entirely new to Big Ed, as he had been assigned by Col. Abcede to observe these Jap movements, and tentative plans were being made for a raid before the Japs could bring power launches to haul away their loot.

Sun Li stood up from the table and clapped his hands together one time. At this signal the elderly lady served us a very sweet wine, almost like a liqueur, and bowed out of the room. We talked further small talk that finally got around to the cock-fight, at which time Sun Li laughed and said to me, "It not good to have a friend to lose his shirt." I think I grinned and said, "I know," or something of that nature. (I did have on the white but torn shirt, today). Then he said he would like to introduce his niece whom he had brought with him from mainland China. He said his niece had something for me. Boy, did my eyes get big! What, I wondered?

When Sun Li left the room to fetch his niece, Johnny and I looked at each other in amazement and wonder. Big Ed noticed this and related to us that Sun Li was well-respected by his neighbors and was nice to all of them, but he guarded very closely his niece who we were about to meet.

She appeared in the doorway, tall and slim, fair-skinned, a truly beautiful young lady of twenty-two years, in a pale yellow ankle-length silk-dress with Mandarin collar and no belt. The collar was trimmed and bordered in black, and the loose, elbow-length sleeves were bordered in black with green and lavender floral designs. Her curves were in the right places and of proper proportions. When she turned to one side and smiled, she revealed her shiny, waist-length. black hair. I was shocked, delightfully so, to see such beauty here so deep in these mountain jungles. My thoughts flashed immediately to *Terry and the Pirates* and *The Dragon Lady*. Yes! This was the young Dragon Lady! I was brought back to the present when she turned toward her Uncle Sun Li and smiled. At this time, Sun Li introduced his niece to each of us. "This is the joy of my life, Li Lin Shen, the daughter of my dear deceased brother."

After the *glad to meet you's* were passed, Li Lin softly spoke to me, saying, "So sad you lose shirt. I fix." At this, she turned again to the doorway to meet the elderly servant lady who held a folded, pale blue silk garment. Li Lin took the silk garment and came over to me with a smile saying, "Now you have new shirt...do not lose on cockfight." At this we all had a good laugh. It was a slipover-style shirt with three buttons. I was dumbfounded and at a loss for words, but I believe she knew how I felt.

Later, that same day, Sun Li told us that Li Lin was to have been married four years ago when she was eighteen, but her parents and her intended husband had been killed for hiding their silk cloth that the Japs were trying to take from them. It seems that her parents, as well as her Uncle Sun Li, were in the silkfinishing business. When Suri Li and Li Lin had escaped China, they had brought as much of their silk as possible with them. By early evening we had thanked our gracious host and beautiful hostess and were back to base camp.

Admiral Intengan was head of the Information Gathering Bureau and had his flotillas of *bonhas* (small-to-medium outrigger boats with sails) and *balsas* (smaller outriggers without sails) busy patrolling the southern shores of Negros. These boats were primarily for fishing. The Japs took part of each catch and thus paid little or no attention to whatever else these harmless boats might be up to. The crews, along with their fishing activities, were watching very closely every step their enemy made; where they were storing rice or sugar and especially any combustibles such as gasoline or kerosene. All of this information was reported and catalogued with Admiral Intengan at base camp back in the mountains where the Japs feared to come.

A two-pronged raid was in the planning by Col. Abcede. I now had lost right much weight from dysentery and dengue, but felt strong enough to go along on this raid. I had walked twenty kilometers from base camp, spent the night sleeping *in* the jungle and had had no more swelling in my left foot (now that I was wearing the Jap pilot's boots), so I assured Col. Abcede that I was up to the task.

Our plan was to attack both warehouses at the same time. It would be on a Saturday night when the Japs were sacked out with *sake*. We were to kill the guards, six of them, quietly, if possible, with knives or clubs, or both; recover as much of the rice as possible; then set the rest on fire. No attempt would be made to recover any of the sugar...just set it on fire.

I had never been on a patrol with more than twelve men. But now, if we were going to try to recover some of the rice, a very large contingent would be needed; half to move the rice and half to do the rest. We figured two groups of thirty plus a third group of riflemen to position themselves in the jungle near the Jap quarters to cover our retreat and kill as many Japs as possible. We were to move out any civilians anywhere near our proposed raid (very few civilians or anyone stayed in the area of the Japs, anyway.)

Gasoline was a scarce item, a small quantity had been stolen from Jap supplies each time they were struck by U.S. air raids, most of which were by the U.S. Navy. Kerosene had been a popular cooking fuel before 7 December 1941, but by now it too was scarce. The only real gasoline in quantity was that used by the Jap power patrol boats; but that was just too risky a source to try to tap. A bit of alcohol was to be had, most every village made its own brand of vermouth, rum, or whatever, and there was always some on hand. This was collected from all until forty-five gallons of high grade alcohol was in our possession. With all our efforts, only about one-third of the needed amount of gasoline and kerosene could be found. it was decided to use most of this on the rice that could not be recovered and to use the balance of this plus the alcohol to flame the sugar storage.

I had hoped that our raid would be on 7 December 1944, but a heavy tropical storm changed all this. Besides, the Japs had started moving their troops away from the warehouses. We figured the fewer that remained, the better our chances of success. On 10 December, Col. Abcede gave the word to prepare to strike at midnight. We were to place ourselves into position by 2330 hours. Kerosene cans had been gathered and filled either with alcohol or a kero-gas mixture and each of the first thirty carried a four liter can with him. The riflemen went ahead and positioned themselves first, then the thirty who were to kill the guards and recover the rice, then the torch men. By the time all positions were taken, we became aware that there were only four guards stationed, and possibly no more than a dozen remaining Jap troops about.

At the appointed hour, 1200, on 10 December, four Jap guards gave their all for the Emperor. Thirty-some Filipinos swarmed upon the rice storage, scooped up as many bags of rice as they could and headed for the hills. About the same time, the riflemen opened fire on the remaining Jap, troops. Now, all the Jap troops had done their thing for the Emperor. Thus, with no resistance left, there was no need for the flame team to hurry, so they in turn carted off as much rice and sugar as they could, even the riflemen joined in this effort. By daybreak all of the rice had been moved up into the mountains and now, it seemed that some of the sugar would also be recovered. This latter attempt was discarded as we heard fighter aircraft in the distance and quickly disarmed the Jap corpses, piled their bodies upon the remaining stacks of sugar, soaked them thoroughly with alcohol, then topped it off with the kero-gasoline mixture. One of the flamers lit a gasoline soaked rag and torched the warehouse. The blaze was seen ten kilometers away, and black smoke from the burning sugar lasted several days.

The total outcome was much better than we had expected. They recovered all the rice, we had expected to get less than one half; and we had recovered some sugar when we expected none. We also wiped out two platoons of Jap troops, got their weapons and supplies, and brought back to base camp most of the kero-gas mixture and a little of the alcohol. Since it was grain alcohol, I kind of expect that not all of it was used to start a sugar fire.

The fighter planes came into sight just over the mountain top. We could now see it was a dog fight between Navy F4F's and Jap Nates. We watched as long as they stayed in sight, but soon the battle zone had removed itself from us. With our heavy loads of rice and sugar, we headed back to base camp and arrived there exhausted at 1530 hours on 11 December 1944. What did I do during this raid? I stood in the edge of the jungle with a carbine in my hands ready to shoot, if needed. These were my orders from Col. Abcede. I was a spectator.

During my time away with the raiding party, Johnny Duarte had been working the radio receiver. He believed he had made a reception on an ATC (Air Transport Command) frequency and had tried to set up the transmitter to the same frequency. Today, he would try again. I stayed for a while, but I seemed to be getting a fever. I was beginning to feel pretty bad. I was getting light-headed, and my body was overcome with uncontrollable shakes. Johnny looked over at me. "Man, your eyes are glassy. you act like you have the D.T.'s or something. What's wrong?" I answered, "I've got dysentery and dengue, but it never bothered me this way." I was now shaking so badly that I could not walk across the room, so I just sat down and held my head in my hands as I leaned over the radio table. Johnny called in the two men that were cranking the radio generator just outside. When they saw me, both at the same time said, "Malaria. He's got malaria."

The next thing I recall is that I was in a hut that was used as a *sick bay* with a native nurse asking me how I felt. I was not shaking now and said to her that I felt pretty punk. She gave me a cup of water that was pretty strong with cinko flavor. I drank it and laid my head down again. I was getting dizzy all over again and sweating like a horse. The nurse said that truly I did have a bad case of malaria. She said, "My name is Estrellita Dela Rosa. I'm a nurse who used to live in Bacalod, up north on Negros." Then, after she had cooled my forehead with a damp cloth, she said, "I'll take care of you, right now you need to just lay still and try not to get up. I'm going to get some medicine for you." I don't know what was in the cinko water that I just drank, but suddenly I became extremely drowsy and just faded off into a semi-conscious world.

The next morning, I was awakened by someone shaking me. It was Estrellita, again, (Stella, she said, is what I'm called). "I have some pills for you to take. They are quinine tablets, they are very bitter so try to swallow them whole without biting or chewing them." She gave me the pills; they were about the size of an antacid tablet. They were hard to swallow, but I did get both of the pills down with plenty of the cinko water. We kept up this regimen three times a day for three days without any food but with plenty of cinko water.

By the evening of the third day, Stella asked me to stand up and try to walk. I did, and to my surprise, I didn't feel dizzy at all. I also noted that I felt pretty hungry and told Stella that I'd like something to eat. She told me that if I could keep food down it would improve my strength greatly. I was served soupy rice sweetened with coconut milk (not the water) and brown sugar. It felt good going down. I had just a hint of nausea which disappeared in about ten minutes. By the evening of the fourth day, I was feeling pretty good again. I continued taking the pills and cinko water for three more days for a total of a full week.

Johnny told me that while I was sick, he had tried an uncoded message on the ATC frequency to notify the 23rd Squadron, 13th Air Force, to try to contact Mahanes/Duarte on this frequency after 1800 hours, but had gotten no reply.

16 December 1944: Early this morning two C-47 transports, escorted by four P-38 fighter planes circle over the flat valley at the foot of our mountain. A number of cargo parachutes are discharged from the first C-47. On the second pass over the valley, sixteen paratroopers jumped from the second airplane. They all seem to be in good order when we lost sight of them in the jungle foliage. We learn by native message runners that this is an advanced, American liason detachment. They are setting up radio equipment to monitor and report enemy action in our area. By mid-day, Big Ed and I were already down in the valley. We surprised the U.S. detachment with our unannounced arrival. They asked if we were the two missing airmen from the 23rd Squadron. I nodded yes, then explained that I was Mahanes and that Big Ed was my Filipino aide. I also told about Johnny's radio call to A.T.C, but that we had had no response back. A young

captain by the name of Alexander was in charge and questioned me about other possible U.S. airmen that might be in our general area. I didn't know of any.

The captain had two staff sargeants, one buck sargeant, two corporals and the remainder of his detachment were P.F.C.'s. All were U.S. Army Signal Corpsmen.. After a detailed discussion concerning the safety of our location, the captain told me that as soon as his equipment was set up and operating, he would alert U.S. rescue PBY's on Morotai Island to come to our aid. I thanked the captain and told him that I would get him a troop of perimeter guards from our base camp. Col. Abcede had already anticipated this action and had twenty-four Filipino scouts already on the way to us.

Back at base camp, Johnny said he had worked the radio transmitter at intermittent periods for the last hour and a half. He thought that he had gotten some kind of garbled response, but was not at all sure. He said that the last transmission ended with a word that he made out to be *Crawfish*. By golly! This was the nickname of my A.T.C. friend, radioman Dick *Crawfish* Pendleton from Shreveport. The transmission said, "Relayed to 23rd." Johnny had made contact, first. I was elated and congratulated Johnny and his men who had faithfully cranked the hand generator for him.

At the evening meal at base camp. I told Col. Abcede what had occurred in the valley and that we (Johnny and I) would probably be picked up by PBY soon. After the meal, the Colonel summoned me into his private quarters and began speaking to me in a very serious manner. *Boop*, he said, "I know how much vital information you have gathered about Jap movements, and it is good. But Admiral Intengan has been doing this for a long time. He is the chief intelligence officer for the island of Negros, P.I. In fact, he has learned that on 1 November, when you were shot down, no less than seventy Jap fighter planes were to land at Alicante Airdrome that your squadron had just bombed. Now that the landing strip was ruined, many of the Jap fighters had to crash land or ditch into the sea due to lack of fuel. The remainder that had fuel were the ones that attacked your planes. Many pilots in this latter group were kamikazes."

17 December 1944: Col. Abcede had a mail sack three-fourths filled with handwritten intelligence reports. He asked me for my reports (also handwritten), along with several gifts that my friends had given me. He put all of this into the bag and pulled the rope closure together. Then, he looked me straight in the eye and said, "Boop! Usually, the rank of O-three is required to carry such sensitive material. I'm not authorized to make you a captain, but as you have acquired much of this yourself, I feel that you can safely handle its transportation to its proper destination."

18 December 1944: We were instructed by the signal people, who had relayed our position to air/sea rescue, to go to the mouth of a small river that opened into the ocean. This we did and waited until 1400 hours when we heard the distinctive sound of PBY engines. The PBY was south of us and seemed to be circling. It continued to do this for about twenty minutes; then the engines' sound faded away. We had missed our contact.

19 December 1944: We were instructed to go south an additional five kilometers to the mouth of a larger river. This we did. Again, at about 1400 hours, we heard the PBY engines, but also, we could hear Jap fighter planes coming toward the PBY—a second lost contact. The PBY did not show up, but we did hear the machine-gun fire of both U.S. and Jap aircraft in the distance. This gun-fire continued on-and-off for about twenty-five minutes or more; then it abruptly ceased. We heard one fighter crash into the mountains, but couldn't tell if it was friend or foe But, in a few minutes, a Navy F4F headed south and came into

view over the mountains. It was trailing heavy, black smoke from its engine and losing altitude rapidly. We watched the stricken F4F pass over us headed for the sea. Suddenly, the engine burst into flames and nosed over onto its left. The pilot bailed out of the burning aircraft, but we could not see his parachute open. We all figured he must be over the ocean when this happened. It was now near dusk when we reported this to Admiral Intengan. He sent out *bankas* and *balsas* (small outriggers) the next morning to search for the downed Navy pilot.

20 December 1944: We started out early to reach our rescue rendezvous point. We took a different trail, wider, and had far less undergrowth. Although a longer trail, it was easier walking. As we were beginning to leave the more dense part of the jungle, I heard a moaning sound in the not too far distance. We stopped in our tracks and ducked low in unison. There! We heard it, again. Big Ed was the first to move forward for a look see. I was two steps behind with my .45 in my hand. We heard the mournful sound again, over head, this time. I pushed the foliage above me aside and saw the source of the moaning was the Navy pilot hanging in the shrouds of his parachute which had become entangled in the tree limbs. The pilot was ten or more feet from the ground and was obviously hurt. We threw a weighted rope through his parachute cords and gently lowered him to the ground. The poor fellow had an injured ankle and broken left arm. We had no pain medication with us, but we did have canteens of water which the injured pilot begged to have. After resting him on the ground for ten minutes or more, probably more, we tried to construct a makeshift stretcher. This we did with two bamboo poles that were criss-crossed with rope over which our shirts were tied. Not much, but it worked. When our patient was able to talk he told us his name was Lt. J.G. Richard Williamson, and he had been in a dog fight with three Jap Zeros the previous day. His wingman had been hit earlier and headed back to the flat top leaving him without any protection. Williamson had flamed one Zero, and it crashed into the mountain, but he, too, had been hit and was headed for the sea when his engine quit on him. He had hurt his ankle leaving the F4F and fractured his left arm in the tree top as he fell. With nothing to stabilize his broken arm we laid it folded across his chest and tied a cord loosely around it and onto his belt to keep down movement as we carried him to our new contact area.

For the third time in as many days, we were instructed to be at the contact sight, the same place as the day before. This time we were to build a fire and *smoke it* at 1400 hrs. By the assigned day and time, the bonfire was going strong and the Scouts had armfulls of wet coconut hemp to smother the flames, creating heavy, white smoke. We heard airplane engines in the distance, fighters first, then, yes!, the great sound of those good ol' reliable, PBY engines. Our smoke signal was doing just great and, suddenly, a big ol' P-38 came over the mountain crest and headed for our smoke signal, then another and another until there were four beautiful P-38's circling overhead. Then, our PBY came into view. Excitement is too mild a word to use. I guess ecstatic with joy would more correctly express my feeling. Johnny, too, was in an active tizzy, waving a U.S. flag as hard as he could.

As the PBY landed and began maneuvering up into the mouth of the river, I turned to speak to Big Ed. He was in an emotional state; he was happy for me to be rescued but hated to part our friendship which had become very close in the last few weeks. He gave me the mail sack with all our goodies inside, grasped my right hand and forearm, and wished me and Johnny *Godspeed to safety*. I held Big Ed's hand and thanked him for all that he had done for me. I was trying to think if there was anything I could give him, then I looked at my .45. It had been John Emig's gun. He had given it to me the day we set out to find help. I

thought, he will need it more than I will, so without a moment's delay, the gun and holster had a new, grateful owner.

As the PBY taxied up into the mouth of the river close enough, we motioned that we had an injured man on our stretcher. As soon as the props on the PBY were still, our scouts closed the short distance between shore and plane quickly in their *balsas*. The medical officer aboard was Col. Campbell. He thought that it was me on the stretcher; our radio contact had mentioned Mahanes was sick because I was recovering from my malaria attack. Col. Campbell set about getting Lt. Williamson comfortable. After determining that his patient was not in a state of shock, morphine was administered, the left arm stabilized with a splint. We carefully lowered the Lt. into the *balsa* and ferried him out to the PBY where we had a little difficulty getting him inside. By now, the morphine was doing its job. Lt. Williamson was resting comfortably on *cloud nine*. Johnny and I bid a last farewell to our friends and boarded the PBY with our mail bag of intelligence material. Aboard, Col. Campbell questioned me about my wounds and of the severity of my recent Malaria attack. I had lost a lot of weight, but felt O.K. now.

Our pilot quickly started up both engines, first a spit and cough of the exhaust, then a full, powerful roar. I looked out of the window and saw that our friends in their little balsa were now close to shore and were briskly waving goodbye to us. As we gained altitude, I could see the outlines of Palawan, the long island to the west of Negros. This is one of the sites of a Jap, prisoner-of-war camp. I wondered the fate of those U.S. and British P.O.W.s being held there. Did they see the big-flights of B-24's that passed over each day? What would the Japs do; kill all prisoners, or make life better for them now that the Americans were retaking the Philippines? I hoped for the latter. Col. Campbell took my temperature and pulse and listened to my heart beat. He said I still had a little temperature. Across on a bunk on the other side of the plane, Lt Williamson was sleeping soundly. Johnny was seated next to him, nodding with his eyes half closed. I relaxed and at the suggestion of the Colonel, went to sleep too.

We arrived at Morotai about 1800 hrs. Our amphib PBY landed smoothly on the coral strip. The landing jarred all of the sleepers awake. We watched as the plane came to a stop and turned off the runway and down the long taxiway to the revetment where several military ambulances staffed by medical people awaited us. There was Capt. Funkenstein, Corporal Nunez, and my hometown friend, Sargeant John Hill of our 23rd Squadron Flight Surgeon Staff.

We moved Lt. J.G. Williamson off first. He opened his eyes as we were moving him, but once in the ambulance, smiled and went back to sleep. we were greeted warmly by Doc Funkenstein and his staff. While we were talking to the flight surgeon, a jeepload of M.P.'s drove up. They questioned us about an intelligence bag that they were to pick up. I told them I had it but needed to get some of my personal things out. I had removed my note pad, an embroidered wash cloth that Stella Delarosa, the nurse, had made for me, a pink and white sun shirt made of hemp, and was reaching for my silk shirt that Li Lin Shen had given me. Before I could do so, one of the M.P.'s grabbed the bag, closed it and said to me, "You'll have to come to headquarters to get anything from this bag; it's top secret." I complained that I had gathered the top secret material, but I wanted my shirt. He said, "Sorry, Mack," and departed in his jeep in a hurry.

On our way to the group hospital, Doc Funkenstein said he would help me get my shirt back. At the hospital I got first class treatment, a soft water shower, fresh new underclothes, a G.I. bathrobe and a good meal with real, fresh, baked bread. Johnny remarked that he had eaten so much rice in the past two months that he sort of expected some now.

We stayed in the group hospital two days. Both of us had lost weight, Johnny just a few pounds, but my weight had dropped from 167 pounds down to 117 pounds. On the next night, 23 December, I went to the movie with my friend, Medic Sgt. John Hill. We had an air raid, John *Bunker* Hill grabbed me by my arm and pulled me into the nearest fox hole. Yep! I'm back in Moratai again!

Several days later, Doc Funkenstein called for Johnny and me to come to the Flight Surgeon's tent. When we arrived he was all smiles and had good news for us. Lt. John Emig and three of our crew had been picked up in Borneo and were now at Group Hospital. We piled into his Jeep and headed for the hospital. I expected to see the worst. To my delighted surprise, all four seemed in pretty good shape. All had lost a lot of weight and all sported very long beards. Emig and Gillisie were bed patients. I was told that Gillisie had a live Jap shell-imbedded in his right thigh (this I already knew). Davies and Desmarais, although worn and thin, looked pretty good in spite of their thirty-three days on the life raft. Emig was being treated for his multiple chest and body wounds. It was a grand reunion.

2 January 1945: I boarded the hospital ship *Torrens* for a twenty-three day sea voyage back to San Francisco. During most of this time I was ship librarian. There I went over the notes of my P.I. experience and brought my diary up to date.

This about concludes my last active days as a member of the 23rd Bomb Squadron. Some of the questions put to me since are as follows:

Q: Were you afraid?
A: Hell, yes!

Q: Did you ever think you might not make it out alive?
A: I never doubted I would come back alive.

Q: What did you think of the Island food?
A: Great, and the people were too.

Q: Did you shoot down any planes on 1 November 1944?
A: I know some were hit; they ran directly into our line of fire. There is no way of ascertaining who shot down how many. I know Desmarais hit two, and I believe Gilliesie got two. No way I can be sure. I fired point blank until my turret was hit.

Q: What was your most important mission?
A: On 18 June 1944 our lone B-24 crew in Lil' Jo Toddy (all ass, and no body) flew a 16-hour search and weather from Wakde into the Philippine Sea. There we spotted the remains of the Jap fleet. I radioed our find and this was confirmed six hours later at 1800 hours by an Allied sub. This set off the Great Mariannas Turkey Shoot, 19-20 June, the last major battle of WWII. Some books tell of this event, but identify us only as a lone B-24 crew.

Q: Did you ever again have contact with Col. Abcede, Big Ed, or Admiral Intengen?
A: Yes. After the war I corresponded several times with Col. Abcede, who lived in Bakalat on the island of Negros and became the Governor of Negros. I sent vitamins to his wife, who was quite ill. After awhile I received no reply and figured he had died. Admiral Intengen, who was G-2 during the Jap occupation, was living on Luzon, and I heard that he went on active duty with the U.S. Navy and eventually retired. I was unable to contact Big Ed. He almost certainly left the mountain area and returned to his pre-war village.

VETERANS

5TH BOMBARDMENT GROUP (H)

13th Air Force headquarters in the Philippines. Twelve of these seventeen men are Bay area soldiers and have won two Distinguished Unit Citations as members of the Bomber Barons. (l to r) Front row: unknown, Lt. John Colville, Lt. John A. Thompson, Lt. Edward Winthers, Lt. D. G. Injraham, and S/Sgt. Ben Winnikoff. Back row: F/O James Shallenberger, F/O Arthur Sobol (KIA), Cpl. Henry Faglians, unknown, Lt. William Mason, Sgt. John A. Miles, Mag. Ray Ungermach, unknown, unknown, unknown, and Sgt. F. N. Butler.

RICHARD AH-TYE, Staff Sergeant, born Stockton, CA on February 27, 1924. Entered the U.S.A.A.F. on March 25, 1943. Took basic training at Jefferson Barracks, St. Louis, MO; Armament School at Denver, CO; Gunnery School at Harlingen, TX; and combat crew training in Walla Walla, WA. Assigned to Capt. Lance Pitts crew as Armament Ball Gunner on B-24. Joined the 72nd Sqdn., 5th Bomb Grp., 13th Air Force.

Flew missions from Morotai and Samar, Philippines and completed 44 missions. The crew was being sent home to the States. While waiting at Manila that day to fly home, their orders were held up. Japan had surrendered so all flights were changed and occupational forces headed for Japan. While overseas the intelligence officer suggested sewing an American flag on Ah-Tye's flight jacket because of his Chinese-American descent to insure his safety. He was discharged on November 28, 1945.

After the military, Ah-Tye became a cartographer with the U.S. Geological Survey for 27 years until retirement in 1989.

ERNEST LEE ALEXANDER, born in Wilson, OK on January 12, 1921. Enlisted U.S. Army 1st FA, Ft. Sill, OK on February 27, 1939. In July 1941 went to U.S. Army Air Corps, 14th Fighter Grp. (P-38's and P-36's), March Field, CA. Appointed W.O. (Jg) May 1942; graduated OCS, Miami Beach, FL on December 9, 1942; sent overseas by Liberty Boat in 1943 through the Panama Canal to Noumea, New Caledonia; to HQ Sqdn., 5th Bomb Grp. in January 1944 at Guadalcanal. Group personnel officer and assistant adjutant with a dozen additional duties supervising service activities. 31st Sqdn. Adjutant for Everett B. Thurlow for a short time.

Returned to U.S. from Samar in October 1945 as captain assigned to USAF Bombardment School, Mather Field, CA; to Scott Field, IL; and to Randolph Field, TX. In 1953 to the 75th Air Depot Wing, Chinhae, Korea; 1954 to USAF Special Weapons Command, Sandia Base, NM and Medina Base, San Antonio, TX; 1957 to USAF Deputy IG, Norton AFB, CA; 1962 to 4th ATAF (NATO), Ramstein Air Base, Germany; 1965 to Air Material Command, Norton AFB, CA.

Retired October 31, 1967 as Lt. Colonel Trust Administrator for Security Bank, Bank of America, and Bank of California. Retired from Bank of California in 1984. Real estate sales (commercial) until 1995. Now retired full time, except for golf, computers, reading, and some traveling.

CARLTON E. ALLWARDT, born in Calhoun County, MI on June 10, 1918. Entered the U.S. Army on May 19, 1943. Assigned to the Army Air Force. Took basic training at Sheppard Field; Radio School at Sioux Falls, SD; Gunnery School at Yuma, AZ; and took crew training at Walla Walla, WA. Joined flight crew at Hamilton Field, CA. Assigned to the 13th Air Force, 5th Bomb Grp., 31st Bomb Sqdn. Flew 44 missions from New Guinea to Philippines. Last base was Samar, Philippines as Airborne Radio Operator/Gunner.

Awards received were Air Medal with two Oak Leaf Clusters, Asiatic-Pacific Theater Ribbon with one Silver and two Bronze Battle Stars, Presidential Unit Citation, Good Conduct Medal, and the Philippine Liberation Medal with one Bronze Battle Star. Highest rank achieved was Tech/Sgt.

Allwardt retired in 1992 from business. He is an active volunteer at Fort Custer National Cemetery in Battle Creek, MI.

FORREST AVERBECK, born December 5, 1920 near Fond du Lac, WI. Enlisted in the Army Air Force in September 1941. Took basic training at Jefferson Barracks, St. Louis, MO and Air Mechanic School at Chanute Field, IL. After graduating in April 1942 took train to Fresco and the USS Cleveland to Oahu, HI. After more basic, shipped to the 23rd Bomb Sqdn. at Mokeleum, a new camp. First assigned mechanic ground crew, Tech/Sgt. Flanagan crew chief.

There was a shortage of enlisted flyboys, something Averbeck wanted, so he threw his hat into the ring and got it. The new kid got to fly a lot. In September 1942 went to Espiritu Santo with new fresh crew, Pilot Captain Raines and Sgt. Hooten, Flight Engineer. Was attached to the 72nd Bomb Sqdn. After about six missions off Guadalcanal, malaria and acute dysentery knocked out several crewmembers forcing the crew to break up.

Flew fill-in on missions with the 72nd and 31st. Also rode shotgun for bombardier on search missions. The most rewarding events were when Anton Schmidt, Radio Operator and Averbeck became Captain Tex Burn's crew members. Tex was Sqdn. Commander of the 23rd. Never admired a person more than Burns. The whole crew was first class. Flew about 40 missions with Burn's crew. Had about that many prior missions also. Took a few licks, but am here today with all my parts. Decorated with the Distinguished Flying Cross with Oak Leaf Cluster and Air Medal with two Oak Leaf Clusters. Returned Stateside in September 1943, ending up at Amarillo Airfield as flight instructor on B-17. Discharged in October 1945.

Averbeck was a GI apprentice in carpentry. For 22 years was self-employed as a carpenter in houses and kitchens. For 24 years, he was superintendent of buildings and grounds for a small college until retirement in 1991.

MERLIN D. AVERETT, Staff Sergeant, Airplane Armorer/Gunner #612, 5th Bomb Grp., 31st Bomb Sqdn., 13th Air Force. Lived in Camden, AR and enlisted in Arkansas National Guard in 1938. His unit was a regiment of the 206th Coast Artillery (anti-aircraft). They were federalized on January 6, 1941. Trained at Ft. Bliss, El Paso, TX. Deployed to Fort Mears, Dutch Harbor, AL. At Dutch Harbor for the air raids on June 3 and 4, 1942 to start the Battle of Midway.

Applied for Aviation Cadet Training, Pre-flight training at San Antonio, TX, Primary Flight School at Sikeston, MO. Washed out and went to Armament School at Lowery Field, Denver, CO and Gunnery School in Laredo, TX.

Assigned to Willie Marten's crew at Muroc Army Airfield for crew training on April 11, 1944 and arrived at Guadalcanal for combat training at the 13th Bomber Command. Flew 42 combat missions from Guadalcanal, the Admiralty's, Wakde, Noemfoor, and Morotai. Outstanding targets we hit were Truk, Balikpapan oil fields, and Brunei Bay.

CLYDE E. AVERY, born in Polk County, MN on August 30, 1921. Moved West in 1939 and was drafted in November 1942. Went into the Army Air Force and took Pilot training in December 1942. Took Pre-flight at Santa Ana, Primary Oxnard, CA; basic training, Lancaster, CA; Advanced in Marfa, TX; and B-24 training at Albuquerque, NM and Muroc AAB.

Joined the 31st Bomb Sqdn. in July 1944 at Manus Island just prior to the group move to Wakde. Flew missions from Wakde, Noemfoor, Morotai, and Samar. Avery flew 44 missions that included two Balikpapan and a naval strike at Brunei Bay. Discharged on December 31, 1945.

All crewmembers had returned stateside uninjured which considering the holes in their B-24's was quite remarkable. Recalled to active service in January 1951 and flew C-124s and B-29s. Also passed the Air Force Instrument Instructor School in Valdosta, GA. Avery left the Air Force in December 1953.

In 1981, he retired from the U.S. Postal Service San Francisco Regional Office. Presently active with the Wickenburg, AZ Sheriff Posse, Search and Rescue in the desert area.

ROBERT L. BEESON, native Californian, born on May 31, 1917. Married and working for Shell Oil Company in Sacramento, CA in 1942 when he passed the Army Air Corps examination for pilot training at Mather Field AAF Base. Beeson took all of his pilot training in Texas. The crewmembers were assembled in Tonopah, NV. On December 1, 1944, they flew a new B-24 M from Fairfield-Suisun AAF (now Travis) to Biak Island.

The crew was assigned to the 13th AAF, 5th Bomb Grp. (Heavy), 72nd Bomb Sqdn. Flew 47 combat missions out of New Guinea, Morotai, and Samar. Logged 425 hours pilot combat time, 1,280 hours total pilot flying time (all types

of aircraft). Discharged in October 1945 at Camp Beale, CA and returned to Shell Oil Co. and retired after 33 years of employment.

LEE BENBROOKS, born on August 11, 1919 in Cove, AR. Joined the Army Air Force in October 1939 and served in the Pacific Theater. Assigned to the 23rd Bomb Sqdn., 5th Bomb Grp., he completed 58 missions. Memorable experiences include on December 7, 1941 at Hickam Field, the exciting Battle of Midway, the bombing run on carrier at 2,500 feet, and the Guadalcanal campaign.

Awards and decorations he earned include the Silver Star, Distinguished Flying Cross, and Air Medal. Discharged in May 1945 with rank of Master Sgt.

Benbrooks is retired and living in Murrieta, CA.

DONALD T. BERKUS, born in St. Paul, MN on July 7, 1922. Moved to Los Angeles, CA in 1929. Enlisted AAF in 1942. Training bases include: Santa Ana, CA; Oxnard, CA; Merced, CA; Marfa, TX; Albuquerque, NM; and Tonopah, NV. Joined the 23rd Bomb Sqdn., 5th Bomb Grp., 13th Air Force in November 1944 at Morotai. Flew 44 combat missions and came home in August 1945.

His most memorable mission was to Cebu. The Marines had landed but were bottled up. The Japanese had gun emplacements on both sides of the valley that the Marines had to go through. The gun locations were camouflaged. Berkus was assigned a colorblind observer and they flew many hours back and forth through the valley 200 feet above the ground. The observer would tell where a gun was and Berkus would tell his gunners where to shoot. He would then radio a Marine Dive-Bomber Sqdn. flying above them to drop where their tracers were hitting - which would be the end of the gun placement! Another Marine squadron took over when the first squadron ran out of bombs and etc., until all the gun emplacements were destroyed. That mission put Berkus on the front page of the L.A. Times.

His highest rank attained was captain. Today, he is retired and keeping busy as a docent at the Museum of Flying in Santa Monica, CA.

REUBEN W. BLACKBURN, born on August 3, 1920 in Port Arthur, TX. Married to Ima Grace Warren on December 24, 1939. They had one son in 1941 and one daughter in 1944. Volunteered for pilot training in January 1943, finished, and received his pilot's license in November 1943, Class 43-J. He completed his term as a B-24 pilot in Tonopah, NV. Received the following crew: Alvin Z. Levine, Co-pilot; Frank H. Lossing, Navigator; John R. Rapp, Bombardier; Carl Valentino, Leonard F. Noack, George R. Hartman, Kenneth M. Foster, Thomas J. Katin, and William S. (Bill) Chipman.

In May 1944, they flew a B-24 to Guadalcanal. They joined the 13th Air Force, 5th Bomb Grp., 31st Bomb Sqdn. and began flying bombing missions from New Guinea to all over the South Pacific from Yap Island to Borneo and Cavite in the Philippines. On March 13, 1945, after 43 missions, all four officers in the crew and four enlisted men returned home. Two enlisted men, Carl Valentino and William S. Chapman were lost in combat. 1st Lt. Reuben W. Blackburn retired from duty on July 12, 1945.

A graduate of Texas A&M College on June 12, 1951, he became a certified public accountant on August 8, 1952. He formed an accounting firm. Lawrence Blackburn, Meek & Maxie shortly thereafter and retired on August 3, 1989. He now has five grandchildren and three great grandchildren.

ERNEST W. (BILL) BLAIR, was born in Tonopah, NV on November 10, 1922. Grew up in Fallon, NV, which is now the home of one of the Navy's top gun schools. Married Margaret Crehore, his high school sweetheart. Has two daughters, three grandchildren, and two step-grandchildren.

Joined the USAAF in December 1942 while a freshman at the University of Nevada in Reno, NV. Went through pilot training in the Western Training Command, Class 44C; Pre-flight, Santa Ana, CA; Primary, Hemet, CA; Basic, Taft, CA; and Advanced, Ft. Sumner, NM. Was assigned to a B-24 crew as copilot. Their pilot was Terry Spivey. Received combat crew training at Muroc AAB, CA.

Flew a new B-24 to South Pacific and was assigned to the 13th Air Force, 5th Bomb Grp., 72nd Bomb Sqdn. Overseas stations were Admiralty Islands, Wakde, Noemfoor, Morotai, and Samar. Participated in 40 missions, mostly against targets in Borneo and the Philippines. His crew led group in strikes against Cavite Naval Base, Nichols Field, and Corregidor.

Returned to the States in May 1945 and was assigned to pilot AT-11 bombardier trainers in Big Spring, TX. Received honorable discharge in October 1945 as a 1st Lieutenant. Awarded the Air Medal with Oak Leaf Clusters, Asiatic-Pacific Medal with one Silver and two Bronze Stars, Philippine Liberation Medal, and the Presidential Unit Citation.

Graduated from Caltech with BS in Electrical Engineering in 1949. Spent most of his career with IMC Magnetics, Western Division, manufacturer of electro-magnetic components for the aerospace and computer industries. Now retired and residing in Pasadena, CA. His hobby is collecting and restoring mechanical music machines.

DONALD E. BONE, born Garland, UT on January 3, 1922. Graduate of Bear River High School in 1939. Graduated from the University of Utah in 1949 with a BS degree in Electrical Engineering. Employed by FMC Corporation. Married Wilma Morris 1945. Two daughters, seven grandchildren.

Entered military service with the Utah National Guard March 1941. Transferred to Air Corps Cadet training program (Class 43-E) August 1942. Graduated at Columbus, MI, May 1943. Transitioned in B-24 at Smyrna, TN July 1943. To Davis-Monthan August 1943, then to Pueblo, CO September through December 1943. Assigned to the 13th Air Force, 5th Bomb Grp. (H), 394th Bomb Sqdn. in South Pacific. Participated in 43 missions. Was 394th leader on first Balikpapen, Borneo (Pacific Ploesti) mission on September 30, 1944.

Trained as a communications officer at Chanute and Scott Fields after return from combat. Left active service November 1945 and the Air Force Reserve as a major in 1957. Retired from FMC in January 1986.

JEROME K. (JERRY) BORAK, was born in Chicago, IL on October 4, 1924. He attended Von Steubon High School and Wright Junior College before enlisting in the Army Air Corps. After basic training at Keesler Field, MS, he was assigned to Scott Field Radio School from

where he was accepted into the Aviation Cadet Program. He attended Kingman Arizona Gunnery School and graduated from Kirtland Field Bombardier School, Albuquerque, NM in the Class of 44-12. B-24 training at Casper, WY, Pueblo, CO, and Walla Walla, WA was a prelude for his bomber crew flying a new B-24 to Biak, New Guinea.

The crew was being ferried to the Philippines, when the C-46 lost an engine on takeoff. After circling the Biak Bay in an attempt to land, they crashed in the jungle, just 30 feet short of a row of parked and gassed fighters. The plane exploded and caught fire, but everyone was able to get out. Undaunted, another C-46 carried the crew to Clark Field and then to Samar, Philippines where they were assigned to the 23rd Bomb Sqdn., 5th Bomb Grp., 13th Air Force.

Their missions took them to Formosa (nine hours going and nine hours returning with heavy flak over the target), Borneo oil fields, Japanese troops holed up in Luzon (marked by an Army spotter plane), and targets in China.

WALTER S. BRALLEY, was born in Sydney, Australia in 1919. In 1941 he graduated from Virginia Tech. Reported for active duty in the Army Air Force in January 1942 to the U.S. Ordnance Dept. Served as Ordnance Officer with the 31st Bomb Sqdn. (H), from August 1942 until April 1944. Saw action in the South Pacific at Admiralty Island, Wakde Island, Noemfoor, and Morotai.

Decorated with the Bronze Star Medal, two Presidential Unit Citations, nine Battle Stars (Pacific Theater), Joint Service Commendation Medal, and the French Legion of Honor. Bralley remained in the Air Force and served until 1969 when he retired as a Lt. Colonel. Post WWII he served in the CO Statistical Control Unit; Adj. 1100th M&S Grp. and Co. 1103 Maintenance Sqdn, Bolling Field; Dir. Reserve Affairs, HQ Command; CH. Franco-American Affairs,

USAFE, Paris, France; Instructor College ROTC; Dir. Adm. Svs., Amarillo, Tech. Training Center; Adj. General JTF-8, (Nuclear Testing Task Force); and retired in 1969.

Bralley is married and his family includes three sons and one daughter. Son is CDR. USN, Ret.; son, Albuquerque police officer; son, Colonel, US Army; and daughter, E-7, CA-Army National Guard. Currently, he is retired in Albuquerque, NM and is traveling.

GEORGE W. BRITT, JR., born August 6, 1925 in Magnolia, AR. Moved to Galveston, TX in 1939. Graduated from high school in 1943 and was drafted into the Army. Completed Gunnery School at Laredo, TX and crew training at Tonopah, NV. Transferred overseas and assigned to the 13th Air Force. Completed 43 missions starting from Nadzab, New Guinea, and ending at Samar in the southern Philippines.

Postwar service consisted of flying as Central Fire Control Gunner in B-29s, working as an Armorer on F-80 and F-84 aircraft, and instructing NATO students on the A1CM radar gunsight during the Berlin Airlift. Returned to the States in 1951 and worked as training NCO and first sergeant until discharged in 1953. Enlisted in Texas Air National Guard Hall of Honor, November 1988, and retired from Dickinson Independent School District, Dickinson, TX in 1990.

LOUIS M. BROCKLY, Chicago, IL, born September 9, 1921. Graduated from high school in June 1940 and enlisted in AAF as a Radio Operator Mechanic with duty in Hawaii. Arrive Hawaii in December 1940 aboard the USS Grant. Assigned to HQ and HQ Sqdn., 5th Bomb Grp., Hickam Field. Finished Wheeler Field Radio School on December 5. Back to Hickam on December 6, on the third floor of the barracks, when the Japanese attacked on December 7, 1941.

Qualified as Aviation Cadet Class 43-K, Santa Ana, Santa Marie, Lancaster graduated on December 5, 1943 from Luke AAF as 2nd Lt. Duties Mariana, Randolph, Turner AAF with 31st TFW, Great Falls C-54 and Vittals training HQ Pac Div MAS Hickam, HQ MATS Andrews, RAF station South Rusilip, ADC Minot, HQ NORAD, RTAF Air Operation Bangkok, Thailand. Air Staff Pentagon. Retired at Lt. Col. on July 31, 1970. Returned to Colorado Springs, CO.

RICHARD L. BRUNET, ASN6146121. Enlisted in the U.S. Army in June 1938, arriving in Hawaii in September. Took basic training at Ft. Kamehamehao. Transferred to Luke Field, Ford Island, Pearl Harbor in February 1939. In October 1939 was transferred to the 4th Reconnaissance. The 5th Bomb Grp. moved to Hickam tentcity in September 1939 and Luke AAF Base was all Navy.

On February 1, 1940 moved into new barracks at Hickam. Brunet made PFC Spec. 3/C and attended AM School from February to May 1940. June 1940 passed AM test and made corporal on September 12, 1940. 4th Reconnaissance, flying B-18s around the island seven days a week in the daylight hours. On October 3, 1940, returned to mainland and was discharged in June 1941.

Re-enlisted on December 17, 1941 for Keesler. Arrived Keesler on December 25, 1941, pit latrines. Hickam AM test put Brunet in training command February 1942. Worked on BT-13s until May 1944. Was crew chief, hangar chief, line chief, and made M/Sgt. on January 1, 1943. Arrived in Europe, July 1944.

Assigned to the 15th AFB 17 Grp., 97th Bomb Grp., 340th Bomb Sqdn. as a crew chief until VE-Day. Returned to the U.S. in September 1945 and was discharged on October 11, 1945. In 1946 passed FAA A&E tests. Worked for TWA until December 1946.

Attended Kansas University from 1947-1951, received BS degree in Aeronautical Engineering. Worked at Boeing for 18 years as an engineer. Had wonderful career in aviation from 1939-1969.

JAMES F. BURNS, born August 22, 1922 in Johnstown, PA. Inducted into the service on January 23, 1943. Took basic training at Miami Beach, FL, went to Gunnery School in Tyndall Field, FL, and Air-plane Mechanic School at Sheppard Field, TX. Went to Salt Lake City and was assigned to Tom Cline's crew. Started combat crew training in Salt Lake City and was transferred to the Mojave Desert where they finished training.

Shipped out to Fairfield-Suisun, CA; picked up a B-24 and was assigned to the 13th Air Force, 23rd Bomb Sqdn., and flew to Guadalcanal, arriving on April 10, 1944. Flew 40 missions from Guadalcanal, Admiralty Islands, Wakde, Noemfoor, and Morotai, as an Engineer/Gunner with rank of S/Sgt. Decorated with the Air Medal with six Oak Leaf Clusters and the Asiatic-Pacific Theater Ribbon with six Bronze Stars. Discharged on October 5, 1945.

BERNARD B. BUSKA, born in Mosinee, WI on November 14, 1923. Inducted into the military on March 1, 1943. Sent to Camp Sheridan, IL. Next stop was Keesler Field, MI for basic training and then onto Airplane Engine Mechanic School (747). Sent to Oklahoma City for a C.T.D. Course. Eventually ended up on the west coast to a P.O.E.

Shipped out on the USS *General Black* on March 1, 1944 to New Caledonia, Solomon Islands, the to Los Negro. Assigned to the 5th Bomb Grp., 72nd Bomb Sqdn., then shipped to Wakde Island, next was Moratai, then Samar. A short stint on Palawan. War ended August 1945. Arrived back in the U.S. in December. Discharged December 28, 1945.

Civilian jobs. First ten years spent as a gear machinist. Twenty-eight years as a building engineer for the Milwaukee School system. Retired in 1984.

DENVER DEA CAMPBELL, born Isleton, CA on April 10, 1922. Lived entire life, except during Air Force duty, in California. Enlisted in the AAF, September 1942. Primary training, Phoenix, AZ; basic training, Merced, CA; advanced training and commissioned in Yuma, AZ. Phase training, B-24s Muroc, CA.

In Guadalcanal assigned to the 13th Air Force, 5th Bomb Grp., 23rd Bomb Sqdn. Flew 39 missions from Wadke, Noemfoor, and Morotai. Returned to U.S. April 1946. Ferry Command training Long Beach, CA. C-54 training in Homestead, FL. Assigned ATC at Fairfield-Suisun AF Base to fly C-54s.

Flew numerous trips into the Pacific ending up in Okinawa to fly occupational troops into Japan. Next to Kermatola, India carried cargo and occupational troops to Kunming, Shanghi, and other Chinese cities. Awarded the Distinguished Flying Cross with one Oak Leaf Cluster. Discharged in January 1946.

Joined Mobil Oil Co. for 38 years. Production/construction. Involved construction offshore platforms and production facilities. Retired September 1, 1984 to Palm Springs, CA.

WILLARD J. CARLSON, born Spokane, WA on May 6, 1923. Entered the Army Air Force in November 1942 and served in the South Pacific Theater. An AAF pilot, he was assigned to the 31st Bomb Sqdn., 5th Bomb Grp., 13th Air Force.

Credited with 35 missions from Morotai Island, Samar, and the Philippine Islands over Manila and Borneo areas. Decorated with the Air Medal with Oak Leaf Cluster. Discharged in January 1946 with rank of 1st. Lieutenant.

Carlson is Chairman of the Board and owner of Evergreen Memorial Gardens Cemetery and Funeral Home in Vancouver, WA.

RICHARD ALEN CLACK, (Deceased) born Nash County, Rocky Mount, NC on October 8, 1921. Lived in Rocky Mount through high school and attended Apprentice School in Newport News, VA (shipbuilding). Volunteered and enlisted in the service on August 27, 1942. Trained in Utah and Buckley Field, CO. Technician in Norden bombsight and C-1 Automatic Pilot. Served in Central Pacific, New Guinea, northern Solomons, and Bismarck Archipelago.

Earned the Good Conduct Medal, Distinguished Unit Citation with two Oak Leaf Clusters, Philippines Liberation Ribbon with one Bronze Star, Asiatic-Pacific Theater Campaign Medal with seven Bronze

Stars. Unit Citations for April 18 and May 15, 1944, Los Negros, Admiralty Islands, task of neutralizing Woleai Island Group, key base in Japanese inner defense circle. September 30, 1944, maximum effort bombing gasoline and oil refineries at Japanese base of Balikpapan, Borneo. Discharged on October 15, 1945 as Staff Sergeant.

Recalled from Reserves for one-year active duty from August 1950 to 1951 during Korean activity. Stationed at Randolph Air Force Base in Texas. Spent 22 years in reserves and became Master Sergeant, Supervisor.

Worked as director of Neighborhood Youth Corps, Nash-Edgecombe Economic Development, Inc. Work Experience and Employment and Training Programs, Department of Labor, U.S. Govt. Retired in 1983 and died in 1996. A Mason and Shriner, active in the American Legion, Baptist Church, Volunteer Fire Dept., and N.C. and National Manpower Associations. His family includes two children and six grandchildren.

JOSEPH D. CUMMINGS, born McDonough County, IL on January 7, 1925. Inducted into service, April 13, 1943 at Camp Grant, IL. Basic training at Atlantic City, NJ. Radio Operator/Mech. School AAFT, Sioux Falls, SD. Flexible Gunnery School, YAAF, Yuma, AZ. Flight crew training, TAAB, Tonopah, NV. Assigned to the 31st Bomb Sqdn., 5th Bomb Grp. (heavy), 13th Air Force. Served with the "Bomber Barons".

Flew missions to the Philippines, New Guinea, Weewak, Morotai, Netherlands East Indies, Woleai in the Carolines, Balikipapan, and Borneo. Completed 45 missions. Sent home August 1945 from Manila on the John S. Lykes. Discharged on October 26, 1945 from Camp Grant, IL.

Married in 1953 with two children and two grandchildren. Employed for 37 years with Northern Illinois Gas Company before retirement on February 1, 1985. Residence is Crystal Lake, IL.

ROY ALBERT DAVENPORT, born November 3, 1918 in Denver, CO. Joined AAF on October 21, 1941; Airplane Mechanic School, Chanute Field, IL, April 1942; 4th Recon/394th Bomb Sqdn., 5th Bomb Grp. (H), 7th AAF, 13th Air Force, January 1943. Thirty-three months combat

duty Hawaii to Morotai. With Colonel Marion Unruh, developed practice turret system August 1943. Colonel introduced Davenport to General Henry (Hap) Arnold.

In September 1943 hospitalized at 39th General Hospital, Auckland, New Zealand; returned to squadron. October 16, 1944 with Captain Campbell Larrson and crew of 50, prepared to bivouac Morotai for squadron move. Released to come home December 16, 1944, 85 air raids during this period. Assigned to Nellis Air Base, Las Vegas, NV on February 2, 1945. Discharged Buck Sergeant, Turret Specialist, September 18, 1945.

Awarded the Good Conduct Medal, American Defense Medal, Asiatic-Pacific Theater Ribbon, 10 Campaigns, two Presidential Unit Citations, and the Philippine Presidential Citation.

Career automotive mechanic, retired on December 29, 1978 as Chief Mechanic United States Postal Service.

LEE R. DAVIS, born in Abbott, TX on January 14, 1921. Moved to south Texas in 1927, settling in Sinton and attending public schools there. Sworn into the Air Corps on August 21, 1941 at Ft. Sam Houston, TX. On September 3, 1941 arrived Oahu, HI. Basic training, Bellows Field; assigned to Wheeler Field, October 1941; and sent to Hickam on November 25, 1941 to attend Gunnery School. On November 28, the school was discontinued; students formed ground defense battalion.

On December 7, 1941, the Japanese attacked. Sent back to Wheeler on December 12, 1941 and in August made S/Sgt. Sent to the 11th Bomb Grp. on December 21, 1942 on Espiritu Santo. Transferred to the 31st Bomb Sqdn., 5th Bomb Grp. Guadalcanal, arriving on March 3, 1943. Per CO's request, Davis grounded himself to work in Armament Section. April 1943 made Tech/Sgt. April 1944, 5th Bomb Grp. went to Admiralty Islands. Returned Stateside in August 1944 after a 21-day leave to Key Field, MS. Discharged in September 1945.

Re-upped in November 1945. Career spent in SAC. November 30, 1962 as M/Sgt. from 305th B-58 Hustler Bomb Wing. November 1963 to work for Navy Polaris Program. On January 14, 1975 retired WB 12 Civil Service.

ALFRED E. DAYWALT, born Annapolis, MD on April 8, 1915. Inducted into service on March 27, 1943. Took basic training AAF Miami Beach, FL; Airplane and Engine Mechanic School, Gulfport, MS; and Gunnery School, Laredo, TX. Assigned to Lt. Bolton's crew as a third engineer at Muroc AAF Base, Muroc, CA. Flew out of Hamilton Field, CA. April 8, 1944 for Guadalcanal. Assigned to the 13th Air Force, 5th Bomb Grp., 23 Bomb Sqdn. Flew about five missions to Rabaul. Moved up to the Admiralty Islands. Was reassigned to another crew to fly as 2nd Engineer. Lt. Bolton and crew shot down and strafed over Truk Naval Base a few days later.

Moved on to Wakde, Noemfoor, and Morotai, from there they knocked out Balikpapan oil fields and naval ships in Brunei Bay, Borneo. Daywalt finished his 40 missions from Samar, Philippines. Came back on Dutch ship Wiltevreden. Arrived Angel Island, USA on April 23, 1945.

Medals awarded: Good Conduct Medal, Asiatic-Pacific Service Medal with four Battle Stars, Philippine Liberation Medal with one Star, WWII Victory Medal, Air Medal with seven Oak Leaf Clusters, and the Presidential Unit Citation with one Star. Discharged as Staff Sgt. on June 5, 1945.

BASIL D. DEBNEKOFF, born South Bend, IN on April 17, 1922. Family moved to Chicago, IL in 1927. Enlisted in the U.S. Army Air Corps on September 22, 1941. Basic training Jefferson Barracks, MO. Graduated Radio-Op. Mech. School, Scott Field, IL. Arrived Hickam Field, Oahu, HI in May 1942. Assigned to the 7th Bomber Command, 5th Bomb Grp., 23rd Bomb Sqdn. (H), Territory of Hawaii, August 18.

In December the 5th Bomb Grp. transferred to Espitiru Santos, New Hebrides Islands to join the 13th Air Force.

Assigned as radio operator on crew of Captain (later Major and Squadron Commander) Burton H. Burns. Missions flown out of Guadalcanal began on December 21, 1942 and continued until August 1943. Flew 52 sorties included both search missions for shipping as well as bombing missions. Targets included Buka and Kahili Airfields, Bougainville Island; Rabaul Harbor, New Britain Island; Munda Point, New Georgia Island; Ballale, Villa Plantation, Rekata Bay, St. Isabella Island, and Kolumbangara.

Returned Stateside in September 1943. Assigned Troop Carrier Command George Field, IL as instructor. Discharged August 1945. Attended UCLA and Long Beach State University. Received BA and Master's degrees. Retired from Los Angeles School District as school administrator in 1982. Moved to Whidbey Island, WA in 1983. Living the "Life of Riley".

RUDOLPH V. (RUDY) DEPAOLA, born in Baltimore, MD on July 26, 1925. Enlisted in AAF from high school on July 19, 1943. Basic training, Keesler Field, Biloxi, MS; Gunnery School, Harlingen, TX; and crew training March Field, Riverside, CA. Assigned as tail gunner to Robert E. Grey crew. Picked up B-24 at Fairfield-Suisun, CA and became gravely ill and was left behind. Finally, DePaola caught up with his crew several weeks later in Nabzab, New Guinea.

After combat training missions, assigned to the 72nd Bomb Sqdn., 5th Bomb Grp. in November 1944. Flew 25 missions from Morotai (in Halmaheras) against the Philippines, Borneo, and other islands.

After the war, went to college on the GI bill. Became a teacher and later a principal in public, Catholic, and private schools. Retired in July 1983. Now spends summers in Baltimore and winters in Florida. Still a duffer in golf but loves it.

LAWRENCE W. DISMORE, born in Scott County, IN on September 9, 1921. Enlisted on May 13, 1942. Reported for active duty on October 21, 1942. After classification at Nashville, it was pilot preflight at Maxwell Field, then pilot primary at Tuscaloosa. Aerial Gunnery at Tyndall

Field and Navigation School at Selman Field. On December 4, 1943, Dismore received his wings as a Navigator and commissioned a 2nd Lt. in the Army.

Upon completion of three months of B-24 training with First Pilot Edgar Lynch, they proceeded to Hamilton Field where they picked up a new B-24, 092, which was later named Squirrely Shirley. This plane made a name for herself. They reported to the 31st by way of Guadalcanal and the 13th Bomber Command.

Who remembers June 7, 1944 when the 5th Bomb Grp. sent 24 B-24s to Truk, the big Japanese Naval Base? Due to extremely bad weather, only six planes, five from the 23rd and one from the 31st dropped their bombs on Truk. The 31st lost their Pilot, Edgar Lynch and Co-pilot Ward Anderson flew them home without any relief! The windshield and most of their instruments were shot out.

Recently, Dismore learned that the 23rd plane off of their left wing was named Patches. A Japanese fighter plane out of control cut off most of the left rudder. "I don't know the names of any of the 23rd crew that flew that day. Does anyone know the 23rd crew that flew that day?" If so, contact me at (317) 398-7637. Address is 1222 Ruby Drive, Shelbyville, IN 46176-3200.

JAMES W. DOTY, born Big Sandy, TN on May 22, 1925. Enlisted in the Army Air Corps on May 5, 1943. Basic, Keesler Field; Gunnery School, Tyndall Field; C.T.D., University of Tennessee; Pre-flight, Maxwell Field; Bombardier training, Carlsbad, NM, class 44-13 and O.T.U., Walla Walla AAF Base. Assigned to James R. Baker B-24 crew. Assigned to the 31st Bomb Sqdn., 5th Bomb Grp., 13th Air Force in early 1945. Bombing missions from Samar, Philippines over Formosa and bypassed islands until A-bombs, and then sixteen-hour patrol missions along Formosa and China coasts. Crew returned Stateside via Sunset project, October 1945. Discharged Camp Chaffe, AR effective February 24, 1946.

Entered the University of Tennessee on GI bill and graduated with a degree in Mechanical Engineering in 1950. Retired from Tennessee Valley Authority, assistant superintendent, Sequoyah Nuclear Plant after 34 years of service. Married Billie Sandefur in 1954 and have two children, one a writer and one music teacher. Other family includes grandson in University of Tennessee. Presently golfing, fly fishing, and volunteer work.

JOHN J. EAGAN, JR., born in Brooklyn, NY on March 3, 1923. Enlisted in AAF on September 2, 1942 from New York City. Basic training Miami Beach, FL; Aircraft Armorer School, Buckley Field, CO; and overseas infantry training course, Kearns, UT. Shipped out of San Francisco aboard the USS Republic for New Caledonia. Landed in New Hebrides on April 1, 1943. Assigned to the 72nd Bomb Sqdn., 5th Bomb Grp., 13th Air Force.

Served on Guadalcanal; Munda, New Georgia; Admiralty Islands; Wakde; Noemfoor; Morotai; and then onto Samar, Philippine Islands, March 1945. Sent to replacement camp on Leyte, September 10, 1945. Waited 20 days for ship home. Landed in San Francisco October 17, 1945. Discharged October 29, 1945 at Ft. Dix, NJ.

Married Lorraine Sullivan on May 3, 1947. Three daughters, Maureen, Maryelizabeth (deceased), and Kathleen. Worked as newspaper pressman for the New York Times from 1947 until 1990. Retired and living in Oak Run, Ocala, FL. Have three granddaughters and three grandsons. Never received ribbons or medals earned.

WILLIAM R. EATON, born Garber, OK on October 8, 1922. Moved to Borger, TX in 1926 and then to Pampa, TX in 1933. Enlisted in the Army Air Corps on November 13, 1939, for duty at Hickam Field, HI, arriving there on December 21, 1939. Assigned to the 72nd Bomb Sqdn. February 1, 1940. Aerial Armorer School May 1940. Asst. Armament Chief when Japan attacked on December 7, 1941.

Assigned to B-17 task force May 1942, under Navy command in New Caledonia. Moved to Australia and New Guinea with 19th Bomb Grp. June and 43rd Bomb Grp., September 1942, flying 48 bombardment missions from New Guinea bases.

Awarded the Silver Star Medal, Distinguished Flying Cross, Air Medal, and six Distinguished Unit Citations. Returned to U.S. in September 1943, B-29 Turret Systems School May 1944 assigned to Herington AAFB, KS, processing B-29s for overseas. Discharged on points on May 23, 1945.

Entered Northwestern University and marriage to Mary Louise Bailey in September 1945. Awarded BS degree in Electrical Engineering, August 1948. Employed with General Electric Co. as engineer through general manager in research and development businesses concerned with military avionics, nuclear power generation, nuclear warheads, ballistic missiles, re-entry vehicles for Atlas and Titan ICBMs, communications satellites, space life support systems, NASA support services for Apollo, worldwide computer time sharing and data processing services. Left GE in 1970 heading-up mass transit operations for the Philadelphia area. Early retirement 1978, consulting in various specialties, moving to Denton, TX in 1983. Six children, eight grandchildren.

JOHN H. ELMORE, born in Clark County, MO on June 17, 1924. Entered military service on April 22, 1943. Took basic training at Kearns, UT; Radio School, Sioux Falls, SD; and Gunnery School, Las Vegas, NV. Assigned to James (Bull) Rowden's crew as a Gunner at Muroc Air Base, Mojave Desert, CA for three months training.

In May 1944, flew from San Francisco to Guadalcanal by way of Hawaii and Canton Islands. Assigned to the 23rd Bomb Sqdn., 5th Bomb Grp., 13th Air Force. Flew missions in B-24s, ours named "Red Butt" from Guadalcanal, Admiralty, Wadke, Noemfoor, Morotai, and Samar in the Philippines. Hit targets on the islands of Rabaul, Bougainville, New Georgia, New Guinea, Mandate Islands, Truk, Yap, Palau, Balikpapan oil fields on Borneo, Brunei Bay, and Philippines. Fifty-nine total mis-

sions and only one was a turn-back for engine trouble. In December 1944, had a nine-day rest leave in Australia. Returned for duty on Morotia.

Most memorable missions include Bolipapan oil fields and Brunei Bay Japanese ships. Returned to the U.S. in May 1945 as Staff/Sgt. Had a seven-day layover in Hawaii. Honored to wear the Air Medal with three Oak Leaf Clusters, Bronze Stars for New Guinea, Mandated Islands, Philippines, and Luzon campaigns. Went to Miami Beach for a month of R&R and was discharged last of July 1945.

Retired on June 1, 1990 as owner of Tavern and Recreation Center.

ROGER M. FAKE, born Allentown, PA on January 12, 1922. Moved to Palmyra one year later. After graduation, worked briefly assembling shoes before starting work for Hershey Chocolate. Enlisted as a cadet in July 1942 and called January 1943 for training at San Antonio, TX. Flight training was at Brady, Waco, and Brooks Field, TX, graduating in Class 43-K on December 5, 1943. Trained as pilot at Tarrant Field, Ft. Worth, TX before crew training at Muroc, CA.

Fake chose his officers (Stan Gnacek, Gerry Getson, and Vincent Dougherty) and was assigned his enlisted crewmembers (Vance Sawry, Perry Sanford, James Reid, Joseph Tribble, James Goldsberry, and James Shaw) at Fresno, CA. They left from Fairfield-Suisun in a new B-24 on May 22, 1944. They flew to Hawaii, Canton, and finally Guadalcanal. Assigned to the 394th Bomb Sqdn, 5th Bomb Grp., 13th Air Force on May 31, 1944.

James Goldsberry was wounded on a mission to YAP and returned to the US, being replaced by Ray Slater. Fake and the crew flew missions from Admiralty Islands, Wakde, Noemfoor, and Morotai, completing 41 missions. Left group when it moved to Samar, PI. After waiting several weeks at Biak, boarded USS Pueblo on March 11, 1945 bound for the States. About 23 days later arrived at Angel Island, San Francisco, CA on April 3, 1945. After leave, reported to Memphis, TN to ferry B-24s to storage, also one C-54 to Karachi, India. Discharged on October 27, 1945 from Ft. Dix, NJ, after achieving rank of 1st Lieutenant.

Returned to Hershey Chocolate until recalled for the Korean War. Was a purchasing officer and later an instructor in liaison planes at San Marcos, TX. Returned December 9, 1952 to Hershey Chocolate and retired from his job as cost estimator in 1987.

STUART (BUD) FELTON, enlisted on December 8, 1941 from Louisville, KY; opened Anaheim cadet cadre, 42-J; Primary Pilot training, Visalia; Wings as Navigator Class 43-B, Mather, Sacramento. Assigned to the 13th Air Force combat crew, Oahu B-17s, February 23, 1943. Joined the 5th Bomb Grp., 23rd Bomb Sqdn. in Guadalcanal. Crew Pilot, Marion Holt. Then 394th. Promoted to lead Navigator in 72nd in B-24s, Pilot, J. J. Faunce. Completed 62 combat missions: Munda, Bougainville, Rabaul, and Truk. Stationed as bases in Guadalcanal, Solomon Islands, New Ireland, New Caledonia, Espiritu, Fiji, and Rabaul (New Britain).

Awarded the Air Medal with four Oak Leaf Clusters, Distinguished Flying Cross, and two Presidential Unit Citations. Flew in B-26s, B-25s detached duty from New Guinea. Led by Colonel Unruh, Adjutant Major John Dewey. Fellow 43-B graduate and 394th Navigator Major Larry Walton.

Survived several missions where flight loss and abort ratio exceeded 60 percent. Many low altitude oceanic flights, encountered severely unfavorable weather conditions. Usually without escort, the majority of missions experienced enemy interception and flack fields at targets. One key target, Truk, was uncharted. Numerous missions were factored by fuel consumption (radius of actions). Indoctrinated crews for Balikpapan. Rotated to Victorville as Navigator/Bombardier Instructor to B-29 crews. Inactive September 1945.

Post war civilian activities: teacher, author, stockbroker, investment consultant, inter-faith youth groups, and insurance advisor. Indianapolis resident-remain professionally active at 77.

OSCAR C. FITZHENRY was born August 3, 1921, at Big Brushy Creek, Yoakum, Texas. The following is a Summary of his military experience:

Texas National Guard, 1937-1940.

Commissioned as 2nd lt. Aviation Cadet in Class 42-H on September 6, 1942 at Lubbock, Texas, at 21 years of age.

Served in Solomon Islands as 1st Lt. In 72nd Bomb Squadron, commanded by Major Byron Sansom, from May 1943 to January 1944, flying 46 combat missions while attached to the 72nd. Flew additional 12 missions with 394th Squadron as a Captain and OPS officer for a total of 58 missions. Served under commanding officer Major Bill McKinley, who flew a total of 53 missions; their combined total of 111 combat missions set a record for the 1943-1944 Solomon Islands campaign.

Returned to United States on May 6, 1944, which he later discovered was the day his classmate, Major Jerry Cass, had been shot down and killed.

Was assigned to 72nd/46th Recon Squadron as B-29 pilot and photo officer at Ladd Field, Alaska in 1946-1947.

Stationed at Travis Air Force Base from 1950-1953, where he served as a B-29 Aircraft Commander and Adjutant with 23rd Squadron and also as Aircraft Commander flying RB-36s in the 31st Squadron.

Was squadron commander and flew the GRB-36 that carried the F-86 parasite in 1957 at Fairchild AFB, Washington.

Assigned as Commanding Officer of SAC B-47 CCT Squadron at McConnell Air Force Base, Kansas, from 1960-1962.

Retired after 20 years of service at the rank of Lt. Colonel in October of 1962.

Since his retirement, Fitzhenry has lived in Charleston, South Carolina, with his family. He has been self-employed as an investment consultant and real estate developer.

Awards and Decorations: Distinguished Flying Cross with one oak leaf cluster; Air Medal with one silver oak leaf cluster and four bronze oak leaf clusters; three Pacific Theater battle stars; Presidential Unit citation.

Notes of Interest: Has 1500 feet of 16-mm color film covering the Kahili, Rabaul, and Truk raids (copyrighted). Also has detailed diaries of Pacific experiences, 1943-1944 (copyrighted).

Was group leader on Kavieng raid in which an attack by 25 Haps and Zeroes resulted in a 55-minute air battle with no loss of life or aircraft on his side.

Served much of his military career in 5th Bomb Group; flew B-24s in both the 72nd and 394th Squadrons in the South Pacific Command; flew B-29s and B-36s in the 23rd and 31st SAC Squadrons at Travis Air Force Base.

Led rescue effort on December 31, 1943, when Colonel Unruh's aircraft and crew of eleven was shot down. Found and photographed Col. Unruh and his crew on a beach in New Ireland, but subsequent rescue attempts over the next few days by PB-2Ys failed. Two of Col. Unruh's men were drowned at bailout, two starved to death in prison, and six were executed by the Japanese. Of the crew, only Col. Unruh survived the prison camps, and later died in a plane crash in Pretty Prairie, Kansas; he had built the airplane himself after his retirement.

Personal statement: "I know that it was only by the grace of my Lord, who was ably assisted by two of the finest Commanding Officers that I ever served under (Major William McKinley and Colonel Marion Unruh), that I became one of only two out of ten of my close-knit group of friends who survived. Luck or skill had nothing to do with it."

LYNN C. FOXWORTHY, born October 11, 1919 in Indianapolis, IN. Enlisted in the Army Air Corps on September 14, 1942 at Ft. Harrison, IN. After qualifying tests for Tech Schools in St. Petersburg, FL assigned to Armament School, Buckley Field, Denver, CO. Then went to overseas training center at Kearns, UT and Camp Stoneman, CA. Shipped overseas in February 1943. Foxworthy served from March 1943 through the island chain from New Caledonia to Samar, Philippines in August 1945. Discharged as Corporal on October 26, 1945 from Camp Atterbury, IN.

Decorated with the Purple Heart/ Morotai Island on November 22, 1944, Army Good Conduct Medal, American Campaign Medal, Asiatic-Pacific Theater Ribbon with ten Battle Stars, WWII Victory Medal, Presidential Unit Citation with Oak Leaf Cluster, Philippine Liberation, and Independence Medals, Philippine Presidential Unit Citation, and China Commemorative Medal.

Married Hazel Shaw in May 1947 and celebrated their 50th wedding anniversary in May 1997. They have two sons, one daughter, and four grandchildren. Retired from Eli Lilly and Co. after 36 years of employment.

ALEXANDER FRAMARIN, Tech Sgt., Flight Engineer/Gunner. Born in Vicenza, Italy on April 22, 1923. Lived in the Chicago area on the Southside (Pull-

man). Drafted into the AAF on March 23, 1943. Took basic training at Miami Beach, FL; Airplane Mechanic School, Seymour Johnson Field, NC; and Aerial Gunnery School, Ft. Myers, FL.

Shipped to California for more training, then to Tonopah, NV for overseas training, flew to Fairfield-Suisun, CA and picked up a new B-24 and headed for Hawaii. Island hopped to Guadalcanal, then to Negros Island and joined the 5th Bomb Grp., 394th Bomb Sqdn. Flew missions from Guadalcanal, Admiralty Islands, Wakde, Noemfoor, Morotai, and Samar in the Philippines. Flew 43 missions and grounded in March 1945. Sent to California by boat, onto Ft. Snelling, MN, and discharged on June 17, 1945.

Awards and decorations include the Good Conduct Medal, Philippine Liberation Medal, Asiatic-Pacific Theater Ribbon with five Battle Stars, and Air Medal with four Oak Leaf Clusters. The pilot of our plane was Lt. Virgil Blase.

ARMANDO C. FRANCO, born in Guanajuato, Mexico on October 23, 1921. Entered in the U.S. in 1926. Inducted U.S. Air Corps, October 20, 1942 at Ft. MacArthur, CA. Took basic training at St. Petersburg, FL; Radio-Op School, Scott Field, IL; Radio Mechanic School, Truax Field, WI; and Radar Mechanic School, Boca Raton, FL. Became a U.S. citizen on November 27, 1942 in Tampa, FL.

Embarked overseas from San Francisco, CA on June 7, 1944. Arrived Noumea, New Caledonia, June 30, 1944. Assigned to the 23rd Sqdn., 5th Bomb Grp. Island hopped to unit at Morotai Island, by way of Guadalcanal, Hollandia in New Guinea and Noemfoor Islands. Performed first and second echelon maintenance and repairs to radio and radar equipment on aircraft. Returned Stateside on November 20, 1945 with rank of Staff/Sgt. and was discharged on December 16, 1945 at Ft. Bliss, TX.

Now retired in San Antonio, TX after 45 years as a machinist with the Southern Pacific Railroad.

CARL H. FRANZEN, born in Beloit, WI on November 20, 1922. Moved to Bloomington, IN in February 1923. Enlisted in the AAC on September 9, 1942, Ft. Benjamin Harrison, Indianapolis, IN. Clearwater, FL for assignment to Pursuit Armament School at Buckley Field, CO. Graduated December 1942. Kearns, UT for overseas assignment.

Arrived in New Caledonia in March 1943, went to Espiritu Santo and was assigned to the 72nd Sqdn. Rotated with the 31st Sqdn. at Guadalcanal. Lost Colonel Unruh, the 5th Bomb Grp. Commander, in December 1043 on a raid to Rabaul from Munda, then next to the Admiralty Islands (Manus), Wakde (7,000-feet airstrip), Noemfoor where the Balikpapan oilfield raids were made. At that time the longest flight was attempted. Then onto Morotai and finally Samar in the Philippines.

At the end of the war in August, Franzen went to a transfer center on Leyte and was put on a ship, arriving in the States in October 1945 and was discharged from Ft. Knox, KY as a corporal on October 15, 1945. Served as a journeyman apprentice at Diamond Chain in Indianapolis, IN and went to work for Western Electric, Indianapolis. Stayed there until they closed the plant. Retired in 1985 with 36 years service as an associated engineer (engineer without a degree). Married Margaret A. Gustin in September 1948 and they have two girls and two boys.

WILLIAM H. GATES, born in Brockton, NY on February 29, 1924 and moved to Canton, NC in 1934 and Bradenton, FL in 1936. Volunteered for Army Air Force on January 11, 1943. Completed basic training, Jefferson Barracks, MO; B-17 Mechanics School, Amarillo, TX; and B-17 Factory School, Boeing, Seattle, WA. Assigned B-17 engine mechanic at Rapid City, SD and B-29 engine mechanic at Harvard, NB until April 1945. Assigned to the 72nd Bomb Sqdn., 5th Bomb Grp. on Samar, Philippine Islands.

June 1945 as assistant crew chief on B-24. Assigned to the 69th Bomb Sqdn., 42nd Bomb Grp. as crew chief on B-25 in Palawan, Philippine Islands. Re-enlisted for one year in Palawan. Assigned to the 316th Troop Carrier Grp. at Pope Field, NC as crew chief on C-47 and C-82, March 1946. Discharged in December 1946.

In March 1947, earned private pilot's license. April 1947 started Aeronautical Engineering School at Northrop Tech., Hawthorne, CA. Married in June 1947. Graduated Northrop 1949 and 1961 with BS degree in Aeronautical Engineering. Retired chief scientist for Hughes Aircraft on December 1, 1989 after 33 years. Moved to Midland, TX in November 1992. Two children and four grandchildren. Member of Confederate Air Force.

RICHARD T. GLEW, Sgt., born in Trafford, PA on January 25, 1923. Moved to Oakmont, PA in 1935. Enlisted in the Army Air Force on December 13, 1942. Took basic training, Miami Beach, FL; Radio-Op Mech. School, Sioux Falls, SD; Gunnery School, Yuma, AZ; and First and Second Phase combat crew training, Mountain Home, ID.

Assigned to Phillip Bauer's crew as Radio Operator/Waist Gunner. Left for Philippine Islands by boat on July 24, 1945, arrived on August 30, 1945. Assigned 31st Bomber Sqdn., 5th Bomb Grp., 13th Air Force, September 1945. Flew missions from Samar, Philippine Islands over Formosa and China.

Returned Stateside on December 24, 1945. Discharged from Camp Atterbury, IN on January 6, 1946. Enlisted in the U.S. Air Force Reserve in July 1947, discharged in July 1950. Glew has been married for 46 years, with two sons, and he is a retired letter carrier.

LATIMER WILLIAM (BILL) GLOWA, born in New York City, NY on October 8, 1908. Married to Mary C. Duff. They have two children, one son, and one daughter. In 1932, Glowa earned a BS degree from MIT. In April 1940, received executive orders to report to War Department, Washington, DC, to organize and maintain a plan to collect airfield information in the world. Named "Father of the U.S. Air Attache System". This project is still in operation today in 1998.

Joined the Army Air Force as 1st Lt. in January 1943. Assigned to HQ USAF, the Pentagon, 1943-1947; U.S. Air Forces in Europe, 1947-1950 as S-2 61 Troop Carrier Wing, "Berlin Airlift" Operations at Rhine-Main Air Base, West Germany, 1948-1949; the Pentagon, 1950-1953; U.S. Air University, Maxwell AFB, AL, 1953; Air Technical Intelligence Center, Dayton, OH, 1953-1954; Far East Air Forces, 1954-1956; CINCAP, Hawaii, 1956-1958; Inspector General and Chief-Operational Intelligence Division, (concurrent assignments), 5th Bomb Wing, B-52 (G), Travis AFB, CA, 1958-1963. Retired as colonel on May 31, 1962. NSA, Ft. Meade, MD, 196-1993.

HENRY A. GORDON, born in Vernon County, MO in March 1922 and graduated from Bronaugh High School in 1942. Drafted into the Air Force at Ft. Leavenworth, KS in October 1942. Served in the Ordnance Dept., 5th Bomb Grp., 72nd Bomb Sqdn. Supervised at one time, thirty munitions workers. Went to the Central Pacific in February 1943, served in the Solomons, Bismarck Archipelago, New Guinea, Philippines, Eastern Mandates, and China.

Awarded the Good Conduct Medal, Asiatic-Pacific Theater Ribbon, Philippine Liberation Ribbons, nine Battle Stars, and the Presidential Unit Citation with Oak Leaf Cluster. Discharged as a sergeant in October 1945.

Retired from 3M Coin in 1984. Married Glenna Bley in July 1948 has two sons and two daughters. Currently lives in Moundville, MO.

RAYMOND E. GOTT, born March 6, 1922 in Lafayette, IN. Enlisted on September 10, 1942 in the Cadet Program and received pilot wings on June 24, 1944 as Flight Officer at Ellington Field, Houston, TX Class 44-F.

Assigned to B-24 crew of 2nd Lt. Charles Shearer as a co-pilot at Hamilton Field, CA. Ordered to leave for overseas duty on November 7, 1944. Joined the 31st

Bomb Sqdn., 5th Bomb Grp., 13th Air Force at the Island of Morotai on December 25, 1944. The crew flew missions on Philippine bases and airfields, Corregidor, Cavity Naval Base, Balikpapan, and Borneo oil refinery. We moved to Samar Island, Philippines to finish their tour of duty with a total of 44 missions.

Promoted in January 1945 to 2nd Lt., 1st Pilot in May 1945, and 1st Lt. in June 1945. Decorated with the Air Medal with three Oak Leaf Clusters, Philippine Liberation Medal with one Battle Star, Asiatic-Pacific Theater Medal with four Battle Stars. Gott was aboard ship in the middle of the Pacific Ocean when Japan surrendered. Discharged on September 7, 1945.

Retired after working as a toolmaker, toolroom foreman, and tool design engineer after 47 years. Gott was the only married member of his crew.

SOLON A. GREEN, born on February 28, 1925 at Park Rapids, MN. Enlisted in the Army Air Corps on February 9, 1943. Took basic training at Jefferson Barracks, MO and CTD training at the University of Minnesota. Classification and pre-flight at Santa Ana, CA; Gunnery School, Las Vegas, NV; graduated Bombardier School, Victorville, CA; and took combat crew training March Field, CA. Green married while there in August 1944.

On December 7, 1944 left the U.S. and joined the 23rd Bomb Sqdn., 5th Bomb Grp., at Morotai in January 1945. Flew 41 missions from Morotai and Samar. Re-assigned Stateside on August 24, 1945. Released from active duty on January 15, 1946 with rank of 2nd Lt.

Graduated from the University of Minnesota in August 1948. Went into the insurance business at Wadena, MN. Joined the National Guard and formed a truck company in Wadena. Called to active duty on September 25, 1950. Released from active duty from Camp McCoy, WI on November 7, 1951.

Joined Shell Oil Co. on December 15, 1951. After several marketing assignments, retired on December 31, 1981. Have enjoyed life in Park Rapids, MN since with wife, Harriet, their three children, eight grandchildren, and one great grandson.

MELVIN E. GREGORIUS, born Appleton, WI on April 28, 1921. Settled in Baldwin County, AL in 1935. Entered the Army Air Corp. on July 11, 1942; basic training, Miami Beach, FL; and Photography School, Lowery Field, CO. Based in Guatemala, Central America, Aerial Reconnaissance Patrol, Panama Canal Zone.

Entered pilot training and graduated as a pilot at Ellington Field, Houston, TX, September 1944. Joined crew and flew B-24s transitional training, Walla Walla, WA, as co-pilot, Lt. Clarence Hofer as pilot. The crew was assigned to the 31st Bomb Sqdn., 5th Bomb Grp., 13th Air Force, Samar, Philippines, May 9, 1945. Completed 19 missions over Borneo and Formosa areas and one patrol mission to Hong Kong after peace was declared. Returned stateside and discharged on February 6, 1946 at Ft. Sheridan, IL.

As a civilian, worked in various positions with the Air Force and then the Navy Dept. of Defense. Retired on July 2, 1976. Presently living in Daphne, AL with his wife of 45 years. They have four children and eight grandchildren.

JOHN T. GROLLIMUND, born on October 15, 1924 at Rutherford, NJ. Enlisted in AAF on November 17, 1942. Basic training, Atlantic City, NJ and Maxwell Field, Montgomery, AL. Spent the next year or more at various flying schools in Florida and Georgia. Too many cadets training as pilots. Re-assigned to San Marcos, TX for Navigator training. Graduated as 2nd Lt. in December 1944. Assigned to Gerard Kanopa's crew on B-24 Liberator, Pueblo, CO. Flew to Biak, New Guinea via Hawaii, then onto Morotai.

Joined the 23rd Bomb Sqdn., 5th Bomb Grp., 13th Air Force. Seventeen missions out of Samar, Philippine Islands. War ended. Awarded five Battle Stars and two Philippine Liberation Ribbons. Shortage of navigators. Re-assigned to the 403rd Troop Carrier Grp. Rest of crew went home. Finally sent stateside in May 1946. Separated from service, but no discharge until 1955.

Attended the University of Michigan, September 1946 until June 1950. Awarded Bachelor's degree in Pharmacy in June 1950. Retired in October 1984.

ROBERT H. (BOB) HAMILTON, born on March 19, 1925 in China, to parents who were missionaries. Attended Shanghai American School, Atlanta Boys High, and Davidson College. Enlisted in the AAF on May 4, 1943; Primary Pilot, El Reno, OK; Flexible Gunnery, Harlingen, TX; Navigation School, Monroe, LA; and appointed 2nd Lt. Navigator on October 2, 1944. B-24 combat crew training, Tonopah, NV (1st Lt. Marvin C. Seitz, Pilot). Crew flew ATC to Pacific on March 4, 1945, stationed at Nadzab (New Guinea), and Samar, Philippines.

Assigned to the 394th Bomb Sqdn., 5th Bomb Grp., 13th Air Force. Flew 24 combat missions, bombed Rabaul, Balikpapan, Tarakan, Brunei Bay, and Formosa. Decorated with the Air Medal with Oak Leaf Cluster. Assistant squadron navigator, promoted to 1st Lt. Flew B-24 to California in November, discharged on December 31, 1945.

Became airline navigator and flew the Pacific with United Airlines and California-Eastern Airways. Completed A.B., M.A., University of California at Berkeley, Th. M. Dallas Theological Seminary. Taught History, Philosophy at Milliken University, IL, and Columbia College, CA, retired in 1985. Had three children and two grandchildren. Living on lakeshore near Atlanta with wife, Jeanne, enjoying family visits, writing book about his wartime adventures overseas.

RUSSELL E. HANNA, born March 5, 1924 at Cuyahoga Falls, OH. Entered U.S. Army Air Force Pre-cadet Program in October 1942 from Barberton, OH. Attended flight training programs at Mississippi State College; Preflight School; Primary; Basic Pilot; and Advanced Pilot, graduating at Victoria, TX, commissioned a 2nd Lt., single engine, checked out in P-40.

Assigned instructor, single pilot. Transferred to B-24 bomber transition training at Walla Walla, WA. Ferried B-24 to Southwest Pacific Theater as co-pilot, then promoted to 1st pilot and 1st Lt. Commanded B-24 crews in successful missions against enemy in New Guinea, Western Pacific, China Offensive, and Southern Philippines. Flew 27 combat missions in Asiatic-Pacific, 13th Air Force, 5th Bomb Grp., 31st Bomb Sqdn., logging 286 combat hours and 900 hours B-24 flying time hours.

Awarded the Presidential Unit Citation with one Oak Leaf Cluster, Asiatic-Pacific Theater Ribbon, five Battle Stars, Air Medal with one Oak Leaf Cluster, Philippine Liberation Ribbon, and WWII Victory Medal. Ferried B-24 back to U.S. and was discharged on December 20, 1945.

Graduated from University of Akron, BS degree, and Western Reserve University, MA degree, attending on GI Bill. Retired to Phoenix, AZ in 1983 after a successful career in industry as human resource director.

JOHN (JACK) W. HAYES, born in Naperville, IL on February 13, 1922. Enlisted in the Army Air Corps Reserves in August 1942. Active duty as an Aviation Cadet SAAC, San Antonio, February 1943; Pre-flight, Ellington Field; Navigation training, Hondo, TX; graduated 2nd Lt. October 1943; Phase training, Boise, Pocatello, Mountain Home, ID and Muroc, CA; and Fairfield-Suisun April 1945 to the 13th Air Force at Guadalcanal.

Joined the 31st Bomb Grp. on Manus, thence Wakde, Noemfoor, and Morotai. Flew 44 combat missions. Received the Air Medal with six Oak Leaf Clusters. Returned Stateside in April 1945. Took pilot training as a student officer Goodfellow, Perrin, and Luke Fields and earned pilot wings in May 1946. Discharged as captain in November 1946.

Resumed civilian career with CB&Q Railroad, joined Santa Fe Railroad in Chicago 1947. Rose from transportation clerk to vice president and corporate secretary.

Retired in September 1984. Married to wife Jean and celebrated 54 years of marriage in February 1998. They have four children and four grandchildren.

HERBERT B. HENDERSON, born on February 6, 1921 at Tyrone, PA. Worked at Middletown Air Depot, Olmstead Field, PA, overhauling aircraft engines for the Army Air Force. Entered military service with the Army Air Force on September 2, 1942. Attended B-24 Mechanics School at Keesler Field, MS; B-17 Specialist School at Lockheed-Vega, Burbank, CA.

Left USA from Camp Stoneman, CA on USS Wharton for New Caledonia. Assigned to the 31st Bomb Sqdn., 5th Bomb Grp., 13th Air Force on August 23, 1943. Stationed at Henderson, Carney, and Koli Fields, Guadalcanal. Moved to Munda, Admiralty Islands, Wakde, Noemfoor, Morotai, and Samar as crew chief and flight chief. Departed Leyte, Philippine Islands on October 6, 1945 on USS General Hann for Ft. Lawton, WA. Discharged from Indiantown Gap, PA as Staff Sgt. on October 29, 1945.

Worked for Hughes Aircraft Co. in the Test Flight Division, Culver City, CA, as flight line crew chief on USAF and USN aircraft. Licensed FAA aircraft and powerplant mechanic. Retired on September 9, 1977.

RICHARD J. HERREMA, born December 11, 1923 in Lucas, MI. Enlisted in the Army on March 17, 1943 in Grand Rapids, MI. Took basic training, Camp Robinson, AK; transferred to Air Corps; CTD at Western Reserve University; Flexible Gunnery School, Harlingen, TX; overseas training, 4th AF, Walla Walla, WA; and B-24 combat crew training, Tonopah, NV.

Flew ATC to Pacific March 4, 1945, stationed at Nadzab, New Guinea, and Samar, Philippines. B-24 Ball Turret Gunner on 1st Lt. Marvin C. Seitz's crew, assigned to the 394th Bomb Sqdn. 5h Bomb Grp., 13th Air Force. Flew 210 combat hours, 21 combat missions, bombed Rabaul, Balikpapan, Tarakan, and Brunei Bay. Awarded the Air Medal with Oak Leaf Cluster and promoted to Staff Sgt. in July 1945. Returned Stateside in November, discharged on December 31, 1945.

Became painter, then painting contractor in Grand Rapids, MI. Retired to Byron Center, MI with wife Lorraine, enjoying golf, and visiting children and grandchildren.

JAMES C. HILL, born on April 7, 1918 in Akron, OH. Married Anne on October 28, 1939, one pre-war daughter, Jackie (the first of five children). Drafted in October 1943; Basic training, Keesler Field, MS; Primary Pilot training, MS, which ended at the convenience of the government; and Flexible Gunnery School, Harlingen, TX; B-24 combat crew training, Tonopah, NV.

Flew ATC to Pacific on March 4, 1945, stationed at Nadzab, New Guinea and Samar, Philippines. B-24 Tail Gunner on 1st Lt. Marvin C. Seitz's crew, assigned to the 394th Bomb Sqdn., 5th Bomb Grp., 13th Air Force. Flew 23 combat missions, bombed Rabaul, Balikpapan, Tarakan, and Brunei Bay. Earned the Air Medal with Oak Leaf Cluster. Promoted to Staff Sgt. in July 1945. Returned stateside by ship, discharged in January 1946. A memorable event was floating down river in New Guinea to Lae, making friends with the Aussies there.

Hill was a media specialist for Timken Roller Bearing Co. in Canton, OH until retirement. Enjoys portrait painting, golf, and visits with family.

ROBERT L. HILL, born Akron, Oh on November 15, 1922. Enlisted in the Army Air Corps in November 1942. Took basic training at Miami Beach, FL; CTD at Slippery Rock College, PA; and Primary Pilot training at Panama City, FL. Graduated from Bombardier School at Carlsbad, NM in October 1944. Crew training at Walla Walla, WA with Lt. Jack Pease as pilot. Flew from Hamilton Field, CA to Biak, New Guinea.

Assigned to the 394th Bomb Sqdn. at Samar, New Guinea in March 1945. Bombing missions were to various targets in the Philippines, Sarawak, Southern Borneo, and Formosa. Flew 23 combat and four reconnaissance missions. Flew back to U.S. in B-24 in October 1945. Awarded the Air Medal and several campaign ribbons.

Graduated from Akron University in 1948. Retired from Schrader-Bellows Co., June 1986. Immediate family has been wife, Janet (deceased), son, Jim, and current wife Rosemary.

RUSSELL W. HOOVER, born in Amity, PA on October 20, 1924. Joined the Army Air Corp on November 5, 1942 and served in the South Pacific Theater. Assigned as a Ball Turret Gunner to the 394th Bomb Sqdn., 5th Bomb Grp., 13th Air Force

Completed 50 missions on a B-24 from December 1943 until August 1944. A member of Capt. Harold W. Moshy's crew, Hoover saw action at Rabaul, Truk, Biak, Yap, and Woleai. Decorated with the Air Medal with six Oak Leaf Clusters, Good Conduct Medal and Asiatic-Pacific Theater Ribbon. Discharged on October 10, 1945 with rank of Staff Sgt.

Currently retired from the U.S. Postal Service and residing in Washington, PA.

REGINALD J. HOUSE, born in Clare, MI on September 10, 1915. Attended high school and Central Michigan College. Worked four years at airfield. Enlisted into the Army Air Corps in October 30, 1940. Arrived overseas on December 5, 1940 and was assigned to the 23rd Bomb Sqdn., 5th Bomb Grp. at Hickam and survived the Japanese attack with broken ribs on December 7, 1941. Did not receive Purple Heart, as records were lost.

In September 1941 moved to the 13th Air Force at Midway. Served at Espirtu Santo, Guadalcanal, then to Munda Point, Northern Solomons, Manus group at Momote Air Field, and New Guinea. Earned seven Battle Stars. Held for 3 1/2 years the rank of TSgt. as section chief.

Returned from overseas in September 1944 and relocated to Boca Raton, FL, transferred to Sioux Falls, SD Air Base, and mustered out in August 1945. Worked as a machinist. Farmed own farm for 30 years. Retired from Central Michigan University. Married on November 19, 1955 to Janet Lutz. Three children: Thomas, an electrician, David G., an electronics engineer, and Linda S. Stebbleton, computer analyst.

JOSEPH J. HUBKA, born in Wilson, KS on September 11, 1920. Enlisted in the AAF on January 11, 1940. Basic training at Hickam Field in Hawaii and assigned to the 31st Bomb Sqdn., 5th Bomb Grp. Worked in group personnel until December 1942. Commissioned a 2nd Lt. at Miami

Beach, March 3, 1943. Resigned commission after the war ended while stationed in Hawaii with the 7th Fighter Wing and re-enlisted as a master sergeant. Recalled as an officer in October 1950.

Retired as major on June 30, 1961 while serving as deputy director of personnel in the Aeronautical Systems Command, Wright Patterson AFB. Worked for the Boeing Airplane Co. as a senior supervisor in industrial relations. Retired for the second time in November 1974 and lives in the Cascade Mountains of Washington State with wife.

JULIAN BURRELL HUDGINS, born December 6, 1919 at Flowery Branch, GA. Attended North Georgia College and the University of Georgia School of Law from 1936 until 1940. Enlisted in the Army Air Corps on January 7, 1941. Entered Aviation Cadet Pilot training on December 8, 1941 and graduated from Pilot School on June 23, 1942 as a 2nd Lt. and Army pilot. In August, September, and October 1942, completed Phase I, II, and III Combat Crew Training Program at Tucson, El Paso, and Topeka.

Transferred to the Southwest Pacific Theater of Operations in early November 1942 and assigned to the 431st Bomb Sqdn., 11th Bomb Grp., 13th Air Force on November 20, 1942. Was co-pilot to Lt. George Roberts and Capt. Warren Wilkinson. Transferred to the 23rd Bomb Sqdn., 5th Bomb Grp. and joined Lt. Flavel Sabin's crew as co-pilot on March 1, 1943.

On April 13, 1943, Lt. Sabin's crew ditched off of the Southeast tip of Santa Isabel Island at 2:45 a.m., the Bombardier, Lt. Sarratt, and flight engineer, Tech/Sgt. Harvey were fatally injured in the landing. The ditching was made in zero-zero weather conditions with rain and fog at night. Only an outstanding performance by Lt. Sabin prevented the fatality number from being much higher.

Assigned to Major Tex Burn's crew as co-pilot on July 1, 1943. Hudgins became an aircraft commander of his own crew on September 1, 1943, returning to the States on December 13, 1943. His most enjoyable duty was his final six years at Elgin AFB, FL as Chief of Bombardment Section in Test Operations of the Air Proving Ground Center, from 1957 through 1963. He retired from USAF on January 1, 1964 as Lt. Colonel with 23 years of active duty.

ANTON (TONY) IMHOF, born in St. Louis, MO on November 4, 1924. Enlisted in the Signal Corp Reserve on December 4, 1942. Entered active duty on July 5, 1943. Took basic and lineman training in Sacramento, CA. Transferred to Army Air Corps on December 20, 1943; Radio-Op Mech. School, Scott Field, IL; Gunnery School, Yuma AAB; and B-24 combat crew training, Tonopah, NV (1st Lt. Marvin C. Seitz, Pilot).

Crew flew ATC to Pacific on March 4, 1945 and was stationed in Nadzab, New Guinea and Samar, Philippines. Assigned to the 394th Bomb Sqdn., 5th Bomb Grp., 13th Air Force. Flew 23 combat missions, bombed Rabaul, Balikpapan, Tarakan, Brunei Bay, and Formosa. Awarded the Air Medal with Oak Leaf Cluster. Radio Operator/Gunner promoted to Tech. Sgt. on July 15, 1945.

Worked for U.S. Army as a civilian and retired in September 1977. Married on November 24, 1945, four children living, and ten grandchildren. Celebrated 50th wedding anniversary in November 1995 and travel extensively.

ALBERT W. JAMES, see page 142.

EDWARD F. JOKSCH, (Deceased), born in Richardton, ND on September 23, 1916. Enlisted at Ft. McDowell on November 29, 1940 and was sent to Hawaii as a tractor driver assigned to the 394th Bomb Sqdn. Eventually was sent overseas to New Guinea, Guadalcanal, and the Northern Solomon's, among others.

Served as possible crew chief on Facinatin Woman and/or Tim-ber. Discharged as a Tech/Sgt. on September 12, 1945 at Camp Beale, CA. Recalled to active duty between January 1951 and October 1952 at McClellan AFB. "Papa" died in 1980 of a stroke. Written by Michael Cozad, grandson.

W.C. JONES, born in Redland, AR on September 12, 1919 and raised in the Texas Panhandle. Moved to California in 1940. Worked for Douglas Aircraft. Took cadet exam and went into Army Air Corps in 1944. In basic training, a truck in which he was riding overturned. His injuries eliminated his hopes of becoming a pilot. Jones then attended Gunnery School in Laredo, TX and became a Ball Gunner and crewmember on a B-24. First phase combat training was completed in Boise, ID.

The crew picked up a B-24 and island hopped to Biak Island. They spent time in Nadzab, New Guinea, where it rained most of the time, but they managed to complete a couple of missions. Transferred to Samar, Philippines and assigned to the 23rd Bomb Sqdn., 5th Bomb Grp., 13th Air Force and flew eight missions before the war was terminated. Transferred to the 321st Air Service Grp. and traveled by ship to San Francisco. Sent to El Paso, TX for discharge as a Buck Sergeant in 1946.

Retired in 1980, after working for the military as a supervisory quality assurance representative. In 1995, Jones managed to get the crew together. They met in Dayton, Oh and again in 1996. In 1997, they met in Branson, MO. There are currently seven living members.

JACK S. KENDALL, born in Florence, SC on July 4, 1924. Inducted into the Army on April 14, 1943. Received his Navigator Wings from Selman Field on October 2, 1944, Class 44-12, Flight 28-B. Kendall flew 24 combat missions on B-24s in WWII in the South Pacific with the 31st Bomb Sqdn., 5th Bomb Grp., 13th Air

Force. Separated from service in December 17, 1945 with rank of 1st Lt. and lead navigator of his squadron.

The private life of Kendall included his graduation from Georgia Tech with a BS degree in Civil Engineering in 1948 and in 1981 from the University of South Carolina with a Master of Engineering degree. His work included concrete dam construction, plant construction, hospital construction, pre-stressed concrete manufacturing, concrete products, and environmental engineering. In December 1988, he retired. Kendall married Ida Sikes on May 27, 1950 and is still married. He has one son and one daughter, but no grandchildren.

JOHN P. KING, born in Wilmington, NC on August 9, 1922 and moved to Jacksonville, FL in August 1925. Assigned to the Army Medical Corp in February 1943 at Camp Blanding, FL. Took basic training at Camp Joseph T. Robinson, Little Rock, AR and made PFC. Surgical Technician training was at Fitzsimmons Hospital in Denver, CO. Volunteered for Aviation Cadet program in April 1944. Went to Keesler Field, Biloxi, MS; University of Tennessee at Knoxville, Pre-flight at Maxwell Field, AL; Primary flight training at Avon Park, FL; Cochran Field, GA for basic, graduated on August 4, 1944 from Spence Field, GA as flight officer, single engine pilot. Completed B-24 Co-pilot School at Tyndall Field, Panama City, FL and ORTU at Tonopah, NV.

Flew B-24 from Mather Field to Biak, New Guinea and missions at Nadzab. Joined the 23rd Bomb Sqdn., May 1945 at Samar, Philippines. Flew 23 missions, commissioned in field as 2nd Lt. on July 30, 1944. Checked out as 1st pilot. Flew B-24 from Clark Field, Philippine Islands to Mather Field, CA in October 1945. Discharged at Chapel Hill, NC in January 1946. Five years Army Air Force Reserve Troop Carrier Squadron.

Married for 52 years with four children and three grandchildren. Held elected public office for fourteen years. A life insurance agent, life member of the American Federation of Musicians Local #444, and Morocco Temple Shrine.

CHARLES KOLESZAR, Staff Sgt., 394th Bomb Sqdn., 5th Bomb Grp., 13th Air Force. Service time, November 1942 until September 22, 1945. Born in

Hartshorne, OK on September 23, 1922. Graduated from high school at Haileyville, OK in June 1942. Joined the Army Air Corps in November 1942 at Tulsa, OK. Took basic training at San Antonio, TX; Armor School, Lowery Field, Denver, CO; and Gunnery School, Wendover, UT. Joined flight crew in Boise, ID and was then sent back to Wendover Field for flight training. Next stop was Herrington, KS to pickup their B-24D, from there to Hamilton Base, near San Francisco, CA. Had the name and picture of Pistol Packing Mama painted on ship

Then to Hickam, Espiritu Santos, and from there assigned to the 394th Bomb Sqdn., 5th Bomb Grp., 13th Air Force in November 1943. Moved to Guadalcanal and flew several missions from there. Moved to Munda Island. There the crew flew with Pappy Boyington and the Black Sheep as cover. The next move was to Admiralty Island (Manus) and moved onto Wakde Island. The war moved farther North, so we moved to Morotai, by now Koleszar had flown 51 missions and 1,440 hours flight time.

Some of the missions he participated in were Wadi, Biak, Yap, Lakuna, Rabaul, Borpopo, Bougainville, Moen, and Truk Island. He was a member of Capt. Harold Mosby's crew and the Nose Turret Gunner and credited with two and a half kills. They lost three crewmembers and returned Stateside in January 1945. Took leave and then shipped to Las Vegas Gunnery School as an instructor for B-29 flight crews. Discharged in September 1945 at Camp Chaffee, AR. Currently lives in San Jose, CA.

GEORGE E. KUHMAN, born in Bellevue, PA on August 27, 1920. Joined the Army Air Force in August 1942 and served as Navigator in the South Pacific with the 5th Bomb Grp. Credited with 23 combat missions, completed 235 combat hours, and accumulated 756 hours flight time. His decorations include the Air Medal with Oak Leaf Cluster and six Battle Stars. On December 20, 1945 he was discharged with rank of 2nd Lt. Kuhman is retired and living in Mesa, AZ.

JAMES KYLE, born in Barton, MD on October 19, 1918, one of 13 children. Enlisted in the Army Air Force on June 18, 1939. Took Armament School in early 1940. Was Sergeant Armorer Gunner on Decem-

ber 7, 1941 at Hickam Field. Transferred with the 72nd Bomb Sqdn. to Bellow Field on December 10, 1941. The barracks were severely damaged by direct hit bombs.

Attended Bombardier School at Hickam Field early 1942. After the Battle of Midway, assigned to the 394th Bomb Sqdn. as Bombardier of Ripley, Pilot and Gene Roddenbery crew. All combat missions from Guadalcanal in B-17. Total five years in Central, South, and South Pacific as Bombardier, Armorer, and Gunner Master Sgt.

Awarded the Distinguished Flying Cross, Air Medal with one Oak Leaf Cluster, four Bronze Stars for Guadalcanal, Central Pacific, Northern Solomon's, and Papuan Campaigns, American Defense Service Ribbon and Bronze Service Star, and Good conduct Medal. Served as Flight Officer and Bombardier instructor in B-24s at March Field until October 10, 1945.

After the military, Kyle was a broker/ dealer in investment securities and mutual funds for 25 years.

WILLIAM G. (BILL) LAMB, born in Charleston, WV on March 6, 1923. Lived all his life in the Akron, OH area, living in Cuyahoga Falls for 35 years. Enlisted in the Army Air Force in October 1942 and reported for active duty in February 1943. Took basic training at Miami Beach; CTD at Catawaba College, Salisbury, NC; and received his pilot wings at Columbus, MS AAFB, Class 44E.

Joined the "PITTS" crew at Walla Walla, WA in August 1944. Served as co-pilot with an outstanding crew. On November 1, 1944, flew a new B-24 L to Townsville, Australia, then to Nadzab. Joined the 5th Bomb Grp., 72nd Bomb Sqdn. in December 1944. First mission was to Morotai on December 13, 1944. Completed 43 missions. Returned to the USA from Samar in the Philippines in July. Decorated with the Air Medal with two Oak Leaf Clusters and promoted to 1st Lt. in March 1945.

Married to college sweetheart in November 1945, now married 52 years. Two boys, one a printer and the other is a Pharmacist. Graduated from the University of Akron in June 1948. Retired from own wholesale company in 1988. Attended the first A.F.A. convention in Columbus, OH.

THOMAS B. LA MON, born on October 6, 1921 in Mackay, ID. Joined the military on July 16, 1942. Served as an Army Air Corp Navigator with the 31st Bomb Sqdn. Flew 42 missions mostly on Frank Bates, crew aboard Squirrelly Shirley. The worst missions were Truk, Balikpapan, and with G. Lucchessi, Pilot on aircraft Patches. Received 80 holes due to a fire. Limped into Middleburg Fighter Strip. Decorated with the Air Medal with eight Oak Leaf Clusters. Discharged in September 1945 with rank of 1st Lt.

Retired weapons designer and teacher, living in Mackay, ID.

LESTER W. LAPPEN, born in Hartford, CT on April 14, 1925. On July 28, 1943 joined the Army Air Corps. Served at Samar Island, Philippines as an Aerial Engineer with the 72nd Bomb Sqdn. Involved in approximately 35 missions from New Guinea and Samar against targets in Borneo, the Philippines, China coast, and Formosa. Lappen was decorated with the Air Medal with one Oak Leaf Cluster. Discharged on November 10, 1945 with rank of Tech/Sgt. Graduated from the University of Connecticut in 1951. He is married with three children and two grand-children.

Employed as Chairman of the Board of Randolph Paper Company, Inc. in Taunton, MA. Currently retired and living in Florida.

DAGFINN T. (DAG) LARSEN, born August 21, 1924 in Philadelphia, PA. Raised in Brooklyn. Enlisted in the AAF in October 1942. Basic training Atlantic City, NJ. Airplane Mechanic School of Aeronautics, Newark, NJ. Aviation Cadet program January 1943. Graduated Navigation training at Selman Field, LA, February 1944. At Hammer Field in Fresno, CA formed combat crew of pilot (Bornus), co-pilot, (Shkurensky), bombardier (Hudspeth), and navigator (Larsen), all flight officers. To South Pacific in B-24s, 5th Bomb Grp. Flew 44 missions.

After WWII in SAC, ATC, AFCC. Stationed at MacDill, Berlin, Munich, Harlingen, TX, Guam, and Scott AFB. Retired as major in 1962 at age 38.

Employed with Computer Sciences Corporation for 22 years as a communications engineer and program manager on various military projects. Project manager for communications and control systems

for subway systems in Washington, Atlanta, Baltimore, Chicago, Miami, and Seoul, Korea. Active in 394th Bomb Sqdn., 5th Bomb Grp. Association activities.

ARTHUR E. LASHER, born in Greenville, NY on December 3, 1920. Moved to Washington, DC in 1933, then to Silver Spring, MD in 1937. Attended the University of Maryland from 1938 until 1940. Went to work for Washington Suburban Sanitary Comm., Surveys Division. Enlisted in the AAF on June 22, 1942 at Ft. Meade, MD; went to Miami Beach, FL; then to Aircraft Armorer School, Buckley Field, Denver, CO.

After graduating on September 26, 1942, was sent to Jefferson Barracks, MO for overseas placement. In December went to Camp Stoneman, Pittsburg, CA and shipped out of San Francisco on December 30 for Noumea, New Caledonia. Onto Espiritu Santos-New Hebrides, onto Guadalcanal, and assigned to the 31st Bomb Sqdn., 5th Bomb Grp., 13th Air Force. Lasher was with the 31st Sqdn. while it operated from the following: Guadalcanal, Munda, Los Negros-Admiralty Island, Wade, and Noemfoor, off of New Guinea, Morotai-Halmaheras, where he was slightly wounded during a Japanese air raid on November 22, 1944. After rest leave in McKay, Australia, moved from Morotai to Samar, Philippines. Left the Philippines, July 20, 1945 and arrived in San Francisco, August 22, 1945 (34 days). Discharged at Ft. Meade, September 1, 1945 as a corporal.

Returned to the Surveys Section. Married Jeanne Hoffman in 1947. They have three children, seven grandchildren, and two great granddaughters.

CAMERON K. LYON, born in India of American parents on July 23, 1923. Enlisted in AAF, November 30, 1942. Pilot training in Central Flying Training Command, followed by combat crew training in Walla Walla, WA. As pilot, picked up a new B-24 M at Hamilton Field, flew to

Fairfield-Suisun Army Air Base and then on December 24, 1944 (in five stages) to Nadzab, New Guinea. Was assigned to the 31st Bomb Sqdn., 5th Bomb Grp.

Flew 44 missions from Morotai and Samar to the Philippines, Borneo, Celebes, and Sulu Archipelago. Returned to the U.S. in August and was discharged as a 1st Lt. in December 1945. Remained in the Air Force Reserves until resigned as captain in April 1955. Earned Ph.D. at Northwestern University in 1951, then worked as research chemist at Dupont and U.S. Department of Agriculture until retirement in Orinda, CA in 1986.

Married Lorraine Duckworth in 1948. They have three children and seven grandsons.

DONALD B. MACALLISTER, born Arthide, MN on December 29, 1918. Moved to Texas in 1923. Joined the Army Air Corps at Ft. Brown, Brownsville, TX on November 7, 1941. Transferred to Cadet Training. Graduated as 2nd Lt. Bombardier at Kirtland Field, Albuquerque, NM on September 26, 1942. Requested combat. Sent to Geiger Field, Spokane, WA. Joined crew with 2nd Lt. William R. McKinley, Pilot. Trained at Geiger Field, Casper, WY and Salina, KS. Sent to Hamilton Field then to Guadalcanal, Solomon Islands, in 1943.

Flew 48 missions off Guadalcanal with the 31st and 394th Bomb Sqdns. Awarded the Distinguished Flying Cross, Air Medal, Asiatic-Pacific Campaign Medal with two Bronze Stars, American Campaign Medal, and WWII Victory Medal. Upon return to the U.S. served as instructor, flight leader, and squadron commander in Bombardier and Autopilot Schools in Deming, Carlsbad, and Hobbs, NM. Left active duty in October 1945. Remained in Reserves until May 1973 and received an Honorable Discharge as Lt. Colonel.

Taught, farmed, and ranched in Texas, served as county commissioner, raised four children, and obtained BS and Master's degrees. Now happily married. Own ranch in Oklahoma. Raise registered Brangus and gaited horses. "I love my country deeply. I am proud to have served my country and proud to be an American."

GEORGE H. MAGRUDER, born on May 6, 1920 in Rome, GA. Educated at the University of Georgia, earning a BS degree in Business Administration in 1942 and the University of Oklahoma, earning a BS de-

gree in Eng. Physics. Enlisted in the Army in May 1942. Assigned to Airplane Mechanics School at Keesler Field, MS. Selected to attend Engineering Cadet School at Chanute Field, IL in November 1942 and commissioned a 2nd Lt. in December 1942.

Assigned to Officer Training School at Miami Beach, F: and returned to Chanute Field in January 1943 for overseas shipment. Assigned to the 23rd Bomb Sqdn. as Asst. Eng. Officer, New Hebrides, March 1943. Returned to U.S. from Samar, Philippines in November 1945. Separated in February 1946 as major in the Air Force Reserve.

After the military, Macgruder attended the University of Oklahoma from 1947 until 1950. Employed with the Tennessee Division of Eastman Kodak, Kingsport, TN as a Physicist from 1950 until 1953. Vitro Corp. at Eglin AFB, FL as Physicist/ Engineer and later Manager of Engineering from 1953-1961. Pan Am World Airways, Aerospace Service Division, Patrick, AFB, FL from 1961 until 1982. Retired as Manager of Range Instrumentation Engineering 1982.

In retirement, Macgruder and his wife divide their time between the Bahamas and Melbourne, FL until her death in 1996.

WESLEY W. MANSIR, born in Cambridge, MA on November 26, 1922. Enlisted in the U.S.A.A.C. on November 18, 1942. Basic training, Miami Beach, FL; Airplane Mechanic School, Gulfport, MS; Aerial Gunnery School, Laredo, TX; First Phase combat crew training, Gowan Field, Boise, ID; and Final phases at Muroc, Dry Lake, CA. Then was stationed on Guadalcanal and attached to 13th Air Force, 5th Bomb Grp., 31st Bomb Sqdn., April 1944. From Koli Field flew missions from Admiralty Islands, Wakde, Noemfoor, Morotai, and Samar - completing 43 missions.

The 13th Air Force was known as the "Jungle Air Force", a well-deserved title. Entertainment in the Pacific (with the exception of a visit from Bob Hope) was supplied by themselves, teaching some of the local natives to sing "Lay That Pistol Down" was fun (and punishment for any Japanese who could hear the wailing). Also made sailboats out of discarded drop gas tanks.

March 1945 left from Biak, New Guinea aboard the U.S.A.T. Pueblo, converted from a German ship, where Mansir was inducted into the "Shellbacks", and ancient order of the Trident. An honor for an airman crossing the equator aboard ship. Arrived stateside on April 3, 1945 after three weeks at sea. Two days to Pacific and three weeks to home. Honorable discharge received on May 18, 1945 and receiving five Campaign Ribbons and a dozen or so decorations and citations.

I am now retired and spend time with my grandsons and frequent volunteer work at E.N.R. Memorial Veterans Hospital. One lasting impression from my tour in the Pacific was the close cooperation of all branches of service.

ROY L. MARSTON, was born in Gresham, OR on November 29, 1921. Enlisted in the Army Air Force in 1942. Took Basic training and A & M training, Sheppard Field, TX; Pre-flight, Kelly Field, TX; Primary School, Stanford, TX; Basic Flight, Greenville, TX; Advanced Flight and graduation, Frederick, OK; and B-24 training, Ft. Worth, TX.

Picked up a B-24 at Hamilton Field, CA and left Fairfield-Suisun, CA on December 24, 1944. Assigned to the 13th Air Force, 5th Bomb Grp., 23rd Bomb Sqdn. Completed 43 missions and returned stateside on November 7, 1945. Released from active duty on November 19, 1945.

As a Reservist, served with the 403rd Troop Carrier Wing, Portland Air Base, Portland, OR. Called back to active duty on April 1, 1951. Trained as a B-26 pilot at Perrin Air Force Base, TX and Langley Field, VA. Sent to Korea in July 1952. Assigned to the 5th Air Force, 17th Bomb Grp., 95th Bomb Sqdn. Completed 54 missions by December 1952. Released from active duty in January 1953.

Retired Reservist with rank of major. Retired in 1984 from Portland General Electric.

JOHN G. MCDONALD, (birth name John G. Ramey), born on June 18, 1920 in Vincennes, Knox County, IN. Grew up in Daviess County, IN and Jasper, IN. Enlisted in the AAF on January 2, 1942 in Evansville, IN. Sworn in at Fort Benjamin Harrison, Indianapolis, IN on January 5, 1942. Basic training, Sheppard Field, TX and attended Aircraft Mechanics School there. Attended Boeing B-17 Specialist training, Seattle, WA; overseas training at Jefferson Barracks, MO, October - November 1942; and Camp Stoneman, CA in December 1942.

Debarked from San Francisco on December 31, 1942 on troop ship Rochambeau, a former French luxury liner. Arrived in Noumea, New Caledonia on January 18, 1943; joined the 5th Bomb Grp. in Espirtu Santo, New Hebrides in February 1943, and the 31st Bomb Sqdn. on March 2, 1943 at Henderson Field and assigned to a crew on B-17 as mechanic. Later changed to B-24s. After some time, McDonald was made ground crew chief on B-24 #944 at Koli Field, Guadalcanal. From there they moved to Los Negros, Wakde, Noemfoor, and Morotai.

Returned stateside on March 17, 1945 for a 45-day T.D. rest leave. Married on April 4, 1945. Discharged on the point system on May 20, 1945 at Camp Atterbury, IN with rank of Tech/Sgt. Wife Dorothy and he have four children and 11 grandchildren. Retired from Prudential Insurance Company in August 1982.

JACK B. (MAC) MCEWAN, born on January 8, 1920 in Salt Lake City, UT. Drafted on September 30, 1941, elected to join Army Air Corps instead, stationed at Jefferson Barracks, MO. Entered the flight training in January 1942 and took Primary training at Tulare, CA in the Class of 42G, Basic training at Merced, CA, and Advanced training at Luke Field, AZ. Commissioned 2nd Lt. and received pilot's wings on July 26, 1942.

Responded to a request for 100 immediate volunteers for foreign duty. Sent to Hickam Field, HI as a single engine pilot, however, was assigned to 72nd Bomb Sqdn., then the 394th of 5th Bomb Grp. H. In October after 15 hours co-pilot time in a B-18 and two hours, 15 minutes co-pilot time in a B-17E, was sent into combat in the New Hebrides and Solomon Islands and flew as co-pilot to Captain J.J. Charters in the 98th Bomb Sqdn., 11th Bomb Grp. H.

Assigned again to the 394th Bomb Sqdn. when the 11th Bomb Grp. was relieved. Flew as co-pilot to Captain William Ivey in the B-17 Poison Ivey until becoming first pilot. Received the Distinguished Flying Cross, two Air Medals, and the Presidential Unit Citation Ribbon. Became base operations officer with rank of captain at Kearney Army Air Base, NE, staging B-17s and B-29s, until discharged from active duty on points just before the close of the war.

Married Betty Clark in 1948 and this year they celebrated their 50th wedding anniversary. The McEwan's have three sons and fifteen grandchildren. Practiced dentistry in Arcadia, CA where they live.

REX T. MCKY, born in Junction City, OR on July 13, 1918. Enlisted at Ft. Lewis, WA in October 1941 in the Airforce. While in St. Louis, he met his wife to be Mary F. Teubner and they married on March 15, 1942. Took basic training at Chanute Field and was sent overseas to Hawaii in April 1942.

His group was the first Airforce recruits on the island. While there, he joined the 394th Bomb Sqdn. and went to Fiji Island in December 1942. Sent to Guadalcanal, the captain asked him if he wanted to go on a night mission over Bougainville. After accepting they were the second plane over the target and after the bombs were dropped, it was light up in the sky. After that experience, McKy decided to stay on the ground!

A crew chief on B-17 and B-24, he was sent to Wakde Island and onto Noemfoor. He made flight chief and master sergeant. Received the Good Conduct Medal, Asiatic-Pacific Theater Ribbon with three Bronze Stars, and American Defense Medal, and five overseas Service Bars. Sent home in 1944 and discharged on September 1945 at Ft. Lewis, WA.

BILL T. MEYER, was born in Omaha, NE on August 24, 1924. Joined the military on December 11, 1942 and served in the South Pacific. A member of the Army Air Corps, Meyer was a Navigator with the 72nd Bomb Sqdn., 5th Bomb Grp., 13th Air Force. Credited with 44 missions. On January 10, 1946 he was discharged with rank of 1st Lt. Meyer is currently retired and living in Tucson, AZ.

CLARENCE C. MORRISON, born on August 21, 1921 in Wrightsville, PA in York County. On June 1, 1940 he enlisted in the Army Air Corps and served as a decontamination equipment operator #809. Saw action in he Central Pacific, Guadalcanal, and Northern Solomon Islands.

Wounded on December 7, 1941 during the Japanese attack on the Hawaiian Islands at Pearl Harbor. Morrison lost his hearing in one ear and suffered burns on his back

and legs. A Staff/Sgt. with the 64th Army Air Force Base Unit, he was decorated with the Purple Heart, Good Conduct Medal, American Defense Medal with one Battle Star, and the Asiatic-Pacific Theater Medal. Sent to the 6th Bomber Command and separated on December 15, 1944.

Married for 54 years, and has one daughter and one son. He lives in Mt. Joy, PA. Worked for Armstrong Marietta as a security guard.

KENNETH L. MOWLES, born in Roanoke, VA on July 31, 1925. Moved to Salem, VA in 1927. Enlisted as Aviation Cadet in November 1943. Sent to Basic Training Center #10 at Greensboro, NC. Qualified for Pilot Cadet Training-by mistake sent to Tyndall Field, FL for Aerial Gunnery School, 1944. Completed training and sent to Gowen Field, Boise, ID for advance training as Ball Turret Gunner on Lt. Richard Nesossis' crew. After advance training, picked up a B-14 at Hamilton Field, CA. Island hopped to Nadzab, New Guinea. Member of the 13th Army Air Force, 5th Bomb Grp., 72nd Bomb Sqdn.

Flew 34 missions, 21 as ball gunner, and 13 as nose gunner. Missions flown over Borneo, Dutch East Indies, North and South Philippines, China, Formosa, etc. One bailout, lost three crew members: Robert M. Shannon, Signal Mt., Tennessee-Top Turret Gunner; James Golmon, LA-Tail Gunner; and Edward J. Tebbetts, Manchester, NH-Nose Gunner. Overseas home bases were New Guinea, Morotai, and Samar. Last mission flown was August 1, 1945. Returned stateside and discharged in June 1946.

Attended college. Married former Nancy Ann Hurt and reared five children, Lysa Ann, Rebecca Kay, Kenneth Lyon, Jr., Allison Wallace, and Matthew Lewis. Worked for Norfolk Western Railway as chemist, research and test engineer for 34 years. Founder and past president of Mow-Dev Corp. Retired August 1985 and bought a farm. Enjoying farming and traveling.

THOMAS C. MUSGRAVE, JR., the son of the late Colonel Thomas C. Musgrave and Olive Dodge Musgrave of Washington and San Antonio, TX. A graduate of the U.S. Military Academy at West Point in 1935 and later from the Air Corps Flight Training School, the Air War College, and the National War College.

In 1944, he became the commander of the 5th Bomb Grp., 13th Air Force in the Pacific. He participated in General MacArthur's island hopping strategy and led his B-24 group through the campaigns of the Bismarck Archipelago, Eastern Mandates, New Guinea, Western Pacific, North Solomons, South Philippines, Leyte, and Luzon.

Among the missions he planned and led, were the destruction of the heavily defended oil refineries at Balikpapan, Borneo-the last major refineries left to the Japanese. Prior to the B-29s, these were the longest and most heavily loaded formation missions ever flown.

In a thirty-day period his group was credited with sinking over 130,000 tons of Japanese merchant and warships. During the Cold War, General Musgrave commanded all strategic air forces in Europe, North Africa, and Iceland, and all atomic support to the Supreme Allied Commander of Europe.

He was awarded the Distinguished Service Medal, Distinguished Flying Cross, Legion of Merit, Purple Heart, Bronze Star for Valor, Air Medal with Oak Leaf Cluster, and Presidential Unit Citation with Oak Leaf Cluster.

In 1962 he retired as Director of Legislative Affairs for the Air Force, spent a short time with a brokerage firm, and then became president of Textron, Inc. In 1969, he resigned to handle family affairs. He was a member of the Atlantic Council of the United States; the Washington Institute of Foreign Affairs; the Alibi, Burning Tree, Chevy Chase, and Metropolitan Clubs of Washington; and the Argyle and San Antonio Country Clubs of San Antonio, TX.

His family includes wife, Josephine Bennett Musgrave, a son, Thomas C. Musgrave III of San Antonio, TX, a daughter, Jamie Musgrave Hall of Aspen, CO, four grandchildren, and two great grandchildren.

RICHARD L. NESOSSIS, LTC, USAF, Ret., born in Beaumont, TX on December 23, 1922 and entered the U.S. Army Air Force on September 23, 1942. He received his Pilot's wings in Class 44-C and after completing B-24 transition, he joined the 72nd Bomb Sqdn., 5th Bomb Grp., 13th Air Force at Morotai and flew 52 combat missions with 450 hours of flight time. Returning to the States and being separated, he continued in the active reserves, retiring in 1965.

During his business career in the life insurance industry and as a real estate broker, he attained the designation of Chartered Life Underwriter and is past-president of he Mississippi Association of Life Underwriters; Gulfport Lions Club; Metropolitan Dinner Club of the greater Mississippi Gulf coast; Harrison County Association for Retarded Citizens; and remains active in the Bay Vista Baptist Church, having been "born again: as a Christian believer; a 24-year member of the Gideons International.

He and his wife Myrtle are the parents of five children, nine grandchildren, and four great grandchildren. His hobbies include golf, gardening, restoring cane seats in chairs, and making cast nets. He now resides in Biloxi, MS.

ROBERT E. NOBLE, born in Kansas City, MO on August 19, 1923 and moved to Minneapolis, MN in 1929. Entered service on April 10, 1943 and took basic training at Sheppard Field, TX. Joined the 394th Bomb Sqdn. H, 5th Bomb Grp. H, 13th Army "Jungle" Air Force, December 1943 at Guadalcanal, working in the ground forces.

It took two years of island hopping from the Admiralty Islands, Wakde, Noemfoor, Morotai, and Samar in the Philippines. When the atomic bomb was dropped, the group was packing up to move to advance bases and to bomb the Japanese islands. Thanks to Harry S. Truman, they came home early. The Jungle Air Force was involved in seven campaigns in the Southwestern Pacific. Noble was discharged at Camp McCoy, WI on December 18, 1945. He retired in 1983, with 38 years in the trucking industry as a driver.

JOHN W. NORRIS, born in Colfax, WA on September 29, 1925. Lived in Washington until 1943 moved to Bonners Ferry, ID. Drafted into service 1943. Entered Army Air Corps and took basic training at Buckley Field, CO. Sent to AACS ground radio operator, Scott Field, IL. Wanted to fly, signed up for Gunnery School at Harlingen, TX. Graduated tail gunner met the John A. Buchanan crew, Lemoore Air Field, and CA. Overseas training Walla Walla Air Base, Walla Walla, WA in B-24s.

Left the States in Navy convoy to Leyte. Left Tacloban airstrip by C-46, flew Mindanao, Morotai, Biak, back to Samar before locating the 5th Bomb Grp. Assigned to the 72nd Bomb Sqdn., flew 14-hour missions to Formosa and China coast. End of war, eight members of the crew flew a B-24 home. The armorer gunner and Norris had to remain. Moved to Dulog, Leyte and made an automotive supply clerk until able to return home. Discharged on March 22, 1946. Took Pilot training at Bonners Ferry upon his return, received a commercial license, and flew crop dusters for eight years. The rest of his working years was spent as an operating engineer.

DALE G. OLESON, born in Woodbury County, IA on March 20, 1923. Enlisted in the AAF Cadet Program on December 12, 1942. Took basic training in Wichita Falls, TX; Classification and Preflight at Santa Ana AAB, CA; Gunnery School at Las Vegas AAF (Nellis), NV; Bombardier School at Deming AAF, NM; and combat crew training at Davis Monthan AAF, Tucson, AZ, where he was assigned to John J. McHugh's crew.

After training, they proceeded from Fairfield-Suisun AAF (Travis) to New Guinea where they were assigned to the 394th Bomb Sqdn., 5th Bomb Grp., 13th Air Force. They flew out of Morotai and Samar in the Philippines. Oleson flew 42 missions and returned to the U.S.A. late in 1945. He was separated from active duty and joined the AAF Reserve in 1946, where in 1972 he retired with rank of Lt. Colonel. In civilian life, he worked as a design engineer.

THOMAS C. OLIVER, JR., born in Austin, TX on February 14, 1919. Attended Choate School and Yale University. Enlisted AAF, August 1941. Radio-Mechanic School, Scott Field, IL; and Radio School 2, Morrison Field, FL as Cpl., Radio Operator, flew with B-27D to Espiritu Santo, June 1942. Flew 27 missions in B-17Ds and B-17Es from Buttons Field and Cactus

(Henderson Field). Returned stateside Staff/ Sgt., April 1943, married Helen Steffen, June 1943. Radio Instructor, Dalhart, TX, and Rapid City, SD. Honorable discharge in October 1945. Awarded the Air Medal with Oak Leaf Cluster, and Distinguished Unit Badge.

B.E.E., June 1948, Brooklyn Polytechnic Institute. Westinghouse Corporation 1952-1964. Data Master Div. (Amer. Chain & Cable), 1964-1976. Two daughters, Catherine (1950), and Steffenie (1952).

Most memorable wartime experience was walking down the isle aisle in June 1943. Second most memorable wartime experience was the return flight to Buttons after receiving 20mm hits from the nose to the bombay. After landing, assessment of damage to starboard wing root rendered ship unserviceable.

MAX L. OLSON, MAJ, USAFR, S/ N0785607, was born November 28, 1925 at Conroy, IA. Entered service from high school April 1943 and served until October 1946. Basic training at Sheppard Field, gunnery at Tyndall Field. Awarded commission and bombardier rating September 2, 1944 at Carlsbad, NM. Bomb crew training in B-24s at Gowen Field, ID.

Olson served with the 5th Bomb Grp., 23rd Bomb Sqdn. in the Pacific Theater and also with the 307th Bomb Grp., 370th Bomb Sqdn. His campaigns included Western Pacific, Air Combat Borneo, Philippines, and China Offensive. When the war ended, he was assigned to the 570th Service Grp. at Clark Field.

After graduation from the University of Iowa, Olson's civilian career has been organizational work and international marketing. He has retired as director, International Trade Promotion for the state of Iowa.

HAROLD L. PAGE, born Monroe County, NY on November 20, 1921. A resident of Henrietta, NY all of his life, Page entered the military on October 17, 1942. Took infantry training at Camp Craft,

SC and was transferred to AAG. Took Pre-flight training at Maxwell Field, AL and Jackson, TN. Went to CAAF Childress, TX, Class 43-16 for Bombardier training, graduated and was commissioned a 2nd Lt. on December 24, 1943. Went to Bemis, TN and married Lela Brunette Myracle. Took RTU at Tonopah, NV and Fairfield-Suisun and picked up a B-24. Sent to Hawaii, Canton Island, and onto Guadalcanal. Assigned to the 31st Bomb Sqdn., 5th Bomb Grp., 13th Air Force.

Flew missions from Admiralty Islands, Wakde, Noemfoor, and Morotai. Missions to Yap, Palau, Balikpapan, Brunei Bay, Truk, Celebes, Corregidor, plus naval ships. Flew 46 missions and returned stateside in March 1945. On January 15, 1946, a daughter was born to Page. Separated from service in October 1945. Stayed in the Reserves and became a captain. Employed by New York State, retiring in 1977. A volunteer firefighter for over 50 years. Chief of Dept. for 11 years and of District for three years. His nickname while overseas was Salvo.

THOMAS PALMER, JR. born November 26, 1925 Big Run, PA. Graduated Big Run High School 1943. Enlisted AAF October 1943. Basic training Miami Beach, FL. Aerial Gunnery, Harlingen, TX, May 1944. Assigned 420th AAF Base Unit, March Field, CA as Ball Turret Gunner, Crew B-28 trained in B-24. South Pacific September 1944—landed New Guinea. Assigned 13th Air Force, 5th Bomb Grp. (H), 72nd Bomb Sqdn (H). 44 combat missions tail gunner on B-24 to Borneo, China, Celebes, Halmahara and Philippines. Discharged Chanute Field, IL October 1945 Staff/Sgt.

Graduated Franklin College, Franklin, TN 1950 BA Business Administration. Married Mary Pyle August 1950 moved to Warren, OH. Have two daughters, one son, and four grandchildren. PRR 1950-1952. Grinnell Corp. 1952-1960. Assistant Traffic Manager; Heltzel Company 1960-1982

Traffic Manager, started T&M Transportation Services 1982. Sold the business 1988. Worked several years Transportation Consultant. Retired. Live six months Cortland, OH and six months in Seminole, FL. Enjoy golf, hunting, fishing, traveling, and my grandchildren.

HAROLD R. PARKER, born August 3, 1923 in San Antonio, TX. Left Texas in 1930 with his family for Los Angeles, CA. Attended school in Los Angeles. Drafted into the U.S. Army on December 30, 1942. Inducted at Ft. MacArthur, San Pedro, CA. Basic training Air Corp. unassigned St. Petersburg, FL. Radio Operator and Mech. School, Sioux Falls, SD. Radio Mech. School, Truax Field, Madison, WI. Radar Mech. School, Boca Raton, FL. At graduation, he became a corporal. First assignment was at McDill Field, Tampa, FL. Received overseas assignment to the 13th Air Force. Landed in New Caledonia. After much island hopping, finally joined the 5th Bomb Grp., 23rd Bomb Sqdn. at Wakde. From there moved to Samar in the Philippines. They set up the airbase to receive the four groups of B-24s. Parker's basic duty was to maintain communications and radar equipment on all four of the squadron's airplanes.

On Samar, April 8, 1945, he received a shrapnel wound that did damage to the sciatic nerve. Wound was the result of a Marine Corsair that had been moved from an aircraft carrier onto the base. This Corsair was returning from a strike in the Lingayen Gulf, with a 500 lb. Bomb hung up under his wing. On landing, the bomb became dislodged from the hooks, and tumbled end over end under the aircraft until it exploded. After he was hit, Parker was taken to a field hospital. Eight weeks later he returned to duty. Flight Surgeon Funkensten sent Parker to the Leyte General Hospital. Was sent by ship to Letterman General Hospital in San Francisco, CA; Hammond General Hospital, Modesto, CA; and to Santa Ana, CA Convalescent Hospital. Nine months after entering hospital he was discharged on January 16, 1946.

Employment was difficult to obtain due to service connected disability until 1959 when he had an opportunity to obtain employment as an electronic technician with North American Aircraft. At North American Aircraft and Rockwell International, Parker did research and development work on many interesting projects. He ended his career with Rockwell International as an engineer after 30 years on January 6, 1989. Active with the D.A.V. as a disabled American veteran. In addition, he enjoys gardening and traveling.

On October 21, 1997 after 52 years, Parker was finally awarded the Purple Heart. The award was presented during Retreat Service at Ft. MacArthur, San Pedro, CA. Ironically; this is the base where he was inducted into service in December 1942. The award was a longtime in being awarded due to a mistake made on his discharge papers while being discharged from the Air Corps.

CONO (CONNIE) PASOUA, born Bridgeport, CT, 1925. AAF November 1943. Basic training, Miami Beach, FL, Gunnery School, Harlingen TX, combat crew training, Walla Walla, WA. Joined Doug Faulkner crew as a replacement tail gunner September 1944. Flew 44 missions with 72nd Bomb Sqdn. from Noemfoor, Morotai, and Samar. Discharged September 1945.

Graduated Rensselaer Polytechnic Institute, 1950 BS Management Engineering, Married Peggy McLoughlin, 1948. Three children, two grandchildren. Started career in engineering with Hamilton Standard, shifted to Procurement, then on to Lear Siegler, Control Data, Fairchild Semiconductor, and LSI Logic. Retired 1990 as vice president of World Wide Procurement.

HENRY B. PECHER, Master Sgt., (Deceased) born Fairfield, Adams County, PA on February 10, 1919. Enlisted in the AAF, June 1, 1939. Took basic and technical training as aerial engineer, with airplane and engine mechanics ratings at Luke/Hickam Fields, HI, and assigned to the 72nd Bomb Sqdn. until September 1941. Worked with Douglas B-18 bombers, then the B-17 Flying Fortresses. Transferred with the 14th Bomb Sqdn, 19th Bomb Grp. to Clark Field, Philippines and survived the December 7, 1941 Japanese attack.

Flew as an engineer/gunner on missions from Java, the Dutch East Indies, and Broome, Australia. On March 12, 1942 returned as one of four Fortresses to provide emergency supplies and to remove General MacArthur from the Philippines. The plane hit the water while attempting to locate the darkened, radio-silent landing site near Mindanao. Five of the seven-crew members survived and succeeded in swimming to shore after four hours in the water, despite Pecher's head and chest injuries. Captured in late May 1942 at the fall of Corregidor and transferred to Kawasaki POW camp near Tokyo and soon after, liberated at Sunva POW camp with 230 others on September 7, 1945.

Returned stateside to Valley Forge Hospital in October 1945. Awarded the Distinguished Flying Cross, 1950; the Philippines Presidential Unit Citation; and POW Medal, 1988, among others. Separated/re-enlisted 1947, serving with AFRIC in Reading, PA and New Castle, DE. Assigned Wheelus Field, Tripoli, Libya, 1953-1954; Aberdeen Proving Grounds, then Dover AFB, DE as Aircraft Maintenance Tech/Supervisor, 1607th Maint. Grp. Retired Air Force on August 31, 1959 and Civil Service 1975 at Dover AFB. Five of Pecher's children served in the Army and Air Force during the Viet Nam era; two made the military a career and a third died on active duty. Pecher passed away on July 29, 1990 in Fairfield, PA.

RAPHAEL PENZENIK, ASN 6988817, born in Nanticoke, PA on January 3, 1919. Enlisted in the Air Corps on April 19, 1939. After Radio School at Wheeler Field in Oahu, he eventually wound up in the 23rd Bomb Sqdn. After the Pearl Harbor attack, the 23rd was based at Mokulea. In the afternoon of June 6, 1942, the 5th Bomb Grp. took off for Midway.

North of the Hawaiian Island Archipelago is an area of magnetic interference through which radio signals cannot be transmitted. Penzenik was the radio operator on the lead plane, and happened to be over that area when he picked up radio signals from Pearl Harbor and an out-to-sea net control, trying to contact each other. Each seemed desperate to contact the other. When the out-to-sea station broke from code and used clear language, viz., "Anyone, Anyone", he obtained permission from the pilot to act as the relay station. After a while of the five letter code transmissions, the crew received orders to change course and intercept the Japanese fleet at approximately 3,000 feet. Their flight scored a near miss on the rear of an aircraft carrier. The next day they hit the Mogami.

The 5th Bomb Grp. flew the Solomon's in search/strike operation until they were declared unfit to fly (most likely because they refused to switch to B-24s). On his second tour, this time in B-26s, Penzenik was on the mission that hit Houfilleze at the Battle of the Bulge. Pulled 55 missions with the 9th Air Force when the war ended. Discharged on November 11, 1945. Awarded the Silver Star, Purple Heart, Distinguished Flying Cross with Oak Leaf Clusters, Air Medal with Oak Leaf Clusters, Southwest Pacific Campaign Medal, and the European Theater of Operations Campaign Medal.

Currently retired Russian Orthodox priest.

JOSEPH M. PHILLIPS, born in Louisville, KY on March 31, 1924. Enlisted in the Army Air Corps on August 5, 1942. Assistant Radio Operator/Gunner on O. G. Adam's crew (#68-16); 72nd Bomb Sqdn., 5th Bomb Grp., March 1943 until April 1944. Flew 54 missions.

Most memorable mission was November 3, 1943. Bombing a Japanese convoy at 7,000 feet jumped by Zeros coming off a bomb run. With two engines, the hydraulic system knocked out, and manual control cables inoperative, "Skipper" Adams flew and landed the Hugger Mugger on automatic pilot. He was awarded the Silver Star. After 47 days in the hospital in Auckland, New Zealand, Phillips returned to duty, sometimes flying as photographer. Decorated with the Distinguished Flying Cross, eight Air Medals, Purple Heart, and five Battle Stars. Returned to U.S. and reclassified as Control Tower Operator. Discharged on July 22, 1945.

Married Katie Lou Beam on January 27, 1945. Six children, 14 grandchildren, and two great grandchildren. Retired as advertising director, Falls City Brewing Co., July 1979 on disability.

WALLACE F. PICKARD, 2nd Lt., U.S. Army, 5th Bomb Grp., 4th Recon. Sqdn. was born August 2, 1919 in New York. Entered service as a flying cadet on March 14, 1941. He was commissioned a 2nd Lt. and earned wings as a pilot on October 31, 1941 at Maxwell Field, AL. His first orders took him to Hawaii and Hickam Field. Assigned to the 5th Bomb Grp., 4th Recon Sqdn., he was wounded on December 7, 1941 when Japanese high

level bombers hit Hickam on the second wave attack. Returned to the States early March 1942. He was a patient at Walter Reed Hospital in Washington, DC.

In August 1942, after many operations and the start of reconstructive surgery on his right arm and hand, he was assigned to the Office of the Chief of Staff, Gen. George C. Marshall, as an aide. He was responsible for daily operational briefings to the General, among other duties. In November 1943 he had a final operation on his hand and was retired as a captain, but was called back to duty as executive officer of the newly formed 20th Air Force, with B-29s created to carry the war to the Japanese homeland. With this assignment he was promoted to major.

On November 4, 1945, his retirement was made effective and he returned to civilian life. In March of 1944, Pickard married Trudy Tuskey, a 1st Lt. in the Army Nurse Corps, whom he had met while a patient at Walter Reed. They had three children, Patricia, Nancy, and Wallace F. Jr., who is a Brigadier General and a Wing Commander in the New Jersey Air National Guard.

Major Pickard was in the pharmaceutical business and later in insurance. For the last 12 years he has owned a restaurant in Ocean Beach, NY. He now resides in Lighthouse Point, FL.

He was awarded the Purple Heart, Pacific Theater Ribbon with one Campaign Star, American Theater Ribbon, European African Theaters, American Defense Ribbon with one Campaign Star, and Pearl Harbor Commemorative Medal.

WILLIAM G. RAMSEY, born in Bloomington, IN on October 25, 1923. Entered the military on February 1, 1943. Assigned to the 394th Bomb Sqdn., 5th Bomb Grp., 13th Air Force as a Navigator, he saw action in the South Pacific. Credited with 28 missions. Discharged on November 1, 1972 with rank of Lt. Colonel. Presently retired and living in Bloomington, IN.

DAVE E. RENFRO, born in Gorman, Eastland County, TX on November 3, 1925 and moved to Austin, TX in 1938. Enlisted in the USAAF on December 8, 1943, basic training Sheppard Field, TX; Gunnery School, Harlingen, TX. Assigned March Field, combat crew assembled with George J. McDowall, Pilot. Completed replacement training, crew transferred to Hamilton Field and were flown (island hopped) in a C-54 by ATC to Nadzab, New Guinea.

Assigned to the 13th Army Air Force, 5th Bomb Grp. (H), 23rd Bomb Sqdn., October 1944. Flew missions from Noemfoor, Morotai (Dutch East Indies),

and Samar (Philippine Islands). Completed 45 missions with 408 combat hours. One mission stands out-Brunei Bay, Borneo. Their 5th mission, November 16, 1944, a shipping strike turned out to be the Japanese fleet. Mac was and is a heck of a pilot. The squadron lost three planes over target and had to salvage the other upon return to base, but he brought their plane back, ripped bomb bay and all.

Returned stateside (APA 272 USS Cape Johnson) August 3, 1945. Discharged on October 16, 1945. Readjusted to civilian life and worked for the U.S. Post Office in Austin. Attended Southwest Texas State College. Worked for Phillips Petroleum Co. 19 years. During this time he became the proud father of three daughters and one son. Now scattered from Massachusetts to Florida. Employed by Stone and Webster Engineering for 15 years.

Worked in several countries, India, Belgium, Netherlands, France, Wales (UK), Saudi Arabia, and Malaysia. While on assignments took the opportunity to visit several other countries, also revisited Sydney, Australia. King Cross still the same, Bondi Beach/Harbor Bridge still pretty as ever. The Renfro's retired to their home in Leander, TX on July 1, 1994. On some of their assignments, they lived in trailers, mobile homes, and motor homes. So they bought a motor home and now travel around the USA quite a bit.

DONALD J. RICHARDS, born in Stratford, WI on February 13, 1921. Moved to Wells, MI in 1922. Joined Enlisted Reserve Corps on September 14, 1942 at Flint, MI. Took basic training at Miami Beach, FL; Gunnery School, Tyndall Field, FL; Cadet training, Maxwell Field, AL; and Bombardier training, Carlsbad, NM. At Lincoln, NE, assigned to Charles F. Ownby's crew for B-24 combat crew training, moving to Gowen Field, Boise, ID. At Mather, Sacramento, given a B-24, they flew to Salinas, CA and under sealed orders to Nadzab, New Guinea.

Assigned to the 13th Air Force, 5th Bomb Grp. (H), 394th Bomb Sqdn. The crew hit targets in the South Pacific Theater to include the Philippines, Borneo, and the Bismarck Archipelago. Flew three sea sweeps from Clark Field to Hong Kong, up the China coast to Amoy to Formosa. Orders were bomb any powerboat, although they only saw sail boats. They jettisoned their #2,000'ers at sea. As these missions were after V-J Day, they were deleted from their combat record. Richards was on Clark when the atomic bombs were dropped. In November 1945 the crew flew a B-24 back to California and was released on their points.

Stayed in the active Reserve, his last assignment was Federal Preparedness Liaison Officer, DCPA Region 4, Battle Creek, MI. Retired on February 25, 1975.

B. JACK RIEDEL, was born in Minneapolis, MN on October 5, 1923. Enlisted in the AAF Reserves in July 1942. Called to active duty in January 1943. Attended Carroll College, Wakesha, WI for CDT training and onto San Antonio Aviation Cadet Center, TX. Primary training, Enid, OK and advanced training, Atlas, OK. B-24 training at Liberal, KS. Picked up crew at March Field, CA. Went overseas in January 1945 to New Guinea.

The crew missed their connection at Hollandia and stayed in the convoy to Leyte, Philippines. Back to New Guinea for training and to Samar, Philippines. Assigned to the 72nd Bomb Sqdn., 5th Bomb Grp., 13 Air Force. Flew 23 missions and returned Stateside after the war.

Married to Pearl in 1946. They have been blessed with six sons, six daughters-in-law, and 17 grandchildren. Stayed in the Reserves and retired in 1973 as Staff Communications Officer with rank of Major. Retired from his career in the Telephone Company in 1974. Bought an appliance business and sold it in 1986. Now busy seeing the U.S., Canada, and renewing old friendships from the war years with his crew and attending reunions.

LOUIS R. RIVAS, born August 25, 1923 near Anadarko, OK. Attended Verden and Chickasha schools. Enlisted in the AAF on October 29, 1942. Basic training, Sheppard Field, TX; Aerial Gunnery, Laredo, TX; Airplane Mechanics, Keesler Field, MS; and Airplane Instrument, Chanute Field, IL.

Assigned to Donald Bone crew as a Ball Turret Gunner with the 394th Bomb Sqdn., 5th Bomb Grp., 13th Air Force. Completed 48 missions returning stateside in January 1945. Discharged on October 18, 1945 with rank of Staff/Sgt. Battles and Campaigns were Bismarck Archipelago, New Guinea, and Northern Solomon's.

Citations include the Asiatic-Pacific Theater Service Medal with three Bronze Battle Stars, Good Conduct Medal, Air Medal with four Oak Leaf Clusters, Lapel Button, and ASR Score. Most memorable mission was the long over water flight to bomb the oil fields on the island of Borneo.

Retired and residing in Manitou, OK.

LEON H. ROCKWELL, born in Las Vegas, NV on December 22, 1919. Graduated from Las Vegas High School in 1937. Attended the University of Utah for two years. Spent a short stint in Engineering Department at Douglas Aircraft, entered Aviation Cadet Training Thunderbird I Primary School, June 1941; Basic training, Gardner Field, Taft, CA. Received Pilot wings and 2nd Lt. commission at Luke AFB, Phoenix, AZ on January 9, 1942.

On December 7, 1941, Rockwell volunteered with eight other classmates to fly B-18 and B-17 bombers in 7th Air Force in Hawaii and Battle of Midway. Assigned to 13th Air Force, 5th Bomb Grp., 31st and 23rd Bomb Sqdns. as combat pilot in Solomon Islands (Guadalcanal) and New Hebrides and Fiji Islands until November 1943 (22 months in the South Pacific).

Stateside assignments: ASC Central Test Pilot School, Kelly Field, TX; Air Force Airborne Radar Officers School, Boca Raton, FL. Upon completion of Test Pilot and Radar School, his assignment was with Airborne AAFTAC Communications Branch, Orlando AFB, FL. Duties: Flight testing airborne radar on fighters, medium, and heavy bombers. Honorable separation from service July 1945. Rank: Major. Decorations: Distinguished Flying Cross with

one Oak Leaf Cluster, Air Medal with three Oak Leaf Clusters, and Asiatic-Pacific Medal with three Bronze Battle Stars.

Civilian life: Western Airlines pilot for three years. Graduate education: BA degree California State University, Fresno; DDS, Northwestern University Dental School, 1953; MBA, Pepperdine University, 1975, Ph.D., University for Humanistic Studies, Holistic Health, San Diego, CA, 1986. Professions: Airline pilot, general and pediatric dentistry, commercial real estate development and property management. Married to Margaret McLaughlin for 56 years. Three children, Rosemary R. Waters, Richard Allen Rockwell, deceased 1995, Robert L. Rockwell, and seven grandchildren.

LELAND RODGERS, born Bryan County, OK on January 13, 1923. Enlisted in the Army Air Force on October 22, 1942. Basic, Perrin AB, TX; Sheppard AB, TX Aircraft Mech. School; Tyndall AB, FL Gunnery School; Clovis AB, NM First Phase B-14 training; and assigned to Barney Clary crew as a Tail Gunner/Asst. Engineer; Pueblo AB, CO; Second and Third Phase; and Topeka AB, KS waiting overseas. Departed by C-54 Hamilton AB, CA on February 19, 1944 for Hawaii. By C-87 through Canton Island to 394th Bomb Sqdn., 5th Bomb Grp., 13th Air Force on Guadalcanal on February 26, 1944.

Flew 44 combat missions from Admiralties, Wakde, Noemfoor, and Morotai. Relieved on January 10, 1945 and arrived in USA on March 4, 1945. Discharged as Staff/Sgt. on June 16 1945 at Camp Chaffee, Ft. Smith, AR. Re-enlisted on May 2, 1946 at San Francisco, CA. Love Field, TX; Topeka AB, KS; and Westover AB, MA in Maint and Ops (Changed to Admin Field); Castle AFB, CA in Ops 93rd Bomb Grp. (B-29s & B-50s) (seven months and three months TDY to Mildenhall, England); Offutt AFB, NE NOIC Intelligence Admin HQ SAC; Overseas June 24, 1958 until November 20, 1959 Clark AB, Philippine Islands as NCOIC Admin SAMAP; Wright-Patterson AFB, OH as NCOIC Admin School of Logistics, then First Sergeant, AF Institute of Technology. Overseas November 3, 1964 through April 18, 1968 Manila, Philippine Island as NCOIC Det 22 APRFE; then Nellis AFB, NV as NCOIC Admin Comptroller. Retired there on November 1, 1969 as Master Sergeant.

CHARLES F. (CHUCK) ROSS, Staff/Sgt., born in Mt. Airy, NC on April 27, 1925. Moved to Graham, NC in 1941. Entered service on January 6, 1944. Basic training, Miami Beach, FL; Gunnery School, Harlingen, TX; and crew training March Field, CA.

In September 1944, crew flew from California to Nadzab, New Guinea aboard a C-87 (cargo/passenger model of B-24). Left Nadzab after 13 days, on Friday 13th on plane #113, and assigned to the 13th Air Force, 5th Bomb Grp., 72nd Bomb Sqdn.

In the first month overseas, 15 - one half of the enlisted who bunked with his crew at March Field - were killed either by enemy action or by flying accidents. Flew 44 missions as a Top Turret Gunner from bases at Noemfoor, Morotai, and Samar. Returned to the States in June 1945. Discharged at ORD Greensboro, NC in October 1945.

Married Frances Frazier in July 1947. Retired from AT&T after 33 years. Family includes three children and nine grandchildren.

RICHARD D. ROUX, born in Marion County, OH on February 3, 1916. Joined the military in September 1942. Served in the USAF as a B-24 Bombardier with the 394th Bomb Sqdn., 5th Bomb Grp., 13th Air Force in the South Pacific.

One of his first missions was a flight to Brunei Bay, Borneo against the Japanese Fleet. The flak was heavy and Roux saw two B-24s hit and go down. His plane was hit and lost an engine, but got home safely. Credited with 47 missions. Decorated with the Air Medal with three Oak Leaf Clusters. Discharged as 1st Lt. in December 1945.

A retired Ford dealer, Roux is living in Marion County, LaRue, OH.

ERNEST C. RUIZ, born on September 15, 1918 in Santa Barbara, CA. Started flight training in Oxnard, CA in March 1941. Basic training Bakersfield, CA and advanced training at Luke Field. Received commission and Pilot wings October 30

1941. Assigned to Hawaiian Air Force. B-18 Pilot, 31st Bomb Sqdn., 5th Bomb Grp., December 7, 1941. Transferred to the 72nd Bomb Sqdn., B-17 Co-pilot, May 1942. 50 missions in Guadalcanal Area (Solomon Islands). Shot down off the Island of Narau. Adrift for 15 days. Lived in Carteret Island with natives 51 days before rescue.

Pilot B-17, B-24 Instructor, C-47. Engineering Officer, Operations Officer at March Field, Weights and Balance Officer. Mess Officer with 72nd Bomb Sqdn. Received the Silver Star, Distinguished Flying Cross, Purple Heart, Air Medal, and various other campaign medals. Relieved from active duty in December 1945.

In 1946, joined his dad in the concrete and plastering business in Santa Barbara, CA. Became sole owner in 1960 and retired in 1987. Married for 55 years and have one son.

JOHN S. RUSTEMGYEN, born in Bonesteel, SD on January 27, 1921. Enlisted in the service on June 2, 1942. Served in the South Pacific with the 13th Air Force as Photo Gunner, HQ. Participated in 36 missions and was wounded on fifth mission over Alicante A/D Negros Island.

Received the Purple Heart, Good Conduct Medal, Air Medal with two Oak Leaf Clusters, Philippine Liberation Medal, and Southwest Pacific Ribbon with seven Battle Stars. Returned home in April 1945 aboard the USS Pinkney. Discharged with rank of Staff/Sgt.

Presently retired and living in Bonesteel, SD.

ROCCO SANSONE, (Deceased), born on September 7, 1914 in Philadelphia, PA. Inducted into the service in 1934 at Ft. Hoyle, MD, 6th Field Artillery; Amateur Radio Operator License; Schofield Barracks, Hawaii, 13th Field Artillery. In 1941 transferred to Hickam Field 7th Communications HQ AACS. Japanese planes attacked Pearl Harbor/Hickam Field on Sunday, December 7, 1941. His duty station during the attack was HQ Communication Tower.

In January 1942, established AACS station Canton Island; given direct commission 2nd Lt. Army Air Corps, command of 7th AACS Sqdn., 5th Bomb Grp (H), and Legion of Merit when mission accomplished.

Executive Officer 70th AACS Grp.; Commander 145th AACS Sqdn; Commander 71st AACS Grp; Executive Officer 1801st AACS Grp., Air University Maxwell AFB; ACS Communication/Electronics Staff Officers School, Gunter AFB; CEO Communications CONAC Mitchell Field; George Washington Field; Commander Far East 1956th AACS Grp., Japan; Commander Far East AACS Region; Chief Electronics AFORQ/R&D-Pentagon to retirement November 1956; 30 years service; Colonel USAF-Regular Air Force. 1966-1975 Page Communications, Inc., Washington, DC.

Awards and decorations: Legion of Merit, Air Force Commendation with Oak Leaf Cluster, Army Commendation, Good Conduct Medal, American Defense Medal, American Campaign Medal, Asiatic-Pacific Campaign, WWII Victory Medal, National Defense Medal, and Air Force Service with Silver Leaf and Bronze Oak Leaf Cluster.

Honors/Memberships: Pearl Harbor Survivors Inc.; Air Force Museum; Air Force Academy Blue/Silver Club; Life Member Retired Officers; Life Member Bolling Officers Club, Honor Roll 70th AACS Grp.; Honorary Admiral Texas Navy (Gov. William P. Clements, Jr.); Honorary Award President Ronald Reagan; Honorary Award President George Bush; Pearl Harbor Medal (Virginia Congressman Frank Wolfe); and USAF Sharp Shooter Small-arms Marksman.

On Sunday, July 1, 1945, Major Rocco Sansone and Cordelia Grantham were married in the Church of the Cross Roads, Honolulu, Hawaii. Reception was held at Hickam Officers Club. Cordelia was a government clerk from McClellan Air Depot, Sacramento, CA before transfer to Hickam Field 1944. She was the only child of Rodney and Addie Grantham of Texas. Rocco, the youngest child of Dominico and Teresa Sansone, was orphaned by the death of his mother when he was two years old. Both parents were born in Italy, where Dominico served in the Royal Army of Umberto I King of Italy.

Rocco Sansone was stricken suddenly by a massive bloodclot to the brain and died in hospital on December 1, 1988. Burial with full honors in Arlington National Cemetery, VA. Only his widow survives, they have no children.

EARL M. SCHAEFFER, M/Sgt., born in Reading, PA on April 25, 1922. Enlisted on July 1, 1940. Retired October 31, 1962. Flew as Radio Operator on B-18, B-17, and B-29s. Earned the Silver Star, Distinguished Flying Cross with Oak Leaf Cluster, and Air Medal with three Oak Leaf Clusters. Saw action in Pearl Harbor, Midway, and Solomon Islands.

Married Rozella Olson on June 23, 1945. They have three sons, Steven, Robert, and Gary and four grandchildren. Retired on April 26, 1986 from Salina Planing Mill as office manager. Currently living at Assaria, KS.

EDWARD SCHEFFELIN, entered Bombardier training from Coshocton, OH in April 1942 and graduated in April 1943 from Midland, TX, Class 43-6. Commissioned a 2nd Lt., S/NA0678472. He reported to Davis-Monthan Airfield for crew formation and combat crew training, completed in November 1943.

With a new B-24J aircraft, his crew flew the Pacific in four days and joined the 13th Air Force, 5th Bomb Grp., 72nd Bomb Sqdn at Espiritu Santo, New Hebrides. After two weeks of training, they moved to Guadalcanal in the Solomon Islands. On Christmas Day, 1943, he flew his first combat mission to Rabaul Harbor, the Japanese southern "Pearl Harbor".

During the next ten months, he flew 44 combat missions and over 400 combat flying hours to Japanese strongholds in the Bismarck Archipelago, central Pacific, Dutch East Indies, Philippines, and Caroline Islands. He was awarded the Distinguished Flying Cross and Air Medal with seven Oak Leaf Clusters.

In December 1945, he became a civilian and attended Ohio State University in Columbus, where he met Margaret Ann Merrick. They were married in August 1947 and raised a family of eight children: Susan, Catherine, Andrea, Marianna, Joseph, Thomas, Julia, and Paul. He was recalled and flew in B-29s for four years. He changed his specialty code to training and retired from the Air Force with 22 years of service. He founded the Visual Tutor Company in Carmichael, CA and continues as president.

LOCKWOOD B. SCOGGIN, born in Conehatta, MS on February 6, 1923. Joined AAC on December 11, 1942. Completed Pilot training Stuttgart, AR, May 1944. Completed B-24 Aircraft Commanders Maxwell AFB and combat crew training at Tonopah, NV. Joined the 72nd Bomb Sqdn., 5th Bomb Grp. on Samar, Philippines in May 1945. Flew 26 missions as aircraft commander then flew a B-24 to California on October 28, 1945.

Graduated from Mississippi State in 1948 with a degree in Aeronautical Engineering. Re-entered the Air Force in 1949 to study weather and spent 17 years as a weather forecaster. From 1958 until 1960, the Air Force sent him to Florida State University to study Meteorology. Re-called as a pilot in 1966 to go to Vietnam and fly EC-47. Last assignment was flying C-141 at Norton AFB for three years re-supplying Vietnam. Retired in 1971 as Lt. Colonel to Montgomery, AL.

Awarded the Distinguished Flying Cross, Meritorious Service Medal, and Air Medal with 11 Oak Leaf Clusters. Spent 15 years as a building contractor and in real estate.

LEROY E. SHANKLIN, born on April 15, 1923 in Fork, MD. Joined the Army Air Force on December 10, 1942. Graduated from Class 44-H in Blytheville, CA and assigned to the 23rd Bomb Sqdn., 5th Bomb Grp., 13th Air Force. Saw action in the South Pacific at Samar, Philippines. Co-pilot on B-24 for Lt. Peyton Woods and crew. Flew seven missions before Japan surrendered. Flew to the USA on the Sunset Program. Discharged on March 19, 1946 with rank of 2nd Lt. Decorated with the Philippine Liberation Medal, five Battle Stars, and the Asiatic-Pacific Service Medal.

Retired from Baltimore Gas and Electric Company where he built power lines as a general foreman. Presently flying Cessna 172s, 152s, etc.

JOHN S. SHARKEY, born in Boston, MA in April 1925. Enlisted in the Aviation Cadet Program in February 1943. Called to active duty, June 1943. Trained at Greensboro, NC and Kent State University, OH. After washing out, attended Armament School at Lowry Field, Denver, CO and Aerial Gunnery School in Harlingen, TX.

Joined Terry Spivey's crew in Muroc, CA as a tail gunner. Joined the 72nd Bomb Sqdn. in the Admiralty Islands and flew missions from Wakde, Noemfoor, Morotai, and Samar. Flew 39 missions with the regular crew and one mission with Col. Haviland and a pickup crew. The most memorable missions were Balikpapan, Alicante on Negros Island, and Brunei Bay.

After discharge in September 1945, earned a Bachelor's and Master's degrees in Business Administration at Northeastern University and then worked as an industrial accountant until retiring in 1989.

JOHN L. SHEPHERD III (Deceased), born in Rockledge, PA on September 12, 1924. On June 24, 1944, he entered the Army Air Corps. Navigated a B-24 bomber in 1944 and 1945. Flew 48 missions in the Southwest Pacific-600 hours over Negros, Galela, Borneo, Halamahara, Luzon, Bantangas, Corrigedor, and Celebes.

Served as Air Force Chaplain from 1952 until 1972, retiring in 1972 with rank of LTC Chaplain. His decorations include the Air Medal. While serving as Navigator on the Jungle Air Force against Japan, held bases and shipping in the Southwest Pacific with the 13th Air Force B-24 Liberator Bomber 2 Barons. Passed away on February 21, 1995.

GEORGE C. SPITZNER, born October 4, 1925 in Philadelphia, PA. Inducted into the service on December 18, 1943; Air Cadets, Miami, FL; Gunnery School, Harlingen, TX; and F/O Anderson's crew formed March Field, CA, July 1944. On September 26, 1944 flew new B-24 J form Fairfield-Suisun, CA arriving in Townsville, Australia on October 1. Assigned to the 394th Bomb Sqdn. at Noemfoor.

On November 22, 19444, returning from a ten-hour mission to Bacalon A/D Negros Island to Morotai Island, ran out of gas approximately twenty minutes from base. Eleven men bailed out and six were lost in the Pacific Ocean. Picked up by Navy PBY crew four hours later. Completed 46 missions, returned to the States in August 1945 and discharged.

Joined the Pennsylvania Air National Guard, 111th Bomb Grp., 117th Bomb Sqdn. L, July 1947. Activated into Korean service in April 1951. Stationed at Langley, VA, training A-26 combat crews for Korea. Released from duty on July 10, 1952.

Worked 44 years as manufacturing planner for ITE Circuit Breaker Co., Philadelphia, PA. Retired in March 1991.

ISAAC T. (STEVE) SPIVEY, born in Hansford County, TX on March 11, 1921. Enlisted at Lubbock, TX on July 21, 1942. Took Flight training on the West Coast, B-24 instructor at Kirtland Field, Albuquerque, NM. Assigned to the 72nd Bomb Sqdn. and flew 50 missions in the Southwest Pacific. Received flying experience in the shadow of Captain Bob Hannagan. Crew was grounded after 38 missions. Stayed three extra months as Assistant Operations Officer to Art Cader. Flew 12 more missions including two recon missions over Saigon, Indochina with Russell Massey and his crew on March 3 & 4, 1945.

His most memorable day was also the blackest. When Howard Sanders (his best buddy) of the 23rd Bomb Sqdn. was killed by a Kamikaze fighter attack on mission to Alicante A/D Negros Island on November 1, 1944.

Discharged from the Air Force Reserve on August 24, 1966 with rank of major. Earned the Distinguished Flying Cross on March 3, 1945, but award was lost in red tape almost 42 years. Finally, it was presented on November 24, 1986. Retired on October 1, 1985.

For 28 years, he was a boat dealer and part-time boat racer. Living now in Farmington, NM, Spivey is a snowbird in Parker Dam, CA at River Lodge Resort for five months during the winter. His family includes wife, Jessie Hatch Spivey, three daughters, Terry Elaine, Dixie, and Jana, and one son, Scott. Other family members include 17 grandchildren and three great grandchildren.

ELWOOD D. (BUD) STORRS, JR.,
born Philadelphia, PA on June 2, 1924. Entered service in December 1942 in Hempstead, NY for Aviation Cadet training. Graduated Class 44-E, Napier Field, AL.

Flew P-40s at Napier and Gunnery Elgin, FL. Whole class assigned B-24 transition. Went to South Pacific with the 72nd Bomb Sqdn., 5th Bomb Grp., 13th Air Force. Completed 39 missions and returned to the States.

Got out of the service in September 1946 and returned in October 1947. Instructor in T-6s Randolph AFB, TX December 1947 until June 1950. Korea with 21st Troop Carrier Sqdn., Kyushu Gypsies, flew 144 missions returning to the States in November 1951. Other overseas tours include Morocco and Panama, where he was commander 605th Air Commando Sqdn.

Awarded the Distinguished Flying Cross, Air Medal with five Oak Leaf Clusters, BSM, AFCM, AFOUA one Oak Leaf Cluster, ROKPUC one Oak Leaf Cluster, PLR, APCM, five Battle Stars, KSM one Arrow and three Battle Stars, UNSM, NDSM one Battle Star, DUC one Oak Leaf Cluster, PRDUC, and ALFSA one Oak Leaf Cluster.

Retired Lt. Colonel on August 1, 1970, San Antonio, TX. Married for 52 years to former Betty Jane Cornell. Children: Pamela Kasper and Sharon Gore, three grandchildren the Kasper girls, Kristin, Kimberly, and Jennifer.

FLOYD L. STREEPER, born Jones
County, IA on August 21, 1924. Moved to Rock Island, IL in 1933. Enlisted in the Army Air Force on December 9, 1942. Basic training, Miami Beach, FL; Radio-Op Mech. School, Scott Field, IL; Gunnery School and 1st Phase combat crew training, Davis-Monthan, Tucson, AZ; and 2nd and 3rd Phase CCT, Blythe, CA. Assigned to Walter D. Lucas' crew as Radio Operator. The crew picked up their B-24 at Herington, KS flew to Fairfield-Suisun (Travis), CA then island hopped to Guadalcanal.

Assigned to the 23rd Bomb Sqdn., 5th Bomb Grp., 13th Air Force, January 1944. Flew missions from Guadalcanal, Munda, New Georgia, Admiralty Islands, Wakde, Noemfoor, and Morotai. Completed 38 missions returning Stateside February 1945. Discharged September 1945 and re-enlisted in November 1947 making a career of the Air Force in the field of Aircraft Electronics, serving at all levels from NCOIC Sqdn. Shop to Depot Maintenance, also instructing Comm-Nav maintenance and shop supervision. Last Air Force assignment, Avionics Superintendent, HQ, 4th Air Force. Retired on August 1, 1969. Worked for Harold Hofman to organize the first 5th Bomb Grp. reunion held in 1983.

B.D. THOMAS, born in Oklahoma
and reared in Wichita Falls, TX. Enlisted on November 3, 1943 at University of Texas at Austin. Finished Pilot School at Fort Sumner, NM in Class 44-E. Flew B-17 at Las Vegas, NV and B-24 at Tonopah, NV. Overseas on December 25, 1944 and arrived in Nadzab, New Guinea at 4:00 p.m. on December 31, 1944. Joined the 5th Bomb Grp., 72nd Bomb Sqdn. on January 20, 1945 on Morotai. Flew 20 missions as co-pilot, 20 as pilot, and five as instructor/pilot.

Assigned to Jack Nichols' crew as co-pilot, early on became pilot. Flew missions to Borneo and Philippine Islands. Longest flight 10:30. At Samar from March 1945 until October 1945. Acquired some gray hair on last mission to Northern Formosa from Samar, Philippine Islands. Came back to USA from Clark AFB, arriving on December 23, 1945.

Graduated from the University of Texas at Austin with a degree in Geology. Retired from the state agency that regulates oil and gas, well drilling, and production. Married for 47 years with two children.

PAUL D. THOMPSON, Captain,
Ret., as born on September 7, 1920 in Ft. Wayne, IN. He entered the service in the Aviation Cadet Program on October 13, 1942 at Baer Field, Ft. Wayne and was put on Air Force Enlisted Reserve. Called to active duty on February 20, 1943, San Antonio, TX Aviation Cadet Center.

Bombardier rating awarded on December 24, 1943 in Childress, TX. Sent to Tonopah, NV for RTU training. Assigned to the 31st Bomb Sqdn., 5th Bomb Grp. H, 13th AAF based at that time in Los Negros, Admiralty Islands. Flew 47 missions in the 15-month tour of duty. Started as lead bombardier in November 1944. Appointed squadron bombardier in January 1945. Targets for the tour included, Truk Island, Woleai, Ceram, Ulithi, Yap, Palau, Halmahera Island, Balikpapan, Borneo, Tarakan Island, and many targets in the Philippine Islands. Last mission was a storage area in Balikpapan, Borneo. Last base was Samar, Philippine Islands. Squadron bomber last six months of tour. Also 31st Bomb Sqdn. Mgr. Officer Club on Samar.

Campaigns: Bismarck, New Guinea, South Philippines, Eastern Mandates, Western Pacific, Luzon, China Defense, and China Offensive. Awarded the Air Medal with Oak Leaf Cluster, Presidential Unit Citation, and the Philippine Liberation Medal. Separated from service at the same time SAACC in January 1945 where he had entered the service three years earlier. Highest rank attained was captain.

Married Cile on February 16, 1946. They have two children, Barbara and Douglas. He retired on October 1, 1982 as a sales representative after 42 years from Nabisco Brands, Inc. His hobbies are making beautiful items in stained glass and traveling.

THOMAS E. THOMPSON, born in
Bradford, IL on October 28, 1921. Enlisted in the Illinois National Guard, 33rd Division, Galva, IL, 1938. Enlisted in the Army Air Corps on July 29, 1940. Attended Radio Operator and Mechanic School, graduated and taught in the school for 14 months before attending Aviation Cadet School, graduating Class 43-F, June 1943, Craig Field, Selma, AL as a fighter pilot. Was transferred to Idaho for training on B-24s and sent to Espiritu Santo, Southwest Pacific as a co-pilot in the 394th Bomb Sqdn.,

5th Bomb Grp., 13th Air Force in November 1943. Later, he was checked out as a first pilot and flew 47 missions returning Stateside in December 1944. Discharged as 1st Lieutenant in September 1945.

An incident that Thompson would like to relate occurred while returning from a mission to Los Negros, Admiralty Islands in July 1944. The Tactical Bulletin No. 6, HQ. 5th Bomb Grp., dated August 4, 1944 tells the story fairly well except for a couple of exceptions.

We had lost our radio in addition to the hydraulic system. We did buzz the strip, as well as a B-24 can buzz anything, and threw out a message describing our plight. The use of parachutes to slow down a plane with damaged hydraulics had been discussed before during briefings, but since no one had tried that particular technique, it was mostly speculation. I knew we had at best one application of brakes from pressure supplied by the hydraulic accumulator, which I learned while teaching Hydraulic Systems back at Wendover, UT while awaiting assignment to an air crew. I know I learned more than the flight engineers I was teaching.

I talked our situation over with Lt. Sam Magee, co-pilot and Jim Hope, bombardier. We developed a plan and Jim was in charge of running things in the rear of the plane. It was our idea; not tower advice on the actions that we would take. No offense intended.

The landing approach wasn't exactly normal; since we landed S to N coming in over the water at about 50 feet hanging on our props with extra power applied and literally dropped it on the end of the runway. Things worked out fine after that.

DONALD WAYNE TYLER, (Deceased) born on November 9, 1921 in Merrick County, NE. Enlisted in the AAF in July 1942, West Coast Training Center. Received commission and Pilot's wings at Marfa AAB. Assigned to the 72nd Bomb Sqdn., 5th Bomb Grp., 13th Air Force as co-pilot. May 1944, Lt. Tyler and crew flew B-24 to Guadalcanal, then Admiralty Islands. Flew missions from there to Morotai. His diary on June 15 reads: "Raided Eton Island, Truk. Target closed. Used too much gas. Jettisoned all flight equipment. Stood by to bail out. Lost No. 1 engine on final approach to an unfinished landing strip, out of gas, but landed OK."

Other rough missions included the 14-hour strike on Balikpapan oil fields and shipping strike to Brunei Bay, Borneo in October. Checked out as 1st pilot on November 27. Flew last of 42 missions to Philippines in January 1945. Returned Stateside in May 1945, assigned to Ferry Command. Joined Reserve in March 1946. Honorably discharged as captain in 1955.

Passed away on February 15, 1998 in Central City, NE.

SIDNEY ULMER, see page 143.

MARVIN L. VORPAHL, Tech./Sgt., born in Green Bay, WI on February 11, 1920. Inducted into the service on July 18, 1942. Assigned to the 95th Infantry Division at Camp Swift, TX. Trained at various camps and other locations in the U.S. Left the 95th Infantry Division in October 1943 from Camp Coxcomb, CA. Served 16 months.

Qualified for Aviation Cadet (Air Crew) training, November 9, 1943. Arrived at Buckley Field, CO on December 14, 1943. From there, he was sent to Sioux Falls, SD in January 1944. Attended Radio Operator/Mechanic School. Graduated June 20, 1944. Next stop was Yuma, AZ to attend Flexible Gunnery School. Graduated August 12, 1944. To Lemoore Field, CA for assignment. Onto Tonopah, NE where he was assigned to John Ellenbecker's crew as Radio Operator/Mechanic Gunner. December 8, 1944, our crew transferred to Hamilton Field, CA (Processing Unit).

Left the States on January 16, 1945 for combat in the Pacific Theater. Assigned to the 394th Bomb Sqdn., 5th Bomb Grp., 13th Air Force. Completed 42 missions. Returned Stateside on October 18, 1945. Discharged on October 27, 1945 at Baer Field, Ft. Wayne, IN.

Decorations and Citations include the Asiatic-Pacific Service Medal, Air Medal with one Oak Leaf Cluster, and the Philippine Liberation Ribbon.

RUSSELL L. WALDRON (GATTY) was born on 8 April 1910 in Wellston, Ohio. He was the first born child of Matthew Hoadley Waldron and Sadie Lorena (Blagg) Waldron. His parents were born and reared on farms in southern Ohio. His father died of tuberculosis in 1914. He was employed at the time as a cager-elevator operator at the Milton Iron Furnace in Wellston, Ohio. Gatty, at the age of nine, became an orphan when his mother died of tuberculosis in 1919.

He then went to live with his grandparents on a farm in Richland Township in Vinton County, Ohio. He graduated from High School in 1926. Upon completion of one year of Normal School Training he taught in one room country schools (all eight grades) for two years in Vinton County, Ohio – beginning at the age of seventeen. In 1930, after completing two and one half years of College he enlisted as a buck private in the Army Air Corps.

Within eight months he obtained an appointment as a Flying Cadet and graduated from the Advanced Flying School of the Army Air Corps at Kelly Field, Texas in February 1932. He was then Commissioned a Second Lieutenant, Air Corps Reserve, and rated as a military airplane pilot. After one year of active duty he continued his college education for a short while and then re-enlisted as a buck private in August of 1934 in order to improve his chances to obtain a Regular Commission. During this tour of duty he was an enlisted military pilot with base pay of $21.00 a month. On July 11, 1935 he was commissioned as a Second Lieutenant in the Regular Army Air Corps.

On December 7th, 1941 he was the Commander of the 31st Bombardment Squadron and a Pearl Harbor Survivor at Hickam Field, Hawaii. He had two tours of Combat Duty in World War II and flew 50 Combat and Enemy Search Missions. For nine months of World War II he was the Commander of the 11th Bombardment Group (Heavy) in the Island Hopping Campaign across the Pacific. During this period of time the 11th Bombardment Group (Heavy) was based at Kwajalein and Guam. During his military career he commanded a Bombardment Squadron, a Bombardment Group, a Flying Training Wing, two Air Transport Divisions, and The Western Transport Air Force (now the 15th Air Force). He also had three tours of duty in the Pentagon, all of which were in Personnel. At the time of his retirement he was Assistant Deputy Chief of Staff for Personnel for the United States Air Force.

His military awards and decorations include the Distinguished Service Medal, the Legion of Merit, the Distinguished Flying Cross with one Oak Leaf Cluster, The Air Medal with three Oak Leaf Clusters, and the Commendation Ribbon with one Oak Leaf Cluster. His foreign Decorations and Awards are: The Order of the Cloud and Banner from Nationalist China, The Knight Commander of the Most Noble Order of the Crown of Thailand, and The Order of the Rising Sun from Japan (Third Class).

He was awarded an MBA Degree by the Harvard School of Business and is a graduate of the National War College. After thirty years of active duty he retired from the United States Air Force on 1 July 1962 with the rank of Permanent Major General.

He retired eight years prior to mandatory retirement from the Air Force in order to attend the Church Divinity School of the Pacific in Berkeley, California as a Special Student. In 1965 he was ordained as a Deacon and in 1966 as a Priest of the Episcopal Church. He served in the active Ministry until 1972. During this period of time he initiated and established the Mission of our Holy Redeemer. In February of 1967 he was installed as Rector of Ascension Parish. Both the Mission and Parish were in Vallejo, California

He is the father of six children. He and his wife, Ruth, now reside in Fairfield, California.

WILLIAM E. WALKER, born in Waterbury, CT on December 4, 1926. Enlisted in the AAF on November 27, 1942 after lying about his age. Attended Radio School, Truax Field, Madison, WI and Gunnery School at Laredo, TX. Underwent Phase training at Biggs Field, El Paso, TX. Joined the 31st Bomb Sqdn. with Ray C. Stubblefield's crew as Radio Operator/Mechanic Gunner on Guadalcanal in March 1944.

Flew missions against Bougainville, Truk, Wolei, Yap, as well as 1st and 3rd missions against Balikpapan, Borneo for a total of 44 missions. The move from Noemfoor to Morotai ended in a C-47 crash which broke up the crew. Returned to the States in January 1945 and was hospitalized until discharge in September 1945.

Received college education under the Disabled Veterans Rehabilitation-Public Law 16 and with additional education enjoyed a career in Physical Instrumentation until retirement in August 1990. Residing in Danbury, CT since discharge.

LAWRENCE H. WALTON, enlisted in the AAF for Cadet training in January 1942. Sent to Mira Loma Flight Academy, Oxnard, CA for Primary Flight training after indoctrination at Williams AAFB, AZ. Washed out of primary and was transferred to Santa Ana AAFB, for testing and reassignment. Detailed to Mather AAFB for Navigation training, from which he graduated in February 1943. Ordered overseas upon gradu-

ation, as one of three graduates assigned to the Pacific Theater. Stations there in the Pacific were Oahu, Fiji Islands, Guadalcanal, Munda, and Admiralty Islands.

Tours of duty ended in March 1944 after having flown 900 plus hours on 117 missions, of which 55 were strikes against targets from Bougainville to Rabaul to Truk. On his, first combat bombing mission (which was a night mission). He flew with a Captain John Pitts, up in the slot, to bomb Bougainville. When the nose of that B-17 got lit up by the searchlights, Walton sort of freaked out and yelled over the intercom "They've got us in the lights", The response from Capt. Pitts was to stand up and take a bow! That humorous response really relieved any anxiety that Walton had and it served him well then and continues to do so today.

Upon return to the States, he was ordered to Walla Walla AAB as an Instructor/Navigator, and was discharged in July 1945.

Recalled to active duty in 1950, and remained on active duty through tours at Randolph AFB, Forbes AFB (RB-47s), and the USAF Academy, where he served as an instructor from 1955 until 1959, when he fell ill, and went before a Physical Evaluation Board. The Board found him unfit for further flying duty, and Walton chose to accept retirement (physical), and has been retired since 1960.

Awards received were the Distinguished Flying Cross, Air Medal with 11 Oak Leaf Clusters, two Presidential Unit Citations, and pertinent Pacific Theater and Longevity Ribbons.

Highest rank held was Major and aeronautical rating was Master Navigator.

DAN WEENER, born in Chelsea, MA on September 27, 1923. Entered the military on April 19, 1943. Trained at Miami Beach, FL; Biloxi, MS; Harlingen, TX; and Muroc, CA. Served in the South Pacific Theater as an Engineer/Gunner with the 31st Bomb Sqdn., 5th Bomb Grp., 13th Air Force.

Flew on missions over Brunei Bay, Borneo and two missions over Balikpapan oil fields, for a total of 41 missions. Discharged on September 13, 1945 with rank of Tech./Sgt. Decorated with the Air Medal.

Retired and living in Needham, MA.

CHARLES W. WERNTZ, born on August 11, 1916 in Huntsville, MO. Enlisted Army Air Corps on October 21, 1939,

Jefferson Barracks, MO. Arrived Hickam Field, December 1939. Assigned to HQ and HQ Sqdn., 5th Bomb Grp. Schooled in Aircraft Maintenance. Sqdn. Instrument Chief prior to December 7th. Was looking out his third floor barracks window, in the direction of Pearl Harbor, and saw his first Japanese torpedo plane. No way, a torpedo could be as long as it looked at that moment at eye level and about 200 feet away.

Assigned to the 31st Bomb Sqdn., June 20, 1942 as LB-30-B-24 maintenance instructor. Embarked Honolulu with the 31st Bomb Sqdn., 5th Bomb Grp., for a Pacific tour, October 1942-Guadalcanal, Munda, and Admiralty Islands. Assigned to HQ, 5th Bomb Grp. as Chief Technical Inspector, July 1943. Returned Stateside, July 17, 1944. Joined B-29 group in September 1944. Discharged July 21, 1945. Awarded five overseas bars-Good Conduct, American Defense with one Battle Star, Asiatic-Pacific with five Battle Stars, and the American Theater Victory Medal.

ROBERT J. WHITE, born in Howarden, IA on June 29, 1919. Moved to California in 1935. Enlisted in AAF on January 7, 1942. After completing basic training was assigned to the 5th Bomb Grp. Battles and Campaigns he fought in were: Eastern Mandates, Western Pacific, Luzon, China, South Philippines, Central Pacific, New Guinea, Guadalcanal, Northern Solomons, and Bismarck Archipelago, White spent seven months and five days in the USA; three years and seven days in Europe; and overseas duty form June 15, 1942 until June 25, 1945. Separated from the AAF in Santa Ana, CA on September 18, 1945 with rank of Sergeant.

Special remembrances include monthly pay in 1942 of $21.00 and after laundry and insurance expenses; he netted about $7.00. Driving loaded munitions trucks over Pali in Hawaii, Wash Machine Charlie raids in Guadalcanal, and going through a hurricane aboard ship returning to USA.

141

White retired from Armour & Co. in 1980 after 33 years of service.

STANLEY WIEC, born in Detroit, MI on October 16, 1925. Joined the Army Air Force on December 28, 1943 and served in the Philippines. An Aerial Gunner with the 394th Bomb Sqdn., 5th Bomb Grp., 13th Army Air Force. Wiec participated in the last mission of the war for the 394th Bomb Sqdn. Decorated with the Air Medal and discharged from military service on January 11, 1946 with rank of Staff/Sgt.

Retired Dearborn Heights, Michigan founder of Yankee Air Museum.

ARTHUR E. WILLIAMS, born in Ritzville, WA on October 21, 1921 and raised there on wheat ranch. Graduate of Ritzville High School, 1939. Entered Washington State College and majored in Music Education, graduating in 1946. Taught in Washington public schools for 30 years before retiring in 1979.

Enlisted in the Reserve on September 4, 1942 at Geiger Field, Spokane, WA. Activated in spring 1943. Received basic training, Lincoln, NE; Flight training, Boseman, MT, Santa Ana, CA, King City, CA, and Mariana, AZ. Took Radio School at Scott Field, IL; Gunnery School, Yuma, AZ; and assigned to Del Hagberg's crew as Radio Operator at Lemoore, CA. The crew received combat crew training in a Liberator at Walla Walla, WA.

On December 7, 1944 they headed for Nadzab, New Guinea where the crew was assigned to the 72nd Bomb Sqdn., 5th Bomb Grp. (H), 13th Air Force. They joined the group at Morotai. Williams finished his flying tour in Samar, Philippine Islands. Credited with a total of 44 missions, the longest being 15 1/3 hours long.

Although most of the crewmembers lost contact with each other, in 1990 Williams had located all ten of the crew. Nine of the crew was present at the first of several reunions. Two of the crew are now deceased. Currently, he is living in Centrailia, WA.

WILLIAM B. (BILL) WINKS, Lt. Col., USAF Res., Ret., born in Cushing, OK on August 2, 1922. Entered the Army Air Corps on March 12, 1941 and spent seven years active and 18 years Reserve. A bomber pilot, Winks flew 60 missions in 25 B-17s, 35 B-24s.

Assigned to the 23rd and 31st Bomb Sqdns., 5th Bomb Grp., 13th Air Force. Flew missions out of Espiritu Santo, Guadalcanal, Fiji, Munda, and Funafuti. All missions flown as co-pilot. Field commissioned as 2nd Lt., January 1944.

The two missions that stand out in his memory include when the crew followed Col. Unruh down to 10,000 feet in Rabaul Harbor to bomb a cruiser; they missed and were lucky no one was shot down. In July 1943, they flew to Funafuti Island and hit Tarawa at dusk. On their return flight to Funafuti, they ran out of gas on the final approach going against traffic to land. What an experience! Decorated with the Air Medal with six Oak Leaf Clusters, three Battle Stars, and other Ribbons.

OSCAR A. ZILLIG, born in Bronx, New York City, NY on January 16, 1924. Inducted on March 3, 1943. Basic training at Miami Beach, FL; Airplane Mechanic School, Amarillo, TX; Gunnery School, Las Vegas Air Field, NV; and combat crew training, Muroc AFB, CA.

Assigned to the 31st Bomb Sqdn., 5th Bomb Grp., April 1944. Flew missions from Guadalcanal, Admiralty Island, Wakde, Noemfoor, and Morotai. Completed 44 missions returning Stateside on April 3, 1945. Discharged on September 6, 1945.

Worked for the New York Telephone Company, retired 1985.

ALBERT W. JAMES, born in National City, California, 27 April 1916. After two years of schooling in a joint program offered by San Diego State College and Ryan School of Aeronautics, he joined the Army Air Corps Flying Cadet Program in September 1939. He graduated from Kelly Field in June 1940 as a rated pilot and a newly commissioned 2nd Lieutenant. His first military assignment was to the 7th Bomb Group at Hamilton Field, near San Francisco.

In October of 1941, he was detailed to the Fairfield Air Depot at Patterson Field, Ohio as head of a crew to run test flights of the new B-17E Flying Fortress. Crews were assigned to perform flights for each of the several areas identified in the total performance envelope. He was given the high altitude assignment, i.e. fly at 30,000 feet for four hours in a simulated bombing mission. This required flight in an unpressurized, unheated, aircraft at an elevation substantially higher than the highest pinnacle of Mount Everest. Human life could be sustained only by the constant use of oxygen.

In December of 1941 he found himself at Manchester, New Hampshire with an airfield full of DB7s—a British version of our A-20 which they had planned to use as light bombers or night fighters. They had been stopped enroute with our declaring war against Japan and Germany. Because of the submarine menace along our east coast the 45th Bomb Group had been given an anti-submarine patrol role—to be implemented immediately. James was made operations officer for the squadron, which included deriving tactics, scheduling patrols, training new graduates of flying schools, and overseeing effectiveness of operations. Initially patrol flights were staged through Mitchell Field on Long Island to Langley Field in Virginia. Our squadron was moved to Dover Delaware, then to Langley Field, where we were equipped with B-18s with radar. Then to Opa Locka Naval Air Station in Miami, and somewhat later to Miami's 36th Street Airport. With the radar, the B-18's were limited to strictly night-time patrols. Other non-radar equipped planes were given the day-time patrol responsibility. On one occasion James was obliged to make a dead-stick landing while flying one of the B-18's while still in almost total darkness. The location was about 20 miles to the east of Holywood, Florida. The normal patrol altitude was 500 feet, so that when hings went awry, there were only seconds remaining to solve the problem.

In late 1944 James found himself in possession of orders to the 13th Air Force/5th Bomb Group after probing relentlessly for an assignment to a B-29 Group. Even though orders to B-29s did belatedly come through, he elected to stay with the "orders in hand" rather than risk another dissappointment. After arriving at the 5th Bomb Group's location on Morotai island, James soon found himself filling the role of Group Commander, since Colonel Musgrave was destined to take an overdue R&R in Australia, and upon the Colonel's return, he barely had time to change his clothes before he was off to his new assignment in Washington, D.C.

It seemed that no sooner had Colonel Musgrave departed for stateside than James had been alerted to move the 5th Bomb Group to Samar in the Philippine Islands. The task of keeping the operations going on regular basis was eased by the presence of an exceptionally competent staff in every area of essential activity, from technical maintenance, health, food, housing, recreation, flight operations, intelligence, religion, security and morale. Bombing missions were conducted routinely throughout the Philippines, aiding in the on-going cleaning the Japanese out of the various islands where they had established their presence either by direct assualt or psychological discouragement. This also included the island of Borneo, especially Balikpapan, Tarakan, and Brunei.

Lt. Col James, assigned to Headquaraters 4th Air Force in San Francisco, was given the asignment of contacting the Adjutants General of each of the states west of the Mississippi River and briefing them on the potential available to them of participating in the (Newly) to be created Air National Guard. Four such contacts had been made when James found himself to be on PCS Orders to the Fourteenth Air Force Headquarters at Orlando, Florida At James' new station he became aware of an announcement spelling out the reactivation of the Air Force Institute of Technology at Wright Field in Ohio James elected to make application for admission to fulfill his educational goals, interrupted by the war. He was accepted forwith. PCS orders were issued for his transfer of himself and family to Ohio. After two years and graduation from USAFIT in August 1948, he was accepted for two more years at the University of Texas at Austin, with the goal being a BBA. James was graduated from the University of Texas in June of 1950 with a BBA with honors, and in August of 1950 with an MBA with a commendation from USAFIT.

James then found himself in New York City, sent there to establish and head-up the New York Regional Procurement Office— to speed up the acquisition of much needed war materiel in support of the Korean War effort. Another of Jarnes responsibillities was the Sikorsky plant in Connecticut where

they were producing the H-19 Helicopter in quantity for the Army. Four years later lie was sent to the San Antonio Air Material Area in Texas, where as Director of Procurement and Production was responsible for the timely production of a myriad of weapon systems, amongst which were the B-36, B-58, F-102, F-106, C-131, Solid Propellant JATO bottles, the ATLAS Missile, engines for the C-131, and all of the Jet Engines for the B-52 and the KC-135, both of which were in full production. In addition James oversaw the recurring maintenance of the entire SAC B-36 Fleet—our primary deterent against nuclear war.

Then James was sent to Europe as U.S. Liaison to the F-104 Consortium, composed of Germany, Italy, Belgium and the Netherlands, to aid in the construction of one thousand F-104 Fighter aircraft in a joint, integrated production program. The Honorablr Joseph Imrie, Assistant Secretary of the Air Force told James that it was his job to see that he kept the "Stripped Pants" types out of it. Two years later when James returned stateside he was assigned as Director of Procurement at Patrick AFB, Florida. In that role, he was directed to create a joint DOD/NASA Wage Stabilization Board for the stability of all construction wage rates to be applicable for the duration of the construction effort just beginning for what was to be later known as Kennedy Space Center. James chaired the Board which met regularly with representatives of all the various unions involved in construction work. Rates thus arrived at were published in governmental procurement regulations—with the proviso that any government contract calling for construction within Brevard County would call-out the applicable published rates.

James retired from the Air Force in late 1965, and took employment with the Boeing Company in 1966 in thr role of Contracts Manager for the Saturn Five/Apollo (Moon Shot) Program.. When the Saturn Five program reached reasonable maturity Alected to accept Boeings' offer of further employment in Seattle on the Minuteman Program which had now ascended to our most important and reliable deterent to nuclear war.

SHIRLEY SIDNEY ULMER, born North, South Carolina, April 15, 1923.

Enlisted in U.S. Army Signal Corps, December 4, 1942. Transferred to U.S. Army Air Force, August 20, 1943. Basic Training, 51st Training Group, Class 221, Keesler Field, Biloxi, Mississippi. Gunnery school, Laredo Air Force Base, Laredo Texas. Combat Crew training, Tonopah Air Force Base, Tonopah, Nevada. Assigned to Pat Earhart crew as an Assistant Radio operator -- Gunner, May, 1944. Sent to Hamilton Field, California for overseas processing. Departed for Guadalcanal on May 18, 1944. Assigned to the 13th Air Force, 5th Bomb Group, 31st Bomb Squadron. While completing 44 missions with 500 combat hours, Ulmer flew strikes from Guadalcanal, Los Negros, Wakde, Noemfoor and Morotai.

Most memorable missions were the first mission to Balikpapan on September 30, 1944 and the strike at Brunei Bay on November 16, 1944. During his service Ulmer was awarded the Air Medal with four oak leaf clusters, the Philippine Liberation Medal, and the Asiatic Pacific Campaign Medal with seven battle stars. Ulmer returned to the states by ship in April 1945. He was subsequently assigned to service as a military policeman at La Junta Air Force Base, La Junta, Colorado. In June he was transferred to the Las Vegas Air Force Base to command a detachment of MP's. He served there until transferred to Seymour Johnson Field in North Carolina for separation from the service in the rank of Staff Sergeant on Oct. 12, 1945. Subsequent to his discharge Ulmer got a Ph.D. in Political Science at Duke University. He then pursued a teaching career at the college level for 32 years. During this period, he lectured at many universities across the country while holding permanent faculty appointments at Michigan State University for 7 years and the University of Kentucky for 25 years. He served as Chairman of Political Science departments at both institutions. He has been retired since 1988.

Index

This index includes key words and surnames from the general history text only. The profile section is alphabetized.

CPSIA information can be obtained
at www.ICGtesting.com
Printed in the USA
JSHW020301080222
22645JS00004B/121